SPACE LAW

Space Law

By

C. WILFRED JENKS

FREDERICK A. PRAEGER
Publishers
New York · Washington

This book is set in 12 pt
Bembo on 14 pt

First published in 1965 by
Stevens & Sons Limited of
11 New Fetter Lane, London.

Published in the
United States of America in
1965 by Frederick A. Praeger,
Inc., Publishers, 111 Fourth
Ave., New York 10003, N.Y.

Printed in Great Britain
by Staples Printers Limited
at their Rochester, Kent,
establishment

Library of Congress
Catalog Card No. 65-17859

To
PHILIP C. JESSUP
Pioneer of Law and Justice
in Space as on Earth

Contents

vii

Contents

Contents

APPENDICES

Preface

WITH the launching of Sputnik I on October 4, 1957, activities in space ceased to be a speculative possibility and became one of the outstanding achievements of the scientific and technological progress of our time. The law governing activities in space remained for a time almost wholly speculative. That phase has now passed. With the unanimous adoption by the General Assembly of the United Nations on December 13, 1963, of the Declaration of Legal Principles Governing the Activities of States in the Exploration and Use of Outer Space space law ceased to be a speculation of jurists and became a body of principles recognised by States.

The present volume is an attempt to state tentatively the law as it now stands. While giving a brief account of the historical, scientific and political background of activities in space and a general picture of the already voluminous literature of space law, it consists primarily of an analysis of the extent to which there is now a recognised body of law on the subject accepted as such. The Declaration of Legal Principles represents the Twelve Tables or Ten Commandments of Space Law. It is, indeed, hardly too much to describe it as the Magna Carta of space.

GENEVA,
December, 1964   C. WILFRED JENKS

Acknowledgments

I HAVE, with his permission, dedicated this volume to Judge Philip Jessup, whose friendship and encouragement have meant much to me for upwards of a quarter of a century. For me to say anything here of his general contribution to the growth of international law in our time would be quite presumptuous, but it is not out of place for me to pay tribute to *Controls for Outer Space and the Antarctic Analogy* as a model of legal craftsmanship working on scientific materials, an unfamiliar and all too often uncongenial task which the international lawyer must increasingly assume under contemporary conditions. Philip Jessup's work on space law represents a landmark in the development of a new approach to international legal problems and remains a continuing source of inspiration for future workers in the field.

My other debts in connection with this volume are numerous and heavy.

To Lord McNair I owe the encouragement and counsel on which I have drawn so heavily in all my work.

I am particularly appreciative of the generous co-operation in my studies of space law of Professor Eugene A. Korovin, Chairman of the Research Committee on the Legal Problems of Outer Space of the Academy of Sciences of the U.S.S.R., and Professor Grigori Tunkin, Legal Adviser of the Soviet Foreign Office. I have also had the benefit of consultation with Professor Manfred Lachs, Chairman of the Legal Sub-Committee of the United Nations Committee on the Peaceful Uses of Outer Space. Professor Eugène Pépin, now of the *Institut International d'Etudes et de Recherches Diplomatiques*, Paris, and currently President of the International Institute of Space Law, whose unique experience of air and space law extends over fifty years, has allowed me to profit from his wise advice. Among other old friends, Professor Myres S. McDougal of the Yale Law School and Sir Kenneth Bailey, Solicitor-General of Australia, have made special contributions in many discussions to the development of my own views on the problems of space law. Professor R. Y. Jennings, Whewell Professor of International

Law in the University of Cambridge, Professor B. A. Wortley, Professor of Jurisprudence and International Law in the University of Manchester, and Mr. J. E. S. Fawcett, Fellow of All Souls College, Oxford, have all made suggestions which have been of great value.

The present volume has grown out of a report prepared for the Institute of International Law and I owe a special debt to my colleagues in the Institute Committee for their counsel and co-operation. From 1959 to 1963 my colleagues in this Committee were Messrs. Léon Babínski, Erik Brüel, R. Y. Jennings, Philip Jessup, Herbert Kraus, Josef Kunz, Antonio de Luna, Paul de La Pradelle, Rolando Quadri, Grigori Tunkin, Haroldo Valladão and J. H. W. Verzijl. As reconstituted in 1964 the Committee now consists of Sir Kenneth Bailey and Messrs. Léon Babínski, Charles Chaumont, J. E. S. Fawcett, C. Wilfred Jenks, R. Y. Jennings, Philip Jessup, Manfred Lachs, Paul de La Pradelle, Riccardo Monaco, Rolando Quadri, Grigori Tunkin and Haroldo Valladão.

The international lawyer who ventures to discuss the problems posed for the law by new scientific and technological developments cannot hope to attain more than a reasonable familiarity with the general nature and significance of these developments; many of their technical complexities lie beyond his ken and the constantly accelerating rate of development defies his bravest attempts to keep track of what is happening. He is therefore dependent in an exceptional degree on the indulgent co-operation of outstanding scientists who share his preoccupations and are prepared to give him the benefit of critical advice based on a unique knowledge and experience available only to those who are in constant touch with the latest developments. In the early stages of my study of the matter the late Professor F. J. M. Stratton, Fellow of Gonville and Caius College, Cambridge and Secretary of the International Astronomical Union, gave me invaluable advice. More recently, I have had the privilege of the suggestions and criticism of Sir Harrie Massey, Chairman of the British National Committee for Space Research, Sir Bernard Lovell, Director of Jodrell Bank Experimental Station, and Dr. F. Graham Smith of the Mullard Radio-astronomy Observatory of the University of Cambridge. To all of them I extend my most sincere thanks.

I am likewise indebted for advice and information to many colleagues in the international organisations of the United Nations family, and in particular to Oscar Schachter, Director of the General Legal Division of the Secretariat of the United Nations; Gerald Gross, Secretary-General of the International Telecommunication Union; D. A. Davies, Secretary-General of the World Meteorological Organisation; and P. K. Roy, Director of the Legal Bureau of the International Civil Aviation Organisation.

I have also greatly profited at various stages from information supplied by and the suggestive criticism of Mr. P. J. Beaulieu, Executive Secretary of COSPAR (the Committee on Space Research of the International Council of Scientific Unions); Mr. Andrew Haley, General Counsel of the International Astronautical Federation; Professor John Cobb Cooper, formerly Legal Adviser of the International Air Transport Association; Professor D. Goedhuis, Reporter on Space Law of the International Law Association; and Professor Maxwell Cohen, Director of the Institute of Air and Space Law at McGill University.

I need hardly add that none of these gentlemen has any kind of responsibility for my errors and omissions or for the views which I have expressed.

I am indebted to the Bureau of the Institute of International Law for permission to embody in this volume substantial parts of reports to the Institute which have been published in French in Volume 50 of the *Annuaire de l'Institut de Droit International* and have also, with the permission of those on whose invitation they were prepared, made use of certain parts of an introductory lecture delivered in Stockholm on August 16, 1960, before the Third Colloquium on the Law of Outer Space held in connection with the XIth International Astronautical Congress and published in the Proceedings of the Congress and of an address delivered before the *Société Suisse de Droit International* at Berne on May 9, 1964, which is to appear in the *Annuaire Suisse de Droit International* for 1964.

I am also grateful to COSPAR for permission to include among the appendices to this volume the text of the COSPAR *Guide to Rocket and Satellite Information*, to the David Davies Memorial Institute of International Studies for permission to include their *Draft Code of Rules on the Exploration and uses of Outer Space* and *Draft Rules concerning Changes in the Environment of the Earth*, and to the Association of the Bar of the City of New York for permission to include the text of the *Tentative Provisions for International Agreements* proposed in 1960 by their Committee on Astronautics.

C.W.J.

PART I

THE BACKGROUND

I

The Birth of Space Law

───────

PRIOR to October 4, 1957, the legal status of activities in space was a speculative matter rather than an immediate practical problem.

Since that date the political, military and economic implications of activities in space have been a constant and growing preoccupation of practical statesmanship.

Until December 28, 1961, the law on the matter continued to be almost wholly speculative. From that time onwards there have been far-reaching developments which have now given us a solid core of generally accepted principle and practice around which the law can grow. By Resolution 1721 (XVI) of December 20, 1961, the General Assembly of the United Nations unanimously approved the general principles that "international law, including the Charter of the United Nations, applies to outer space and celestial bodies" and that "outer space and celestial bodies are free for exploration and use by all States in conformity with international law and are not subject to national appropriation". A deadlock speedily developed in the United Nations Committee on the Peaceful Uses of Outer Space when its Legal Sub-Committee was entrusted with the task of framing more detailed proposals for the regulation of the legal problems which may arise from the exploration and use of outer space. On September 11, 1963, the unanimous adoption by the Institute of International Law of a resolution concerning the legal régime of outer space symbolised the breaking of the deadlock. On December 13, 1963, the General Assembly adopted unanimously a Declaration of Legal Principles Governing the Activities of States in the Exploration and Use of Outer Space which was submitted for its approval as representing the maximum area of agreement possible at the time.

Proposed international agreements on international liability for space vehicle accidents and assistance to and repatriation of astronauts and space vehicles are under consideration by the United Nations Committee on the Peaceful Uses of Outer Space.

During the same period there have been important advances in the framing and acceptance of technical arrangements and regulations governing space activities.

A United Nations Register of Orbital Launchings has been maintained in virtue of Resolution 1721 (XVI) of December 20, 1961, since March 7, 1962.

The arrangements governing the exchange of information and data concerning rockets, satellites and space probes, originally agreed for the International Geophysical Year, were, in May 1962, placed by COSPAR (the Committee on Space Research of the International Council of Scientific Unions) on a more permanent basis. While not technically constituting a legal obligation, these arrangements are the *de facto* basis of the international interchange of space data.

Space telecommunication regulations, which will become legally binding when approved by the Members of the International Telecommunication Union, were adopted by an Extraordinary Administrative Radio Conference on November 8, 1963, to govern space telecommunications as from January 1, 1965.

Arrangements for co-operation in the use of meteorological satellites were approved by the Fourth World Meteorological Congress in April 1963.

A Bilateral Space Agreement of June 8, 1962, between the Academy of Sciences of the U.S.S.R. and the National Aeronautics and Space Administration of the United States, supplemented by a Memorandum of Understanding of March 20 and May 24, 1963, provides for a co-ordinated meteorological satellite programme, joint participation in passive communications satellite experiments, and a co-operative magnetic field survey through the use of artificial satellites.

Bilateral agreements concerning such matters as launching and recovery arrangements in the Cape Canaveral–Bahamas area, space vehicle observation, tracking and communication stations and facilities throughout the world, upper atmosphere research, and intercontinental testing in connection with experimental communications satellite have been concluded by the United States with a wide range of countries, including Britain, Canada, Australia, South Africa, France, Spain, Chile and Ecuador.

By Resolution 1802 (XVII) of December 14, 1962, the General Assembly of the United Nations endorsed basic principles for the operation of sounding rocket facilities under United Nations sponsorship.

The Convention establishing a European Organisation for the Development and Construction of Space Vehicle Launchers of March 29, 1962, and Convention establishing a European Space Research Organisation of June 14, 1963, have established a legal and institutional framework for the co-operative participation in activities in space of the United Kingdom, France, Germany, Italy, other West European States and Australia.

Significant if tentative progress has also been made towards the legal demilitarisation of space.

The general principle that "the sending of objects through outer space shall be exclusively for peaceful and scientific purposes" was approved by the General Assembly of the United Nations by Resolution 1148 (XII) of November 14, 1957, but no further progress in the matter was made until 1963.

By the Treaty Banning Nuclear Weapons Tests in the Atmosphere, in Outer Space and Under Water, signed at Moscow on August 5, 1963, on behalf of the United States, the United Kingdom and the U.S.S.R., and subsequently signed on behalf of more than 100 governments, each of the parties undertakes "to prohibit, to prevent and not to carry out any nuclear weapon test explosion, or any other nuclear explosion, at any place under its jurisdiction or control, in the atmosphere, beyond its limits (including outer space) or underwater".

By Resolution 1884 (XVIII) of October 17, 1963, the General Assembly of the United Nations welcomed "expressions by the U.S.S.R. and the United States of their intention not to station in outer space any objects carrying nuclear weapons or other kinds of weapons of mass destruction" and solemnly called upon all States "to refrain from placing in orbit around the Earth any objects carrying nuclear weapons or any other kinds of weapons of mass destruction, installing such weapons on celestial bodies, or stationing such weapons in outer space in any other manner".

This volume is an attempt to state in its context the body of law and practice which has already developed on the basis of these decisions and arrangements and to discuss some of the problems which the further growth of the law around the core which now exists will pose.

The task presents a number of characteristic difficulties.

The space lawyer has been confronted from the earliest speculative stages of the development of the subject with an inescapable dilemma – that of weighing the possible dangers of attempting to crystallise the law too soon against the certain dangers of waiting too long. This dilemma remains acute. The Declaration of Legal Principles Governing the Activities of States in the Exploration and Use of Outer Space, adopted by the General Assembly of the United Nations on December 13, 1963, while epoch-making as a stage in the development of the law, does not purport to be more than a statement of "the maximum area of agreement possible at this time". As Ambassador Plimpton of the United States said before the United Nations Committee, the Declaration "is not the last word; it is one of the first". Ambassador Morozov of the U.S.S.R. described it in similar terms as "only the very first step, which can and must be followed by other steps". The problem of how far and how fast will therefore remain with us for some considerable time to come. How far should we anticipate and systematise? How far should we be empirical and await further knowledge and experience? Some reasonable compromise between these contrasted approaches is clearly desirable. As I ventured to say when first writing on the subject in 1955:

"While it is healthy that the evolution of the law should follow rather than anticipate that of life, there are circumstances in which the possibility of developing the law on sound principles depends primarily on an initiative being taken in the matter before *de facto* situations have crystallised too

6

far. . . . Law and policy on the subject will necessarily interact upon each other from the earliest stages of development, and the future of the law on the matter, in addition to being profoundly influenced by, may also exercise some influence upon, the general course of international politics."[1]

This general approach has now become the accepted policy of responsible governments; as Secretary of State Dean Rusk of the United States has said, "the right time to subject activities in space to international law and supervision is now, before possibly untoward developments occur";[2] Soviet spokesmen have also laid stress on the need to define the legal principles governing activities in space, and this common approach of the leading space powers constitutes the basis of the series of unanimous decisions taken by the General Assembly of the United Nations. These decisions are in general terms; they have been designed to avoid mortgaging the future unduly in all matters of detail; there are significant ambiguities and omissions; but they provide the necessary general framework for the future development of the law.

There has been some continuing argument concerning the extent to which the principles relating to the exploration and use of space formulated by the General Assembly should be regarded as hard law. There have not been lacking voices to argue, partly on the ground that the General Assembly is not a law-making authority, partly on the basis of the form of the General Assembly resolutions as statements of principle, partly out of dislike for what the resolutions say or fail to say, that they are at most a programme for the future and not a statement of the existing legal obligations of States.

My own view remains as I stated it in 1958:

"There is now a fleeting opportunity to establish the principle that all activities in space, whether pooled or operated independently by individual nations, are subject to the direct regulatory authority of the United Nations, exercised by an appropriate body to be created for the purpose. If the principle is established the details can be evolved at leisure. . . . Why cannot the United Nations, by action of the General Assembly, collectively assume jurisdiction in space in relation to all its Members? Hitherto no

[1] *The Common Law of Mankind*, 1958, p. 384, reproducing "International Law and Activities in Space", 1956.
[2] Speech at Seattle, May 25, 1962.

State has effectively exercised jurisdiction in space. There would therefore be no interference with any existing jurisdiction. Such action would be entirely without precedent, but the circumstances are equally unprecedented. . . . Such a departure would be as epoch-making as the creation of the United States, the development of the British Commonwealth into a partnership of equal States, the establishment of the European Communities, the reorganisation of the Empire of all the Russias as the U.S.S.R., or the abolition of the Caliphate of Islam, all of which involved a change in fundamental legal conceptions, but it would be a worthy political and legal foundation for man's venture into space."[3]

It is premature to claim that any such development has taken place; but is it not perhaps in process of taking place, and is not such a consummation "most devoutly to be desired?"

The responsibility of the international lawyer when confronted with such a possibility is to devote his skill to enabling a new world to be born. While he cannot create law by imagining it, he can prevent or disastrously retard its creation by failing to be imaginative. When he cannot advise with confidence that a firm legal obligation exists he can at least refrain from asserting that no such obligation exists in such a manner as to destroy or greatly delay its coming into being. In such a situation the most reasonable course to follow may be to attach decisive weight to unanimous approval by the General Assembly of the United Nations and where no such approval has yet been given to formulate a body of principles and rules which commend themselves on their merits, recognising that they are law in the making and that their precise status therefore remains open to debate. Future experience will determine the respective contributions of General Assembly action, new treaty obligations, the practice of States, international adjudication and scholarly appraisal to giving these principles and rules an authoritative character.

We should, therefore, not be over-concerned that we cannot yet determine what proportions of the necessary regulation of activities in space will be constituted by recognised legal obligations, political understandings and rules of scientific practice respectively. All three forms of regulation are necessary and they will interact upon each other

[3] *The Common Law of Mankind*, 1958, pp. 406-407.

8

as they develop. In the present phase of development we cannot give an intelligible picture of the law of space as it is now taking shape without paying considerable attention to political understandings and rules of scientific practice which may not in themselves constitute rules of law but may well be the raw material out of which the law will evolve in much the same manner in which maritime and commercial law evolved out of maritime and commercial usage. The impossibility of foreseeing with any accuracy what will be regarded in future as having the force of law and what will remain political understanding or scientific practice may be of relatively little practical significance for the purpose of stating the code of conduct applicable to current activities in space.

The process of development will inevitably be a long, though not necessarily always a slow, one. The problems which confront us are new or arise in a new form; the solutions envisaged for them have not yet been tested by experience and must therefore be regarded as continuing to be in some measure tentative even when they have been generally accepted; the scale and complexity of the problems themselves and in some cases their very nature remain conjectural or largely unknown. But we now have a reasonably settled point of departure from which the law can evolve. We can substitute for the almost purely speculative approach to which there was no alternative in the earliest phase of the development of space law a more reasonable balance between what is and what may be. "What is" is no longer limited to a plausible body of sensible doctrine; it now includes a significant proportion of authoritatively recognised legal principle on to which further developments can be grafted as fuller experience becomes available and a larger measure of international agreement is reached.

We must, however, before attempting to state tentatively the law as it now stands, first give some brief account of the historical, scientific and political background of activities in space, and then give a general picture of the already voluminous literature of space law, which has made a significant contribution to the degree of agreement which now exists in the matter.

9

2

The Centuries of Speculation and
Decades of Planning

PRIOR to October 4, 1957, activities in space were generally regarded as a fancy of enthusiasts rather than as an immediate practical possibility or problem.

SPACE TRAVEL IN IMAGINATIVE WRITINGS

The possibility of space travel had, of course, fascinated imaginative writers for centuries.[1] Plato, Cicero and Plutarch had somewhat indistinctly foreshadowed it; Lucian of Samos writing in A.D. 160[2] had described a visit to the Moon; the seventeenth and eighteenth centuries had produced a copious literature on the subject, Cyrano de Bergerac,[3] Defoe[4] and Voltaire[5] being only the most famous of the many writers on cosmic voyages,[6] while in more recent times the tradition had been continued by Edgar Allan Poe,[7] Jules Verne,[8] H. G. Wells,[9] and C. S. Lewis,[10] and not least by Konstantin Ziolkowsky[11] who bridged

[1] The imaginative literature of the subject is admirably surveyed in Marjorie Hope Nicolson, *Voyages to the Moon*, 1948.
[2] *True History.*
[3] *L'autre Monde ou les Etats et Empires de la Lune et du Soleil*, 1656.
[4] *The Consolidator*, 1705; *A Journey to the World on the Moon*, 1705; *A Letter from the Man in the Moon*, 1705; *A Second and More Strange Voyage to the World in the Moon*, 1705.
[5] *Micromegas*, 1752.
[6] *e.g.*, Francis Godwin, *Man in the Moon*, 1638; John Wilkins, *A Discourse concerning a New World*, 1640; Atterly, *Voyage to the Moon*, 1827.
[7] *The Unparalleled Adventure of One Hans Pfaal*, 1835.
[8] *From the Earth to the Moon*, 1865; *All Around the Moon*, 1876; *To the Sun*, 1878; *Off on a Comet!*, 1895.
[9] *The First Men in the Moon*, 1901.
[10] *Out of the Silent Planet*, 1938; *Perelandia*, 1944.
[11] *Beyond the Planet Earth*, 1920, translated 1960.

personally the gap between fantasy and rocket engineering. But astronomers, with the notable exception of Kepler,[12] had been sceptical, and until rocket power of a thrust previously inconceivable became available in the mid-twentieth century these fancies remained no more than fancies.

THE IMPACT OF MILITARY TECHNOLOGY

It was the impact of war and military preparedness on technology resulting from the First and Second World Wars and the events following the Second World War which revolutionised the position. As President Eisenhower has said "It has been the military quest for ultra long-range rockets that has provided him with machinery so powerful that it can readily put satellites into orbit".

While the history of rocketry[13] goes back to ancient times, the First World War gave a substantial stimulus to the basic pioneer work on which modern rocketry has been based.

The Second World War gave the further stimulus which produced the V2 and made rocketry a major factor in military calculations.

The political strain following the Second World War resulted in the development of Intercontinental and Intermediate Range Ballistic Missiles capable of furnishing the thrust required to permit of the exploration of space.[14]

PIONEERS OF PEACEFUL DEVELOPMENT

While these developments were occurring the International Astronautical Federation (established in 1951 as a federation of national

[12] *Somnium*, 1634.
[13] The history of rocketry is summarised in Andrew G. Haley, *Rocketry and Space Exploration*, 1958; the classical works on rocketry include Robert H. Goddard, *A Method of Reaching Extreme Altitudes*, 1919; *Rockets*, 1946; *Rocket Development*, 1948; Hermann Oberth, *The Rocket in Planetary Space*, 1923; *Wege zur Raumschiffarht* (*The Way to Space Travel*), 1924; *Man into Space*, 1957; Robert Esnault-Pelterie, *L'astronautique*, 1930; *L'astronautique complément*, 1935.
[14] Some of the military developments are described in United States Air Force ROTC, *Fundamentals of Aerospace Weapons Systems*, 1961; United States Air Force Manual 52–31, *Guided Missiles Fundamentals*; General G. I. Pokrovsky, *Science and Technology in Contemporary War*, 1959 (originally published in Moscow by the Military Publishing House, Ministry of Defence, U.S.S.R.); M. N. Golovine, *Conflict in Space*, London, 1962; General Pierre Gallois, *Stratégie de l'Age Nucléaire*, 1960.

astronautical societies) pioneered a wider interest in the potential peaceful uses of outer space.[15]

When the International Council of Scientific Unions made plans for the International Geophysical Year of 1957–1958 it included therein provision for rocket and Earth satellite programmes, the initiative in suggesting the inclusion of an Earth satellite programme having been taken by the International Scientific Radio Union and the International Union of Geodesy and Geophysics; the United States and the U.S.S.R. agreed to undertake the responsibility for launching instrumented Earth satellites. A Special Committee for the International Geophysical Year Conference on Rockets and Satellites, which met in Washington D.C. from September 30 to October 5, 1957, held detailed discussions on plans for satellite research and culminated with the announcement on October 4 of the first successful launching of an instrumented Earth satellite by the U.S.S.R.[16] These arrangements had the inestimable advantage that activities in space, in marked contrast to the development of atomic energy, were initiated within a framework of organised international scientific co-operation, doubtless imperfect and inadequate but nevertheless of fundamental symbolical and substantial practical importance.

[15] The origin and development of the International Astronautical Federation are described in Andrew G. Haley, *Rocketry and Space Exploration*, 1958, pp. 229–237; the annual proceedings of the Federation are published.

[16] The IGY arrangements and programmes are described in detail in *Annals of the International Geophysical Year*, Vol. VI, 1958, IGY *Manual on Rockets and Satellites*, edited by L. V. Berkner, published by Pergamon Press. More recent accounts of the scientific results secured are contained in James A. Van Allen (ed.), *Scientific Uses of Earth Satellites*, 2nd rev. ed., 1958; H. E. W. Massey and R. L. F. Boyd, *The Upper Atmosphere*, 1958; Desmond King-Hele, *Satellites and Scientific Research*, 1960; L. V. Berkner and Hugh Odishaw (ed.), *Science in Space*, 1961; Ari Sternfeld, *Soviet Space Science*, 1959; Ari Sternfeld, *Soviet Writings on Earth Satellites and Space Travel*, 1959.

3

The Basic Scientific Facts

ACTIVITIES in space make calls upon all the sciences from mathematics to biology and psychology, but the basic scientific facts fundamental to an understanding of the problems presented by such activities for the international lawyer can be conveniently summarised under four heads, namely, two of the fundamental sciences, astronomy and geophysics, and two of the outstanding developments of modern technology, rocketry and electronics.

ASTRONOMY

The Earth is one of the nine known planets revolving around the Sun, a medium small star, some 30,000 light years from the centre of our galaxy of some 200,000 million stars, which is itself only one of the millions of galaxies in the telescopically observable expanding universe which extends at least 2,000 million light years from us in all directions. The nearest galactic neighbour of our solar system is the star system Alpha Centauri at a distance of about four light years or some 25 trillion miles. The speed of light is about 186,000 miles per second, the distance of the Sun from the Earth being approximately $8\frac{1}{3}$ light minutes. Velocities of spacecraft are of the order of five to ten miles per second, corresponding roughly to the velocities of Earth satellites and spacecraft designed to escape the gravitational pull of the Earth and the Sun. The velocity of a spacecraft leaving the solar system would in fact be greatly reduced by the gravitational pull of the sun, but even if a velocity of ten miles per second could be maintained the journey to Alpha Centauris would take over 70,000 years. We may therefore, for reasons of distance alone, limit our ambitions in space to the solar system for an indefinite time to come. Instruments beyond the atmosphere of the Earth may make a major contribution to our further knowledge of the universe beyond the solar system in the near future, but the likelihood of our being able to despatch instruments to other star systems and receive telemetered readings from them is altogether remote and the possibility of manned space travel by thermonuclear or some equal power at speeds approximating to the speed of light remains an imaginative fancy not matched by any hard core of reality in our present knowledge and techniques.

Even within the solar system the distances are so great as to defy any real understanding. Whereas the distance of the Moon from the Earth is only about 240,000 miles and the mean distance of the Earth from the Sun 92,900,000 miles, the diameter of the orbit of Pluto is 7,300 million miles. All of the planets move round the sun, in the same direction and in nearly the same plane, in ellipses of low eccentricity. Their positions in relation to each other are therefore constantly changing. Thus, the distance between the Earth and Venus varies from 25 million to 160 million miles; that between the Earth and Mars from 35 million to 220 million miles, the range when the Earth and Mars lie in the same direction from the sun varying from 35 million to 60 million miles. The interval between two successive close approaches of the Earth and Venus is some nineteen months; that between two successive close approaches of the Earth and Mars slightly over two years. Mars at its closest is more than a hundred times as distant as the Moon. For a journey to Venus a long elliptical approach is necessary to escape the gravitational attraction of the Sun. In the case of the outer planets the differences between their closest approaches and furthermost distances form a much less significant proportion of their mean distance from the Earth by reason of the relative nearness of the Earth to the Sun. The mean distance of Jupiter from the Sun is 480 million miles, that of Saturn 890 million miles, that of Uranus 1,800 million miles, that of Neptune 2,800 million miles and that of Pluto 3,700 million miles. The scope for space travel within the solar system therefore depends partly on the distances involved and partly on the extent to which the necessary precision of timing can be achieved. For practical purposes we can limit even our most ambitious speculations concerning the foreseeable future to the Moon, Venus and Mars.

The problems of distance and timing affect space probes by instruments as well as manned flight. When we come to envisage manned flight it is necessary to consider a wide range of further questions: the structural stability of the various celestial bodies; their temperature; whether and to what extent they are gaseous, liquid or solid; their mass and gravity; whether they have or lack an atmosphere; the gases composing their atmosphere and the presence or absence of water; their relative exposure to radiations and micrometeorites; their possibility of sustaining life. In some cases the answers to these questions may differ for a planet and one or more of its satellites. While there has been much speculation on all these questions, the existing knowledge of astronomers and astrophysicists is based on what they have learned by mathematical calculation based on telescopic and spectroscopic observation and radioastronomy. Information secured by space exploration by instruments may substantially modify our present beliefs concerning the Moon, Venus and Mars, before manned space travel puts our theories to the test. Of Venus, which has a mass and escape velocity comparable to those of Earth, we had little reliable knowledge until the results of the scientific experiments made by Mariner II during the flight past Venus in December 1962 became available; it was generally assumed to be enveloped by a cloudy atmosphere which prevented us from securing any knowledge of conditions on the surface and might veil either a lifeless desert or a moist and humid tropical world;[1] we now have important data which indicate that Venus has no significant magnetic field or radiation belt, that she has a surface temperature of about 800°F, and that the cloud layers have a temperature of about − 30°F which is curiously the same on both the light and the dark side. Mercury, on the other hand, a small rocky sphere which always keeps the same side turned towards the Sun, is not known to have any atmosphere and is believed to have temperatures as high as 750°F on the sunlit side and approaching absolute zero on the side which is in per-

[1] *Cf.* Patrick Moore, *The Planet Venus*, 3rd ed. 1961.

petual darkness.[2] Mars is assumed to have an appreciable atmosphere, believed to consist largely of nitrogen and with an atmospheric pressure at the surface estimated at eight to twelve per cent of Earth sea-level normal. The temperature is believed to vary from 80° to 90°F in a tropical noon to − 100°F before dawn. The surface markings of Mars exhibit seasonal changes in coloration, and, while there appears to be no free oxygen and little, if any, water, some form of vegetable life is thought to exist.[3] Human life on Mars would require extensive local environmental modifications, but the possibility of a self-sustaining colony there does not appear to be ruled out. The outer planets (excluding Pluto) are assumed to be massive bodies of low density and large diameter consisting of a small dense rocky core surrounded by a thick shell of ice and covered by thousands of miles of compressed hydrogen and helium, with methane and ammonia as minor constituents and temperatures at the visible upper atmospheric surfaces ranging from − 200° to − 300°F.[4] Some of their satellites may be more hospitable, but little is known about them. Earth's moon has no appreciable atmosphere and little gravity; its surface is probably dry, dust-covered rock; the face of the Moon is covered with many large craters, the origin of which is a matter of debate. The Sun itself we may think of as a thermonuclear furnace with a remarkably constant outflow of light and heat (probably varying by no more than 0.5 per cent from the average) but a variable outflow of ultraviolet radiation, radiowaves (solar static) and charged particles (cosmic rays); the peak intensity of the cosmic rays may rise to one thousand times the average. All usable forms of energy on the surface of the Earth, with the exception of atomic and thermonuclear energy, are directly or indirectly due to the storing or conversion of energy received from the Sun. Physical structure and temperature apart, the gravitational attraction of the Sun, which is over 300,000 times as massive as the Earth, precludes any close approach and subsequent separation by a spacecraft even without any attempt at landing. The physical characteristics of the celestial bodies,

[2] *Cf.* Werner Sandner, *The Planet Mercury*, 1963.
[3] *Cf.* Gerard de Vaucouleurs, *The Planet Mars*, 1950; *Physics of the Planet Mars*, 1952.
[4] *Cf.* Bertrand M. Peek, *The Planet Jupiter*, 1960; A. F. O'D. Alexander, *The Planet Saturn*, 1962.

as we at present surmise them to be, therefore set limits to the opportunities for manned landings in space roughly coinciding with those set for any immediately foreseeable technology by considerations of distance alone.

Our knowledge of the nature and hazards of interplanetary space is also highly tentative. The Van Allen Radiation Belts, for instance, were identified by satellite experiments. But the general concept of space beyond the atmosphere as a relative void of sparse but omnipresent gaseous matter with an unknown content of cosmic radiation and dust seems unlikely to be fundamentally changed, and the orbits and rotation of the celestial bodies, including Earth, necessarily involve a constantly changing relationship between them, and even more markedly between any one point on any one of them, and the space through which they all move.

How far forms of intelligent life diverging from the human pattern may exist within the area of space accessible to us, or in more distant areas having access to our area, remains a wholly speculative matter.[5]

GEOPHYSICS

While the facts of astronomy constitute the setting of all activities in space, the activities in space with which we are primarily concerned for as long a time to come as we need consider as a practical matter are Earth based. As Jessup and Taubenfeld have said:

"Earth is still the launching site and the base for sending and receiving communications. The needs or desires which inspire the exploration of outer space are Earth-born and Earth-centred. The use or misuse of outer space of which we speak is man's use or misuse. In speaking of controls for outer space we are thinking of man-made and man-applied controls; of controls not *of* space, but of man-made objects and also of men *in* space, and ultimately of men on planets in space."[6]

While the astronomical facts set limits to what can reasonably be envisaged, the geophysical facts are the point of departure of all activity in space.

[5] Sir Harold Spencer Jones, *Life in Other Worlds*, 1940.
[6] *Controls for Outer Space and the Antarctic Analogy*, 1959, p. 4.

The Basic Scientific Facts

The more important of the relevant geophysical facts are those relating to the atmosphere and those relating to gravity.

The Atmosphere

The Earth is enveloped by an atmosphere the density of which decreases progressively with distance from the Earth. In addition to furnishing the air we breathe, the atmosphere offers air resistance to motion through it, consumes by ignition objects entering it at high speed, and reflects radiation. It thereby provides the aerodynamic lift which makes possible aviation and protects us against the dangers from outer space represented by micrometeorites and cosmic radiation. The layers of the atmosphere are generally known as the troposphere, the stratosphere, the mesosphere and the thermosphere (also called ionosphere with its fringe region known as exosphere). The troposphere, which extends upwards some ten miles at the equator and about five miles at the poles, contains about three-fourths in weight of the gases composing the Earth's atmosphere and is characterised by continually decreasing temperatures with increase of altitude. The stratosphere extends from the top of the troposphere (known as tropopause) to some thirty to thirty-five miles from the surface of the Earth. In the stratosphere the temperature generally increases with height. The mesosphere extends from the top of the stratosphere (known as the stratopause) to about fifty miles from the surface of the Earth. In the mesosphere the temperature generally decreases with height. The stratosphere and the mesosphere together contain slightly less than one-fourth in weight of the Earth's atmosphere. The thermosphere (or the ionosphere) extends from the top of the mesosphere (known as the mesopause) to some four hundred to five hundred miles from the surface of the Earth. Throughout the ionosphere, temperature is believed to increase continuously with height; the ionosphere has been described as a zone of "free electrical discharges".

Gravity

The mutual attraction known as gravity is a fundamental law of astrophysics and geophysics alike. It explains both the orbits of the celestial bodies and the falling of the apple to earth. The gravitational attraction between two bodies depends on their masses and the distances between them. To escape from this gravitational attraction an object must leave a planet with a velocity exceeding a minimum value, known as the escape velocity. A lower velocity suffices to launch an Earth satellite, which remains in the gravitational field of the planet.

ROCKETRY

Space flight has been made practicable by the contemporary development of rocketry resulting from military programmes. Conventional aircraft cannot operate beyond the point at which there continues to be a sufficient density of atmosphere to give the aerodynamic lift necessary for their operations; nor can they attain a sufficient velocity to escape the gravitational attraction of the Earth. Rocket thrust, which may be described as the reaction force produced by expelling particles at high velocity from a nozzle opening is independent of aerodynamic lift and can give the velocity necessary to escape the gravitational attraction of the Earth. Once a space object has been placed by rocket thrust in orbit beyond significant atmospheric drag or has been carried beyond the gravitational attraction of the Earth it will continue upon its course at a consistent speed until deflected therefrom by the intervention of some new factor. The problem of launching objects into space therefore resolves itself into one of securing the initial thrust required to give the space object the velocity necessary to hold its course by the inertia of its motion. Present-day technology has solved the problem by the use of multi-stage rockets and of a variety of solid and liquid chemical propellants as fuels and oxidisers; experiments are also taking place into the possibility of using nuclear or thermonuclear reactions to obtain rocket power and into the possible use of solar and ion propulsion and plasma rockets. The technicalities of these propulsion systems need not detain us; it is sufficient for our purpose to note that their present or potential availability has given altogether new dimensions to the possible range of human action and adventure.

ELECTRONICS

The existence of rocket power which can place satellites in orbit and give space probes the thrust necessary to attain escape velocity would, however, be of little practical value in the absence of effective practical means of tracking space objects, receiving information from them, and giving directions to them. These achievements, in many ways more striking than the development of rocket thrust itself, have been made possible by developments in electronics. These developments have made it possible to use a combination of radiotelegraphy, sound broadcasting, television, infra-red detection, radar, electronic memory devices and computers for the purpose of guiding space objects, tracking them, storing in them and receiving from them the information recordable by the scientific instruments which they carry, recalling or destroying them, computing necessary adjustments and effectuating such adjustments automatically, receiving, storing and processing on the ground data received from space, and, in the case of manned operations, maintaining constant contact between the astronaut and the ground. The world of electronics lies as much beyond the general experience of international lawyers as that of astronomy, geophysics or rocketry and it is unnecessary for our purpose to enter into these matters in more technical detail, but it is the existence of these new techniques which makes possible, and defines the nature and limitations of, the activities in space out of which the legal problems arise.

4

The Breakthrough—1957-1964

SINCE the launching of Sputnik I on October 4, 1957, developments have occurred so rapidly that only those professionally concerned with developments in space can hope to keep track of them. For a systematic account of these developments reference must be made to the appropriate technical publications and periodicals.[1] All that is possible here is to indicate some of the leading landmarks, which I may perhaps be forgiven for describing as spacemarks.

SPACEMARKS

Sputnik I was launched by the U.S.S.R. on October 4, 1957.

Sputnik II, which carried the test dog "Laika", was launched by the U.S.S.R. on November 3, 1957.

Explorer I, which discovered the radiation belt round the Earth identified by Van Allen, was launched by the United States on January 31, 1958; further data on radiation belts were later secured by Explorers III and IV and Sputnik III.

Vanguard I, which was launched by the United States on March 17, 1958, provided geodetic observations including the determination that the Earth is slightly pear-shaped.

---

[1] See in particular the *COSPAR Bulletin*, such periodicals as *Planetary and Space Science* published by the Pergamon Press and *Space Science Reviews* published by D. Reidel, Publishing Co., Dordrecht, *Space Research*, sponsored by COSPAR and published annually by the North Holland Publishing Company, and *Progress in the Astronautical Sciences* issued by the same publisher. *Space Handbook – Astronautics and its Applications*, by Robert W. Buckheim and the Staff of the Rand Corporation, 1959, continues to be an invaluable comprehensive guide; a useful chronology of events to December 1960 is contained in United States National Aeronautics and Space Administration, *Aeronautics and Astronautics, 1915–1960*.

Pioneer I, which was launched by the United States on October 11, 1958, provided the first measurements of the interplanetary magnetic field.

Project Score, which was launched by the United States on December 18, 1958, was the first satellite to transmit a recording of the human voice from space.

Lunik I, which was launched by the U.S.S.R. on January 2, 1959, was the first successful deep space probe and entered into orbit around the Sun.

Discoverer II, which was launched by the United States on April 13, 1959, was the first satellite to carry an instrument package designed to be recoverable but not in fact recovered.

Lunik II, which was launched by the U.S.S.R. on September 12, 1959, was the first lunar impact, having travelled 236,875 miles in thirty-five hours.

Tiros I, the first purely meteorological satellite, was launched by the United States on April 1, 1960; the Tiros satellites carry television cameras for photographing the world's cloud systems and infra-red sensors for making measurements of a variety of atmospheric elements.

Transit IB, which was launched by the United States on April 13, 1960, demonstrated the feasibility of a navigation satellite.

Discoverer XIII was launched by the United States on August 10, 1960, and a man-made object was successfully recovered from space for the first time when a data capsule was recovered from the sea on August 11; Discoverer XIV was launched on August 18 and a space object successfully recovered by snatch in the air for the first time.

Echo I (a 100-foot inflatable sphere) was launched by the United States on August 17, 1960, to demonstrate the use of radio wave reflection for global communications.

Courier IB was launched by the United States on October 4, 1960, to test the feasibility of an active global communications system with a capacity of 68,000 coded words per minute.

A Venus Probe was launched by the U.S.S.R. on February 12, 1961.

On April 12, 1961, Major Yuri Gagarin orbited the Earth in a Vostok launched by the U.S.S.R.

On May 5, 1961, U.S. Navy Commander Alan B. Shepard, Jr., piloted a Mercury capsule through space to an altitude of 116.5 miles over a distance of 302 miles down range at a maximum speed of 5,036 miles.

Midas III was launched by the United States on July 12, 1961, for the detection of missile launchings with satellite borne sensors.

On August 6 to 7, 1961, Gherman Titov orbited the Earth seventeen times in a Vostok launched by the U.S.S.R.

Ranger I was launched by the United States on August 23, 1961, for the development of spacecraft systems for future lunar and interplanetary missions.

On February 20, 1962, Colonel John H. Glenn, Jr., orbited the Earth three times in Friendship 7 launched by the United States.

On April 26, 1962, the first United Kingdom satellite, Ariel, was launched by the United States.

The first Orbiting Solar Observatory was launched by the United States on March 7, 1962.

On July 3, 1962, it was announced that the United States National Aeronautics and Space Administration had approved a plan for a Lunar Excursion Module, designed to permit astronauts visiting the Moon to leave their spacecraft in orbit around the Moon while visiting the Moon in a lighter rocket ship able to surface upon and depart from the Moon more easily.

On July 10, 1962, the United States launched Telstar, a communication satellite launched and tracked by the National Aeronautics and Space Administration but built and operated by the American Telephone and Telegraph Company; Telstar, the first commercial space vehicle, was designed as a demonstration of the capability of a future communications satellite system girdling the world, and has been used both for a wide range of experimental purposes and for television relays between the United States and Europe.

On July 15, 1962, it was announced that the United States National Aeronautics and Space Administration had a plan for Lunar Logistics Carriers, radio-controlled from Earth, to serve as mobile caches of supplies and instruments for both normal and emergency use.

On July 22, 1962, the National Aeronautics and Space Administration of the United States issued the first of a series of geological maps of the surface of the Moon for use by astronauts.

On August 12, 1962, Vostok III piloted by Cosmonaut A. G. Nikolaev and Vostok IV piloted by Cosmonaut Popovitch achieved a near rendezvous in orbit and carried out the first group flight in orbit.

Mariner II was launched by the United States on August 27, 1962, to make close range observations of Venus; its course was corrected on September 4 when it was at a distance of 1,500,000 miles from the Earth and on December 14 when flying by Venus at a distance of 21,564 miles it successfully made and transmitted back 36 million miles to Earth observations which have given us a fuller knowledge of Venus than was available from centuries of astronomical observation.

On September 29, 1962, the first Canadian satellite, Alouette, was launched by the United States.

On November 1, 1962, the U.S.S.R. launched Mars I for the purpose of taking photographs of the surface of Mars and transmitting them to Earth.

On December 13, 1962, the United States launched Relay I to test microwave communications between North America, Europe and South America; it receives and retransmits to Earth radio signals and telephone traffic.

On May 15–16, 1963, Major L. Gordon Cooper orbited the Earth twenty-two times in Faith 7 launched by the United States and, on failure of the automatic control system for re-entry, successfully effected with close precision a manual retrofire and re-entry.

On June 16, 1963, the first woman astronaut, Valentina Tereshkova, was placed in orbit by the U.S.S.R.

In July 1963 the United States launched Syncom II into a near synchronous equatorial orbit as a prototype of a system of global communication satellites in stationary orbit above the equator.

On September 20, 1963, President Kennedy, addressing the General Assembly of the United Nations, called for "further joint efforts" by the United States and the Soviet Union "in the regulation and exploration of space" and said "I include among these possibilities a joint expedition to the Moon"; the suggestion was renewed on behalf of President Lyndon Johnson in December 1963.

In October 1963 the United States launched a nuclear test detector satellite designed to detect any breach of the Treaty of August 5, 1963, Banning Nuclear Weapons Tests in the Atmosphere, in Outer Space and Under Water.

On December 10, 1963, the United States Secretary of Defense announced plans for the development of a manned orbital space laboratory.

On December 29, 1963, the U.S.S.R. announced that the Crimea Deep Space Tracking Station had successfully bounced radar echoes off the planet Jupiter when the planet was at a distance of 370 million miles from the Earth.

On January 25, 1964, the United States launched Echo II, an inflated balloon passive communication satellite, designed for the experiments provided for in the United States – U.S.S.R. Bilateral Space Agreement involving the co-operation of the Gorky Observatory in the U.S.S.R. and the Jodrell Bank Station in the United Kingdom.

On January 29, 1964, the United States launched Saturn I, a super-rocket of 562 tons which propelled into orbit an 84-foot-long satellite weighing 37,700 pounds.

On January 30, 1964, the U.S.S.R., using a single carrier rocket, launched Electron I and Electron II, unmanned satellites for the study of radiation belts, into widely different orbits.

This breathtaking chronology gives some indication of the rate of development, but must be supplemented by a brief analysis, necessarily summary in character, of the nature of the results secured and in prospect.

TYPES OF CURRENT ACTIVITIES IN SPACE

Current activities in space (excluding any undisclosed activities of a military character) fall into three main types; the use of instruments for purposes of scientific research; the use of instruments in space for operational purposes in communication, meteorological, navigation, missile warning, and nuclear test detection satellites; and manned space travel.

Scientific investigation by instruments

Earth satellites and space probes as tools of scientific research have already opened up far-reaching new horizons to the scientific investigator. We have already learned much from them, and may reasonably hope to learn much more, in regard to such matters as the shape and detailed measurement of the Earth, the distribution of weather systems as revealed by clouds and knowledge of the meteorological data obtained from measurements of infra-red radiation, the density, composition and temperature of the upper atmosphere, irregularities in the atmosphere (including variations of density, winds, and the vagaries of the ionosphere), the zones of radiation which satellites have detected high above the Earth, the magnetism of the Earth, cosmic rays, the radiation of the Sun, the traffic density of meteors, and the effects of weightlessness on animals. This information has been secured by four methods: by tracking the orbits of satellites and space probes, optically and by radio and radar; by radio-recovery of the readings of satellite and space probe borne instruments, frequently made more valuable by telemetering and electronic memory devices; by radio photography; and by the recovery of data capsules ejected from satellites. Orbit tracking supplemented by the mathematical interpretation of the data obtained thereby has been particularly important as a source of geodesical information and has also thrown light on the basic properties of the atmosphere; for other purposes the other methods have been, and will increasingly be, more important. Orbit tracking can be undertaken by any State within reach of which a satellite or space probe passes which has the necessary organisation and scientific equipment; information from radio transmissions and radio photography by satellites and space probes is available directly only to States which can receive and interpret it; data capsules afford information directly only to States which recover them and can interpret their contents.

Improved instrumentation, which may include satellite-borne telescopes, spectroscopes and other instruments, will make possible a wider variety of new and more complex observations.

The range of scientific investigation by instruments may also be expected to be extended by the placing in orbit of artificial satellites of the Moon, the Sun, the nearer planets and possibly certain comets, and by the maintenance of contact with them for substantial and increasing periods.

Instruments in space for operational purposes

The use of instruments in space for operational purposes is emerging from the experimental phase in degrees varying for different types of satellites. The existing communication satellites, while designed as experimental, have already been used for a wide range of operational purposes, including television relays of the death of Pope John XXII and enthronement of Pope Paul VI, the conferment upon Sir Winston Churchill of honorary citizenship of the United States and the assassination and funeral of President Kennedy. Meteorological satellites have already provided data of great operational value and the United States Weather Bureau has made arrangements through the World Meteorological Organisation for the dissemination of cloud observations made by satellites on a world-wide and day-to-day basis by the meteorological telecommunications network; these have been in operation since July 1961. Such data have been used for the detection of tropical storms in the early stages of their development, for synoptic analysis and forecasting over oceanic areas from which meteorological observations are normally unobtainable or meagre, and for ensuring that manned satellites are launched in the most favourable weather conditions. The use of instruments in space for operational purposes will become fully operational with the placing in sufficiently stable orbits of a number of communication, meteorological and navigation satellites adequate to permit of dependable telecommunication relays, meteorological services and navigation aids. Astronomical observation satellites may place certain types of scientific experiment in space on a continuing operational basis. Missile launch detection warning satellites take us into the military field but may have an important place in internationally agreed arrangements for mutual warning against surprise attack. Nuclear test detection satellites are already being used by the United States to satisfy itself that there is no violation of the Treaty Banning Nuclear Weapons Tests in the Atmosphere, in Outer Space and Under Water.

27

Man in space

Man has already orbited the Earth and achieved a near rendezvous in space. It remains to be seen how much further he will travel, what range of activities he will undertake in space and how quickly such activities will develop. Manned space travel involves biological and other human problems our picture of which is still largely conjectural, but intensive research and experiment on the subject are in progress.[2]

Any prediction in the matter is liable to err by a wide margin of excessive optimism or excessive caution. It follows that the political and legal problems which man's venture into space will bring with it cannot be foreseen with any accuracy until we know much more of the nature and extent of his probable activities in space. Scientific expeditions, military activities, and exploitation of the resources of space in a manner still undefined would create entirely different situations and problems; brief ventures into space, continuous residence in space for substantial periods, and permanent residence in space with reproduction of the species there would likewise involve wholly different problems. The first phase will presumably be one of hazardous and intermittent exploration with at most a handful of people in space at any one time. In this first phase we cannot reasonably hope to have evolved either adequate institutional arrangements or sufficiently fully accepted legal principles to meet longer-term needs, nor will it be practically necessary that we should have done so, but it will be vital to have established the position that such arrangements and principles will be evolved by common agreement on the basis of growing experience as they become necessary and that meanwhile no unilateral claim to extra-terrestrial sovereignty or jurisdiction or to exclusive access to or use of any extra-terrestrial place or resource will be recognised.

In the light of the developments of recent years the elaborate plans for orbital relay stations and extra-terrestrial settlements adumbrated by pioneer writers on space travel[3] during the years preceding the

---

[2] See, for instance, Kenneth F. Gantz (ed.), *Man in Space*, 1959 (with a Preface by General Thomas D. White, Chief of Staff United States Air Force) and James S. Hanrahan and David Bushnell, *Space Biology – The Human Factors in Space Flight*, 1960.

[3] e.g., Clarke, *Interplanetary Flight*, 1950; *The Exploration of Space*, 1951; Gatland and Kunesch, *Space Travel*, 1953; Ley, *Rockets, Missiles and Space Travel*, 1951, with bibliography of the pioneer literature.

launching of the first Earth satellites can no longer be dismissed as wholly fanciful. Our advance thinking concerning the legal problems of space must reckon with the possibility that these fancies may become realities.

The breakthrough which has taken man into orbit and his instruments to the Moon and the neighbourhood of the nearer planets has already occurred. How much more may lie ahead, and when further developments will occur, remains unknown.

5

Scientific Co-operation in Space and its Limitations

IT is already clear from the foregoing that the background of space law consists of a complex of political, military, scientific and technological considerations, some account of which is a necessary preliminary to any satisfactory account of the legal problems. International co-operation in space began among the scientists and it is therefore appropriate to begin by describing the existing arrangements for scientific co-operation in space.

THE INTERNATIONAL COUNCIL OF SCIENTIFIC UNIONS
AND THE INTERNATIONAL GEOPHYSICAL YEAR

The International Council of Scientific Unions (ICSU) consists of fourteen international scientific unions for different branches of science and fifty-seven adhering bodies; the constituent unions consist of recognised national scientific bodies; the adhering bodies are national academies or similar institutions. ICSU is generally recognised as the authoritative voice of science and has been granted consultative status by the United Nations, by the specialised agencies primarily concerned with scientific matters (notably UNESCO, the World Health Organisation and the World Meteorological Organisation) and by the International Atomic Energy Agency.

In 1952 ICSU constituted the Special Committee for the International Geophysical Year (CSAGI) to implement proposals for intensive observations of the Earth and its cosmic environment which on the initiative of Professor L. V. Berkner had been made in 1950 and 1951 by the International Scientific Radio Union, the International Astronomical Union, and the International Union of Geodesy and Geophysics.[1] The concept was stimulated by the antecedents of the International Polar Years of 1882–1883 and 1932–1933 and developed into a programme of intensive observations by 30,000 scientists and technicians in sixty-six countries for an eighteen-month period selected because it coincided with the peak in the eleven-year sunspot cycle. The programme of investigations covered the Earth (seismology, gravity and longitude and latitude) the interface phenomena (meteorology, oceanography and glaciology), and upper atmosphere physics (solar activity, geomagnetism, cosmic rays, ionospheric physics, and aurora and air glow). There was an unprecedented programme of investigation in the Antarctic and an intensive programme in the Arctic. Rocket research was an important element in the programme from the outset and Earth satellites and space probes became progressively more important as it developed.

The programme was developed by a series of meetings of scientific delegates from national committees established by the adhering bodies of ICSU on the initiative of CSAGI. Each national committee assumed responsibility for the specific nature of its contributions, which were completely voluntary, and within the framework of the criteria established internationally each committee determined the extent of its own work, saw to the raising of funds and provision of logistical support, and directed the overall national effort. To cope with the data collected three world data centres were established, one in the United States under the direction of the National Academy of Sciences, one in the U.S.S.R. under the direction of the Academy of Sciences of the U.S.S.R., and the third distributed by scientific fields in Western Europe, Australia and Japan.

A series of recommendations concerning rocket and satellite programmes were formulated by CSAGI which was assisted in the matter by regional conferences and by a Rocket and Satellite Conference held at Washington D.C. in October 1957. These ultimately took the form

[1] For general accounts of the International Geophysical Year see Werner Buedeler, *The International Geophysical Year*, UNESCO, 1957; Fraser, *The History of the International Geophysical Year*, 1958; Sydney Chapman, *IGY – Year of Discovery*, 1959; Walter Sullivan, *Assault on the Unknown*, 1961; and United States, 85th Congress, 2nd Session, *The International Geophysical Year and Space Research*.

of section XI (Rockets and Satellites) of the CSAGI Guide to IGY World Data Centres.[2] These recommendations envisaged the provision by the IGY authorities effecting a launching of certain information required by co-operating observers; the information was to be published as soon as possible after a launching, but in no case more than twenty-four hours later. All IGY Committees which could co-operate by setting up observing stations (visual, radar or radio) were urged to do so in order to assist in tracking the satellites and improving the predictions of subsequent orbits; their observations were to be transmitted telegraphically within one day to the IGY authority effecting the launching. Codes appropriate for the rapid communication of both visual and radio observations were indicated. The recommendations included a suggested flight information form and a plan for the publication of reports of rocket and satellite experiments. While not wholly effective in practice in the absence of any obligation upon launching governments to implement them, these recommendations provided an invaluable general framework of scientific co-operation.

COSPAR

COSPAR (the Committee on Space Research) is a scientific committee of the International Council of Scientific Unions established to facilitate the continuation on a more permanent basis of the international scientific co-operation in respect of space matters initiated on the occasion of the International Geophysical Year. It is one of four such committees, the others being CIG (the International Geophysical Committee), SCOR (the Scientific Committee on Oceanographic Research), and SCAR (the Scientific Committee on AntarcticResearch). The membership of COSPAR consists of one representative designated by each national scientific institution adhering to the International Council of Scientific Unions which is actively engaged in space research and which wishes to be represented in COSPAR, together with one representative designed by each international scientific union federated in the International Council of Scientific Unions which wishes to par-

---

[2] The full text is available in *Annals of the International Geophysical Year*, Vol. VI. *IGY Manual of Rockets and Satellites*, pp. 465–472.

ticipate in COSPAR. Twenty-six national scientific institutions and ten international scientific unions were represented in 1964, the national scientific institutions being those of Argentina, Australia, Austria, Belgium, Canada, Czechoslovakia, Finland, France, Federal Republic of Germany, German Democratic Republic, Hungary, India, Israel, Italy, Japan, Netherlands, Norway, Pakistan, Poland, Rumania, South Africa, Sweden, Switzerland, United Kingdom, U.S.A. and U.S.S.R.

The purpose of COSPAR, as defined by its Charter, is to further on an international scale the progress of all kinds of scientific investigations which are carried out with the use of rockets or rocket-propelled vehicles. The Charter provides that "COSPAR shall be concerned with fundamental research" and "will not normally concern itself with such technological problems as propulsion, construction of rockets, guidance and control". Its objectives are to be achieved "through the maximum development of space research programmes by the international community of scientists working through ICSU and its adhering national academies and unions". Any arrangements involving national territories are to be made "by bilateral or multilateral discussion between the nations concerned". COSPAR, as a non-political organisation, "shall not, as a matter of policy, recommend any specific assistance of one nation by another" but will "welcome information concerning such arrangements and provide a convenient assembly in which such arrangements may informally be proposed and discussed".

"Recognising the need for international regulation and discussion of certain aspects of satellite and space probe programmes", COSPAR is to "keep itself informed of United Nations or other international activities in this field, to assure that maximum advantage is accorded international space science research through such regulations and to make recommendations relative to matters of planning and regulation that may affect the optimum programmes of scientific research". COSPAR is to report to ICSU "those measures needed in the future to achieve the participation in international programmes of space research, of all countries of the world with those which are already actively engaged in research programmes within the domain of COSPAR".

The methods employed by COSPAR to pursue these objectives include arrangements for mutual notification through COSPAR of the scientific results secured by satellites and space probes; the holding of periodical International Space Science Symposia; more specialised symposia, and working group sessions; and the issue of a regular *Information Bulletin* and other publications and documents.

The International Council of Scientific Unions, in a resolution adopted at a meeting of its General Assembly in London, September 25-28, 1961, invited COSPAR to examine any proposed experiments or other space activities that may have potentially undesirable effects on scientific activities and observations, to arrange for careful, objective quantitative studies, and to make available to unions, academies and governments the facts and analyses needed by them for making wise and proper decisions; it likewise appealed to all governments planning such experiments to make available to the International Council of Scientific Unions information and data about the proposed experiments to make the desired studies.

In May 1962 COSPAR established a Consultative Group on Potentially Harmful Effects of Space Experiments to carry out this responsibility. The Group consists of seven broadly competent scientists named by the President of COSPAR having among them specialised knowledge of astronomy, radiation physics, atmospheric physics and chemistry, communications, meteorite penetration and microbiology. The Group was expected to act as a focal point in the International Council of Scientific Unions for the consideration of all questions regarding potentially harmful effects of space experiments on scientific activities and observations. In this capacity it would examine in a preliminary way all questions relating to possibly harmful effects of proposed space experiments, including but not restricted to questions referred to it by any of the ICSU Unions; would determine whether or not any serious possibility of harmful effects would indeed result from the proposed experiment; would, in consultation with appropriate Unions, appoint and arrange for convening an appropriate *ad hoc* Working Group or Groups to study any expected effects which are considered to be potentially harmful, such Working Group or Groups to include competent scientists in the appropriate specialised disciplines; to receive and consider the conclusions or recommendation of such *ad hoc* Working Groups in a timely manner; and to prepare final recommendations to the COSPAR Executive Council for its further action. Positive or negative recommendations by studies considered appropriate by the Council for dissemination would then be made available to all COSPAR adherents, the ICSU Bureau, the appropriate Unions of ICSU, and appropriate bodies of the United Nations and specialised agencies.

The establishment of the Consultative Group on Potentially Harmful Effects of Space Experiments was precipitated by the concern of radio astronomers regarding the United States "West Ford" experiment. On October 21, 1961, the United States launched for experimental purposes connected with long-distance radio communication and placed in a near-polar orbit a package consisting of a cylindrical block of naphthalene about 45 by 15 cm. in size in which 350 million copper wire dipoles (popularly called needle satellites) weighing altogether about 30 kg. were embedded. The intention to make the experiment was announced in the summer of 1960 and gave rise to prolonged and acute controversy on the ground that the resulting accumulation of material in orbit would cause interference to optical and radio astronomy. A United States Government Policy Statement of August 8, 1961, contained assurances that "no further launching of orbiting dipoles will be planned until after the results of the West Ford experiment have been analysed and evaluated", that "the findings and conclusions of foreign and domestic scientists" would be "carefully considered in such analysis and evaluations", and that "any decision to place additional quantities of dipoles in orbit . . . will be contingent upon the results of the analysis and evaluation and the development of necessary safeguards against harmful interference with space activities or with any branch of science". The International Astronomical Union, meeting at Berkeley (California) on August 24, 1961, unanimously adopted a resolution appealing to all governments concerned with space experiments which could possibly affect astronomical research to consult with the International Astronomical Union before undertaking such experiments and to refrain from launching until it is established beyond doubt that no damage will be done to astronomical research; as regards the West Ford project it expressed appreciation that the plans had been announced well ahead of the proposed launching and that further launching would be guided by the principle that such projects shall not be undertaken unless sufficient safeguards have been obtained against harmful interference with astronomical observations. The International Council of Scientific Unions then adopted its resolution inviting COSPAR to examine any proposed experiments or other space activities that may have potentially undesirable effects on scientific activities and observations. A further report by a panel of the Scientific Advisory Committee of the President of the United States reached the conclusion that the initial test belt of dipoles could be launched without danger to science.[3]

It subsequently appeared that the wire dipoles had not been released from the solid package.[4]

A second experiment, in the course of which the dipoles were successfully released, was made in 1963; COSPAR subsequently found that it had not had significantly harmful results, but that the position should continue to be carefully watched.[4a]

In addition to studying orbiting dipoles the Consultative Group has initiated studies of the pollution of the upper atmosphere with rocket exhaust fumes and other artificially injected materials and on the potential contamination of the Moon and planets.[4b]

The question of space experiments has also been extensively discussed in connection with nuclear testing. In April 1963 the United Kingdom Steering Group on Space Research reported unanimously in the following terms to the Minister of Science concerning the issues of general policy involved:

"(a) serious adverse effects, both on scientific research and on other space activities (*e.g.*, communications, or meteorological satellites), could result from further high-level nuclear tests above the 1 kiloton range,

[3] As regards the whole matter see *COSPAR Information Bulletin*, No. 7, November 1961, pp. 20–21.
[4] *COSPAR Information Bulletin*, No. 8, February 1962, p. 54.
[4a] pp. 408–410, below.
[4b] pp. 406–414, below.

or from other experiments in outer space, which might be undertaken by any country;

(b) the effects of such experiments may, in some circumstances, be difficult to predict. Indeed, it is still difficult to predict the duration of the artificial radiation produced by the high-level test on July 9, 1962;

(c) as far as defence considerations permit, any proposed experiments in outer space which could adversely affect scientific research should be openly discussed with the scientists whose work might be affected."[5]

Their findings concerning the United States high altitude nuclear explosion of July 9 1962 were as follows:

"1. The explosion of July 1962, has changed the charged-particle environment of the Earth in a way which is likely to last for several years. The life history of these artificially injected particles will provide valuable information about the origin of the radiation belts, but it may now be difficult to decide precisely what the natural environment was before the explosion.

2. The modified environment radiates radio waves which interfere with radio-astronomical observations, particularly those made from low latitudes and from artificial satellites. Improvement in observing techniques will render these interfering effects more important, and will make their effects felt over greater portions of the Earth.

3. The charged particles have either interfered with or have stopped the working of some artificial satellites.

4. Explosions with yields of about one kiloton have in the past led to some interesting scientific results without interfering in any known way with other scientific work. Presumably they might do so again in the future.

5. Neither the essential facts about the explosion of 1962, nor the calculations of its probable effects, were made available to world scientists, in spite of the resolutions of the International Astronomical Union."[6]

On the basis of these findings they recommended that if any more high-level nuclear explosions are planned by any country, they should first be discussed by an international group of scientists who would be given the task of advising how the explosion should be planned so as not to interfere with any known scientific researches and so as to pro-

[5] Cmnd. 2029 of May 1963, p. 3.
[6] *Ibid.*, pp. 6–7.

duce the most valuable scientific results, and that a body under ICSU, such as the panel set up by COSPAR to study potentially harmful effects of space experiments, would be a suitable international group. This recommendation must be regarded as having been superseded by the Moscow Nuclear Test Ban Treaty assuming that Treaty to remain generally effective.

The question is also adumbrated in the WMO *First Report on the Advancement of Atmospheric Sciences and their Application in the Light of Developments in Outer Space* which envisage[7] that mankind will eventually have the power to influence weather and even climate on a large scale with far-reaching repercussions in other parts of the earth and points out that it is "imperative that the consequences of any such large-scale interference with the existing climatic balance should be accurately foreseen and evaluated".

Scientific co-operation clearly has a major part to play, and may well be the decisive factor, in resolving the problem of avoiding undesirable effects of space experiments, but it is now widely recognised that a legal principle of general application is already desirable and may increasingly become indispensable. The case for buttressing scientific understandings by a legal principle is reinforced by the increasing extent to which the potentially harmful effects of experiments in space are regarded by scientists as posing a moral issue. Thus Sir Bernard Lovell writes that "the newly acquired technical ability of human beings to launch satellites, space probes, and space ships involves hazards where the judgment between right and wrong is thinly veiled" and that the contamination of space for national interests "is ethically wrong".[8]

THE INTERNATIONAL ASTRONAUTICAL FEDERATION

The International Astronautical Federation, a federation of national astronautical societies in some forty countries, brings a more popular touch to scientific co-operation in space.

While COSPAR is concerned with fundamental research the International Astronautical Federation specialises in applied science and

[7] Appendix E.
[8] Sir Bernard Lovell, *The Exploration of Outer Space*, 1962, pp. 78–79.

technology. It brings together space enthusiasts and pioneers of all types, including administrators and legislative protagonists of national space programmes, rocket engineers, inventors and makers of propulsion and guidance systems and electronic equipment of all types, aviation, telecommunication and other commercial interests, publicists and lawyers. It works through congresses, colloquia, committees and contacts, has provided much of the driving force behind national civilian space programmes, and has played the leading role in the popularisation of such programmes. It sponsors an International Academy of Astronautics and an International Institute of Space Law.[9]

THE LIMITATIONS OF SCIENTIFIC CO-OPERATION

Scientific co-operation is the indispensable basis of the use of space for the betterment of mankind, but, as is recognised by the reference in the COSPAR Charter to the need for international regulation of "certain aspects of satellite and space probe programmes", there are clear-cut limitations to what scientific co-operation alone can achieve. It cannot eliminate the military element from space; it cannot furnish the minimum of legal regulation necessary to buttress understandings among scientists by obligations mutually binding upon governments; it cannot define the legal consequences of occurrences in space; and it cannot provide an adequate measure of regulation of economic interests which may develop in certain space activities. No scientist should, and responsible scientists do not, cherish the illusion that space affords a new opportunity for the withering away of the State before the magic of goodwill among scientists. The existing space programmes are government ventures; the launching facilities which have made them possible have been created and are operated by the military; large commercial interests are becoming increasingly involved in them; we cannot hope to avoid confusion and frustration or to keep power politics out of space unless scientific co-operation and political understandings are translated into firm legal obligations. Only by a close partnership of policy, law, science and technology can the proper scope

[9] For a fuller account see Andrew G. Haley, *Space Law and Government*, 1963, pp. 343–380.

and content of such obligations be determined. This becomes increasingly apparent as examination of the matter proceeds from generalities to specifics.

The constructive possibilities of scientific co-operation may be overshadowed at any time by the use of space for military purposes. We are told, for instance, that it is technically possible to place nuclear weapons in orbit and release them by a radio signal.

In this general situation what role has the law to play and what measures of international control do we require?

Unless space is exclusively dedicated to peaceful and scientific purposes, and a satisfactory inspection system designed to make the exclusive dedication of space to peaceful and scientific purposes effective is introduced, all else will be precarious. This is primarily a problem of the control of armaments rather than a problem of the control of space.

Pending a satisfactory outcome of negotiations for disarmament, what other steps can usefully be taken?

In the first place, legal regulation is a necessary element in the measure of common discipline without which the scientific exploration of space cannot proceed fruitfully. This is most obviously so in respect of space telecommunication, a field in which the International Telecommunication Union has already taken, and must continue to hold, the initiative. It is equally so in respect of measures to minimise the adverse effects of possible biological, radiological, and chemical contamination of and from space, a matter in respect of which the initiative lies for the moment with COSPAR but which may well call for legal regulation to buttress understandings among scientists. Unless clear rules on these matters exist from the outset and are strictly applied, space research will not yield the fruits which we are entitled to expect from it. It is equally important for the same purpose to have clear rules requiring space vehicles to be fitted with instruments permitting their recovery at the end of their useful lives, or where this is impracticable their destruction by the silencing of radio transmission from them, in order to avoid space being cluttered with derelicts the continued observation of which places an impossible burden on the ground tracking networks.

These prospective measures represent a minimum without which nobody will be able to begin to reap efficiently the fruits of the scientific exploration of space; a much larger measure of co-operation will be necessary before anybody can reap the full harvest, the garnering of which involves simultaneous observation in many parts of the world; a still larger measure of co-operation will be necessary to make that harvest available to everybody in such a manner as to eliminate national rivalry from space.

Simultaneous observation in many parts of the world may be partly the spontaneous result of scientific or military curiosity and partly the outcome of understandings among scientists and observational stations, but its successful organisation on a long-term basis calls for an agreed code of rules providing as a minimum for the exchange of full tracking information and of methods of data decoding and ideally for a much more complex exchange of information, including a complete tabulation of reduced, calibrated and corrected data and facilities for verifying matters calling for further enquiry by access to telemeter records.

The further stage of making the full harvest of new knowledge available to everybody has a major bearing on the demilitarisation of space. Mutual protection against surprise attack is the key to making effective the exclusive dedication of space to peaceful purposes; the chief danger of activities in space unleashing war on earth may well lie in some inoffensive space vehicle being mistaken in a radar screen at a moment of heightened international tension for an intercontinental ballistic missile which has been launched for a military purpose. Advance notification of launching sites and firing schedules, the filing of flight plans and of descriptions of weight, load and size, and the use of agreed radio codes for the reception of data from space can all play a significant part in eliminating the element of potential military surprise. The international arrangements desirable for this purpose may well include a special organisation analogous to that which was projected at one stage for the detection of any violation of the comprehensive nuclear test ban then proposed.

The use in artificial satellites and other space instrumentalities of observational equipment involves a major danger of international incident in the absence of clear understandings expressed in the form of clear-cut obligations. The solution of the problems to which it gives rise may perhaps be found in a requirement that information obtained by the use of such equipment shall not be reserved for the exclusive use, whether for military or for other purposes, of the State having collected it, but shall be made available to the whole world. Example may be more effective than precept as a means of inaugurating such a practice, but, except in the meteorological field where it has already been adopted, the practice is not likely to be generally observed despite national pressures to maintain secrecy unless it is fortified by accepted international obligations covering the matter.

The elimination of the military element has a special significance for States which are preoccupied by the possibility that the passage of space vehicles through their atmosphere may be regarded by more powerful States as a breach of neutral duty. While it would appear to be clear that no State can reasonably be held responsible for failure to prevent something which only the most advanced and expensive technology, as yet within the resources of only two powers, can either achieve or prevent, an international agreement which would eliminate the problem is eminently desirable.

The launching, flight and re-entry of space vehicles involve a number of dangers to third parties – dangers from misfires, dangers to aircraft, and dangers from loss of control on re-entry. The question of liability for injury or damage caused by space vehicles is therefore one of high priority. It includes the principle and extent of liability (a problem the solution of which may be found in a combination of absolute liability for injury or damage on the surface or in the air and liability based on fault for injury or damage in space), the question whether liability should be unlimited in amount and if not what limitation of liability should apply, the provision of insurance against liability, and possibly, in certain cases, the question whether liability is joint or several. The possibility of a serious international incident arising from injury or damage caused by a space vehicle cannot be ignored and the question is therefore of urgent political, as well as of legal, importance. An early international agreement settling the law on the subject with some precision, establishing a procedure for the recovery of damages which gives injured persons an effective means of redress and providing for the submission to the International Court of Justice of disputes between States concerning the liability of States for injury or damage caused by space vehicles is therefore desirable. It also seems desirable to formulate at an early stage by international agreement or otherwise as a recognised duty the principle of mutual aid against the common dangers of the unknown and assistance for persons in distress. The principle is fundamental in the ethics of mountaineering and polar exploration and has already received legal expression in the Safety of Life at Sea Convention and the Search and Rescue Annex to the International Civil Aviation Convention.

Operational activities in space for telecommunication, meteorological, navigation and astronomical purposes will call as a minimum for codes of regulations governing their operations, but they may also present an opportunity to organise such activities as world public services rather than as national or commercial undertakings. The International Telecommunication Union, the World Meteorological Organisation and the Intergovernmental Maritime Consultative Organisation are not at present operational bodies, but the possibility of entrusting them with certain operational responsibilities in connection with the operation of such world public services should not be lightly set aside. The opportunity to organise operational activities in space as world public services will be a fleeting one but every effort should be made to grasp it and to exploit it to the full. Success in this respect would be a major contribution to the establishment of an effective international control of space.

In the light of this complex of political, military, economic and legal considerations it is not surprising that within a few weeks of the launching of Sputnik I scientific co-operation in space began to be supplemented by United Nations action.

6

United Nations Action

UNITED Nations action in respect of space co-operation has passed through a succession of phases, beginning with the immediate enunciation by the General Assembly in 1957 of the broad principle of the exclusive dedication of outer space to peaceful and scientific purposes and progressively evolving, though not without setbacks and difficulties, towards positive measures for dealing with specific problems, the main bar to progress being the continuing deadlock in respect of the need for and nature of inspection as a measure of protection against military surprise.

THE EXCLUSIVE DEDICATION OF SPACE
TO PEACEFUL AND SCIENTIFIC PURPOSES

Sputnik I was launched on October 4, 1957.

On November 14, less than six weeks later, the General Assembly, in a resolution relating to disarmament, called for "the joint study of an inspection system designed to ensure that the sending of objects through outer space should be exclusively for peaceful and scientific purposes".[1]

Opinion in favour of the exclusive dedication of space to peaceful and scientific purposes crystallised rapidly thereafter.

On January 12, 1958, President Eisenhower, in a message to Premier Bulganin, proposed that outer space should be used only for peaceful purposes, that the testing of missiles designed for military purposes in outer space should be stopped, and that outer space should be dedicated to the peaceful uses of mankind.

[1] General Assembly Resolution 1148 (XII) of November 14, 1957, para. 1 (f).

44

On March 16, 1958, the Government of the U.S.S.R., while formulating political conditions unacceptable to other States, proposed a plan envisaging prohibition of the use of outer space for military purposes, an undertaking by States to launch rockets only in accordance with an agreed international programme, the establishment within the framework of the United Nations of adequate international control over the implementation of these commitments, and the creation of a United Nations body for international co-operation in the field of outer space research. The functions of this body would have been (a) to elaborate an agreed international programme for launching intercontinental and outer space rockets with a view to investigating outer space and to supervise this programme; (b) to continue on a permanent basis the types of research into outer space carried out by the International Geophysical Year Programme; (c) to serve as a world centre for the collection and mutual exchange and dissemination of information about space research; and (d) to co-ordinate national research plans for outer space and co-operate in their implementation.

No responsible statesman appears to have called in question the general principle of the exclusive dedication of space to peaceful and scientific purposes.

A further General Assembly resolution, adopted in 1958,[2] included recitals "recognising the common interest of mankind in outer space and . . . that it is the common aim that outer space should be used for peaceful purposes only", expressing the wish "to avoid the extensions of present national rivalries into this new field", and stating the belief that "the development of programmes of international and scientific co-operation in the uses of outer space should be vigorously pursued" and that "progress in this field will materially help to achieve the aim that outer space should be used for peaceful purposes only". It will be observed that in this resolution the exclusive dedication of space to peaceful purposes is stated as an aim rather than as an accomplished reality.

There have not been lacking lawyers to argue that the peaceful use of space includes military measures which are defensive in intent and

[2] General Assembly Resolution 1348 (XII) of December 13, 1958.

non-aggressive in character. Any such view, so broadly expressed, would imply that action the whole purpose of which was military preparation would continue to be regarded as a peaceful use of space until the final logical conclusion of such action in the use of space for a military purpose was reached. Clearly that was not what the General Assembly of the United Nations had in mind when it spoke of reserving outer space "exclusively for peaceful and scientific purposes". The use of space instrumentalities as a measure of missile launch detection for warning purposes may be regarded as consistent with the exclusive dedication of space to peaceful and scientific purposes, particularly if it forms part of an agreed or preannounced plan; the placing in orbit of a nuclear weapon which can be released by a radio signal, or other measures the nature of which remains uncertain by reason of military secrecy, cannot reasonably be so regarded.

SPACE IN RELATION TO DISARMAMENT AND NUCLEAR AND THERMONUCLEAR TESTS

The demilitarisation of space is among the subjects under consideration as part of the disarmament negotiations taking place within the framework of the United Nations.

Ten-Nation Disarmament Committee

In the Ten-Nation Disarmament Committee established by agreement among France, the United Kingdom, the U.S.S.R. and the United States on September 7, 1959, which reached a deadlock with the withdrawal of the Soviet representatives and their associates on June 27, 1960, both sides had accepted, but subject to varying conditions which had not been reconciled, the general principle that outer space should be used only for peaceful purposes.[3]

The Western Plan for General and Comprehensive Disarmament in a Free and Peaceful World of March 16, 1960, included proposals for an immediate undertaking of prior notification to the International Disarmament Organisation of proposed launchings of space vehicles

[3] United Nations Document D.C./179 of August 15, 1960.

and the establishment of co-operative arrangements for communicating to the International Disarmament Organisation data obtained from available tracking facilities, and immediate joint studies of (a) measures to assure compliance with an agreement that no nation shall place into orbit or station in outer space weapons of mass destruction, including provision for on-site inspection, and (b) measures to assure compliance with an agreement on prior notification of missile launchings, according to predetermined and mutually agreed criteria, and on declarations to the International Disarmament Organisation of locations of launching sites and places of manufacture of such missiles. On the completion of the joint studies provision would be made for (a) the prohibition against placing into orbit or stationing in outer space vehicles capable of mass destruction to be effective immediately after the installation and effect-ive operation of an agreed control system to verify this measure; and (b) prior notification to the International Disarmament Organisation of proposed launchings of missiles according to predetermined and mutually agreed criteria, and declarations of locations of launching sites, and places of manufacture of such missiles, with agreed verifica-tion including on-site inspection of launching sites of such missiles. Among further measures regarded as necessary for achieving the ultimate goal were measures to ensure the use of outer space for peaceful purposes only and control of the production of agreed categories of military missiles and existing national stocks and their final elimination.

A further Western proposal of April 26, 1960, indicated that a programme of general and complete disarmament under effective inter-national control must "provide for the use of outer space for peaceful purposes only and for the final elimination of weapons of mass destruction and their means of delivery".

The U.S.S.R. proposals for a Treaty on General and Complete Disarmament of June 2, 1960, provided that from the very beginning of the first stage of disarmament and until the final destruction of all means of delivering nuclear weapons, the placing into orbit or stationing in outer space of any special devices should be prohibited, that the launching of rockets should be carried out exclusively for peaceful purposes and in accordance with predetermined and mutually agreed

47

criteria, and should be accompanied by agreed measures of verification, including inspection at the rocket launching sites, and that on-site international control should be established over the destruction of rocket weapons, that rocket launching sites, with the exception of those maintained for peaceful purposes, should be destroyed under the supervision of the international control organisation, and that international inspection teams dispatched by the control organisation should have the right to carry out a thorough examination of rocket devices to be launched for peaceful purposes and to be present at their launching.

A further United States proposal of June 27, 1960, provided for prohibition of the placing into orbit or stationing in outer space of vehicles carrying weapons capable of mass destruction and for prior notification to the International Disarmament Control Organisation of all proposed launchings of space vehicles and missiles and their planned tracks; these measures were to be effective as from the first stage of disarmament.

At this point the negotiations in the Ten-Nation Committee were discontinued.

Eighteen-Nation Disarmament Committee

In the reconstituted Eighteen-Nation Disarmament Committee[4] established by the agreement concerning the composition of a negotiating body between the U.S.S.R. and the U.S.A. endorsed by General Assembly Resolution 1722 (XVI) I of December 20, 1961, the question of the demilitarisation of outer space has continued to play an important role.

The Draft Treaty on General and Complete Disarmament under Strict International Control submitted by the U.S.S.R. on March 19, 1962, provided that all rockets capable of delivering nuclear weapons, of any calibre and range, whether strategic, operational or tactical (except for strictly limited numbers of rockets to be converted to peaceful uses), as well as pilotless aircraft of all types, should be eliminated from the armed forces and destroyed and that all launching pads, silos and platforms for the launching of rockets and pilotless aircraft, other

---

[4] Sometimes described as the Seventeen-Nation Committee because France has not yet occupied her seat.

than those retained for peaceful launchings under the provisions of the Treaty, should be completely demolished.[5] Inspectors of the International Disarmament Organisation were to verify the implementation of these measures.[6] The production and testing of rockets appropriate for the peaceful exploration of space was to be allowed, but the plants producing such rockets, as well as the rockets themselves, were to be subject to supervision by the inspectors of the International Disarmament Organisation.[7] From the very beginning of the first stage of disarmament and until the final destruction of all means of delivering nuclear weapons under the Treaty, the placing into orbit or stationing in outer space of any special devices capable of delivering weapons of mass destruction was to be prohibited.[8] The States parties to the Treaty were to provide advance information to the International Disarmament Organisation about all launchings of rockets for peaceful purposes.[9] The launching of rockets and space devices was to be carried out exclusively for peaceful purposes and the International Disarmament Organisation was to exercise control over the implementation of these provisions "through the establishment of inspection teams at the sites for peaceful rocket launchings who shall be present at the launchings and shall thoroughly examine every rocket or satellite before their launching".[10]

The Outline of Basic Provisions of a Treaty on General and Complete Disarmament in a Peaceful World submitted by the U.S.A. on April 18, 1962, provided that, as part of the first stage of disarmament, the Parties to the Treaty would agree not to place in orbit weapons capable of producing mass destruction and would agree to support increased international co-operation in peaceful uses of outer space in the United Nations or through other appropriate arrangements. With respect to the launching of space vehicles and missiles they would provide advance notification of such launchings to other Parties to the Treaty and to the International Disarmament Organisation together with the track of the space vehicle or missile; such advance notifications would

[5] Art. 5 (1).   [8] Art. 14 (1).
[6] Art. 5 (3).   [9] Art. 14 (2).
[7] Art. 5 (4).   [10] Art. 15 (1) and (2).

be provided on a timely basis to permit pre-launch inspection of the space vehicle or missile to be launched. The International Disarmament Organisation would conduct pre-launch inspection of space vehicles and missiles and would establish and operate any arrangements necessary for detecting unreported launchings. The production, stockpiling and testing of boosters for space vehicles would be subject to agreed limitations; such activities would be monitored by the International Disarmament Organisation. The arrangements for inspection of launchings and the monitoring of other activities would be set forth in an annex on verification.

In the third stage of disarmament the Parties to the Treaty would report to the International Disarmament Organisation any basic scientific discovery and any technological invention having potential military significance, would, where necessary, establish scientific and technical information and free interchange of views among scientific and technical personnel.

After an adjournment the United Kingdom Delegation suggested on July 17, 1962, a list of subjects suitable for discussion in depth which included as point ten "outer space and related measures of verification".

These matters remained until the General Assembly adopted on October 17, 1963, Resolution 1884 (XVIII) welcoming "expressions by the U.S.S.R. and the United States of their intention not to station in outer space any objects carrying nuclear weapons or other kinds of weapons of mass destruction" and solemnly calling upon all States "to refrain from placing in orbit around the Earth any objects carrying nuclear weapons or any other kinds of weapons of mass destruction, installing such weapons on celestial bodies, or stationing such weapons in outer space in any other manner".

In summary, therefore, there has been throughout the disarmament negotiations substantial agreement on the general principles that weapons of mass destruction should not be placed in orbit and that, as a material guarantee of compliance, there should be advance notification of launchings and pre-launch inspection. There have doubtless been many problems in regard to the implementation of these principles, but these have been greatly compounded by other problems relating to disarmament generally rather than to the demilitarisation of space as such. The stage now reached is that the General Assembly has noted a declaration of intent by the two leading space powers that they do not intend to station weapons of mass destruction in outer space and has called upon all States to refrain from so doing.

Conference on the Discontinuance of Nuclear Weapon Tests

The use of satellite systems as a means of detection and indentification of nuclear weapon tests was also being considered by the Conference on the Discontinuance of Nuclear Weapon Tests. The Draft Treaty on the Discontinuance of Nuclear Weapon Tests submitted to the Conference by the United Kingdom and United States Delegations on April 18, 1961, included an annex providing for a detection and identification system, Article 11 of which described a proposed high altitude system of detection in the following terms:

"1. The high altitude systems, which are based upon the recommendations contained in the 'Report of the Technical Working Group on the Detection and Identification of High Altitude Nuclear Explosions', of July 15, 1959, are established for the purpose of providing, when in effective operation, a level of capability not less than that estimated by the Technical Working Group in sections A and B of their Report. The techniques and instrumentation for the detection and identification of nuclear explosions at high altitudes shall comprise apparatus installed at control posts and ground stations as specified in Articles 2, 5 and 6 of this Annex, together with satellite systems.

"Satellite systems shall be so positioned in orbits as to provide maximum capability for detecting nuclear explosions as follows:

"A. One or more satellites (trapped-electron satellites) placed in an appropriate terrestrial elliptical orbit and suitably instrumented with counters for recording electrons trapped in the Earth's magnetic field. A satellite shall be replaced when it can no longer record or transmit the required data to ground stations.

"B. At least six satellites (far-Earth satellites) placed in terrestrial orbits at altitudes of more than 30,000 kilometers so as to be continuously outside the Earth's trapped radiation belts. Three of the satellites shall be nearly equally spaced in the same orbital plane, and three satellites shall be similarly placed in a second orbital plane positioned at approximately right angles to the first. Each satellite shall be suitably equipped with instruments for recording prompt and delayed gamma rays, X-rays, and neutrons. A satellite shall be replaced when it can no longer record and transmit to ground stations the required data from any three of the four methods of detection as set forth in this sub-paragraph. In addition, satellites shall be replaced when the System

(i) no longer provides complete surveillance of the Earth, or

(ii) no longer provides surveillance in all directions in space lying outside the orbits of the System's component satellites by means of the X-ray detection method from at least three satellites.

"C. At least four satellites (solar satellites) placed in appropriate solar orbits and suitably equipped with instruments, including those for recording X-rays. A satellite shall be replaced when it can no longer record and transmit to ground stations the required data on X-ray signals.

"2. Each satellite requiring replacement shall be replaced as rapidly as possible.

"3. Each satellite shall carry apparatus for verifying the performance of its equipment. Each satellite shall be inspected immediately prior to launching to ensure its instruments meet the detection requirements and that the satellite includes nothing which might interfere with the performance of its equipment. After inspection, the launching of each satellite shall be observed. This inspection and the subsequent observation of the launching of the satellite shall be performed by members of the staff of the Organisation selected by the Administrator in accordance with the principles set forth in sub-paragraph 3 C (v) of Article 9."

The Treaty Banning Nuclear Weapon Tests in the Atmosphere, in Outer Space and Under Water signed at Moscow on August 5, 1963, does not provide for any measures of supervision or detection, but the United States has announced that it has placed in orbit satellites for the detection of nuclear weapon tests which appear to be designed to constitute a detection and identification system similar to that envisaged in the Draft Treaty proposed in 1961 but established unilaterally instead of on behalf of an international organisation.

THE COMMITTEES ON THE PEACEFUL USES OF OUTER SPACE

In 1958 the General Assembly of the United Nations established an *Ad Hoc* Committee on the Peaceful Uses of Outer Space.[11] While the

[11] General Assembly Resolution 1348 (XIII) of December 13, 1958.

Committee was handicapped by the refusal of the U.S.S.R. and certain other States to take part on the basis of the composition of the Committee decided by the General Assembly, it adopted a most useful report[12] which, in addition to giving a convenient survey of the potential scope of space activities, the support facilities necessary for the effective conduct of space activities, and the existing arrangements for international co-operation, contains an abundance of practical suggestions concerning matters which should be further pursued.

The 1959 Report of the Ad Hoc Committee

The report distinguished between matters in respect of which international agreements providing for an "open and orderly conduct of space activities" can "form the basis of an international routine" without continuing co-operative action and matters in respect of which "there is need for active co-operative endeavours in which groups of nations assist each other in carrying out various phases of space activities." It envisages international agreements dealing with such matters as the use of radio frequencies, the registration of orbital elements, the termination of radiotransmission at the end of the satellite's useful life, the removal of spent satellites, the re-entry and recovery of space vehicles, the return of recovered equipment, indentification of origin, and measures to minimise the adverse effects of possible biological, radiological and chemical contamination. Among the measures of international co-operation in joint projects contemplated by the report are simultaneous sounding rocket launchings, the international use of launching ranges, co-operation in the instrumentation of satellites and deep space probes, co-operation in tracking, telemetering and data processing, co-operation in the exchange and interpretation of data, and international arrangements to permit of a maximum use of communications and meteorological satellites. The Committee grouped as legal problems susceptible of priority treatment the questions of freedom of outer space for exploration and use, liability for injury or damage caused by space vehicles, the allocation of radio frequencies, the avoidance of interference between space vehicles and co-ordination

[12] United Nations Document A/4141 of July 14, 1959.

53

of launchings and arrangements governing the re-entry and landing of space vehicles; it classed as less urgent the question of determining where outer space begins, the provision of safeguards against contamination of outer space or from outer space, questions relating to the exploration of celestial bodies, and the avoidance of interference among space vehicles. While needing wider support to make them practicable, these proposals represent an invaluable point of departure.

In 1959 the General Assembly established a new Committee on the Peaceful Uses of Outer Space, constituted on a broader basis, with a mandate to review the area of international co-operation in the exploration and exploitation of outer space for peaceful purposes, to study practical and feasible means for giving effect to programmes on the peaceful uses of outer space which could appropriately be undertaken under United Nations auspices, and to study the nature of the legal problems which may arise from the exploitation of outer space.[13] The meeting of this Committee was delayed until March 1962 in order to secure the participation of all its members.

The General Assembly also approved in 1959 the principle of the convocation under the auspices of the United Nations of an international scientific conference for the exchange of experience in the peaceful uses of outer space, analogous in general character to the scientific conferences which have played so important a part in promoting the peaceful uses of atomic energy.[14] No such conference has yet been held.

1961 General Assembly Resolution

In 1961 the General Assembly considered the matter further and on December 20 adopted unanimously a resolution of major importance concerning international co-operation in the peaceful uses of outer space. This resolution (General Assembly Resolution No. 1721 (XVI) of December 20, 1961[15]) recognised "the common interest of mankind in furthering the peaceful uses of outer space and the urgent need to

---

[13] General Assembly Resolution No. 1472 (XIV)A of December 12, 1959.
[14] General Assembly Resolution No. 1472 (XIVB) of December 12, 1959.
[15] The full text of the resolution (excluding certain transitory provisions) is reproduced in Appendix II, pp. 320–323, below.

strengthen international co-operation in this important field" and expressed the belief "that the exploration and use of outer space should be only for the betterment of mankind and to the benefit of States irrespective of the stage of their economic or scientific development". It commended to States for their guidance in the exploration and use of outer space two principles, namely (a) that international law, including the Charter of the United Nations, applies to outer space and celestial bodies, and (b) that outer space and celestial bodies are free for exploration and use by all States in conformity with international law and are not subject to national appropriation. It invited the Committee on the Peaceful Uses of Outer Space to study and report on the legal problems which may arise from the exploration and use of outer space.

In addition to formulating these principles the resolution called upon States launching objects into orbit or beyond to furnish information promptly to the Committee on the Peaceful Uses of Outer Space, through the Secretary-General, for the registration of launchings and requested the Secretary-General to maintain a public registry of the information so furnished. It also requested the Committee on the Peaceful Uses of Outer Space to provide for the exchange of such information relating to outer space activities as governments may supply on a voluntary basis, supplementing but not duplicating existing technical and scientific exchanges, and to assist in the study of measures for the promotion of international co-operation in outer space activities.

The resolution also dealt with the progress in meteorology made possible by advances in outer space and with space telecommunication. It recommended to all Member States and to the World Meteorological Organisation and other appropriate specialised agencies the early and comprehensive study, in the light of developments in outer space, of measures (a) to advance the state of atmospheric science and technology so as to provide greater knowledge of basic physical forces affecting climate and the possibility of large-scale weather modification, and (b) to develop existing weather forecasting capabilities and to help Member States make effective use of such capabilities through regional meteorological centres; it noted with satisfaction that the International Telecommunication Union planned to call a special conference in 1963 to make allocations of radio frequency bands for outer space activities, and recommended that the International Tele-communication Union consider at that conference those aspects of space communication in which international co-operation will be required.

Following the adoption by the General Assembly of this resolution an exchange of messages of March 7 and 20, 1962,[16] between President Kennedy and Premier Khrushchev envisaged a number of initial steps in the direction of a substantial measure of co-operation between the U.S.A. and the U.S.S.R. in space matters.

Method of Procedure of the 1962 Committee

On the basis of the General Assembly resolution the Committee on the Peaceful Uses of Outer Space held its first session in March 1962.[17] The Committee established a Scientific and Technical Sub-Committee and a Legal Sub-Committee to examine in greater detail the matters before it. In reviewing the outcome of the session the Chairman of the Committee noted "that in their statements many delegations have expressed deep satisfaction with the exchanges of messages between the Chairman of the Council of Ministers of the U.S.S.R., Mr. Khrushchev, and the President of the United States of America, Mr. Kennedy, on the prospects of development of concrete projects in the field of explora-tion and use of outer space for peaceful purposes". The Committee agreed "that it will be the aim of all members of the Committee and its Sub-Committees to conduct the Committee's work in such a way that the Committee will be able to reach agreement in its work without need for voting".

1962 Report of the Scientific and Technical Sub-Committee

The Scientific and Technical Sub-Committee held its first session at Geneva from May 28 to June 13, 1962, and reached a considerable measure of agreement concerning the exchange of information, the

[16] *New York Times International Edition*, March 8 and 22, 1962.
[17] The report of the session has been issued as United Nations Document A/5109 of March 30, 1962 and the verbatim records of the meetings as Documents A/A.C.105/PV 2–9.

encouragement of international programmes, and international equatorial sounding rocket facilities.[18]

The agreed recommendations of the Sub-Committee concerning the exchange of information through the Committee covered: the provision on a voluntary basis of information relating to national, regional and international programmes of peaceful space research and exploration; the availability to Member States of documents on technical requirements for establishing small-scale facilities for satellite tracking, telemetry reception, and sounding rocket launchings and on other sources of useful technical information; and arrangements with COSPAR (the Committee on Space Research of the International Council of Scientific Unions) to make available to Member States COSPAR information on its activities and on the activities of the World Data Centres for Rockets and Satellites and to inform the Committee concerning "the organisation, utilisation, functions and purposes of World Data Centres for Rockets and Satellites and the Spacewarn communications network". These agreed recommendations, it will be observed, deal primarily with a wide diffusion of the available information concerning space developments rather than with a fuller exchange by space powers of information not yet available.

The agreed recommendations for the encouragement of international programmes related partly to scientific programmes sponsored by the International Council of Scientific Unions and partly to international co-operation in the fields of space communications and satellite meteorology through the International Telecommunication Union and the World Meteorological Organisation. The scientific programmes included the International Year of the Quiet Sun (a programme of specialised scientific work, during a period of minimum solar activity, in meteorology, geomagnetism, aurora, air glow, solar activity, cosmic rays, aeronomy and other disciplines pertinent to space research, exploration and use), a world magnetic survey, and programmes for synoptic rocket and polar cap experiments. The recommendations concerning space communications and satellite meteorology were

[18] The report of the Sub-Committee has been issued as United Nations Document A/AC.105/C.1/L.2/Rev.2 of June 14, 1962.

57

essentially an endorsement of the action being taken by ITU and WMO.[19]

Proposal for International Equatorial Sounding Rocket Facilities

Sounding rockets are the only means of taking direct measures of the atmosphere at levels between about 30 and 200 kilometres, *i.e.*, above the ceiling of balloons and below the operational altitude of satellites. COSPAR contemplates extensive sounding rocket programmes, but there are major gaps in the world coverage of sounding rocket launching sites, notably the equatorial region and the southern hemispheres. The Sub-Committee accordingly recommended "that a sounding rocket launching facility on the geomagnetic equator be established as soon as possible, as a first step in creating and using international sounding rocket facilities under United Nations sponsorship". It summarised the potential usefulness of international sounding rocket launching facilities in the following terms:

> "Sounding rocket launching facilities, freely available to all interested Member States, will serve the interests of the international scientific community, and of all Member States, and will contribute to international co-operation by creating new opportunities for peaceful technical and scientific research.
>
> "Such facilities would open possibilities for nations which wish to enter the field of space research and would provide opportunities for practical instruction and training in this field. They would also make possible such research by Member States which are unable, because of economic or technological factors, or the unsuitability of their territories, to support sounding rocket programmes except through co-operative efforts. They would also allow States already possessing facilities to conduct research in other regions, for peaceful scientific purposes."

The necessary facilities would include "a launching site and impact area, buildings, launchers, power, an adequate range safety system, tracking, telemetry, timing equipment and meteorological services"; additional specialised equipment which could advantageously be added would include "an ionosonde, magnetometer, optical trackers, environ-

---

[19] Described below at pp. 64–70.

mental testing facilities, and a data reduction system". United Nations sponsorship of the facility would, the Sub-Committee suggested, facilitate the release to States which do not have appropriate sounding rockets of such rockets for use at the international sounding rocket facilities. The Sub-Committee therefore recommended that the United Nations Committee on the Peaceful Uses of Outer Space should take early steps to prepare a "broad charter" for the creation and operation of international sounding rocket launching facilities on the lines of basic principles which it indicated.

The recommendations of the Scientific and Technical Sub-Committee were endorsed by the full Committee in September 1962 and transmitted to the General Assembly.

1962 Report of the Legal Sub-Committee

The Legal Sub-Committee held its first session at Geneva from May 28 to June 20, 1962, but did not succeed in reaching a comparable measure of agreement. The Sub-Committee recorded in its report[20] four substantive proposals which had been submitted to it. The U.S.S.R. submitted a proposal for a Declaration, to be signed on behalf of Governments, of the Basic Principles governing the Activities of States pertaining to the Exploration and Use of Outer Space and a proposal for an International Agreement on the Rescue of Astronauts and Spaceships making Emergency Landings. The U.S.A. submitted proposals concerning assistance to and return of space vehicles and personnel and concerning liability for space vehicle accidents. No agreement was reached on any of these proposals. Nor was it possible to reach agreement on proposals formulated by India and Canada respectively for the purpose of recording the stage reached in the discussions. There was initial disagreement both concerning the relative priority of a general declaration of legal principles and a series of agreements dealing with immediate practical problems and concerning the respective roles of inter-governmental agreement and action by General Assembly resolution. Apart from these preliminary questions of approach, there were

[20] United Nations Document A/AC.105/C.2/3; see also the Summary Records of the Sub-Committee, A/AC.105/C.2/SR 1–SR 15.

four main substantive issues in respect of which conflicting views could not be reconciled and which it proved impossible to defer in order to permit of agreement on other points. These were four U.S.S.R. proposals to declare illegal the use of observation satellites for the purpose of military intelligence, to prohibit "the use of outer space for propagating war, national or racial hatred, or enmity between nations", to provide that activities in space "shall be carried out solely and exclusively by States", and to specify that measures which may hinder "the exploration by use of outer space for peaceful purposes by other countries" shall "be permitted only after prior discussion of and agreement upon such measures between the countries concerned". Other legal problems which it was suggested during the proceedings should be considered at a later stage, but which were not discussed, included demarcation between outer space and atmospheric space; jurisdiction and law applicable to men in outer space and manned stations on celestial bodies; measures to prevent interference with space projects due to scientific experiments or other space activities; prevention of contamination of or from outer space and celestial bodies; control over the launching and orbits of spacecraft and artificial satellites; United Nations control of radio and television programmes through outer space instrumentalities. In these circumstances the Legal Sub-Committee confined itself to reporting back to the Committee on the Peaceful Uses of Outer Space. The full committee, meeting in September 1962, was unable to take the matter beyond the stage reached by the Legal Sub-Committee, and had to content itself with reporting the position to the General Assembly.

1962 General Assembly Resolution

On December 14 the General Assembly adopted unanimously a further resolution concerning international co-operation in the peaceful uses of outer space (Resolution 1802 (XVII) which reaffirmed that "the activities of States in the exploration and use of outer space should be carried out in conformity with international law including the Charter of the United Nations, in the interest of friendly relations among nations", stressed "the necessity of the progressive development of international law pertaining to the further elaboration of basic legal principles governing the activities of States in the exploration and use of outer space, to liability for space vehicle accidents and to assistance to, and return of, astronauts and space vehicles as well as to other legal problems", and, noting with regret that the Committee on the Peaceful Uses of Outer Space has not yet made recommendations on legal questions connected with the peaceful uses of outer space, called upon all Member States to co-operate in the further development of law for outer space and requested the Committee on the Peaceful Uses of Outer Space to continue urgently its work.

The resolution endorsed the recommendations set forth in the report of the Committee on the Peaceful Uses of Outer Space concerning the exchange of information, noted with appreciation that a number of Member States had already, on a voluntary basis, provided information on their national space programmes, and requested other States and regional and international organisations to do so, and urged effective support to the international programmes mentioned in the report, including the International Year of the Quiet Sun and the World Magnetic Survey. The resolution also endorsed the basic principles suggested by the Committee on the Peaceful Uses of Outer Space for the establishment and operation of a sounding rocket facility, or facilities, on the geomagnetic equator, in time for the International Year of the Quiet Sun under United Nations sponsorship, and affirmed that such facilities, when established and operated in accordance with these principles, would, at the request of the host Member State, be eligible for United Nations sponsorship.

Like the resolution of the preceding year, the 1962 resolution also contained provisions concerning meteorological developments and space telecommunications. It recommended that the World Meteorological Organisation, in consultation with other agencies and organisations, should develop in greater detail its plan for an expanded programme to strengthen meteorological services and research, placing particular emphasis on the use of meteorological satellites and on the expansion of training and educational opportunities in these fields and invited the International Council of Scientific Unions through its member unions and national academies to develop an expanded programme of atmospheric science research which will complement the programmes fostered by the World Meteorological Organisation. It expressed the belief "that communication by satellite offers great benefits to mankind, as it will permit the expansion of radio, telephone and television transmissions, including the broadcast of United Nations activities, thus facilitating contact among the peoples of the world", emphasised "the importance of international co-operation to achieve effective satellite communications which will be available on a world-wide basis", noted the arrangements made for the Extraordinary Administrative Radio Conference to be held in October 1963, and stated it to be "of the utmost importance that this Conference make allocations of radio frequency bands sufficient to meet expected outer space needs".

1963 *Reports of the Committee on the Peaceful Uses of Outer Space*

The Committee on the Peaceful Uses of Outer Space continued its work in 1963.[21] It approved further recommendations made by the Scientific and Technical Sub-Committee concerning the exchange of information, international co-operation in respect of space communications and satellite meteorology, and co-operation with UNESCO in the field of education and training in space activities. It reiterated that "international space communications should be available for the use of all countries on a global non-discriminatory basis". It reviewed the action taken concerning international sounding rocket launching facilities, approved arrangements for the examination of an application for United Nations sponsorship for a facility at Thumba, India; invited COSPAR to review the geographic distribution of sounding rocket launching facilities and their capabilities from information given about them on a voluntary basis, and to advise from time to time on desirable locations and important topics of research, taking into account the need to avoid duplication of effort; and urged that, where there is shown to be a need, Member States in appropriate locations should, either singly or in co-operative groups, consider the establishment of such a launch-

[21] *Report of the Committee on the Peaceful Uses of Outer Space*, United Nations Document A/5549 of September 24, 1963.

ing facility following the basic principles approved by the Committee. It considered the potentially harmful effects of space experiments and recognised "the need for careful preparation for, and conduct of, activities in the exploration and use of outer space in order to avoid potentially harmful interference with other such activities" and recognised "the scientific difficulty and the competence required to assess properly the nature and possibilities of such intereference"; it noted "that the COSPAR Consultative Group on the Potentially Harmful Effects of Space Experiments is composed of authoritative scientists and specialists on an international basis and that their assistance is available to the members of COSPAR, the international scientific unions and bodies of the United Nations" and recognised "the importance of the problem of preventing potentially harmful interference with peaceful uses of outer space".

The Legal Sub-Committee failed to break the deadlock which had frustrated its work but reported some progress. On the question of general principles governing the activities of States relating to the exploration and use of outer space, agreement was reached that they should take the form of a declaration, but there was no agreement concerning the character of the declaration, some delegations favouring a treaty-type document and others a General Assembly resolution. There was some *rapprochement* of points of view concerning the content of the declaration but important differences remained. With regard to two specific issues, namely the rescue of astronauts and space vehicles making emergency landings and liability for space vehicle accidents, a certain *rapprochement* and clarification of ideas was recorded and agreement was reached that the relevant insruments should take the form of international agreements. In these circumstances the Committee, meeting in September 1963, noted the position and expressed the hope that a wider consensus might be achieved by further exchanges among governments before its report was considered by the General Assembly.

Following such further exchanges the Committee met again on November 22, 1963, and adopted an additional report[22] containing an agreed text of a Draft Declaration of Legal Principles Governing the

[22] United Nations Document A/5549/Add.1 of November 27, 1963.

Activities of States in the Exploration and Use of Outer Space and the record of a number of statements concerning this text made by members of the Committee. As this text now constitutes the basis of the law of space and is for this reason fully discussed in Part III of this Volume[23] it is unnecessary to describe its contents more fully at this point.

1963 General Assembly Resolutions

On December 13, 1963, the General Assembly adopted the Declaration of Legal Principles Governing the Activities of States in the Exploration and Use of Outer Space and a series of further resolutions[24] concerning international co-operation in the peaceful uses of outer space. The first of these resolutions recommends that consideration should be given to incorporating in international agreement form, in the future as appropriate, legal principles governing the activities of States in the exploration and use of outer space and requests the Committee on the Peaceful Uses of Outer Space to continue to study and report on legal problems which may arise and "in particular to arrange for the prompt preparation of draft international agreements on liability for damage caused by objects launched into outer space and on assistance to and return of astronauts and space vehicles". The other resolutions endorse the 1963 recommendations on scientific and technical matters of the Committee on the Peaceful Uses of Outer Space and note with appreciation the action being taken by the World Meteorological Organisation and the International Telecommunication Union.

THE WORLD METEOROLOGICAL ORGANISATION

The General Assembly of the United Nations, in Resolution 1721 (XVI) C of December 20, 1961, requested the World Meteorological Organisation to make proposals for appropriate organisational and financial arrangements for taking advantage of the opportunities of progress in meteorological science and technology opened up by advances in outer space.

[23] pp. 182–316, below.
[24] General Assembly Resolution 1963 (XVIII) of December 13, 1963.

In July 1962 the World Meteorological Organisation submitted a report on the subject to the Thirty Fourth Session of the Economic and Social Council.[25] The report, prepared with the co-operation of scientists designated by the U.S.A. and the U.S.S.R., outlines organisational and financial arrangements designed to permit the full exploitation of the new meteorological data which can be provided by artificial satellites by means of a World Weather Watch. The purpose of the proposed system is "to ensure availability to each country of that combination of processed information and observations, including satellite data, best suited to its needs". No joint launching of meteorological satellites is envisaged; launching remains under the plan a national responsibility. What is envisaged is co-ordination of the types and scope of observations, periods and sequence of observations and orbits used to ensure a maximum of operational coverage. This, without involving joint launching, does involve co-ordinated launchings.

The plan is essentially one for the establishment and operation of various centres and stations and the provision of various other facilities (including telecommunications) designed to secure, by the co-ordination of observations and measures to ensure the full availability of the information secured, the optimum utilisation of satellites for meteorological purposes. The main requirements for such optimum utilisation are listed as being:

"The continuous existence of one or more satellites transmitting useful meteorological information; read-out stations in sufficient number and with adequate facilities to ensure accurate reception and processing of data for global coverage and utilisation; interference-free frequency bands for communication with meteorological satellites; further development of techniques for operational use of satellite data; adequate network of conventional and auxiliary meteorological observations to provide the broadscale framework for the detailed observations obtainable from satellites and to help interpret these observations; communication facilities for prompt world-wide dissemination of processed data – both conventional and satellite – for operation purposes; broadening the existing World Meteorological Data Centres A and B and/or setting up of new

[25] World Meteorological Organisation, *First Report on the Advancement of Atmospheric Sciences and their Application in the Light of Developments in Outer Space*, 1962.

World Data Centres to include satellite data and processed data, such as charts and cross sections, with a view to making this information readily available for research purposes; a long-range research programme incorporating data from satellites."

Washington and Moscow have been designated as World Weather Centres which will be maintained by the United States Weather Bureau and the Hydrometeorological Administration of the U.S.S.R. respectively. A third World Centre in the Southern Hemisphere, which may be internationally organised and financed, and a network of regional centres are also envisaged; a comprehensive plan for such centres is to be prepared. A WMO Advisory Committee is to undertake a co-ordinating role.

The Report also outlines a general plan of action for the use of meteorological satellites for scientific and research purposes.

The General Assembly in 1962 recommended the World Meteorological Organisation to develop this plan in greater detail and in 1963 the Fourth World Meteorological Congress took further steps in the matter, notably by establishing the WMO Advisory Committee with a special responsibility to advise on matters relating to meteorological satellites.[26] The practical measures taken by WMO include the preparation for the guidance of practising meteorologists throughout the world of a Technical Note on the *Reduction and Use of Data Obtained by Tiros Meteorological Satellites*; the WMO Congress decided that arrangements should be made for a similar document explaining the technical details of the Automatic Picture Transmission System developed by the United States, by means of which suitably equipped ground stations, costing less than $50,000 (dollars) per unit, can receive from a satellite, whenever it is in sunlight, photographic data of an area roughly 1,600 kilometres in radius immediately surrounding the ground station.

While some of these arrangements may at some stage have to be formalised into WMO procedures and plans, they do not at the present

[26] World Meteorological Organisation, *Second Report on the Advancement of Atmospheric Services and their Application in the Light of Developments in Outer Space*, Geneva, June 1963.

stage appear to raise any problem of wider import of direct concern to the international lawyer. Only if and when the information available from meteorological satellites permits of deliberate action for large-scale weather modification will important legal questions concerning the rights and obligations of States in respect of action by one State affecting the interests of others arise. An appendix to the *First Report on the Advancement of Atmospheric Sciences*[27] refers to this possibility in the following terms:

Modification of Weather and Climate

"1. From current and contemplated research programmes, aided by satellites and other observational techniques, it is reasonable to expect a better knowledge of the general circulation and the heat balance of the atmosphere which in turn will lead to an improvement in our understanding of weather and climate.

"2. Indeed, it is not unrealistic to expect that mankind will eventually have the power to influence weather and even climate on a large scale; for example the artificial melting of the Arctic ice cap has been proposed. It is, however, imperative that the consequences of any such large-scale interference with the existing climatic balance should be accurately foreseen and evaluated.

"3. The complexity of atmospheric processes is such that an artificially induced change in the weather in one part of the Earth will necessarily have repercussions in other parts. This principle can be affirmed on the basis of our present knowledge of the mechanism of the general circulation of the atmosphere. Our knowledge, however, is still very far from enabling us to forecast with confidence the degree, nature or duration of the secondary effects to which a change in weather or climate in one part of the globe may give rise, nor even to predict whether these effects may be beneficial or detrimental.

"4. It must furthermore be borne in mind that a change of climate, even if regarded as beneficial, would necessarily lead to ecological changes in plant and animal life, whose consequences would be felt not only in the agriculture but in the whole economic and social life of the regions concerned.

"5. Therefore, before starting an experiment on large-scale weather modifications, we must be sure of our capability of forecasting accurately

[27] Appendix E.

the expected modification in the heat balance and the circulation of the atmosphere. Otherwise we could face some day the dangerous situation of undesired irreversible weather and climate changes.

"6. Consciously or not, man is engaged in a large-scale contamination of the Earth's atmosphere which is bound to become more serious. We refer not only to contamination of the lower atmosphere by carbon dioxide and other gases, particulates, etc., which may have a significant effect on the Earth's radiational balance, but also to the increasing contamination of the upper atmosphere."

Weather control is, of course, only one aspect of the problem of possible modifications of natural environment resulting from activities in space which may call for some measure of regulation to ensure that irrevocable action is not taken without full consultation of and consideration of the divergent interests involved.[28] This aspect of the matter therefore calls for consideration as part of a more general problem rather than as part of the question of meteorological satellites.

THE INTERNATIONAL TELECOMMUNICATION UNION

The General Assembly of the United Nations, by Resolution 1721 (XVI)D of December 20, 1961, requested the International Telecommunication Union to take appropriate action in respect of space telecommunication.

The Plenipotentiary Conference of the International Telecommunication Union had in fact already accepted the general responsibility for so doing by Resolution 34 of the 1959 Conference.[29]

The 1959 Administrative Radio Conference of ITU considered in detail the requirements for outer space telecommunication from the radio point of view, adopted definitions of the new radio services at stations required for space communication, and allocated frequency bands for research purposes in connection with space and Earth space services.

Longer range action was postponed to an Extraordinary Administra-

---

[28] I have discussed the matter more fully in "The Laws of Nature and International Law" in *Law, Freedom and Welfare*, 1963, pp. 33–49; see also pp. 148–150, below.

[29] *Cf. First Report by the International Telecommunication Union on Telecommunication and the Peaceful Uses of Outer Space*, Geneva, 1962.

tive Radio Conference on the grounds "that until the results of some space research programmes are available, the extent to which space radio communication services and other radio communications services may share frequencies without harmful interference cannot accurately be assessed" and "that additional research experience and the results of studies ... are essential before it will be feasible for the Union to take decisions on firm frequency allocations for space radio communication purposes".

Meanwhile the International Radio Consultative Committee of ITU was commissioned to make certain special studies. In March 1962 a Study Group of the Committee prepared a series of draft recommendations covering the cessation of radio emissions from satellites and other space vehicles; the identification of radio emissions from satellites and other space vehicles; active Earth-satellite communication systems for frequency division multiplex telephony and monochrome television; preferred frequency bands for use in telemetry, tracking, remote control, voice and video in experimental and operation Earth satellites and probes, radio-frequency channelling arrangements for telemetry and remote control in operational satellite relay communication systems; and frequency requirements of radio navigation systems utilising Earth orbiting satellites. In these draft recommendations we have the germ of comprehensive ITU regulations governing space telecommunications.

The Extraordinary Administrative Radio Conference of 1963 was convened to examine the technical progress in the use of radio communication for space research and the results of technical studies concerning Earth satellite systems for operational purposes (communication, radio navigation and meteorology), and in the light of such examination to consider (a) the allocation of radio frequency bands for operating Earth satellite systems, together with bands for the telemetry, command and control facilities necessary for such systems, and (b) whether there is a continuing need for the allocation of certain frequencies for space research purposes, including the associated telemetry, command and control. The terms of reference of this Conference specified that it was "to revise only such provisions of the Radio Regulations, Geneva, 1959, as may be essential for the effective implementation of the decisions of the Conference concerning the technical characteristics and operation of Earth satellite systems and the space research service" and might also consider the frequency requirements for radio astronomy.[30]

The Conference successfully revised the Radio Regulations. The revised Regulations contain new definitions and symbols relating to space systems, services and stations and to space, orbits and types of object in space, and an amended Table of Frequency Allocations allocating frequencies for satellite identification, telemetering and tracking, space research, meteorological satellites, radio navigation satellites, communication satellites and radio astronomy. They include rules governing the technical characteristics of Earth and space stations and providing that space stations shall be made capable of ceasing radio emissions by the use of appropriate means. They provide for the notification and recording in the master international frequency register of frequency assignments to stations in the space and radio astronomy services. While much remains to be done, and new needs and problems will continue to emerge, we nevertheless already have the makings of an effective international regulation of space telecommunications.

THE INTERNATIONAL CIVIL AVIATION ORGANISATION

In the period immediately preceding and following the launching of Sputnik I the International Civil Aviation Organisation was sometimes thought of and described as the body most naturally qualified to undertake the regulation of activities in space. It rapidly emerged, however, that there were two limitations to the part which it can play in the matter. In the first place, activities in space involve a complex of political, military, economic, technical, and legal considerations far exceeding the competence of either the International Civil Aviation Organisation or any other one international body, and involving the assumption of broad responsibilities by the United Nations with complementary action by a number of specialised agencies, including in particular ITU and WMO and other international organisations. In

[30] *Cf.* R. Hanbury Brown and A. C. B. Lovell, *The Exploration of Space by Radio*, 1957; R. D. Davies and H. P. Palmer, *Radio Studies of the Universe*, 1959; F. Graham Smith, *Radio Astronomy*, 1960.

the second place, the U.S.S.R. is not a member of ICAO. These factors, rather than any evaluation of the relationship between flight in the atmosphere and activities in space, have determined the allocation to the United Nations rather than to ICAO of the major responsibility for the international regulation of activities in space. At the Tenth ICAO Assembly held at Caracas in 1956 the ICAO Legal Committee expressed the view that space law fell within the functional competence of ICAO,[31] but at the Twelfth Assembly held at San Diego in 1959[32] the Assembly rejected a Mexican proposal that the ICAO Legal Committee should assume responsibility in the matter and accepted a United States proposal that responsibility for general questions of space law should be left to the United Nations, subject to consultation with ICAO in respect of matters of special concern to it.

ICAO is nevertheless vitally concerned with ensuring that the rules of the road to and from space do not conflict with the rules of the road in the air and that launches and flights are so timed and notified that neither constitutes an unreasonable hazard to the other; this may but does not necessarily imply that the rules on this matter should be framed and administered by the same international body; it certainly requires some appropriate form of co-ordination on an international scale between space launching and aviation authorities comparable to that which it is believed already exists on a national basis in certain States where the matter has become of practical importance. Space communication techniques are of direct interest to ICAO. The use of earth satellites may be an important extension to current techniques of communications with aircraft and the radio navigation service for aircraft; the trend in air/ground communications is towards the use of Very High Frequencies, the range of communications on which is limited, in general, to line of sight distances, and relay via Earth satellites will permit such coverage over areas where this is not now possible, thus greatly increasing the efficiency and reliability of air/ground communication. For supersonic aircraft, satellite based radiation measuring equipment is likely to be necessary for evaluating prevailing levels of

[31] ICAO Document 7712 A10–LE/5, para. 12.
[32] ICAO Document A12–WP/105.

radiation at operating levels. ICAO experience, like maritime experience, may also provide useful analogies for space regulation.

THE INTERGOVERNMENTAL MARITIME CONSULTATIVE ORGANISATION

The Intergovernmental Maritime Consultative Organisation has a potential interest in navigation satellites.

THE INTERNATIONAL ATOMIC ENERGY AGENCY

The International Atomic Energy Agency has a direct interest in such matters as the possible use of nuclear energy for vehicle propulsion and for satellite power systems, the possible contribution of activities in space to our knowledge of radioactivity, the potential bearing of such activities on protection against radiation, and the possibility of radioactive waste disposal beyond the atmosphere; there may also be analogies between the legal problems of liability in respect of space vehicles and liability for accidents involving land-based nuclear installations or nuclear ships.

THE WORLD HEALTH ORGANISATION

The World Health Organisation has an interest in the possible incidence of activities in space on diseases on Earth and in the increasingly important subject of space medicine; the range of this interest includes cosmic biology, genetics and radiation, the physiology and psychology of man in space, and environmental contamination from the transfer of chemical and biological agents to and from the Earth.

UNESCO

UNESCO has a general interest in the bearing of developments in space on scientific research.

A UNESCO meeting of Experts has recommended that "UNESCO take steps to encourage the reservation of those parts and amounts of the broadcast spectrum and related electronic resources necessary to assure for all the transmission and reception of the full range of educational radio and television services, including at the appropriate time the eventual use of artificial satellite communications systems".[33]

ADMINISTRATIVE COMMITTEE ON CO-ORDINATION

The Administrative Committee on Co-ordination, which consists of the Secretary-General of the United Nations and the executive heads of all the specialised agencies, has, at the request of the Economic and Social Council, made a preliminary examination of the steps desirable to promote co-ordination among all the members of the United Nations family which are or may be concerned in the peaceful uses of outer space, and has the whole matter under continuing review.[34]

[33] UNESCO Document ED/190 of April 3, 1962.
[34] Twenty-Fourth Report of the Administrative Committee on Co-ordination to the Economic and Social Council, United Nations Document E/3368 of May 10, 1960, Pt. V, paras. 18–21 and Annex 1.

7

Regional Joint Ventures

ACTIVITIES in space involve expenditures so great that only two States, the United States and the U.S.S.R., have felt able hitherto to undertake on a national basis anything more than the launching of high altitude sounding rockets. A wider distribution of space activities is clearly desirable, both intrinsically and as an element in political and military equilibrium on the Earth. In these circumstances, it is not surprising that steps should have been taken to organise certain regional joint ventures to enable a larger number of States to participate in activities in space, nor that the initiative in the matter should have come from Western Europe from States accustomed to be in the forefront of technological advance until the burden on their resources of keeping pace with development work financed from the military budgets of the U.S.A. and the U.S.S.R. proved to be too great. The European Organisation for Nuclear Research, which operates on behalf of twelve European States a synchro-cyclotron comparable to the facilities available in the United States and the U.S.S.R. afforded an example of what could be done and Conventions providing for the establishment of a European Space Research Organisation and a European Organisation for the Development and Construction of Space Vehicle Launchers, both to be located in Paris, were signed in 1962 and 1963.

Regional joint ventures of varied types may also be necessary for purposes other than that of spreading the cost of activities in space. All activities in space presuppose, if only for purposes of tracking, telemetry and telecommand, the organisation of continuous co-operation from widely scattered points on the surface of the Earth, but the effective operational use of space facilities may require more integrated forms

74

of co-operation on a regional basis, with or without some formal organisation for the purpose. The experimental arrangements made by the American Telephone and Telegraph Company, the North American broadcasting networks, and Eurovision for television relays by Telstar have been followed by the Agreement for a Global Commercial Communications Satellite System.[a] If space vehicles should be launched in regions consisting of relatively small States with high densities of population and air traffic, then regional arrangements analogous to Eurocontrol for co-ordinating launching and flight times and controls would presumably be necessary.

COUNCIL OF EUROPE DISCUSSIONS

The Consultative Assembly of the Council of Europe considered in 1960 a Report on European Co-operation in Space Research and Space Technology and on the basis thereof adopted a recommendation to the Committee of Ministers envisaging a European programme.[1]

EUROPEAN SPACE RESEARCH ORGANISATION

The European Space Research Organisation was established by a Convention opened for signature in Paris on June 14, 1963, which came into force on March 20, 1964, for Belgium, Denmark, France, Federal Republic of Germany, Netherlands, Norway, Sweden, Switzerland and the United Kingdom; the Convention has also been signed by Italy and Spain.

The purpose of the Organisation is to provide for, and to promote, collaboration among European States in space research and technology, exclusively for peaceful purposes.[2] The scientific results of experiments carried out with the assistance of the Organisation are to be published or otherwise made generally available; after prior use by the scientists responsible for the experiments, the reduced data resulting from such experiments are to be the property of the Organisation.[3] Subject to

---

[a] pp. 339–356, below.
[1] Council of Europe, Consultative Assembly, 12th Ordinary Session (2nd Pt.), September 21–29, 1960, Documents, Vol. IV, pp. 1–113.
[2] Art. 2.
[3] Art. 3 (1).

patent rights, the technical results of the Organisation's activities are normally to be published or otherwise made generally available.[4] Member States also give a more general undertaking to facilitate the exchange of scientific and technical information, but a Member State is not required to communicate any information obtained outside the Organisation if it considers that such communication would be contrary to the interests of its security or to its own agreement with a third party, or that it would violate the conditions under which this information had been obtained.[5] Member States likewise agree to facilitate the exchange of persons concerned with space research and technology, subject to the application of their laws and regulations relating to entry into, residence in, or departure from, their territories.[6]

In order to fulfil its purpose, the Organisation is to carry out a programme of scientific research and related technological activities. It may in particular (a) design and construct sounding rocket payloads, satellites and space probes, carrying instruments provided by Member States or by the Organisation itself; (b) procure launching vehicles and arrange for their launching; (c) provide means for the reception, collection, reduction and analysis of data; (d) support research and development as required for its programme; (e) promote and provide for contacts between scientists and engineers, their interchange and advanced training; (f) disseminate information among Member States; (g) co-operate with research institutions in the Member States and assist in the co-ordination of their efforts; and (h) make contractual arrangements for the use of launching ranges for rockets and satellites and other facilities available in Member or other States.[7] The Organisation is to establish and operate the facilities necessary for its programmes; to meet its initial requirements it is to establish and operate a European Space Technology Centre, a research laboratory, sounding rocket launching facilities, and a Data Centre and tracking, telemetry and telecommand Stations.[8] The programme of the Organisation is to provide for the launching of (a) sounding rockets, (b) small satellites in near earth orbits and small space probes, and (c) large satellites and large

---

[4] Art. 3 (2). [6] Art. 4. [8] Art. 6.
[5] Art. 3 (3). [7] Art. 5.

space probes;[9] the number of launchings shall be decided by the Council of the Organisation with a view to providing reasonable opportunities for scientifically valuable experiments, devised by Member States or by the Organisation itself, to be carried out.[10] The facilities of the Organisation may be made available on a reimbursement basis for projects within its scope but outside its agreed programme.[11]

The Organisation consists of a Council and a Director-General assisted by Staff.[12] Each Member State is to contribute to both capital expenditure and operating expenses.[13] Any dispute concerning the interpretation or application of the Convention, which is not settled by the good offices of the Council, shall be submitted to the International Court of Justice, unless the Member States concerned agree on some other form of settlement.[14]

The Space Technology Centre of the Organisation is to be located at Delft, its Data Centre at Darmstadt, and its research laboratory in Italy; it is to have a launching site at Kiruna, Northern Sweden. A programme of scientific round-tables, fellowships and launchings (including the launching of a large orbiting astronomical observatory) has been prepared.

EUROPEAN ORGANISATION FOR THE DEVELOPMENT AND CONSTRUCTION OF SPACE VEHICLE LAUNCHERS

The European Organisation for the Development and Construction of Space Vehicle Launchers was established by a Convention opened for signature in London on March 29, 1962,[15] which entered into force on February 29, 1964, for Belgium, France, the Federal Republic of Germany, Italy, Netherlands, United Kingdom and Australia.

The aim of the Organisation is the development and construction of space vehicle launchers and their equipment suitable for practical applications and for supply to eventual users;[16] it is to concern itself only with peaceful applications of such launchers and equipment[17] and

---

[9] Art. 7 (1).   [11] Art. 8.   [13] Art. 12.
[10] Art. 7 (2).   [12] Art. 9.   [14] Art. 16.
[15] The text is available in United Kingdom Parliamentary Paper Cmnd. 1731 of 1962.
[16] Art. 2 (1).   [17] Art. 2 (2).

the results of its work are to be freely available to Member States in accordance with the provisions of the Convention.[18] The Organisation is to seek to promote the co-ordinated development of techniques relevant to its activity in Member States and is to assist Member States, on request, to make use of the techniques used or developed in the course of its work.[19]

The Organisation is to undertake as its initial programme the design, development and construction of a space vehicle launcher using as its first stage the United Kingdom rocket "Blue Streak" and with a French rocket as its second stage.[20] The design, development and construction of the third stage are to be carried out under the leadership of the authorities and organisations of the Federal Republic of Germany.[21] The design, development and construction of the first series of satellite test vehicles, including the electronic equipment contained therein, are to be carried out under the leadership of the authorities and organisations of the Italian Republic.[22] The design, development and construction of the equipment for the down range ground guidance stations are to be carried out under the leadership of the authorities and organisations of the Kingdom of Belgium.[23] The design, development and construction of the long range telemetry links, including associated ground equipment, are to be carried out under the leadership of the authorities and organisations of the Kingdom of the Netherlands.[24] In the initial programme, the development firings of the first stage and of the complete launcher are to be conducted at Woomera, Australia; the development firings of the second and third stages are to be carried out wherever economic and technical conditions are most favourable.[25] When the Organisation comes into existence, it is to continue the study of future possibilities and the need for launchers and ranges, including experimental research, it being left to the Council of the Organisation to consider what new programme it would be desirable to undertake.[26]

The Convention containing provisions relating to the financial

[18] Art. 2 (3). [19] Art. 2 (4). [20] Art. 16 (1).
[21] Protocol concerning certain responsibilities in connection with the Initial Programme, para. 1.
[22] Para. 2. [24] Para. 4. [26] Art. 16 (3).
[23] Para. 3. [25] Art. 16 (2) of the Convention.

obligations of Members,[27] the use of facilities made available to the Organisation,[28] the distribution of work and placing of contracts,[29] access by Member States to the work of the Organisation,[30] the exchange of information,[31] and similar matters. Each Member State which has contributed to the cost of a programme of the Organisation has the right to procure, for any peaceful purpose of its own, the launchers and equipment jointly developed under such programme or any part thereof; for this purpose, it has the right to call upon the Organisation, or any other Member States in the territory of which such launchers and equipment are or have been in production, to sell such launchers and equipment or to use its best endeavours by means of the framing of the contracts to enable such launchers and equipment to be procured from non-governmental organisations in its own territory; in either case governments are to use their best endeavours to ensure that the cost is calculated on the same basis as the cost of procurement by the Organisation or by the Member State in the territory of which such equipment is produced and are to ensure that contracts placed with non-governmental organisations contain clauses to that effect.[32] Member States which propose to exploit commercially, either alone or in conjunction with non-Member States, a space vehicle launcher jointly developed under a programme of the Organisation are to give all Member States which have contributed to the cost of that programme an opportunity to participate in such exploitation on reasonable terms.[33] The conditions for delivery to States which are not Members of the Organisation, or to international organisations, of launcher and equipment developed by the Organisation are to be decided by the Council of the Organisation.[34]

The tasks entrusted to the Organisation are to be carried out by a Council and a Secretary-General assisted by a Technical Director, an Administrative Director and the necessary staff.[35] The Council is formally to suggest to the European Space Research Organisation the establishment of a joint co-ordinating committee to consider matters

[27] Arts. 4 (3) and 18.
[28] Art. 5.
[29] Art. 6.
[30] Art. 7.
[31] Art. 8.
[32] Art. 9.
[33] Art. 10.
[34] Art. 11.
[35] Art. 13.

of joint concern including the desirability of a merger between the two organisations;[36] it is to transmit an annual report to the Council of Europe.[37]

Subject to the Convention, all operations in connection with a programme of the Organisation are to be carried out in accordance with conditions agreed with the Member State within whose jurisdiction the operations take place.[38]

Disputes not settled by the good offices of the Council are to be referred to an Arbitral Tribunal, appointments to which can be made in the last resort by the President of the Court of Justice of the European Communities at the request of any one of the parties.[39]

It has been announced that the first space vehicle to be launched with a launcher developed by the Organisation will be launched at Woomera, Australia, early in 1965.

TELSTAR ARRANGEMENTS BETWEEN THE UNITED STATES AND EUROVISION

The experimental television relays made possible by Telstar have involved special arrangements among the American Telephone and Telegraph Company (as the operators of Telstar, and of the North American satellite terminal station at Andover, Maine), the North American broadcasting networks, the United Kingdom General Post Office and French National Centre for Space Studies (as the operators of the Goonhilly Down, Cornwall, and Pleumeur-Bodon, Brittany, terminal stations), and Eurovision (the television service of the European Broadcasting Union which is the central organisation of European broadcasting services). The continuing operation of satellite communication systems would probably require the formalisation of such arrangements as permanent machinery which might be international, regional, or partly international and partly regional in character.

[36] Art. 12 (2).
[37] Art. 12 (3).
[38] Art. 17.
[39] Art. 22.

POSSIBLE NEED FOR ARRANGEMENTS ANALOGOUS TO EUROCONTROL

Hitherto space vehicles have been launched over the ocean or in uninhabited areas of States of continental proportions; even so, the United States has found it desirable to negotiate special arrangements with certain of the Caribbean territories as neighbours of the Cape Canaveral launching range; if launching should take place in the future from the territory of a smaller site in a crowded area with a high density of air traffic regional arrangements for the co-ordination of launching and flight control will almost certainly be necessary and Eurocontrol[40] (established by the United Kingdom, France, the Federal Republic of Germany and the three Benelux countries by a treaty of December 13, 1960, for the purpose of exercising joint control of the upper airspace over their territories) may be a suggestive precedent. Eurocontrol exercises joint control of air traffic service in the upper air space of all the participating countries and the whole or any part of the lower air space of any participating country so requesting having regard to practical operational requirements. It operates through a Commission for the Safety of Air Navigation and an Air Traffic Services Agency. The Agency maintains air traffic services for the purpose of preventing collisions between aircraft, ensuring the orderly and rapid flow of air traffic, providing advice and information useful for the safe and efficient conduct of flights, notifying appropriate organisations regarding aircraft in need of search and rescue aid, and assisting such organisations as required.

[40] Eurocontrol has been conveniently described by André Gros in *Comunicaziono e Studi*, Vol. X, pp. 1–12; for the text of the Treaty see *European Yearbook*, Vol. IX, 1961, pp. 726–775.

8

Bilateral Arrangements

BILATERAL arrangements for co-operation in space are based partly on bilateral agreements sufficiently formal in character to have been registered with the United Nations as international engagements and partly on arrangements which have not been expressed in comparable legal form.

The bilateral agreements available by the end of 1963 fall into two groups, agreements concluded by the United States with other countries granting facilities to or co-operating in some other manner with the United States programme, and the first bilateral space agreement between the United States and the U.S.S.R.

The United States agreements with co-operating countries deal with such matters as launching and recovery arrangements in the Cape Canaveral-Bahamas area, space vehicle observation, tracking and communication stations and facilities throughout the world, upper atmosphere research, and inter-continental testing in connection with experimental satellites. Further types of such agreement will doubtless be added as further developments occur.

An agreement between the United States and the United Kingdom acting with the concurrence of the Bahama Islands, concluded on July 21, 1950, provides for the establishment in the Bahama Islands of a Long-Range Proving Ground for Guided Missiles.[1] A similar agreement of January 15, 1952, provides for the extension of the long-range proving ground by the establishment of additional sites in the Turks and Caicos Islands.[2] An Exchange of Notes of April 16, 1959, provides for the use of the Bahamas long-range proving ground on the Island of Grand Turk for tracking artificial satellites and other space vehicles[3]

[1] 97 *United Nations Treaty Series*, pp. 194–224.
[2] 122 *United Nations Treaty Series*, pp. 194–225.
[3] 343 *United Nations Treaty Series*, pp. 12–15.

and grants the Government of the United States "the right to establish, maintain and operate artificial space vehicle tracking equipment" in accordance with the procedure and subject to the terms and conditions set forth in the 1952 Agreement. The 1952 Agreement grants the Government of the United States the right "to launch, fly and land guided missiles" in the range area, to "establish, maintain and use an instrumentation and communications system" there, and to operate "such vessels and aircraft as may be necessary for purposes connected directly with the operation of Flight Testing Range". It provides that the Contracting Governments shall "take all reasonable precautions against possible danger and damage resulting from operations" in the Flight Testing Range, that the rights granted "shall not be exercised unreasonably or so as to interfere with or to prejudice the safety of navigation, aviation or communication within the range, and that these rights shall be exercised in a spirit of good neighbourliness between the Governments concerned", the "details of their practical application" being arranged "by friendly co-operation". The United Kingdom Government agrees to grant "such rights of way as may be agreed to be necessary for the operation of the Flight Testing Range" and such sites for the purpose of the operation of the range as may be agreed to be necessary for the purpose. There are detailed provisions concerning jurisdiction over offences, security legislation, arrest and service of process, the right of audience for counsel, and the surrender of persons charged; and provisions of a more general character concerning the use of public services, the provision of lights and other aids to navigation of vessels and aircraft, immigration arrangements, immunities and facilities, title in and the removal of property, and claims for compensation. Adequate and effective compensation is to be paid by the Government of the United States in respect of valid claims arising out of death, injury, damage or the acquisition of private property or rights affecting such property. The Government of the United States undertakes not to exercise the rights provided for in the Agreement, nor to permit their exercise, except for the purposes specified therein, and not to assign nor part with any of the rights granted thereby.

Agreements relating to space vehicle observation, tracking and communication stations and facilities have been made by the United States with a number of countries, including Australia,[4] Canada,[5] Chile,[6] Ecuador,[7] South Africa,[8] Spain,[9] and the United Kingdom.[10] These agreements are of varied types. Those with the United Kingdom, Australia, Canada and South Africa provide for joint programmes. That with the United Kingdom in respect of Bermuda is an authorisation to establish the required facilities within the leased bases areas provided for by the Leased Bases Agreement of March 27, 1941,[11] (the Destroyer-Bases Deal Agreement). The Agreement with the United Kingdom in respect of Canton Island provides for the construction and operation of the recovery facilities by the United States, for a limited period, within the framework of the 1939 Agreement relating to Canton and Enderbury Islands[12] which provides that the use of any part of either of the Islands or their territorial waters for aviation and other purposes "shall be the subject of agreement between the two Governments". The Agreement with Spain provides for facilities to be established by the United States and operated jointly with Spain. Other agreements grant permission for the United States to maintain certain facilities on either a continuous or a temporary basis. The Agreement with the United Kingdom relating to stations in the United Kingdom provides for a joint programme to be carried out by co-operating agencies designated by the two Governments. The co-operating agencies are to agree, in respect of each station established under the programme, "upon arrangements with respect to the duration of use of the station, the responsibility for and financing of the contruction, installation, equipping, maintenance and operation of the station, and other details relating to the establishment and operation of the station". The

[4] 354 *United Nations Treaty Series*, pp. 96–103.
[5] 388 *United Nations Treaty Series*, pp. 225–235.
[6] 401 *United Nations Treaty Series*, pp. 105–114.
[7] 371 *United Nations Treaty Series*, pp. 56–67.
[8] 388 *United Nations Treaty Series*, pp. 66–73.
[9] 372 *United Nations Treaty Series*, pp. 13–25.
[10] 402 *United Nations Treaty Series*, pp. 154–161; and 404 *United Nations Treaty Series*, pp. 207–213 (in respect of Bermuda); and 404 *United Nations Treaty Series*, pp. 215–225 (in respect of Canton Island).
[11] 204 *League of Nations Treaty Series*, pp. 15–73.
[12] 196 *League of Nations Treaty Series*, pp. 343–348.

Agreement contains provisions concerning the approval of frequencies and avoidance of radio interference. It stipulates that each co-operating agency shall provide to the other, from the data acquired through the operation of each station, such reduced scientific data as the other agency may request for scientific studies it may wish to carry out, and that the results of all such studies shall be made available promptly and in their entirety to both co-operating agencies. Each station established may be used for independent scientific activities of the United Kingdom, it being understood that such activities shall be conducted so as not to conflict with schedules of operations agreed between the two Governments and that any additional operating costs shall be borne by the United Kingdom. There are also provisions concerning immunities, facilities, title to property and similar matters.

Upper atmosphere research agreements may, like that between the United States and Argentina,[13] be somewhat general in character and simply provide that certain facilities and immunities shall be granted to a High-Altitude Sampling Unit or may, like that between the United States and Canada,[14] enter into considerably greater detail and contain provisions relating to such matters as financing and manning, safety requirements, procurement of equipment, ownership of removable property, transport and telecommunication arrangements, and the applicability of the local law, in addition to specifying the facilities to be provided and immunities to be granted.

The Agreements relating to Intercontinental Testing in connection with Experimental Communication Satellites conducted by the United States with the United Kingdom[15] and France[16] take the form of exchanges of notes agreeing to a programme of joint participation in intercontinental testing, designating the agencies which will participate therein, and providing that the details and procedures will be arranged between the designated agencies. The substance of the arrangements envisaged is not contained in the formal exhanges of notes registered with the United Nations.

[13] 315 *United Nations Treaty Series*, pp. 212–213.
[14] 368 *United Nations Treaty Series*, pp. 368–377.
[15] 405 *United Nations Treaty Series*, pp. 108–111.
[16] 409 *United Nations Treaty Series*, pp. 131–138.

We may anticipate that in course of time there will be a much wider and more detailed network of bilateral agreements dealing with these and other matters, including guest payloads, the operation of various types of satellites, and facilities for launching from the territory of co-operating States.

The Bilateral Space Agreement of June 8, 1962, between the U.S.S.R. and the United States consists of a Summary of Understandings between the Academy of Sciences of the U.S.S.R. and the National Aeronautics and Space Administration of the United States, subsequently confirmed by the two Governments and notified by them to the United Nations,[17] and implemented by a First Memorandum of Understanding between the Academy of Sciences and the National Aeronautics and Space Administration of March 20, May 24, 1963.[18] The Agreement provides for a co-ordinated meteorological satellite programme, passive communications satellite experiments, a magnetic field survey through the use of artificial satellites, and future discussions by the scientists of the two countries of scientific results obtained from deep space probes. (Mariner II and Mars I.) The meteorological programme includes exchange of data and of techniques of interpretation and analysis, the establishment of a communication link between the Washington and Moscow World Weather Centres, and co-ordinated launchings of weather satellites.[19] In these arrangements we have perhaps the first practical premonition of what might ultimately develop into a "space for peace pool" transcending political differences "which, without representing a full pooling of all activities in space, would provide for the pooling of a significant segment of such activities and participation therein on a broad international basis".[20]

[17] United Nations Document A/C.1/880 of December 5, 1962, which contains the text, also available in American Society of International Law, *International Legal Materials*, Vol. II, No. 1, January 1963, pp. 195–198, and pp. 378–381, below.
[18] American Society of International Law, *International Legal Materials*, Vol. II, No. 5, September 1963, pp. 902–926, and pp. 382–392, below.
[19] The provisions of the agreement are discussed more fully in Pt. III below apropos of the various subjects to which they relate.
[20] *The Common Law of Mankind*, 1958, p. 406.

9

Private Enterprise in Space?

THE differences of view, and indeed of fundamental philosophy, concerning the respective rôles of government and private enterprise in scientific, technological and economic development which exist among and within States are inevitably reflected in widely varying conceptions of the extent to which there is legitimate scope for private enterprise in space.

There appears to be no disposition anywhere to encourage private enterprise in launching. To this extent subsequent events have confirmed the view which the present writer expressed in 1956 as follows:

> "The possibility of private adventure in, or based upon, space by irresponsible adventurers not subject to any organised political control can perhaps be disregarded in view of the fact that any such adventure would have to have its base within some existing political jurisdiction. The scale of the capital investment involved, the considerable area necessary for a launching station, the degree of preparation required, the need for a substantial measure of public regulation on grounds of public safety alone, and the possible military implication of such developments all combine to make it probable that only States, and perhaps only large States or specially constituted international bodies established by States, will be in a position to undertake the exploration and exploitation of the resources of space."[1]

The danger of piracy or privateering in space can still be regarded as remote. Launching continues to be so closely related to military considerations that one can reasonably assume that it will remain firmly under governmental control, if only to prevent a private adventurer launching an object which when perceived in a radar screen and unidentified led to measures of self-protection or retaliation involving an

[1] *The Common Law of Mankind*, 1957, pp. 390–391.

87

acute danger of war. But we already have in Telstar a case in which the operation, as distinct from the launching, of a communication satellite has been entrusted to private enterprise, and a similar situation may arise as satellites for other purposes become operational or in the event of it becoming possible to exploit commercially any of the resources of space. Big business is heavily involved in the development of space technology. It is natural that it should seek to extend its activities into space as opportunities offer. The question accordingly arises of how much private enterprise should be permitted in space and what kind of international or national regulation is appropriate for such commercial activities as may be permitted.

UNITED STATES COMMUNICATIONS SATELLITES ACT OF 1962

In the United States there was a major controversy on the subject in Congress prior to the adoption of the Communications Satellites Act. In lengthy hearings before the Committee on Interstate and Foreign Commerce of the House of Representatives and the Committees on Foreign Relations and Commerce of the Senate sharply conflicting views were expressed by the partisans of a public corporation analogous to the Tennessee Valley Authority for the operation of a communications satellite system, the partisans of a private corporation for the purpose wholly controlled by telecommunication companies using its facilities, and the partisans of a private corporation stockholding in which is so regulated by law that only 50 per cent thereof is held by such companies.[2] The Act passed is based on the third of these principles.[3]

The Act declares that "it is the policy of the United States to establish, in conjunction and in co-operation with other countries, as expeditiously as practicable a commercial communications satellite

[2] Hearings before the Committee on Interstate and Foreign Commerce, House of Representatives, 87th Congress, 1st Session, on Establishment, Ownership, Operation and Regulation of a Commercial Communications Satellite System; Second Session on H.R. 10115 and H.R. 10138 Bills to Provide for the Establishment, Ownership, Operation and Regulation of a Commercial Communications Satellite System and for Other Purposes; Hearings before the Committee on Commerce, United States Senate, 87th Congress, 2nd Session on S 2814; Hearings before the Committee on Foreign Relations, United States Senate, 87th Congress, 2nd Session, on H.R.11040.
[3] Public Law 87–624, 87th Congress, H.R.11040, August 31, 1962, 76 Stat. 419.

system, as part of an improved global communications network, which will be responsive to public needs and national objectives, which will serve the communication needs of the United States and other countries, and which will contribute to world peace and understanding".[4] The new and expanded international communications "are to be made available as promptly as possible and are to be extended to provide global coverage at the earliest practicable date"; in effectuating the programme care and attention are to be directed "toward providing such services to economically less developed countries and areas as well as those more highly developed, toward efficient and economical use of the electro-magnetic frequency spectrum, and toward the reflection of the benefits of this new technology in both quality of services and charges for such services".[5] In order "to facilitate this development and to provide for the widest possible participation of private enterprise", United States participation in the system is to be "in the form of a private corporation, subject to appropriate governmental regulation", it being the intent of Congress "that all authorised users shall have non-discriminatory access to the system, that maximum competition be maintained in the provision of equipment and services utilised by the system, and that the Corporation created . . . be so organised and operated as to maintain and strengthen competition in the provision of communications services to the public".[6] The Act is not intended "to preclude the creation of additional communications satellite systems, if required to meet unique governmental needs or if otherwise required in the national interest".[7] Subject to federal co-ordination, planning and regulation by the President, the National Aeronautics and Space Administration and the Federal Communications Commission,[8] there is to be created a communications satellite corporation for profit which will not be an agency or establishment of the United States Government but will be governed, subject to the provisions of the Act, by the District of Columbia Business Corporation Act.[9] Stock in the Corporation is to be held in accordance with the terms of the Act in such a manner as to ensure that 50 per cent of it is held by

[4] s. 102 (*a*).
[5] s. 102 (*b*).
[6] s. 102 (*c*).
[7] s. 102(*d*).
[8] s. 201.
[9] s. 301.

telecommunication companies on an equitable basis determined on the basis of the public interest and 50 per cent is issued in such a manner as to ensure the widest distribution to the public with limitations on individual holdings.[10] The board of directors is to consist of three persons nominated by the President of the United States, six members elected by the stockholders who are communications common carriers and six members elected by the other stockholders.[11] The corporation is to be authorised (a) to play, initiate, construct, own, manage, and operate, itself or in conjunction with foreign governments or business entities, a commercial communications satellite system, (b) to furnish, for hire, channels of communication to United States communications common carriers and to other authorised entities, foreign and domestic, and (c) to own and operate satellite terminal stations[12] (defined as "the complex of communication equipment located on the Earth's surface which secures from or transmits to terrestrial communication systems for relay via communications satellites");[13] the corporation may "purchase satellite launching and related services from the United States Government" and "contract with users, including the United States Government, for the services of the communications satellite system".[14] The corporation is subject to the legal obligations of a common carrier;[15] it is required to notify the Department of State of business negotiations with any international or foreign entity.[16] The Articles of Incorporation of the Communications Satellite Corporation spell out these arrangements in greater detail.[17]

Several aspects of these arrangements call for comment. The corporation is designed to be the United States partner in a global system but the Act recognises that the foreign partners in such a system may be either governments or business entities; in this respect the proposed arrangements correspond to those on the basis of which terrestrial telecommunications are at present conducted. The Corporation is designed to operate commercial communication satellite systems, but its function

[10] s. 304.
[11] s. 303 (a).
[12] s. 305 (a).
[13] s. 103 (2).
[14] s. 305 (b).
[15] s. 401.
[16] s. 402.
[17] For the text of the Articles of Incorporation see American Society of International Law, *International Legal Materials*, Vol. II, No. 2, March 1963, pp. 395–416.

is to furnish channels of communication for hire and not to furnish services directly to the ultimate user. The Corporation has no authority to construct or operate launching facilities, the intention being that it will purchase launching and satellite services from the United States Government.

There do not appear to have been any comparable developments in other countries and the fact that most of the other main telecommunication systems are nationally owned makes such developments less probable, though not necessarily wholly excluded, in respect of communication satellite systems. In a Ground Station Committee, representing the United States, the United Kingdom, France, Germany, Brazil, Italy and Japan, formed to co-ordinate technical requirements and plans for the international testing of experimental communication satellites, all of the other initial participants were governmental telecommunication systems.[18]

EUROSPACE

Eurospace is an association for the preparation and publication of studies of the potential contribution of European industry to space programme consisting of industrial firms, associations and organisations in Belgium, Britain, France, Germany, Italy, Netherlands, Norway, Sweden and Switzerland. It published in 1963 *Proposals for a European Space Programme* which envisage European industry playing a part in the construction of satellites, space probes, launching vehicles and ground networks for communication, time-keeping, navigation and meteorological purposes and in the development of space transporter projects and of a recoverable sounding rocket. The proposals neither presuppose nor exclude a measure of private enterprise in space operations. The Eurospace Report suggests "that very considerable advantages would be derived from the formation of a single inter-governmental authority supervising the whole of this extended field" of European space activities[19] and recognises that Eurospace can "only advise governments on

[18] American Society of International Law, *International Legal Materials*, Vol. II, No. 2, March 1963, pp. 335–336.
[19] Eurospace, *Proposals for a European Space Programme*, 1963, p. 13.

an acceptable space programme";[20] as a non–profit–making organisation it "cannot take part in commercial and contractual negotiations of a profit–making nature".[21] The question of how far private enterprise will play any part in European space operations therefore remains an open one.

It is equally premature to attempt to gauge how far private enterprise may play a part in space activities initiated in other parts of the world or in new types of space activity.

[20] p. 90.
[21] p. 96.

Part II

THE LEGAL LITERATURE

Introductory

A voluminous legal literature concerning space problems, highly unequal in quality but containing much of interest and some work of permanent value, has developed rapidly. A comprehensive analysis of this literature would require a large volume, which would almost immediately become dated by reason of new developments. Some account of the literature prior to the decisions and practice which are now tending to place the law on a more positive basis is, however, a necessary preliminary to an exposition of the law as it is now taking shape. This second Part of the present volume is an attempt to give such an account within a reasonable compass. In the nature of the case it is selective and illustrative rather than complete. It begins with brief indications concerning the literature of space law before Sputnik I and the contributions made to the development of space law by leading authorities on air law; it then analyses the literature of the period from 1957 to 1963 by broad geographical areas (an approach which throws into relief the substantial measure of agreement on fundamentals which exists throughout the world and the differences of emphasis and view which exist within all the main geographical areas), summarises a number of proposals made by leading international legal bodies, and concludes by attempting to estimate the general significance of the literature of space law for the future development of the law.

10

The Literature of Space Law before 1957

FORESHADOWED by Emile Laude[1] in 1910 and in Soviet writings from 1927 onwards,[2] the literature of space law begins with a paper entitled *Das Weltraumrecht—Ein problem der Raumfahrt* written by Vladimir Mandl in 1932 which argued that it was not premature to examine the legal problems which space travel would pose. By 1951 the development of high altitude rocket flight had reopened the old question of how far upward in space the territory of a State extends[3] and as the launching of Earth satellites became imminent it became clear that a wide range of new legal problems would require consideration.[4] Oscar Schachter envisaged that "outer space and the celestial bodies would be the common property of all mankind, over which no nation would be permitted to exercise domination" and that "a legal order would be developed on the principle of free and equal use, with the object of furthering scientific research and investigation".[5] Alex Meyer, addressing the International Astronautical Federation in 1952, argued that while the principle of sovereignty over air space had been accepted it could

---

[1] *Revue internationale de Locomotion Aérienne*, 1910.

[2] Eugène Korovine, "La conquête de la stratosphère et le droit international", 1934, *Revue Générale de Droit International Public*, pp. 675–686.

[3] John Cobb Cooper, "High Altitude Flight and National Sovereignty" 4 *International Law Quarterly*, July 1951, pp. 411–418.

[4] Most of the early papers on the subject are available in the invaluable symposium on space law published in 1959 by the United States Government Printing Office (United States Senate, Eighty-Fifth Congress, Second Session, Special Committee on Space and Astronautics, *Space Law – A Symposium*, prepared at the request of Lyndon B. Johnson, Chairman, December 31, 1958; pp. 1–206 consist of papers published before the launching of Sputnik I. A later edition omitting some of the papers from the first edition but also including some early papers not included in the first edition was published in 1961 under the title *Legal Problems of Space Exploration – A Symposium*, United States Senate, Eighty-Seventh Congress, First Session, Document No. 26.

[5] "Who Owns the Universe?", 1952, republished in *Space Law – A Symposium*, pp. 8–17.

not be extended to outer space. The exercise of sovereignty required a space with determinable borders and the possibility of exercising an effective sovereignty; neither condition was fulfilled in respect of outer space. Space bases should, however, be regarded as subject to the sovereignty of the State establishing them on the analogy of sea-dromes.[6] Welf Heinrich, Prince of Hanover, discussed in a doctorate thesis the range of legal questions which activities in space would present.[7] His work, influenced by that of Alex Meyer, developed the same approach in greater detail. He argued that space beyond the atmosphere must be considered free "both on technical grounds founded on the law of nature and for reasons of legal construction and policy". Space vehicles must be regarded as subject to the law of the flag. The pilot of a space vehicle could never be *legibus solutus* even in the absence of special provisions for space traffic "but would have to conduct himself in regions beyond the atmosphere in a manner unlikely to cause damage to third parties or things in accordance with the principle universally recognised both in international law and the national laws of the various countries of an 'obligation to ensure traffic safety' ". Space stations would come "under the dominion of the country which had constructed them or subject to whose order or protection they had been constructed". There was "no obligation to open any completed space station to the general public" but "once released for use by the general public no discrimination whatsoever should be allowed". Andrew Haley's pioneer work,[8] now assembled and amplified in his *Space Law and Government*, appeared at about the same time.

The present writer, in a paper written in August 1955 and published in January 1956, argued that "by reason of the basic astronomical facts, space beyond the atmosphere of the earth is and must always be a *res extra commercium* incapable of appropriation by the projection into such space of any particular sovereignty based on a fraction of the earth's surface". He based this view partly on the consideration that "the

---

[6] *Legal Problems of Space Exploration – A Symposium*, 1961, pp. 9–19.
[7] *Luftrecht und Weltraum*, Hanover, 1953, with English translation in *Space Law – A Symposium*, 1963, pp. 18–76.
[8] See pp. 103 and 112–114, below.

projection of the territorial sovereignty of a State beyond the atmosphere above its territory would be so wholly out of relation to the scale of the universe as to be ridiculous" and partly on two "more fundamental difficulties" which he stated as follows:

"The first is that any projection of territorial sovereignty into space beyond the atmosphere would be inconsistent with the basic astronomical facts. The revolution of the Earth on its own axis, its rotation around the sun, and the motions of the sun and the planets through the galaxy all require that the relationship of particular sovereignties on the surface of the Earth to space beyond the atmosphere is never constant for the smallest conceivable fraction of time. Such a projection into space of sovereignties based on particular areas of the Earth's surface would give us a series of adjacent irregularly shaped cones with a constantly changing content. Celestial bodies would move in and out of these cones all the time. In these circumstances, the concept of a space cone of sovereignty is a meaningless and dangerous abstraction. The second difficulty is that missiles, space stations and space ships moving in space would be constantly changing their position in relation to the subjacent territorial sovereignties at such high speeds that whatever relationship of control might subsist between Earth stations and such objects in space would have no territorial aspect analogous to the control exerted by a State in its air space or territorial waters. Only activities within the atmosphere of the Earth would appear to be susceptible of a degree of control similar in general nature to that which can be exercised in territorial waters or over a wider maritime frontier belt."

The argument was not that space is a *res communis*, an argument which, as later writers have correctly pointed out, would pose the question whether space is any more capable of collective than of individual appropriation, but that it is a *res extra commercium* incapable by its nature of appropriation. In addition to envisaging the adoption at appropriate stages of development of rules governing launches containing such requirements as might be necessary for the protection of aviation, shipping and the territory of other States, a space radio communication code, rules concerning liability for injury to persons or property on the ground, a space rescue code, and rules determining the law applicable to transactions occurring in space, he formulated four submissions which he regarded as having "an immediate practical application" and calling for "full official consideration as a matter of urgency". These were the following:

"1. Space beyond the atmosphere is a *res extra commercium* incapable by its nature of appropriation on behalf of any particular sovereignty.

"2. It is most desirable that jurisdiction over activities in space beyond the atmosphere should be recognised to be vested in the United Nations and that legislative authority over activities beyond the atmosphere of the Earth should be exercised by the General Assembly acting through or on the advice of an appropriately constituted body. If the political difficulties can be overcome, such an international solution of the problem of jurisdiction in space presents no insuperable legal difficulties.

"3. Failing such an international solution of the problem of jurisdiction in space beyond the atmosphere, it will be necessary to determine such jurisdiction on the basis of appropriate criteria inspired by analogies drawn from maritime and aviation law and to develop common international rules and standards governing the wide range of problems which would arise.

"4. Rules governing the extent to which, and manner in which, national authorities may protect themselves against interference from space beyond the atmosphere with matters within their territorial jurisdiction or interfere, by electronic or other means, with activities in space for the purpose of making such protection effective, or for other reasons, will be necessary."[9]

There followed two further submissions which were cautiously described as relating to questions which might "conceivably arise in respect of the moon in the course of the present century". These were the following:

"5. It is most desirable that sovereignty[10] over unoccupied territory in the Moon or in other planets or satellites should be regarded as vested exclusively in the United Nations. Failing this, title to territory would have to be determined by applying the usual rules concerning discovery and occupation, adapted as necessary, and problems of great difficulty, involving serious danger of acute international tension, would arise.

[9] *Ibid.*, p. 101.
[10] See note 11, p. 101, below.

"6. It is most desirable that title to any natural resources of the Moon or of other planets or satellites which may be capable of utilisation should be regarded as vested in the United Nations and that any exploitation of such resources which may be possible should be on the basis of concessions, leases or licences from the United Nations; this principle would not apply to cosmic rays intercepted in space which, if capable of any human utilisation, are *res nullius* which may be utilised, subject to any rules agreed for the protection of third parties, by anyone in a position to do so."[11]

In 1956 submissions of this nature were regarded as highly speculative in character; although the extent to which they are (or were) premature as a practical matter, the measure in which they state or anticipate the law, the nature and validity of the theoretical justification for them, and their precise formulation have been a matter of much discussion and some controversy, these general concepts are now common currency and fall considerably short of what is widely regarded as desirable; the gap between the advanced thinking of 1956 and the commonplaces of 1964 underlines the importance of approaching the international law of outer space in a frame of mind which fully recognises the scope and rate of contemporary development.

[11] pp. 101–102; these proposals were subsequently expanded in *The Common Law of Mankind*, pp. 382–407, in which, at p. 400, the concept of jurisdiction over unoccupied territory in the Moon or other planets or satellites being vested in the United Nations is substituted for that of sovereignty being so vested.

II

The Contribution of Authorities on Air Law

IT is not unnatural that the acknowledged authorities on air law should have been among the leading contributors to the discussion of space law.

Such outstanding authorities on air law as McNair and Lemoine have expressed no view on the questions posed by space exploration as such, but the views which they have expressed on air law have a significant bearing on questions which have now assumed a new form and importance as the result of developments in space.

Among the authorities on air law who have contributed directly to the discussion of the new problems presented by developments in space may be mentioned Eugène Pépin[1] and P. K. Roy,[2] successively legal advisers of the International Civil Aviation Organisation, John Cobb Cooper,[3] Legal Adviser of the International Air Transport Association, Antonio Ambrosini,[4] D. Goedhuis,[5] Robert Homburg,[6]

---

[1] See in particular for an analysis of his *Droit de l'Espace*, pp. 105–107, below; for a bibliography of Pépin's numerous other papers see *Legal Aspects of Space Exploration – A Symposium*, United States Senate, 87th Congress, 1st Session, Document No. 26, (hereinafter cited as *Symposium*), pp. 1370–1371.

[2] *1956 Proceedings of the American Society of International Law*, pp. 94–96.

[3] For a bibliography of Cooper's numerous papers see *Symposium*, pp. 1341–1342.

[4] *Instituciones del Derecho de la Aviacion*, Buenos Aires, 1949.

[5] D. Goedhuis has contributed a series of reports on the limitation of air sovereignty to the International Law Association; see *Report of the 47th Conference*, (Dubrovnik, 1956), pp. 196–215, *Report of the 48th Conference*, (New York, 1958), pp. 320–330; *Report of the 49th Conference*, (Hamburg, 1960), pp. 271–389; *Report of the 50th Conference*, (Brussels, 1962), pp. 31–100.

[6] *e.g.*, "Droit astronautique et droit aérien", *Revue Générale de l'Air*, 1958, pp. 11–16; "Introduction au Droit de l'Espace", *Revue Générale de l'Air*, 1960, pp. 180–207.

R. Y. Jennings,[7] Joseph Kroell,[8] Paul de La Pradelle,[9] Alex Meyer[10] and Bin Cheng.[11]

Another group of writers have become known chiefly by their contributions to the discussion of space law. Of these the leading figure is Andrew G. Haley,[12] General Counsel of the International Astronautical Federation and the American Rocket Society; other members of the group include Aaronson[13] Beresford,[14] Danier[15] and Horsford.[16]

The leading air law reviews frequently contain important and suggestive articles on space law by these and other writers on air law.[17]

McNair, writing in 1931,[18] made a series of comments on the maxim *cujus est solum, ejus est usque ad coelum et ad inferos* which continue to be apposite. "Like most maxims and slogans", he writes, it "has

---

[7] See p. 118, below.

[8] *e.g.,* Eléments créateurs d'un droit astronautique", 1953, *Revue générale de l'Air,* pp. 203–245.

[9] See pp. 117–118, below.

[10] For a bibliography of Alex Meyer's papers on the subject see *Symposium,* pp. 1365–1366.

[11] *e.g.,* "International Law and High Altitude Flights", *Symposium,* pp. 141–155, and "Problems of Space Law", *Symposium,* pp. 666–669.

[12] For a bibliography of Haley's numerous papers, now amplified in his *Space Law and Government,* 1963 (pp. 112–114, below), see *Symposium,* pp. 1350–1352.

[13] Michael Aaronson has contributed a series of articles to the *Law Times,* London, notably "Earth Satellites and the Law", August 26, 1955, pp. 115–116, "Aspects of the Law of Space", October 25, 1957, pp. 219–221, "Towards Control in Space", July 18, 1958, pp. 30–31, and to *International Relations,* London, notably in "Space Law" in Vol. I, No. 9, April 1958, pp. 416–427, "Towards the Peaceful Uses of Outer Space" in Vol. I, No. 12, October 1959, pp. 611–619 and "Comments on Space Law", Vol. II, No. 3, April 1961, pp. 135–142.

[14] Spencer H. Beresford was the author of the *Survey of Space Law* prepared for the Select Committee on Astronautics and Space Exploration of the United States House of Representatives, 86th Congress, 1st Session, House Document No. 89; he has contributed papers regularly to the *Proceedings* of the Space Law Colloquium of the International Astronautical Federation, notably a paper on "Principles of Spacecraft Liability" submitted to the Third Colloquium.

[15] "Les voyages interplanétaires et le droit", *1952 Revue Générale de l'Air,* p. 422; and (with Marcel Saporta) "Un nouveau problème de droit aérien: les satellites artificiels; *1955 Revue Générale de l'Air,* pp. 295–303.

[16] Cyril Horsford has contributed articles on the subject to the *Journal of the British Interplanetary Society* and *International Relations,* London.

[17] *e.g., Journal of Air Law and Commerce, Revue Générale de l'Air, Revue Française de Droit Aérien, Zeitschrift für Luftrecht, Revista de Aeronautica* (Madrid) and *Revista Latino americana de Derecho Aeronautico,* (Buenos Aires).

[18] *The Law of the Air,* 1932; there is no substantial change in the relevant passages in the 3rd edition by Kerr and Evans, 1964, though they are differently arranged; see generally pp. 31–57, and for a history of the maxim see Appendix I, pp. 393–397.

merely been used either to darken counsel or to afford a short cut and an excuse for not thinking the matter out upon a basis of principle . . ."[19] He does not regard the maxim as having in itself any authority in English law:

"I venture to submit the view that the maxim has been grievously misunderstood and misapplied so far as its upward limit is concerned. There is no question that the air and the airspace are two different things. Air is certainly capable of ownership if you can capture it and confine it in a closed space such as a bottle, just as sea-water becomes the property of a shipping company when it is pumped up into a bath on one of its steamers, or of a hotel company when it is pumped into a tank in the hotel. One of the commonest forms in which air becomes the subject of ownership is when it is liquified and put into a bottle."

"But can space – whatever space may be – become the subject of ownership? I have the gravest doubts on that point. Certainly the 'ownable' contents of space may be owned, whether they are minerals below the surface of the Earth or buildings above it. I am not persuaded that the common law is committed to the view that mere abstract space can be the subject of ownership apart from its contents."[20]

The "robust common sense which is so frequently shown by the common law and its guardians"[21] also requires a proper regard for the changing requirements of public policy.

"Further, I submit the view that in deciding whether or not any particular use by a stranger of the airspace superincumbent over a man's land is actionable, either as a trespass or as a nuisance, the common law will, as in other circumstances in the past, pay due regard to the convenience of mankind and to the fact that, as the world's population increases and man's conquest of nature develops, the exclusive enjoyment of all the amenities arising from the ownership of land is continuously and inevitably decreasing."[22]

The concept that space as distinguished from its contents is incapable of ownership, while perhaps not in itself a full answer to the question of the extent of jurisdiction in space in the astronautical sense, is nevertheless the starting point for any reasonable evaluation of the legal

[19] *Op. cit.*, 1942, p. 17.
[20] *Op. cit.*, p. 33.
[21] *Op. cit.*, p. 30.
[22] *Op. cit.*, p. 35.

status of such "space", while the concept of exclusive enjoyment yielding before man's conquest of nature represents the essential key to the effective legal regulation in the common interest of activities in space.

Maurice Lemoine[23] regards both the thesis of the freedom of the air and the thesis of sovereignty based on the maxim *usque ad coelum* as being historical survivals no longer corresponding to current needs. He points out that the conception of an international community with rights binding on all is constantly gaining strength and suggests that the conflicting rights and interests of subjacent and other States can best be reconciled by substituting for the concept of sovereignty in the air one of a right of police of the subjacent State with a sufficiently broad content. This general approach is strikingly similar to that of McNair. Lemoine, like McNair, regards airspace as such as insusceptible of proprietory appropriation; it can be occupied but only to the extent to which occupation of it is a physical possibility.[24]

Among the authorities on air law who have made a direct contribution to the development of space law Eugène Pépin, whose unique experience of international air law goes back to the 1910 International Conference on Aerial Navigation, holds a special place. At the outset of a comprehensive course of lectures on space law given in 1961–1962[25] he poses the question whether we have yet reached the stage at which the law can be formulated on the basis of adequate knowledge and replies by endorsing the view expressed by the present writer that "while it is healthy that the evolution of the law should follow rather than anticipate that of life, there are circumstances in which the possibility of developing the law on sound principles depends primarily on an initiative being taken in the matter before *de facto* situations have crystallised too far".[26] He points out that the first legal regulation in France of the use of balloons was an ordinance of April 23, 1784, adopted within nine months from Montgolfier's first ascent and that

---

[23] *Traité du droit aérien*, 1947, pp. 71–81.
[24] *Op. cit.*, pp. 113–116.
[25] *Le Droit de l'Espace*, Institut International d'Etudes et de Recherches Diplomatiques, Paris, 1962.
[26] *The Common Law of Mankind*, 1958, p. 384.

Fauchille's early work on air law preceded the Wright Brothers' first flight. Pépin introduces the subject with a bird's eye view of the development of air law down to 1961, of early experiments in rocketry, and of the International Geophysical Year and subsequent developments; he describes in some detail the existing national and international space programmes, and gives an account of the discussions concerning space questions in the International Civil Aviation Organisation, the World Meteorological Organisation, the International Telecommunication Union and the United Nations. He then proceeds to an analysis of the legal problems of space and discusses in turn the legal problems of cosmic space, the exploration of space, the utilisation of space, the exploration and exploitation of celestial bodies, responsibility for damage resulting from activities in space, and the future development of space law. He does not consider it either necessary or possible to determine at present for legal purposes where the atmosphere ends and space begins. "Les juristes les plus sages se contentent de dire que l'espace cosmique commence là où finit l'atmosphère, et s'en remettent aux geophysiciens" le soin de dire où est cette limite. Pépin's discussion of the kind of legal problems which may arise in connection with particular type of satellites, including satellites stationary over the territory of another State, orbital stations, and meteorological and telecommunication satellites, is particularly stimulating. He accepts and endorses the principles set forth in the General Assembly resolution of December 20, 1961, that international law, including the Charter of the United Nations, applies to outer space and celestial bodies, and that outer space and celestial bodies are free for exploration and use by all States in accordance with international law and not subject to national appropriation. He does not regard any United Nations sovereignty or trusteeship over celestial bodies as appropriate or feasible and would welcome a treaty analogous to the Antarctic Treaty developing the principles contained in the 1961 General Assembly Resolution in greater detail. In discussing liability for damage resulting from activities in space, he distinguishes direct and indirect damage. He accepts the principle of absolute and unlimited liability for direct damage and suggests that the launching State or States should be liable for damage on the occasion of the launching and the State responsible for the manufacture of the space vehicle for damage on the occasion of its return, with a right of recourse in both cases against any other State or body which may be responsible. Among possible forms of indirect damage he mentions radio interference in violation of international regulations and radio piracy. He envisages that a special procedure of redress may be necessary for liability cases. Pausing to consider the future development of space law, he pauses briefly to discuss the most appropriate terminology and concludes that "space law" is preferable to all of the various alternatives which have been suggested. Space law must be regarded as an autonomous branch of law and as an international or, rather, a world or universal law; it must be solidly based on scientific reality. A convention or declaration setting forth general principles is desirable in the near future. It should proclaim: that space and celestial bodies are free for exploration and use by all the nations of the world for peaceful purposes and in accordance with international law; that space and celestial bodies are not subject to national appropriation; that space vehicles have a right of innocent passage through atmospheric space subject to compliance with regulations requiring them to identify themselves and governing their passage; that space stations not affected to a special purpose should permit technical stops by all space vehicles; that in the event of an emergency landing all States should co-operate in giving assistance, including the repatriation of astronauts and restitution of space objects; that the State or States owning a space vehicle should be absolutely liable for all damage caused thereby; that space vehicles should be identified by marks and signals notified to an international organisation; that there should be advance notification of launchings; that there should be a fair distribution of radio frequencies; that every space vehicle should be fitted with devices making it possible to destroy or silence it on the expiration of its useful life; that there should be provision for the compulsory settlement of disputes; and that there should be provision for a full exchange of space information. Pépin envisages the establishment of a special body for the international regulation of activities in space.

John Cobb Cooper, another acknowledged pioneer in the field, has directed special attention to the demarcation of the boundaries of airspace and outer space[27] and argued this to be the fundamental problem, but other outstanding authorities have dissented sharply from his views. Neither Eugène Pépin[28] nor P. K. Roy,[29] his successor as Legal Adviser of ICAO, nor John A. Johnson, the Legal Adviser of the National Aeronautics and Space Administration of the United States,[30] regards such demarcation as of this order of importance, and general international lawyers have been even less inclined to attach any decisive importance or high priority to the matter.[31]

Cooper's own view concerning the proper basis of demarcation has changed as experience has grown. In 1951 he suggested as the criterion the extent to which the scientific progress of any State in the international community permitted it to control the space above it.[32] In 1956 he abandoned this rule as impracticable and advocated a new international agreement on the subject based on three points: (a) reaffirmation of Article I of the Chicago Convention, giving the subjacent State full sovereignty in the areas of atmospheric space above it, up to the height where "aircraft", as now defined, may be operated, such areas to be designated "territorial space"; (b) extension of the sovereignty of the subjacent state upward to 300 miles above the Earth's surface, designating this second area as "contiguous space" and provision of a right of transit through this zone for all non-military flight instrumentalities when ascending or descending; and (c) acceptance of the principle that all space above "contiguous space" is "free for the passage of all instrumentalities".[33] In 1957 he urged a further extension of sovereignty by agreement up to 600 miles "so as to protect neutral States from the uncontrollable flight of guided missiles on high trajec-

[27] *e.g., Symposium*, pp. 1–7 and 764–772.
[28] *e.g., Symposium*, p. 236.
[29] *e.g., 1956 Proceedings of the American Society of International Law*, pp. 94–96.
[30] Fourth Colloquium on the Law of Outer Space, Washington, 1961, *Proceedings*, pp. 352–360.
[31] *e.g.*, Jessup, p. 119, below, Chaumont, p. 154, below, Quadri, p. 156, below, Yanguas Messia, p. 158, below; Jenks in Third Colloquium on the Law of Outer Space, Stockholm, 1960, *Proceedings*, p. 20.
[32] "High Altitude Flight and National Sovereignty" reprinted in *Symposium*, pp. 1–7.
[33] "Legal Problems of Upper Space", *1956, Proceedings of the American Society of International Law*, pp. 85–94.

tories".[34] In 1958 he was content to note that "no agreement exists as to where the boundary is between the territorial airspace of a State and outer space beyond – nor as to the legal status of the intermediate area . . . in which . . . the presence of a certain amount of gaseous atmosphere may cause the fall of flight instrumentalities",[35] but in 1960 he still held firmly to the view that the rule of law cannot "be established with certainty as to outer space, a finite geographical area, unless the boundaries of that area are known and understood".[36] Cooper has consistently had the courage to adapt his thinking to an unprecedented succession of new scientific and technological developments, but his critics have not unreasonably pointed out that we cannot assume that any finality has been reached in the matter, and that in these circumstances any demarcation is premature, particularly, many would add, as there is no proof of any practical need for such demarcation.

While Cooper's views concerning the practical importance of demarcation do not command general support and have been rejected by two successive United Nations Committees on the Peaceful Uses of Outer Space, his original statement of the grounds on which the extremer claims to sovereignty in space are untenable remains important:

"Under no possible theory can it be said that a State can exercise sovereign rights in outer space beyond the region of the Earth's attraction. The arguments for State sovereignty in space have always gone back to the proposition that it is both the right and the duty of the State to protect itself and that on no other basis can such protection be considered adequate except that it have the right to control, as part of its territory, these regions above it which, if used by other States, may bring damage and loss to persons and property on the State below. Carrying this old rule to its extreme, the outer boundary of the State cannot be further than the point where the Earth's attraction will govern the movement of an object in space so that such object will 'fall' on to the Earth.

[34] "Flight Space and the Satellites", 7 *International and Comparative Law Quarterly*, 1958, pp. 82–91, at p. 90.
[35] "Missiles and Satellites – The Law and Our National Policy", 44 *American Bar Association Journal*, 1958, pp. 317–321.
[36] "Fundamental Questions of Outer Space Law", reprinted in *Legal Problems of Space Exploration – A Symposium*, pp. 764–772.

"On the other hand, this boundary cannot be lower than the upper limit of the airspace. The rule of international law – that the territory of the subjacent State includes at least the region above it known as airspace – need not be challenged. In other words, it would appear that the upper boundary of the State's territory lies at a point between the upper limit of the airspace and the upper limit of the Earth's attraction. Somewhere in this vast intervening region the rights of the State below cease to exist as against other States.

"Certain jurists have insisted that the territory of a State is limited by the ability of that State to make its law effective. This is a harsh rule when applied to sovereignty in space. The richest and most powerful States now have means through high altitude rockets to control more or less effectively the airspace over their surface territories. But the weaker States have no such power. Can we be said to live in such a world where the physical power at any one time of any particular State determines its international right to consider the region above its surface territories as part of its national territory? I may say here that my own belief is and has always been that if the rule of effectiveness is to be applied to determine the limit of State territory in space, then the rule should be that every State, no matter how small or how weak, as a State of equal sovereignty with every other State, has and should be admitted to have territorial rights upward above its surface territories as high as the rights of every other State no matter how powerful.

"Perhaps the rule should be, in the absence of international agreement, that the territory of every State extends upward as far into space as it is physically and scientifically possible for any one State to control the regions of space directly above it."

*   *   *

"I am convinced that we must abandon the theory that the State has the right to claim territory out into space as far as the Earth's attraction extends and that we must admit some such reasonable rules as I have suggested above – namely, that at any particular time the territory of each State extends upward into space as far as then scientific progress of any State in the international community permits such State to control space above it."[37]

More recently, in 1960, Cooper has summarized his views by suggesting "tentative answers" for "four fundamental problems" in the following terms:

[37] "High Altitude Flight and National Sovereignty" reprinted in *op. cit.*, pp. 1–7, at pp. 5–7.

"First, that the boundaries of outer space must be fixed and that the important lower boundary should be at a point above the surface of the Earth where it is possible to put a satellite in orbit at least once round the Earth.

"Second that the legal status of outer space must be fixed and that this could best be done by accepting a status similar to that of the high seas, thus permitting its equal use by all and denying to any State the right to assert sovereignty over outer space or any other celestial bodies therein.

"Third, that the international law right of a State to take action for its self-protection and self-defence must be preserved and acknowledged so far as outer space is concerned, even though no State has a right to claim sovereignty therein.

"Fourth, that the legal status of satellites and of other space craft used in outer space must be determined, and that this status should be that of 'nationality' of the launching State, or other agreed State, otherwise chaos will result."[38]

The question whether demarcation is or is not important is primarily a practical rather than a legal problem, and the practical reasons for not attempting demarcation have been stated with great cogency by Sir William Hildred, the Director-General of the International Air Transport Association and Sir Frederick Tymms, the Master of the Guild of Air Pilots and Air Navigators, in the following propositions:

"1. The exercise of national sovereignty in space is unnecessary for the protection of the interests of any country, because the division of space into national segments would be ineffective for any purpose.
"2. The effective exercise of national sovereignty in space would be absolutely impracticable.
"3. The recognition of national sovereignty in the airspace is something we have to live with for the present, but a practical code of international law does not require a geometric definition of the boundary between airspace and space. Any attempt to define it repeats old errors, is inducive of claims to extended sovereignty, and is dangerous."[39]

Cooper has also made an important contribution to the discussion of responsibility for third-party damage caused by space vehicles,[40]

[38] "Fundamental Questions of Outer Space Law" reprinted *op. cit.*, pp. 764–772, at pp. 771–772.
[39] *Symposium*, pp. 264–270.
[40] See the memorandum reprinted in *Symposium*, pp. 680–683.

notably by his suggestion that, while damage on the surface or in the airspace should give rise to liability without proof of fault, proof of fault should be the rule as to occurrences in outer space as between space vehicles.

Andrew G. Haley has made from the outset a particularly important contribution to the discussion of the legal aspects of space telecommunications and has pioneered the concept of "metalaw", a body of law which will ultimately govern the relationship between man and any extra-terrestrial intelligent beings found in space. His earlier writings focused attention on such matters as the importance of fitting radio equipment sent into space with devices making it possible to terminate transmission, equipping objects placed in orbit with apparatus whereby they may be commanded back to Earth at a safe location, fitting space objects with apparatus rendering them identifiable, and reaching international agreement with respect to the use of television, photography, and observational equipment generally. In *Space Law and Government*[41] Haley has assembled and amplified no fewer than 205 earlier articles, addresses and papers into a systematic presentation of his views. The special quality of his work is the thoroughness of his knowledge of the relevant technology. He discusses in turn national consent to overflight, the limits of national sovereignty, sovereignty over celestial bodies, space vehicle regulations, space communications, liability for personal and property damages in space activities, space medical jurisprudence, and "metalaw". He makes a sustained plea for adequate space vehicle regulations. "Abuses in radio usage; unreported vehicles performing undisclosed functions at undisclosed distances from the Earth; unrecorded launchings; secret payloads; and many other space practices are completely unrestrained to date. Somewhere the nations of the Earth must begin a common system of regulation, identification, registration and licensing".[42] Pre-flight inspection will be difficult to achieve because of its relationship to security but would be a "major accomplishment";[43] regulation of dangerous payloads is another problem of comparable difficulty and importance.[44] Haley's discussion of the technology of space communications gives a particu-

[41] 1963.　　　　[42] p. 137.　　　　[43] p. 140.　　　　[44] p. 141.

larly full and revealing picture of the problems involved, the difficulties which occurred in connection with the early satellites, and the further possibilities and problems which may arise as light-wave and ultra-violet communications supplement the radio spectrum;[45] he lays special stress on the importance of silencing transmission once the useful life of a satellite is ended by means of radiocommand or timing devices[46] and discusses the technicalities of transmission identification procedures.[47] Under the title of "space medical jurisprudence" Haley discusses among other matters the problem of contamination of and from space and formulates a number of recommendations for immediate consideration. These include (a) provision for maintenance of pre-launch sterilisation or else for inflight sterilisation of rocket exteriors unless and until it is proven that life on the rocket exteriors cannot survive the ultra-violet radiation in space; (b) provision for internal sterilisation to avoid contamination from break-up of the rocket or payload on impact; (c) provision for sterilisation of all flights destined to approach the vicinity of celestial bodies, even if not designed for impact; (d) maintenance of sterile conditions within a high probability figure, perhaps one chance in a million; (e) limitation of areas of landing to localise effects of possible contamination; (f) prohibition of explosion of nuclear devices, whether to provide seismic data on the interior and age of celestial bodies or for any other reason, until after tests have been completed which would be endangered by nuclear fall-out (with a maximum limit of fall-out and rigid control of atomic wastes disposal thereafter); (g) prohibition of chemical contamination either by markers or by soft-landings which would so disturb prevailing conditions on the celestial body as to prevent recognition of elements of Earthly origin; and (h) provision that all matter to be returned to Earth from outer space pass inspection at an international quarantine space station.[48] His longer-range recommendations include (i) refraining from any possible major intereference with life systems on other celestial bodies unless the scientific need has been clearly established and international approval has been obtained; (j) establishing rigid controls as to the minimum amount of research that is required to ascertain the

[45] pp. 159–232.   [46] pp. 205–212.   [47] pp. 213–218.   [48] pp. 285–286.

lack of danger of contamination, before any possibly contaminating actions are permitted; (k) acceptance of the principle that if forms of life capable of intelligent communication are discovered on a celestial body the spaceship from Earth should not land until an invitation has been issued based on full and mutual knowledge of the risks involved.[49] In his discussion of "metalaw", the principles applicable to our relations with any sapient life encountered in other worlds,[50] Haley starts from the "principle" that we must treat sapient life elsewhere not as we would wish it to treat us but as it would wish to be treated by us in accordance with the laws of its own nature; "we must do unto others as they would have done unto them"; the Golden Rule has always been regarded as the foundation of morality rather than as being in itself a principle of law, and Haley's Rule of Metalaw is likewise the keynote of a moral approach to a policy rather than a principle susceptible of expression in legal terms; as such it is of fundamental importance. Haley combines with this wide horizon a meticulous examination of some of the immediate problems presented by activities in space for American law, including the status of the Communications Satellite Corporation under the Securities Exchange Act and other federal and State legislation,[51] the extent of absolute liability for damage under the Federal Tort Claims Act of the United States,[52] rights of entry upon land to recover space vehicles,[53] and patent rights arising from work undertaken by contractors with the National Aeronautics and Space Administration;[54] he thereby gives us a glimpse of the extent to which space activities may present new problems throughout the law.

Julian G. Verplaetse's *International Law in Vertical Space*[55] is of considerable interest as an attempt to place air law, space law and telecommunication law in relation to each other which covers a wide range of topics, including, in addition to the legal status of space, spacecraft, and celestial bodies, private law, criminal law and the law of war and neutrality. Verplaetse's general approach is highly conservative; he takes little or no account of contemporary developments in international law and his views on vital points are not generally

[49] p. 286.   [51] pp. 187–205.   [53] pp. 253–257.   [55] 1960.
[50] pp. 394–421.   [52] pp. 245–252.   [54] pp. 336–337.

accepted by authoritative opinion and must be regarded as superseded by subsequent United Nations practice and decisions. He considers, for instance, that the legal status of space will be determined "strictly within the framework of power politics",[56] that artificial satellites are not subject to any regulation of international law,[57] and that satellites and planets are *res nullius* rather than *res communis juris* and are therefore subject to appropriation by effective possession and continuous occupation.[58] He finds it "hard to foresee the rules of private law that will regulate human activity in outer space" and considers that "no sources are available" and "the argument of analogy is very weak".[59] In criminal matters he considers the law applicable to spaceflight to be "the national law of the engines, stations or missiles", with some possible admixture of any international regulation which may be adopted and the law of the place of landing;[60] the criminal law applicable on other planets or satellites will apply to conditions so fundamentally different from those on earth that "no suggestion can be made as to the substantive rule applicable or the way out of cumulative jurisdiction".[61] He denies the present existence of any rules concerning space warfare[62] and questions the applicability to space of either neutral rights or neutral duties. This general approach carries so-called realism to the point of utter defeatism. No legal system has ever grown to maturity in this spirit.

D. Goedhuis[63] enquires into the lessons of value for the development of space law which can be deduced from air law experience in an altogether different temper. He recalls the discussions which preceded the acceptance of the principle of sovereignty over territorial airspace, the subsequent chequered history of freedom of transit and traffic rights, the exclusion from international rules of state aircraft, the requirement that every aircraft have a nationality based on registration in one, and not more than one, country, and the limited success of the conventions on private air law. The clear implication of this record is that

---

[56] p. 156.   [58] pp. 161–164.   [60] p. 427.   [62] pp. 487–489.
[57] p. 159.   [59] pp. 398–402.   [61] pp. 478–486.
[63] "Conflicts of Law and Divergencies in the Legal Régime of Air and Outer Space", 1963, *Recueil des Cours*.

the lessons to be deduced from the experience of air law include warnings as well as analogies and that we must not be the slaves of a past marked by too high a proportion of disappointments and failures. The term "air space" does not include space *ad infinitum*. *De lega lata* the term is used in the 1944 Chicago Convention on International Civil Aviation in its natural meaning; airspace extends as far as the atmosphere and it is for the geophysicist to decide what is the height where a sufficient quantity of air is to be found to give an indication of its presence. *De lege ferenda* it may be desirable that the régime applicable to the airspace should extend only to a part of the airspace. Goedhuis accepts the 1961 General Assembly resolution as a statement of law now having binding force; even before its adoption there was general agreement that international law, including the Charter of the United Nations, is applicable to outer space and celestial bodies and accordingly in this respect the resolution confirms a generally accepted principle. In declaring outer space and the celestial bodies to be free for exploration and use and not subject to appropriation the resolution confirms a "common consent of mankind", already created before its adoption, and based on a general conviction that the interests of mankind are best served by recognition of the principle of freedom and use of outer space and the celestial bodies; we have here "one of the rare examples where the development of the consciousness of a community of interest has kept pace with the technical development by which this community of interest is being created". Spacecraft are outside the scope of the Chicago Convention and in view of the prospective importance of collective international action in space it will not suffice to use, in respect of matters such as nationality and registration, the "old mould used up till now for shipping and aviation". Activities in space "must be carried out with respect for the sovereign rights of other States, including certain sovereign rights a State possesses towards space vehicles and their crews". The legal principle of freedom of outer space for the exploration and use of all States has both positive and negative consequences. It confers on all States the right to draw from outer space and celestial bodies the benefits which the use of this space and these bodies entails and it requires States "to refrain from actions which might influence the use of outer space and celestial bodies in an adverse way". Goedhuis discusses particularly fully and suggestively the question of liability for damage caused by aircraft and spacecraft, examining successively damage on the surface, damage in airspace and damage in outer space. As regards damage on the surface he accepts the principle of absolute liability. As regards damage in airspace he considers that the case for the absolute liability of a spacecraft is weakened by the fact that the gap in speed between a supersonic and a small aircraft is comparable to that between a spacecraft and a supersonic aircraft; the liability of a supersonic aircraft is based on fault; the launching of a spacecraft, if previously made known, does not create any ultra-hazardous risk in the airspace: the principle of fault should therefore apply. As between spacecraft liability should be based on fault. Goedhuis leans towards granting the claimant the choice of presenting the claim to the launching State or the operator or owner State or States. He envisages a limitation of liability where the liability is absolute but not where it is based on fault; an exception to such limitation if there is proof of intention to cause damage or recklessness, and exclusion of liability on proof of negligence or a wrongful act or omission by the claimant or his servants or agents. Where two or more space operators are at fault, they should be liable in proportion to the degree of fault. The question of assistance, salvage and return should be considered in the framework of a general agreement providing for assistance to and by aircraft, spacecraft and ships. The establishment of manned space stations will precipitate a wide range of questions of both public and private law and practical arrangements to guarantee a minimum of order at such stations are therefore indispensable.

The same sense that the past must not imprison the future is expressed by Paul de La Pradelle and R. Y. Jennings. Paul de La Pradelle, in a course of lectures on *Les frontières de l'air* given at the Hague Academy of International Law in 1954,[64] while emphasising the artificial character of frontiers in the air,[65] supported the view that there is no limit to aerial sovereignty[66] but considered that the progress of the law would consist

---

[64] *Recueil des Cours de l'Académie de Droit international*, tome 86, (1954 II), pp. 171–202.
[65] *Ibid.*, pp. 124–125.   [66] *Ibid.*, pp. 126–128.

in opening up space to a maximum extent to the constantly improving means of communication placed by technology at the service of man.[67] R. Y. Jennings has pointed out that the International Civil Aviation Convention, being in the nature of a bargain between States, ignores the possibility of aircraft being operated by an international body, and drawn attention to the need "to provide some special status analogous to nationality for aircraft operated by an international body and to make provision for the enjoyment by such aircraft of the privileges granted in the conventions and agreements".[68] This comment may have a particularly important application to space law.

While a number of writers on space law, notably Valladão, have laid great emphasis on its autonomy from air law, it would be ungracious not to acknowledge the major contribution made by authorities on air law to the early stages of its development. The future will nevertheless pose increasingly a whole series of questions going beyond the scope of air law and involving the responsibility of the general international lawyer. It is therefore natural that the growing literature of space law should reflect this broader approach to an ever increasing extent.

[67] *Ibid.*, pp. 130–131.
[68] "Some Aspects of the International Law of the Air", 75 *Recueil des Cours*, 1949 (II), pp. 559–560; see also Jenks, *The Proper Law of International Organisations*, 1962, pp. 167 and 221–223; some of the possible forms of joint international control and operation of aircraft are described in Bin Cheng, *The Law of International Air Transport*, 1962, pp. 246–288.

12

United States Writers

In the literature of space law envisaged in the context of international law generally *Controls for Outer Space and the Antarctic Analogy* by Philip C. Jessup and Howard J. Taubenfeld[1] holds an outstanding place by reason of the fullness of its historical perspective, the ease and thoroughness of its grasp of the scientific and technological factors affecting the new problems now confronting the law, and a boldness of approach to the problems of the future which never parts company from all-pervading sanity.

The first and second parts of the book discuss international controls of widely varying types in retrospect and international controls for the Antarctic; the third part discusses against the background of inter-national controls for other purposes the question of international controls for outer space. The physical setting of the problem,[2] the extent to which air law and maritime analogies are relevant,[3] the military considerations involved,[4] and the potential uses of space for peaceful purposes[5] are all clearly described succinctly but sufficiently fully to place the essentials in perspective in relation to each other. The authors without attempting to define the boundary between airspace and outer space "assume that at some point there is a limit to the extension of terrestrial sovereignties and that in due course practical international necessities will lead to its definition."[6] They note three views concerning the legal status of the heavenly bodies: the view that

[1] Columbia University Press, 1959.
[2] *Op. cit.*, pp. 194–201.
[3] pp. 201–213.
[4] pp. 222–225.
[5] pp. 225–241.
[6] p. 209.

they are *res nullius* subject to appropriation; the view that they are "free
for the perpetual use of all"; and the view held by "far the largest
group" of writers that space and the heavenly bodies are not subject
to appropriation or control by individual national States but must be
subjected to some international control to prevent misuse of the areas
in question and danger and damage to other persons and nations.[7] Of
the possible maritime law analogies they say that "the very nature of
outer space, the non-existence of definable boundaries or subdivisions
and the ability of craft to move through it at speeds a thousand or more
times as great as those at which vessels can move on the high seas,
presents vitally different problems, especially of defense, and indicates
that a mechanical extension of the law of the sea to outer space, even
if the law of the sea were itself more definite and uniform, is not to be
anticipated and would probably not be desirable"; the practice on the
high seas nevertheless provides instructive precedent for operations in
outer space,[8] but the analogy is relevant "essentially for functional
apolitical problems, even as 'freedom of the seas' is substantially today
a peacetime concept".[9] They deduce from statements by the Legal
Advisers of the State Department and by Soviet lawyers that "both the
United States and the Soviet Union are sparring with problems of
outer space, waiting to see what may develop with the rapidly unfolding
technological advances".[10]

Jessup and Taubenfeld discuss at some length the problem of liability
for damage or injury caused by space instrumentalities;[11] holding that
it would be "an unfair burden to impose upon the person injured the
obligation to prove a defect or negligence in manufacture or in
operation", they consider that "the principle of absolute or strict
liability should be accepted";[12] if the principle of absolute or strict
liability should not be accepted and negligence or intent should be
required, the Anglo-American evidentiary principle of *res ipsa loquitur*
might appropriately be adopted; it would then suffice for a complainant
to show an injury together with circumstances making it so improbable
that such an accident would have happened without the negligence of

[7] p. 210.
[8] p. 212.
[9] p. 213.
[10] p. 221.
[11] pp. 241–247.
[12] pp. 243.

the defendant that a jury of reasonable men could find without further evidence that it was so caused.[13] Provision for an effective remedy against the government responsible would be necessary.[14]

From their description and analysis of the problems which arise Jessup and Taubenfeld proceed to pose the fundamental question of chaos or control.

> "The choice in question is presented to governments in two situations which are unique in that they are the only ones in which the very existence of any valid national or sovereign claim is still in question. The Antarctic is one; outer space is the other. One alternative is to subject the two situations to the same power struggle which has in history characterised the demarcation of national territories on the map of the world. The other alternative is to take time by the forelock and to agree that both situations will be subjected to an international rather than to a national solution or, one might better say, to a series of national solutions."[15]

While there are a number of possible alternative courses of action which States may follow in the treatment of the outer space problem in the years ahead, the possibility that the most radical solution may be the best must not be discarded:

> "The principal States might agree to a solution giving effect to defined and enforceable rights vested in the world community, preferably in advance of the acquisition by one or more States of capabilities permitting effective unilateral occupation of celestial bodies or control of outer space. For the first time on the international scene it might be possible to avoid the giddy cycle of law chasing power but never quite catching up"[16]

A regime of functional co-operation in space would not be adequate:

> "Even if an effective international agreement provided that national sovereignties should not be extended into outer space in order to be exercised over the heavens, and somehow eliminated national rivalries, when man develops the necessary capabilities there will arise questions of occupation, use and exploitation of resources by human beings whether or not in government service, the control of such persons, their comings and goings, and their mutual relationships."[17]

[13] p. 246.
[14] pp. 246–247.
[15] p. 251.
[16] p. 267.
[17] p. 273.

Renunciation of potential sovereignty by national States they regard as a "necessity" but "not sufficient by itself to constitute a viable international solution, since such renunciation is also consistent with a political void in space". A satisfactory international solution therefore implies "a renunciation of potential sovereignty by national States and an assumption of some responsibility for the maintenance of order by some general international organisation".[18] A trusteeship pattern[19] and the "many shadings of international administration which would keep legislative control over outer space and its resources in an international organisation, while using national States for the actual execution of the international will" would be inadequate[20] and some form of direct international administration should be envisaged:

> "Perhaps some totally new organisation should be established outside the framework of the United Nations for the enactment of space codes as needed, the neutralisation of space through ownership, operation and licensing of all space craft, the government of other spheres, and, in general, the advancement of the welfare of all men through activities in outer space. Such an agency could, alternatively, be established within the framework of the United Nations."[21]

A Cosmic Development Corporation, analogous to the great trading companies of the age of discovery on Earth, might be envisaged.[22] "The occasion for a fresh approach has arrived."[23]

Myres McDougal[24] has applied to the study of space law his sociological approach to the study of international law in general. Among the conditions "certain to affect the law of space as it develops over the years" he mentions "the extraordinary interdependence of scientific, military, commercial and other objectives that may be advanced by the same activities in space",[25] the "relation between activities in space and the international political situation" including "the structure of the Earth arena, the position and number of powers, their relative

18 p. 276.   20 p. 279.   22 p. 282.
19 p. 277.   21 p. 280.   23 p. 282.
24 "Perspectives for a Law of Outer Space" by Myres S. McDougal and Leon Lipson in McDougal and Associates, *Studies in World Public Order*, 1960 pp. 912–943 and see also *American Journal of International Law*, Vol. 51 (1957), pp. 74–77 and Vol. 52 (1958), pp. 407–431.   25 *Op. cit.*, p. 915.

technological success, and expectations of violence"[26] and the "changing relative importance of space and time", it being "possible that achievements in space will tend to diminish the importance of space in the positional sense and increase the importance of time for the planning of human affairs".[27] McDougal seeks for a solution of the problems which arise in "mutual tolerance of shareable uses of outer space" restricted by "the attempt to ensure the public order of the world community through devices providing security from military attack, preventing or at least making difficult the activities of unaccountable (flagless) space objects or spacecraft (to be compared with measures against piracy on the high seas), and imposing rules of the road".[28] In "Perspectives for a Law of Outer Space", written in collaboration with Leon Lipson in 1958 and republished in 1960 in *Studies in World Public Order*, McDougal envisages the law developing not by a "Big— Solution—Now"[29] but by "the slow building of expectations, the continued accretion of repeated instances of tolerated acts and the gradual development of assurance that certain things may be done under promise of reciprocity and that other things must not be done on pain of retaliation".[30] His approach at that stage is well illustrated by his discussion of modes of redress for what he describes as deprivation inflicted by space activities. "Whether a rule of absolute liability would be preferable to some form of fault liability; whether there is a place for public or private or mixed insurance schemes; whether an international fund might be set up to accommodate worthy claims; whether efforts should be made to reach international agreement on limits of liability – these questions may abide further experience".[31] McDougal's general conclusion as of 1960 was that "a durable agreement by explicit international convention on anything like a code of law for outer space" was not "something now to be expected or desired" but that one might "expect with rather more confidence a series of agreements, gradually arrived at, on particular subjects.[32] Among possible subjects of such agreement he mentioned "the continuation of the IGY; the

[26] *Op. cit.*, pp. 916–917.
[27] *Op. cit.*, pp. 917–918.
[28] *Op. cit.*, p. 923.

[29] *Op. cit.*, p. 929.
[30] *Op. cit.*, p. 930.

[31] *Op. cit.*, p. 940.
[32] *Op. cit.*, p. 941.

exchange of certain types of information such as tracking data and some signalling codes, beyond present levels; the use or abstention from use of certain radio frequencies; and the co-ordination of launching schedules".[33] Agreement "might be reached – not necessarily by the execution of formal documents – to abstain from the pollution of space, by shrapnel or other 'junk', which might otherwise be thrown up in an attempt to impede the flight of hostile satellites or hostile communications", but "such agreement would probably depend on the assurance either that other means of averting the danger from the hostile activities were adequate or that the activities did not prevent a danger sufficiently great to justify the pollution".[34] The course of development must depend on circumstances:

> "The modes of reaching such agreement cannot now be charted with any precision. Some agreements may be explicit and formal; some may be simply a consensus achieved by the gradual accretion of custom from repeated instances of mutual toleration. Some may be bilateral, others trilateral or multilateral; some may be within the framework of the United Nations, others within some other existing organisation or some machinery yet to be set up. Their details and sequence must, like much else in an indeterminate universe, depend on the order of experience in space as well as on the changing political context."[35]

McDougal nevertheless formulated three suggestions "to help allay anxieties about the possible weapons uses of space satellites and to help lay a foundation for close co-operation in peaceful activities in space for common benefit, a co-operation from which an adequate and effective customary or conventional law might eventually emerge".[36] These suggestions were as follows:

> "1. Each State about to launch a satellite could register its intent to do so with an international agency, filing a flight plan and a description of certain characteristics of the satellite, such as load, weight, and size. This could be combined with willingness to submit to international inspection, to assure that the payload conforms to the description filed. This suggestion could be put into practice by any State, regard-

[33] *Op. cit.*, p. 941.
[34] *Op. cit.*, p. 942.
[35] *Op. cit.*, p. 942.
[36] *Op. cit.*, p. 942.

less of the agreement of any other State, but the decision to do so might well be affected by the communicated willingness of other launching States to agree to corresponding measures.

"2. Agreement might be reached to abstain from the launching of satellites fitted with nuclear or other explosive warheads. Such an agreement probably would have to be contingent on the availability of effective prelaunching inspection of the type that is illustrated by the first proposal above. Whether it should or could be coupled with an agreement on the prohibition of the use of intercontinental ballistic missiles, and whether it should or could be considered as part of a possible general agreement on nuclear or universal disarmament, are matters of strategy, community and national, dependent upon the course of many variables.

"3. States possessing the capability of launching satellites might offer to launch certain types of satellites on behalf of, or even as trustee for, the United Nations. The launching State could retain responsibility for the launching operation, preserving control over the security of its rocketry; the United Nations would decide upon the purpose of the flight, determine the payload, design the instrumentation, and finance the construction of the satellite and its contents. The necessary United Nations decisions could be made by an arm of the United Nations, or authority to make them could be delegated to the launching State or conceivably to some other agent. The existence of such 'trust satellites' would not necessarily preclude national satellites with similar or identical functions."[37]

Law and Public Order in Space, written by McDougal in collaboration with Harold Laswell and Ivan Vlasic and published in 1963, is a major intellectual achievement. It treats space as a theme the discussion of which presents an opportunity for the development of an intellectual method rather than as a subject calling for attention by reason of its intrinsic importance. Nor is it a statement, either *lege lata* or *lege ferenda*, of the law or prospective law of space; it is more in the nature of an analysis of the policy considerations which must be taken into account in weighing the relative advantages of the possible alternative solutions for the political and legal problems which will or may arise. In these circumstances it is the more significant that its conclusions tend as regards the great majority of the innumerable questions discussed to

[37] *Op. cit.*, pp. 942–943.

confirm the consensus of view which has been reached by writers with a more traditional approach to legal problems and expressed in the Declaration of Legal Principles adopted unanimously by the General Assembly of the League of Nations. McDougal and his colleagues use a terminology of sociological rather than legal expressions, the understanding of which requires a special initiation, but they use this terminology consistently and once it has been mastered it is intelligible, clear and reasonably precise. They discuss in turn "inclusive" and "exclusive" uses and competences in space, the "maintenance of minimum order in the Earth-space arena", the nationality of and control over spacecraft, the safe and ordered conduct of space activities, "deprivations" resulting from space activities (including such matters as surface impact damage, collisions, pollution and interference with telecommunications), jurisdiction over space activities and spacecraft, the enjoyment and acquisition of space resources, the "establishment of enterprisory activities", and "potential interaction with advanced forms of non-Earth life". In respect of each of these matters they give their estimate of the "significant features" of the "process of social interaction" affecting the matter, of the "probable types of claims" and of the "basic community policies" on the basis of which "decision makers" must decide and reconcile these claims; their discussion of each subject generally concludes with an "appraisal and recommendation" or "appraisal and alternatives". They discuss extensively, but always with discrimination, the relevance of analogies from the law of the sea, the law of the air, and the law governing the acquisition of territory, and acquisition and enjoyment of resources, on Earth. McDougal's belief that space law must grow out of experiment and experience remains unchanged, but he proceeds much further towards the formulation of firm conclusions than he had thought it prudent or possible to do during the early months of the space age. He and his colleagues describe the growth of a "community expectation about the requirements of inclusive use of space"[38] and accept the position that space and the celestial bodies are not subject to national appropriation on the basis of the existence of "a universally shared conviction that space already *is*

[38] p. 218.

a common domain of the whole mankind, belonging in equal measure to all under shared competence";[39] they reject the varied proposals which have been made for the fixing of boundaries between airspace and outer space and "do not favour the attempted establishment of any boundaries in superincumbent regions unless it can be demonstrated that such boundaries promote inclusive interest".[40] They regard the "fundamental constitutional principle of minimum order so painfully and tentatively established for the Earth arena in recent times by the United Nations Charter" as "no less indispensable, in all its detailed nuances, in man's newer, expanding Earth-space arena";[41] they find that "the common interest of all men, irrespective of their potential and ideological affiliations, in mere survival thus establishes a common interest in minimum order which transcends all other considerations".[42] They advocate a nationality for spacecraft and the right of each State to confer such nationality in its discretion, but recognise that it may be desirable to grant international governmental organisations a competence in the matter similar to that enjoyed by individual States.[43] They accept the principle of absolute liability for surface impact damage,[44] subject to some limitation of the amount of such liability,[45] and more tentatively for cases of collision between spacecraft and aircraft; for damage in space they prefer the view that all of the participants can be presumed to have willingly accepted the risks inherent in space activities and follow the present writer in accepting the principle of "equitable apportionment of the loss, taking into account any evidence concerning relative degrees of fault or lack of reasonable care which may be available".[46] They also regard the principle of liability for ultra-hazardous activity as applicable to claims for injury caused by pollution of or from space. Their discussion of jurisdiction in space and the law applicable in space and on Earth to agreements, dispositive acts, status changes, torts and crimes[47] is particularly full and suggestive. So also is their discussion of the enjoyment and acquisition of space resources;[48] these, which they divide into spatial extension, flow and

[39] p. 243.
[40] p. 359.
[41] p, 407.
[42] p. 510.
[43] pp. 550–556.
[44] p. 558.
[45] p. 619.
[46] p. 624.
[47] pp. 646–748.
[48] pp. 749–871.

stock resources, include, in addition to the void, radiations, radio-frequency spectra, forces, particulate matter (solids, dust and gases) and celestial bodies; their general conclusion is that spatial extension resources in space are not subject to appropriation, that the flow resources of space (being vast in extent and limitless in quantity) are likewise available for enjoyment by all who acquire the necessary capabilities, and that the stock resources of space (such as minerals found on celestial bodies) should be regarded as available to all for exploitation on equal terms, subject to limited rights of exclusive use when investment is necessary for exploration and exploitation; they regard "the authoritative establishment in general community policy of at least unorganised inclusive access to most of the resources of space" as "already an accomplished fact". "Enterprisory activities" will, however, require the development of a wide range of space instrumentalities, the constitution and functioning of which will present a range of problems corresponding to those involved in the functioning of existing international organisations.[49] Prudence demands that some thought should be given to the possibility that "the era of astro politics may bring man in touch with other advanced forms of life".[50] Speculative as the matter may be, it should not be ignored. Intergovernmental organisations need to anticipate the contingency of contact with inferior scientific and technological cultures, and to work out in advance plans capable of meeting the challenge optimistically. Plans should always be at hand for an exchange of basic information with any society whose level of civilisation is similar or higher, and especially for insuring that a provisional arrangement will be made promptly as a means of ensuring smooth initial contact.[51]

Josef Kunz[52] regards the rapid advance of scientific and technological progress as one of the many reasons for the period of flux, crises and transformation through which international law is passing.[53] Like Jessup, he starts from the position that "in order to be able to speak

[49] pp. 872–973.
[50] p. 974.
[51] p. 1021.
[52] "The Law of Outer Space – Its Beginning" in *Völkerrecht und Rechtliches Weltfild – Festschrift für Alfred Verdross*, 1960, pp. 167–184.
[53] *Op. cit.*, p. 168.

about the beginnings of the law of outer space, it is necessary to inform oneself about the present status of natural science concerning space and the expectations of natural scientists in this field for the distant and more remote future",[54] but his general approach is far more conservative. His estimate of the legal literature of space is that "while much is repetitious, different and even antagonistic positions with regard to every single problem can be found"; this, he considers is particularly true as regards the rate at which space law should be developed, the legal advisers of governments and those close to them tending to take the view that the development of space law should accompany the development of space capability, primarily because they are uncertain of the possible military implications of successive steps[55] and partly because it is not known whether there may be advantages to be got in space which cause States to make claims for monopolistic uses.[56] He distinguishes between an original goal of the use of outer space for peaceful purposes only and a current tendency to study and regulate the use of outer space for peaceful purposes without waiting for an agreement on disarmament.[57] Kunz finds agreement that a world-wide treaty should be concluded dealing with "the continuation of the IGY, with the identification of a spacecraft, co-ordination of space research, advance registration of the launching of a satellite, giving a flight plan and a description of the characteristics of a satellite, submission to international inspection, complete exchange of information, and regulation of orbits and flight plans". Whether there is in fact more or less agreement on these practical measures than on the general questions of legal principle which may arise may be debatable. Kunz regards the question whether damages to person or property and interference to property are immediate problems as more controversial. He formulates his general conclusions in six negative and two positive points. The negative points are that (a) there is no general agreement to restrict the the use of outer space to peaceful purposes only, (b) the regulation of the peaceful use of outer space has been separated from the problem of disarmament, (c) there is not yet a general international space

[54] *Op. cit.*, p. 168.   [55] *Op. cit.*, pp. 175–177.
[56] *Op. cit.*, p. 183.   [57] *Op. cit.*, p. 177.

agency, (d) there is no general agreement yet as to the definition, boundaries and legal status of outer space, (e) there is no general agreement yet as to the legal status of the celestial bodies, and (f) there is no general agreement yet as to the more remote problems. The positive points are (g) that "there is general agreement with regard to space exploration during the IGY" and "hope that the IGY will be continued" and (h) that "there is a tendency towards regarding outer space as *res omnium communis* although claims for monopolistic uses may be voiced as well as claims to protect the military security of the States".[58]

The literature of space law issued in the United States is too voluminous for comprehensive analysis,[59] but brief references to the report on *The Law of Outer Space*,[60] prepared by Leon Lipson and Nicholas de B. Katzenbach on behalf of the American Bar Foundation for the National Aeronautics and Space Administration, and to the tentative provisions for international agreements on space activities prepared in 1960 by the Committee on Aeronautics of the Association of the Bar of the City of New York, are appropriate.

The report prepared by Lipson and Katzenbach on behalf of the American Bar Foundation contains an analysis and abstracts[61] of space law literature and proposals; it makes no firm recommendations but concludes with "two points that seem particularly relevant at the present stage of space activity and organisation for space" which the authors express as follows:

"(a) It is at the level of fact, as it seems to us, that an international agency of some kind, able to draw upon the talents of highly-trained scientists to appraise possibilities and alternatives, can play its most useful role promoting legal standards for national or other space programmes. Such a group could help to mobilise the talents of the international

---

[58] *Op. cit.*, p. 184.
[59] An extensive and representative selection will be found in *Legal Problems of Space Exploration – A Symposium*, prepared for the Committee on Aeronautical and Space Sciences of the United States Senate by the Legislative Reference Service of the Library of Congress, with an Introduction by Eilene Galloway, United States, 87th Congress, 186 Session, Senate Document No. 26, pp. xxii–1392.
[60] *Symposium*, pp. 779–983.
[61] The abstracts run to 892 points.

scientific community in making responsible recommendations for the consideration of national States, either as a basis for subsequent formal international agreement or as a consideration that will be relevant to unilateral decisions. It would not thereby supersede national authority and control.

"(b) If an international organisation, existing or to be established, is to conduct any space operations, as to which we likewise make no recommendation, it may usefully begin by appropriate provisional arrangements with States having space capabilities. Such arrangements might take the form of trust agreements, the operation of vehicles being carried out under terms and conditions roughly comparable to those presently applicable to trust territories; or they might take the form of 'guest payloads', prepared by international bodies but launched on their behalf by particular national governments. They might be particularly suited to the operation of space vehicles and space craft for some of the purposes canvassed in sub-section B[62] above, and this operation might promote agreement on norms and procedures applicable to purely national space activities. The 'provisional' arrangements, like other 'provisional' arrangements, might turn out to have unexpected lasting qualities."

These recommendations appear to have had considerable practical influence.

The tentative provisions for international agreements on space activities prepared by the Committee on Aeronautics of the Association of the Bar of the City of New York[63] deal with such matters as freedom of use of space, the principle that the conduct of space activities should be open and orderly, the prohibition of use of space for weapons of mass destruction, the dissemination of space data, notice of launchings, orbital or flight tracks and re-entries, the identification and registration of spacecraft, the repossession of spacecraft and repatriation of personnel, inspection at orbital sites, detection at or near ballistic sites, the establishment of an International Space Agency, World Data Centres, satellite tracking stations, the organisation and direction of joint space

[62] These are radio-spectrum management; conservation of space; radio and television relay satellites; weather forecasting and control; damage to subjacent States, aircraft and vessels, and safety standards; repossession of spacecraft and repatriation of space personnel; observation satellites; and co-ordination of space programmes.

[63] The full text is reproduced in Appendix XI, pp. 440–445.

programmes, radio-spectrum management, the disposal of spent spacecraft, liability for damages, contamination, territorial claims to celestial bodies and the settlement of disputes.

The American Society of International Law has on a number of occasions devoted a part of its annual meeting to the discussion of space law. The record of the discussion is available in the Proceedings[64] of the Society but as a matter of policy no conclusions are adopted. The Society is also sponsoring studies on the subject with the aid of a grant from the Ford Foundation.

[64] 1956, pp. 85–115; 1958, pp. 229–252; 1961, pp. 163–186; 1963, pp. 173–207.

13

Soviet and other East European Writers

THERE are two important Soviet works on space law, a symposium entitled *The Cosmos and International Law*[1] edited by Korovine and a comprehensive treatment entitled *The Way to Space Law*[2] by Kovalev and Cheprov. *The Soviet Yearbook of International Law* contains important articles on space law, including summaries in English; *International Affairs*, published in English in Moscow, contains from time to time articles on the subject; translations of a selection of Soviet, Polish, Czech, Hungarian and Yugoslav articles are available in *Legal Problems of Space Exploration—A Symposium* prepared for the Committee on Aeronautical and Space Sciences of the United States Senate[3]; and studies of the Soviet writers have appeared in the American Journal of International Law.[4] There is also a Soviet collection of Western articles on space law.[5]

Outstanding among the Soviet writers is Korovine who, apart from his general eminence as an international lawyer, is Chairman of the Scientific Research Committee on the Legal Problems of Outer Space of the Institute of Law of the U.S.S.R. Academy of Sciences. Korovine rejects "any mechanical extension of the concept of sovereignty from

---

[1] *Kosmos i mezhdunarodnoye pravo*, 1962; see also *Kosmos i mezhdunarodnoye sotrudnichestvo*, 1963.
[2] *TVa puti K Kosmicheskomu pravu*, 1962.
[3] 87th Congress, 1st Session, Senate Document No. 26, pp. 1011–1218, cited hereinafter as *Symposium*.
[4] Robert D. Crane, "Soviet Attitude Toward International Space Law" in Vol. 56, No. 3, July 1962, pp. 685–723 and "The Beginnings of Marxist Space Jurisprudence" in Vol. 57, No. 3, July 1963, pp. 615–625; see also Robert K. Woetzel, "Comments on U.S. and Soviet Viewpoints concerning the Legal Aspects of Military Uses of Space", 1963, *Proceedings of the American Society of International Law*, pp. 195–204.
[5] *Sovremenie problemi kosmicheskovo prava*, 1963.

the Earth or the global atmosphere to the Cosmos" as "a return from Copernicus to Ptolemy".[6] He notes that "most scholars" from the "capitalist countries" and the "socialist countries" alike "deduce that national sovereignty cannot be extended to the Cosmos (outer space) and thereby reject the right of any country to put cosmic space under its legislation, administration or jurisdiction"; he considers that there are "good astronomical reasons to back this viewpoint" since by reason of the rotation of the Earth and the velocity of its motion "sovereignty in the Cosmos may be enforced only at lightning speed and in continuous movement".[7] Korovine's general conclusion as of 1959 was that "there are as yet no agreed or conventional rules defining the international status of cosmic space" and that "matters pertaining to such status must now be decided in the light of precedents in national and international experience and scientific interpretation of existing international law". This he proposed to do in the following manner:

"On the basis of this material it must be concluded that national sovereignty does not extend to cosmic space. However, it does not follow that space is to be considered as some kind of legal 'vacuum' where no restrictions on freedom of action prevail. All universally accepted rules of international law (inadmissibility of the use of force in solving international disputes, non-injury of foreign citizens, and their property, governmental responsibility for the activities of their representatives, etc.) apply to the Cosmos as well. The presence or absence of separate specialised legal systems corresponding, for example, to international maritime control, cannot abolish the generally recognised principles of law prevailing in our time wherever people are active on land, sea, air or space. Any specialised status can be only a development or improvement of the generally accepted principles and rules. In this, and only in this sense, can one speak of 'freedom of space' or 'open space', that is, the right of each country to use cosmic space as it sees fit without doing harm or causing injury to other States. Of course, 'freedom of space' – as long as imperialism and its inherent contradictions exist – can be only a very relative concept, like all the other 'freedoms' in an antagonistic society. The Cosmos will become a genuinely free arena for the peaceful co-operation of sputniks only when we achieve a durable peace, re-establish international confidence and halt the senseless armament race.

[6] *Symposium*, p. 1064. [7] *Ibid.*, p. 1065.

"There are two opposing political courses on the issue of the international status of space, just as in all contemporary international politics. One course – that of the Soviet Union and all other countries of the Socialist camp – is the path of peace, equality of rights and friendly co-operation among nations and countries, opening broad vistas of learning about our world environment and subordinating the powerful forces of Nature to man's mind and will. The other course – that of the imperialists – is the path of international terror and violence, stockpiling and perfecting all possible means of destruction. They consider the study of cosmic space as a process of saturating the outer space surrounding the globe with military weapons."[8]

Korovine's view was formulated in these terms in January 1959. Writing in March 1956 on balloons alleged to be fitted with special apparatus for aerial photography Krylov had invoked the *usque ad coelum* principle.[9]

The textbook *International Law*[10], edited by Kozhevnikov, of which an English edition has been published by the Institute of State and Law of the Academy of Sciences of the U.S.S.R., states, when discussing airspace, that "the problem of outer space has recently become more urgent", that it is "above all necessary to note that, from the point of view of the existing rules of international law, the question of the upper limit of State sovereignty remains open", and that "the great achievements of science, and in particular Soviet science in conquering space gives the problems of the legal régime of space great urgency and great practical importance from the point of view of scientific progress and international politics".[11]

Grigori Tunkin, in an opening statement before the Legal Sub-Committee of the United Nations Committee on the Peaceful Uses of Outer Space on May 28, 1962, said that the legal problems arising from the exploration and use of outer space "must be settled on the basis of equality and justice, so that all mankind should share in the vast prospects opened up by the peaceful conquest of outer space, so that joint efforts

[8] *Op. cit.*, pp. 1070–1071.
[9] "State Sovereignty in Airspace" by A. Kislov and S. Krylov, translated in *op. cit.*, pp. 1037–1046, at p. 1045.
[10] Undated but apparently published in 1960.
[11] pp. 242–243.

should be made to explore the universe and so that scientific and technical achievements should be made to serve the practical needs of mankind". He pointed out that, according to General Assembly Resolution 1721A (XVI) which was adopted unanimously, international law, including the Charter of the United Nations, extended to outer space and celestial bodies, which were thus free for exploration and use by all States and were not subject to national appropriation.

G. P. Zadorozhny, Deputy Chairman of the Space Law Commission of the Academy of Sciences of the U.S.S.R., argues in *The Cosmos and International Law*[12] that outer space, like the high seas, will cease to be a theatre of military operations only when States establish appropriate norms of international law which provide for general and complete disarmament or at least for the simultaneous liquidation of all means of delivering nuclear weapons, including the liquidation of foreign military bases.

G. P. Zhukov, General Secretary of the Committee on Legal Problems of Interplanetary Space of the U.S.S.R. Academy of Sciences and Chairman of the Space Law Committee of the Soviet Association of International Law, lays emphasis upon the close relationship between international co-operation in the peaceful study and use of space and the prohibition of the military use of space.[13] He contends[14] that the United States space programme is military in character; that it includes provision for spy-satellites, space platforms for the launching of nuclear weapons, and manned rocket-power space craft; that attention is being given to the military use of communications, navigation and weather satellites with the basic purpose of providing a reliable means of communication with American military bases on foreign territory, a system of determining the whereabouts of air or naval units which will function with precision under any weather conditions, and accurate weather forecasting to facilitate the operations of the U.S. Strategic

[12] See also his articles translated in *Symposium*, pp. 1047–1049 and pp. 1072–1084.
[13] "The United Nations and the Peaceful Use of Outer Space", 1960, *Soviet Yearbook of International Law*, pp. 177–185, with summary in English at pp. 186–188; (a primarily descriptive account covering the period from 1957 to 1959).
[14] "American Plans for the Use of Outer Space with Aggressive Purposes and the Security of States", 1961, *Soviet Yearbook of International Law*, pp. 171–202, with summary in English at pp. 202–207.

Air Command; and that plans are being made for the military use of
the moon. He refers to the 1961 General Assembly Resolution, points
out that the principle that the Charter of the United Nations applies
to space implies that States must refrain from the threat or use of force
in outer space, and argues that "any espionage, including that carried
out with the aid of man-made Earth satellites, is, according to the
existing rules of international law, an impermissible violation of the
security of States". The conception that outer space must be used only
for peaceful purposes does not, however, "connote a ban on the use
of outer space for military purposes in accordance with Article 51 of
the Charter of the United Nations which provides for individual and
collective self-defense against an armed attack". In working out rules
of space law States will undoubtedly be guided by their own security
interests.

> "Neither the contemporary international practice of States in the explora-
> tion of outer space, nor the General Assembly Resolution of December 20,
> 1961, solve the question of the limits of outer space. The views expressed
> by authors on this score are scholarly in nature and not obligatory to the
> States. It is only by international agreement and the conclusion of a per-
> tinent treaty that a standard defining the altitudinal limit of State
> sovereignty, obligatory to all States, may be produced. In solving this
> question, considerations of a political, economic, scientific and military
> nature will unquestionably be taken into consideration. In the present
> circumstances vital security interests of States hinge upon the matter.
> People are rightly apprehensive that if the sovereignty of States is extended
> to a relatively small altitude, this will not adequately ensure the safety of
> States from outer space."

But "a State will not feel more secure simply because the military
preparations directed against it are conducted from a great height" and
the only possible solution for the problem is therefore not that "of
extending the sovereignty of each State for an unlimited distance from
Earth" but that "of concluding an international agreement on the
demilitarisation and neutralisation of outer space" as "an organic part
of general and complete disarmament". Addressing the American
Society of International Law in Washington on April 26, 1963,[15]

[15] *1963 Proceedings of the American Society of International Law*, pp. 193–195.

Zhukov said that "Soviet authors, and almost the overwhelming majority of other authors, take the view that certain limits (or qualifications) regarding methods of exploration and freedom of use of outer space should be set". There must be guarantees against the abuse of rights in space, notably in respect of space experiments liable to interfere with the peaceful use of space by other countries, "the use of telecommunication satellites for propagating war, national or racial hatred or enmity between nations", and the use of satellites for intelligence purposes. "There is not and there cannot be 'any right to spy' in outer space or elsewhere". In order to ensure that outer space is governed by the rule of law and to eliminate any chance of irresponsible actions by private persons all space activities should be carried out solely by States. The legal principles governing activities in space "should be embodied in an effective instrument with legally binding force".

The general theme of Kovalev and Cheprov in *The Way to Space Law* is that "the way to international space law is to effectuate the Soviet programme of general and complete disarmament". In an earlier article they argue[16] that the flight of the first Earth satellites did not and could not violate the sovereignty of the States above which their orbits lay since the sovereignty of States over their air space does not extend to the upper atmosphere and outer space and the space in which the orbits of the first sputniks lay was therefore outside the sphere of law regulation in what can be termed a "law vacuum". There had, moreover, been an implied consent of all countries to the launching of satellites, at any rate in respect of the programme of the International Geophysical Year. It is, however, premature to regard the launching of the first satellites as having created any customary rule limiting the right of States to claim an extension of the space limits of their sovereignty above the surface of the Earth. The altitude up to which sovereignty may extend cannot be determined on the basis of the data at the disposal of geophysics. States will determine the altitude limit of their sovereign rights on the basis

[16] "Artificial Satellites and International Law", *Soviet Yearbook of International Law*, 1958, pp. 128–145 with summary in English at pp. 145–149.

of the need to guarantee their security and not on "whether there are traces of the atmosphere at a given altitude and what is the precise density of the gas cloud at one or another distance from the Earth". But it does not follow that a State can, by reason of considerations of national security, extend its sovereign rights to infinity:

"The answer, obviously, can only be in the negative. The supposition of extending to infinity the sovereignty of the State in the space above its territory runs counter to common sense.

"Firstly, no matter what vigilance the State displays in regard to its security there is obviously bound to be in outer space a point sufficiently remote from the Earth completely to exclude the possibility of any harm emanating from it to any particular State.

"Secondly, as a consequence of the daily and annual motion of our planet, the imaginary cone formed by drawing a straight line from the centre of the Earth at a tangent to the border of the given State would envelop different areas of space at different times. Recognition of the claim of the States to the entire outer space, contained within this cone would signify that the Sun, the Moon, and the 'Milky Way' would be regarded as being within range of sovereignty of one country today and of another tomorrow. Moreover, the spaceship launched from the territory of any country into outer space, even in a strictly vertical direction to the surface of the Earth, would be bound to appear quite soon above the territory of another State. These considerations testify that unlimited extension of the range of sovereign rights in outer space would cause confusion and raise such knotty questions that the law would be deprived of any sense.

"It seems the State manifesting the necessary concern for its security should, nevertheless, be guided by some kind of restricted criteria in defining the upper limit of its sovereignty. One of these criteria in all probability would be the ability of the State effectively to control events in the zone of its sovereignty. It would be unthinkable for a State to proclaim sovereign rights to a height so inaccessible that it could not ensure observance of the corresponding law.

"However, the mere application of the criterion of extending State sovereignty would be much more likely to create obstacles to man's further mastery of the cosmos. In defining their attitude as to the limits of their sovereignty, the states should also take care to ensure favourable conditions, including legal possibilities, for scientific exploration. For any State to advance unfounded 'exorbitant' claims to extension of its sovereignty would endanger such exploration."

The maritime analogy suggested by some writers to define the legal status of space does not take into account the physical differences between the two elements, but some of "the rules and theses" of the law of the sea and the law of air space may be applicable. Access to outer space should be open to all countries. In all likelihood, States will "maintain full jurisdiction in relation to their flying apparatuses when they cross the borderline of space", though it "is not excluded that, sometime in the distant future, rules of space navigation and other measures will be worked out to ensure safety of flights". It is premature to attempt to define the status of planets or other celestial bodies, but the principles of "first discovery" and "occupation", characterised in a different way than on Earth may have some application.

G. A. Osnitzkaya[17] takes the view that "it is not at present possible to draw up an integrated system of clearly formulated rules of space law", but that "principles should be formulated which should constitute points of departure".

Osnitzkaya considers that the IGY programme is not a sufficient justification for saying that outer space is free according to the practice of States and that neither the existence of an atmosphere sufficiently dense to sustain the flight of conventional aircraft nor gravitational attraction affords a satisfactory criterion of demarcation.

"Together with other Soviet scholars who have already published articles and other works dealing with this problem, the author of the present article considers that State sovereignty does not extend into cosmic space. In drawing this conclusion, he proceeds not only from the scientific data given to us by astronomers and other scientists, but also from the fact that it corresponds to the policy of peaceful co-existence and co-operation between States. We have already referred to the valuable information regarding the Universe which can be obtained with the aid of sputniks, rockets and other objects launched into the upper layers of the atmosphere and into cosmic space. This information enriches the whole of mankind. A wholly unjustified declaration of sovereignty at such heights would be a brake on this sort of research and would lead to constant disputes between States. With regard to the upper limit of sovereignty, the author primarily

17 "International Law Problems of the Conquest of Space", 1959, *Soviet Yearbook of International Law*, pp. 51–65 with summary in English at pp. 65–71.

believes it necessary to establish a principle which should be the starting point for a discussion of this question, a principle which of course must be based on international law. This principle, or in other words criteria, should, in his opinion, be State security, as was from the outset correctly emphasised by the Soviet lawyers Kovalyev and Cheprov. To take measures to safeguard its security and to protect itself against infringement by other States of its territorial supremacy and independence is a States' sovereign right. Any attempt to draw up a rule which would not ensure the exercising of that right cannot be recognised as being in accordance with the law. In the opinion of the author, all proposals whose adoption would restrict the sovereign rights of a State to safeguard its own security must be rejected. On the basis of this point of view, the author considers that the theory in accordance with which the limit of sovereignty depends upon the ceiling which can be reached by modern aircraft to be completely untenable."

Certain postulates must be borne in mind in settling the question of the legal status of cosmic space:

"It is quite obvious that as on land, on sea and in the air, States must be guided in their activities in cosmic space by the basic international legal principles of peaceful co-existence, which are basic principles of international law. Hence, the activities of States in this field must also be carried out with complete respect for the sovereignty of States, in particular, for their sovereignty over air space as defined by national legislation. The activity of States in space must, therefore, not be utilised for an attack upon other States or in such a way that it creates the threat of such an attack, or in any other way incompatible with the purposes of the United Nations. In the event of the improper use of cosmic space any State has the right to take the measures permitted by modern international law including, in the event of armed attack through space, measures of individual or collective self-defence as provided for in Article 51 of the UN Charter.

"Co-operation between States in the utilisation of space must be based on the principle of the equality of States and their mutual advantage, in accordance with the principles of peaceful co-existence. The Soviet Government rightly rejected the proposal of the United States, which was to consider the question of the prohibition of the use of outer space for military purposes in isolation from the question of the winding up of military bases, since the adoption of the American proposal would have given the NATO countries the advantage of using the bases which they have built on foreign territory against the Soviet Union, while safeguarding them in the event of atomic war against retaliatory atomic attack through space. This would be unequal co-operation, co-operation which would give advantages to one party and run counter to the interests of the other."

An international agreement on the utilisation of outer space may be desirable but should not provide for a supra-state body:

"By their very nature, international law problems arising in the relations between States cannot be settled by any organ standing above them. As is correctly emphasised by G. I. Tunkin, 'States as subjects of international law act in international relations as independent formations, to which no authority is competent to dictate rules of law; international law knows no legislative body laying down rules of international law'.

"This does not mean that the author is opposed to the setting up of an international body which would control or to some extent regulate the activities of States in space. It will be recalled that the Soviet Government in its proposals regarding the prohibition of the utilisation of outer space for military purposes, for winding up foreign military bases and for international co-operation in the study of outer space submitted to the United Nations on March 15, 1958, envisaged the establishment of appropriate international control within the framework of the United Nations. These proposals also envisage the setting up of a United Nations agency for international co-operation in the study of outer space with such functions as the drawing up of an agreed international programme for the launching of inter-continental and space rockets to study outer space and to check the implementation of this programme, the co-ordination of national research programmes in this field, the promotion of the exchange and dissemination of information regarding cosmic research, etc.

"In the opinion of the author, the establishment of the agency proposed by the Soviet Government would provide a good basis for co-operation between States, insofar as such co-operation would be implemented with complete respect for the rights and interests of all.

"The main thing is to achieve agreement on the prohibition of the utilisation of outer space for military purposes on a basis which would ensure the security of all states equally."

Osnitzkaya considers that space objects belong to and must bear the distinguishing mark of the State launching them; that people on board are subject to the legislation and jurisdiction of the State whose marks the vehicle bears; that space vehicles falling in the territory of another State should be returned to the State to which they belong, and that the owner State is liable for damage.

Without considering in detail the possibility of celestial bodies being susceptible of occupation she argues that:

"in order to avoid any possibility of rivalry between States which would be fraught with the threat of a new war, it should be possible to establish that a landing on the Moon, or in future on any other planet, gives no basis for territorial claims. Finally, it is considered to be indisputable that, in accordance with the general rule prohibiting war, planetary bodies must not be utilised for military operations. Provision must be made for freedom of scientific research."

In general, Soviet writers, while discussing critically much of the Western literature on the subject, endorse certain of its conclusions, in particular the tendency to regard space as beyond the reach of sovereignty.

Polish and Czech writers give strong support to this tendency.

Léon Babínski,[18] for instance, elaborates the view that the general principles of international law are applicable to astronautic law. Astronautic law and international law do not coincide and the first is not a subdivision of the second, but, like the various branches of the law of transport, it always includes an international element. The sovereignty of the subjacent State must be rejected in astronautic law, which must be universalist in approach and start from the principle that the general principles of law recognised by civilised nations are applicable among States in respect of cosmic space. The accent must be on the solution of practical problems. It is unnecessary to introduce into astronautic law the innumerable doctrinal controversies of the theory of international law. The objective should be to thread one's way among the difficulties presented by the theory of international law with a view to preparing the ground for the practical solution of concrete problems.

[18] "Quelques réflexions sur les rapports entre le droit des gens et le droit astronautique", *Revue générale de l'Air*, XXIV Année (Nouvelle Série) No. 1961, pp. 59–74; Babínski has also written on the subject in Polish, "Nowy dzial prawa – prawa astronautyezne", *Revue Szczecin*, 1958, livr. 9, pp. 113–122.

Manfred Lachs, in an article on *The Cosmos and Co-existence*[19] regards the 1961 General Assembly resolution as formulating norms which are already valid for all States and call for further development. Among the questions calling for early consideration are the prohibition of space experiments liable to be prejudicial to scientific research or the use of space by other States, assistance to astronauts in distress, the return of space vehicles and liability for damage. The exclusive dedication of space to peaceful purposes is the primary task confronting us and presupposes general and complete disarmament. A course of lectures on *Space Law* by Lachs was delivered by Lachs at the Hague Academy of International Law in 1964.

Jacek Machowski has made a special study of the legal status of un-manned space vehicles[20] in which he reaches the conclusions that "the unmanned space vehicle remains the property of the launching State and should be returned to it after its fall to Earth" and that "the acceptance of liability for injuries or damages caused by an unmanned space vehicle is the logical consequence of adoption of the right of its ownership by the launching State". In this suggested link between the right of recovery and the acceptance of responsibility we may have an idea of substantial importance for the future development of the law.

Jaroslave Zourek,[21] criticising an earlier article by another Czech writer, Michael Milde,[22] rejects the view that sovereignty over space extends *usque ad infinitum*. Roman law is of no help in the matter as the glossators could not visualise the kind of space with which we are concerned and neither the practice of States as evidenced by their legislation nor the treaties governing civil aviation have any bearing on space in general as distinguished from airspace. Sovereignty over the cosmos is inconceivable. "According to the modern conception of the cosmos, based on the relativity theory, it is not at all possible to

[19] "Le Cosmos et la Coexistence", *Perspectives Polonaises*, 6ème année, 1963, pp. 3–9.
[20] Translated in *Symposium*, pp. 1204–1212. Other interesting Polish studies include Marek Zylicz, "Some Problems of Astronautical Law", translated in *op. cit.*, pp. 1157–1163, and Jerzy Sztucki, "Security of Nations and Cosmic Space", translated in *op. cit.*, pp. 1164–1203.
[21] "What is the Legal Status of the Universe?", translated in *Symposium*, pp. 1109–1117.
[22] "Considerations in Legal Problems of Space above National Territory", translated in *ibid.*, pp. 1102–1108.

describe outer space optically. It follows logically that it is also impossible to demarcate any boundaries of imaginary sovereignty there. Outer space is an amorphous " 'continuum', *i.e.*, something which exists and continues without any firm structure whatever, and is subject to constant changes and modifications. - All galaxies are moving away from the solar system and also one from another, so that the possibility of demarcating any boundaries of State sovereignty in this cosmic chaos is completely out of the question." There is the further difficulty that "the possibility of exercising State authority in outer space does not exist". A claim to "consider the infinite cosmos as an accessory of the Earth" would be "almost like the medieval opinion of the Church according to which the Earth was the centre of the universe and all other stars revolved around it". The practical result of the thesis that sovereignty extends to infinity would be that a State carrying out space research "would have to ask all States for authorisation to launch space rockets, as long as these flights were carried out beyond the scope of the IGY Agreement, since the flights of rockets and satellites would then violate according to the above opinion the sovereignty of all States on the globe". Where the altitudinal limits of sovereignty in space are "is a technical problem which can be solved only by States as international law-makers" and has not yet been solved. Outer space is therefore free and jurists can only propose regulations *de lege ferenda*, but international law regulates relations among States irrespective of where they are carried out. The basic principles of international law therefore govern the intercourse of States in outer space. These principles include the prohibition of the use of force or threats of force against territorial integrity and the right of self defence. Nor is there any doubt "about the existence of international responsibility for damage sustained by a State or its citizens in connection with the utilisation of outer space, if for example an artificial satellite, launched for scientific purposes, was destroyed by another State, or if after an unsuccessful launching the artificial satellite or its rocket fell on the territory of a foreign State or on the high seas and caused damage".

One Hungarian study, by Gyula Gál, is available in English.[23] The

[23] "Air Space and Outer Space", translated in *op. cit.*, pp. 1141–1156.

conclusions submitted in it are that "an infinite airspace is a conceptual impossibility", that "the facts of astronautics cannot be squeezed into the conventional framework of international air law", and that "the synthesis of territorial airspace and free outer space can only be assured by an international agreement which can break away from the conventional forms and encompass the activity element of rockets, artificial satellites and planets launched by the States". The "most important task *de lege ferenda* is the explicit prohibition of military employment of space rockets, artificial satellites and planets". Though Soviet emblems "are on the surface of the moon" and "it is the task of international jurisprudence to examine whether this and similar things in the future do mean occupation or not" any "outer space imperialism" which "would start with the occupation of the Moon and would continue in a race for Venus and Mars" must be avoided. An agreement on "the prohibition of the military use of outer space" would make possible "the regulation by treaty of the particular problems in international space law".

This brief and necessarily incomplete analysis of the views of Soviet and other Eastern European writers suggests two general conclusions. Firstly, their views, while having common features, reveal a considerable margin of divergences of view concerning questions of presentation, timing and detail. Secondly, these divergences are in many cases similar to divergences which exist among writers elsewhere. There is no ideological cleavage in respect of the fundamentals of space law, as distinguished from the manner in which these fundamentals are sometimes expressed and the political conditions under which suggested solutions or arrangments are regarded as appropriate or feasible. This will become more apparent as we proceed to examine the work of writers from other parts of the world.

We may begin with the Yugoslav writers who are in a somewhat different position from that of other East European writers.

M. S. Smirnoff is the leading Yugoslav writer. He summarised his views in a proposed convention which he submitted to the International Astronautical Federation in 1959.[24] His draft provides that the use of

[24] *Second Colloquium on the Law of Outer Space*, London, 1959, *Proceedings*, pp. 147–155.

outer space is free for peaceful purposes only; that outer space begins
where propeller and jet planes are no longer able to fly; that a new
international organisation to deal with space matters shall be created as
a specialised agency of the United Nations, shall be informed in advance
of flight particulars, and shall issue all necessary regulations; that there
is no "right of occupation and discovery" in space which is regarded
as *res communis*; that the registration of a spacecraft in a national register
is the basis of responsibility for all damage done thereby; that disputes
shall be referred to the International Court; that space flight shall be
covered by the space convention from the time of launching and the
legal regimes for outer space and airspace ultimately co-ordinated and
that the international organisation shall take precautions against space
contamination.[25]

[25] A bibliography of Smirnoff's articles is available in *Legal Problems of Space Exploration –
A Symposium*, United States Senate, 87th Congress, 1st Session, Document No. 26,
p. 1378, which also contains at p. 1213 another interesting Yugoslav article, "The
Legal Problems of Outer Space", by Duàn J. Milanković who describes outer space
as "a *res communis* open to everyone but with no right of appropriation by anyone".

14

British and Commonwealth Writers

THERE has been a relative dearth of major contributions to the literature of space law by British, Canadian and Australian writers.

McNair's cogent criticism of the *cujus est solum* maxim[1] remains the starting point of English thought on the subject.

The present writer, expanding in 1958 his article on "International Law and Activities in Space" originally written in August 1955,[2] restated an initial programme for the legal regulation of space activities including (a) such immediate practical matters as the registration of launchings,[3] space telecommunications,[4] liability for damage,[5] and the right of property in satellites returning to Earth,[6] (b) a holding action to avoid prejudicing the future "legal status of unoccupied territory in the moon or other planets and satellites, and of any natural resources of such territory which it may become possible to exploit",[7] and "allow appropriate international arrangements to be evolved over a period of time as further scientific and technological progress clarifies the elements in the problem and the possible means of dealing with them",[8] and (c) a "space for peace" pool to provide opportunities for co-operative ventures in space.[9]

In a further study on "The Laws of Nature and International Law", originally written in August 1958[10] and republished in 1963,[11] the present writer discussed, in the context of a wider discussion of the

---

[1] *The Law of the Air*, 1932, p. 17; see pp. 103–105, above.
[2] *The Common Law of Mankind*, 1958, pp. 382–407.   [3] p. 404.
[4] p. 403.   [5] pp. 403–404.
[6] p. 404.   [7] pp. 396–398.
[8] p. 415.   [9] p. 406.
[10] For publication in *Liber Amicorum J. P. A. François*, 1959, pp. 160–172.
[11] *Law, Freedom and Welfare*, 1963, pp. 33–49.

legal aspects of scientific and technological experiment and innovation liable to cause changes in natural environment, the position in regard to space experiments, and suggested a series of seven guiding principles which should be followed in the matter.[12] The first and basic principle was that scientific and technological experiments, tests or development schemes which may have a substantial influence on the natural environment of another State are a matter of international concern. The second principle was that any State proposing to sponsor or permit an experiment, test or development scheme which may prejudice the natural environment of another State should notify in advance the nature and anticipated or possible consequences of the proposed experiment, test or development scheme. The third principle was that any State the natural environment of which may be prejudiced by a proposed experiment, test or development scheme which has been notified should have a recognised right to seek fuller information and, if necessary in the light of the information supplied, to make representations concerning the possible consequences of the proposed experiment, test or development scheme. The fourth principle was that, where the explanations of the State responsible for the proposed experiment, test or development scheme and any representations made by the other State or States concerned do not result in settlement of the matter by negotiation or agreement, it should be open to any State concerned and to appropriate international organisations to call for an impartial international enquiry. The fifth principle was that if an impartial enquiry is requested the proposed experiment or test should not take place or, in the case of a development scheme, the scheme should remain in abeyance, until the State responsible has considered fully th e outcome of the enquiry which should be completed within a reasonable period. The sixth principle was that an appropriate international authority should be entitled to restrain by an injunction procedure, either absolutely or by requiring compliance with certain conditions, experiments, tests or development schemes calculated to modify the natural environment of another State. The seventh principle was that, within limits to be determined, responsibility for loss or damage arising from

[12] pp. 39–43.

changes in the natural environment of a State resulting from experiments or tests made by another State rests with the State making, sponsoring or permitting such experiments or tests, the liability being absolute if the experiment or test has been undertaken without compliance with the notification and impartial enquiry arrangements. These principles, it was suggested, while not yet having the status of established law, are much more than a programme of desirable objectives; "they are an attempt to deduce some of the implications for international law, in the world created by nuclear physics, organic chemistry, and twentieth century technology and engineering, of such fundamental principles of law as *alterum non laedere, nemo judex in re sua, audi alteram partem*, the maintenance *litis pendente* of the existing right of the parties, *ubi injuria ibi jus*, and absolute liability for dangerous activities".[13]

The most important recent British contribution consists of a Draft Code of Rules on the Exploration and Uses of Outer Space and Draft Rules concerning changes in the Environment of the Earth, both prepared by a Study Group of the David Davies Memorial Institute of International Studies with Professor R. Y. Jennings as Chairman and Mr. J. E. S. Fawcett as Reporter. Both the Draft Code and the Draft Rules are accompanied by explanatory commentaries.[14] The Draft Code[15] defines the terms "aircraft", "spacecraft", "airspace", "outer space", "State and international body". "Spacecraft" is defined as meaning "any craft capable of orbital movement or manoeuvre in outer space" and as including "any craft which is being operated as a space station". "Airspace" is defined as meaning "the volume of space between the surface of the air at sea level and an altitude of 80,000 metres above it" and "outer space" as meaning "space outside the airspace" as thus defined. The Draft Code provides that "outer space, and the celestial bodies therein, are recognised as being *res communis omnium*, free for exploration and use by all States in conformity with

[13] pp. 39–40.
[14] See David Davies Memorial Institute of International Studies, *Draft Code of Rules on the Exploration and Uses of Outer Space*, 1963, and *Draft Rules concerning Changes in the Environment of the Earth*, 1964.
[15] The text is reproduced in Appendix X below, pp. 419–430.

the provisions thereof, and that "neither outer space nor the celestial bodies in it are capable of appropriate or exclusive use by any State". It specifies that "all States shall for themselves and for their nationals have equal rights in the exploration and use of outer space, including free navigation by means of spacecraft, the establishment of space stations and other like devices, astronomical and physical observations by optical radio and other methods, and the landing on and exploration and use of celestial bodies". It declares that in the exploration and use of outer space and celestial bodies States and international bodies (a) are bound by international law and by the provisions of the United Nations Charter and other international agreements which may be applicable; (b) should arrange for the greatest practicable interchange of scientific information and personnel; and (c) are not precluded from employing military personnel or equipment for scientific and peaceful purposes. There is a general and somewhat rigid provision concerning changes in natural environment which should perhaps now be regarded as superseded by the Draft Rules concerning Changes in the Environment of the Earth. The Code provides that no spacecraft carrying any type of warhead or otherwise designed as a weapon for use against targets on the Earth or in the airspace, shall be placed in orbit around the Earth or be carried in or launched from any space station or celestial body. A group of provisions relating to celestial bodies specify that "any State or international body may establish stations, manned or unmanned, upon a celestial body for its exploration or use", prohibit the "establishment of military stations upon any celestial body and the use of such stations or of a celestial body for the purpose of war" and the "testing of any nuclear device or the disposal of radioactive waste upon any celestial body", and envisage that "stations on celestial bodies should as soon as practicable be placed under the supervision of the United Nations". There are also provisions concerning radio transmission, the avoidance of contamination and waste, flight through airspace by spacecraft, the registration of spacecraft, liability for injury or loss, the recovery of spacecraft and repatriation of astronauts, the settlement of disputes. The Draft Rules concerning Changes in the Environment of the Earth relate to "changes in the space around the

Earth, by means of the introduction of novel elements or the disturbance of the physical equilibrium or processes which cause reactions upon, or in the vicinity of, the Earth" resulting from "the use of any instrument, device or technique, on the surface of the Earth, in the airspace, or in outer space". The Rules[16] provide that "no State or international body shall engage in, or within the limits of its authority permit, operations which can cause changes in the environment of the Earth" if "the range and scale of these changes cannot be predicted with reasonable precision" or if "the changes may be reasonably expected to have a deleterious effect upon the life, health or growth, of human beings or of animals or plants, to modify the climate or weather of any region of the Earth, or to prevent, or seriously hinder, scientific observation, experiment or research". Where any such operation is planned "the responsible State authorities shall consult an international group of scientists of known competence who shall express a reasoned opinion as to the changes in the environment of the Earth which the operation is likely to cause". If, in the opinion of the group, the range and scale of the changes which can be caused can be predicted with reasonable precision, the changes are confined to changes which may be reasonably expected to prevent, or seriously hinder, scientific observations, experiment or research, the group is to "recommend how the operation may be conducted so as to produce valuable scientific results without interfering with known air or space operations or known scientific researches". If, in the opinion of the group, the range or scale of the changes which can be caused cannot be predicted with reasonable precision, or such changes may reasonably be expected to have a deleterious effect upon the life, health or growth or human beings or of animals or plants, or to modify the climate or weather of any region of the Earth, then it should be open to any Member of the United Nations to refer the matter to the General Assembly. Any operation which can cause changes in the environment of the Earth which is carried out without consultation of an international group of scientists, or after such a group has been unable to predict the range and scale of such changes with reasonable precision, or in disregard of any recommenda-

[16] The text is reproduced in Appendix X below, pp. 430–439.

tion of the General Assembly determining that a deleterious effect upon the life, health or growth of human beings is reasonably to be expected from such an operation, should involve absolute liability to make good or compensate all loss or injury resulting therefrom.

J. F. McMahon has published a study of *Legal Aspects of Outer Space*[17] which is particularly useful as a record of the gradual development of State practice during the six years following the launching of the first sputnik. He discusses at some length the question of reconnaissance satellites and takes the general position that the use of such satellites is not illegal and that "although it may be permissible to destroy an aircraft engaged in espionage in a State's sovereign airspace, it is doubtful whether it would be permissible wholly to destroy a satellite engaged in making observations outside a State's sovereign airspace".[18]

Law and Politics in Space[19] is a symposium edited by Maxwell Cohen which contains valuable papers concerning international arrangements for satellite communications, pollution and contamination in space, space technology and arms control, observation in space, and the prospects for a régime in outer space.

[17] 1962 *British Year Book of International Law*, pp. 339–399.
[18] *Ibid.*, p. 379.
[19] 1964.

15

West European Writers

THE West European literature, like that of the United States, is so extensive and is growing so rapidly that only a highly selective treatment of it is possible.

Charles Chaumont, *Le droit de l'espace*,[1] is particularly valuable as an attempt to discuss basic principles. He starts from the position that activities in space necessarily pose legal problems and discusses in turn the principle of the freedom of space, the legal status (including, in particular, the nationality) of space instrumentalities, the legal consequences of activities in space (including the basis and extent of national responsibility and matters needing international regulation), and the legal status of celestial bodies. His basic thesis is that space should be envisaged not as a place but as a complex of activities. On this basis no question of the limits of sovereignty or the demarcation of zones of jurisdiction arises. Space is at the service of man but does not necessarily belong to him. All that is needful initially is that space should be regarded as dedicated to the general interest; *l'affectation de l'espace a l'intérêt général est donc la contrepartie indispensable de l'abandon, par les Etats sous-jacents de toute souveraineté sur l'espace.* On this basis the international regulations required for the protection of the general interest can be progressively developed, but it is premature to regard the United Nations as having jurisdiction over space or the General Assembly as having any legislative authority over activities there. Ultimately certain activities in space may be conducted by an international public service, but meanwhile the objective should be to combine the renunciation of any territorial claims with a strong re-

[1] *Presses Universitaires de France*, 1960.

affirmation of the independence of States in space. Space instrumentalities must have a nationality (internationalisation being impracticable), such nationality being expressed by registration and an appropriate indentification document. The legal consequences of activities in space are governed by the national law of the space instrumentality except where they occur within the territorial jurisdiction of another State. There is as yet no legal obligation to make known the outcome of space exploration, but the exchange of information on the subject is regarded as good practice. There is no clear rule defining the extent of responsibility for injury or damage to foreign nationals or goods resulting from State activities. There is a prima facie case for letting the loss lie where it falls as a counterpart for the services rendered by space pioneers; there is no State responsibility under customary international law because there is no violation of a rule of international law; nor can the concept of fault be readily applied. On the other hand responsibility may be regarded as an incident of the concept of activities in space as an international public service; while the matter remains unsettled responsibility may be accepted on grounds of moral obligation or with a view to maintaining good relations among States. The celestial bodies cannot be regarded as subject to territorial appropriation by States on the ground that the function which States may be called upon to discharge there are not the functions of territorial sovereignty. States may use, but not appropriate, the celestial bodies. A United Nations sovereignty over celestial bodies is no more conceivable than any national sovereignty, but the exploitation of their resources on the basis of concessions, leases or licences from the United Nations may be a matter for consideration. There is no scope for the application of the trusteeship system in space, but arrangements such as those provided for in the Antarctic Treaty may be appropriate.

Rolando Quadri gave an important course of lectures at the Académie de Droit international in 1959 on *Droit international cosmique.*[2] He expresses a preference for the term "cosmic international law", rather

[2] *Recueil des Cours de l'Académie de Droit International*, tome 98, (1959 III), pp. 505–598; see also "Prolegomeni al Diritto Internazionale Cosmico" in *Diritto Internazionale – Revista Trimestrale di Dottrina e Documentazione*, Vol. XIII, No. 3, 1959, pp. 260–311.

than "space law", "astronautical law", "interplanetary law", "interstellar law" or "metalaw" on the ground that these other expressions, while sometimes used to describe fancies lacking in reality, involve an over-conservative limitation of the general concept which should include everything which is not earthbound. Quadri does not regard the laws of physical nature, the provisions of the international conventions relating to air navigation, or a tacit consent to be deduced from the conduct of States during the International Geophysical Year, as sources of cosmic international law, and perhaps overstresses the extent to which writers whom he criticises (including the present writer) rely on any one of these elements as distinguished from their cumulative effect when combined with other considerations. Sovereignty is governmental authority and cannot therefore extend into space in a territorial sense in any exclusive manner. Neither the law of the sea nor aviation law affords really helpful analogies, the most relevant part of air law being the law of telecommunications. Freedom of access to space is an indispensable condition of any utilisation of space. The problem is not one of determining whether space, or parts thereof, or bodies therein, are *res dominio*, *res nullius*, or *res communes omnium*, but one of determining what activities in space are legal. The concept of space as *res communes omnium*, based on the maritime analogy, would involve both an obligation upon each State to respect in peacetime the freedom of action in space of other States, and the applicability in space of the maritime law of war and neutrality. As the air navigation conventions are inapplicable and no tacit consent can be deduced from the conduct of States during the International Geophysical Year, States enjoy freedom in space except in so far as their freedom is limited by their international obligations. The destruction or contamination of cosmic resources is not a violation of cosmic international law as there exist no legal rights of which such destruction or contamination is a violation. The obligation to refrain from the threat or use of force embodied in the Charter of the United Nations extends to space, but so does the inherent right of self-defence preserved by Article 51. Military activity in space is therefore not illegal, disarmament in space being an aspect of, and governed by the same considerations as, disarmament in general. There is an obligation on space pioneers to avoid interference with aerial navigation, but no corresponding obligation on the subjacent State. Proposals for international inspection prior to launching, prior notification of cosmic voyages, and other measures of internationalisation can unhappily hardly be regarded as realistic. It is premature to envisage space instrumentalities having a nationality; while functioning they are an expression of the cosmic activity of the launching State and the question which may arise in relation to other States is not one of property but of how far such other States may interfere with their functioning; if a space instrumentality falls on the territory of another State it does not become a *res derelictae* but remains the property of the launching State. The concept of absolute responsibility in respect of damage caused by space instrumentalities goes too far and proposals for an international guarantee fund to cover the risk cannot be regarded as promising, but the practical importance of the matter is liable to be exaggerated. There is likewise no urgency about the question of sovereignty over celestial bodies; unless the functions of government can be exercised over such bodies no question of sovereignty can arise, and in the event of settlement on such bodies requiring the continuous exercise of the functions of government the recognition of sovereignty based on, and within the limits of, the effective exercise of governmental functions would be appropriate. Similarly, the legal status of cosmic resources must depend on the extent to which any State succeeds in controlling them, the concept of United Nations concessions, leases or licences being a pure abstraction. States are legally free to use celestial bodies for military purposes and to establish military bases there.

A number of other West European international lawyers, without discussing the questions involved in the same detail as Chaumont and Quadri, have made important contributions to focusing for consideration the questions of principle which arise. Among these Erik Brüel, Erik Castrén, and José de Yanguas Messia.

Erik Brüel[3] points out that whereas the law of the sea evolved from

[3] "Rumrets problemer", *Nordisk Tidsskrift for International Ret*, Vol. 28, 1958, Fasc. 3–4, pp. 321–330. I am indebted to Professor Brüel for an English summary of his article.

the principle of *res nullius* to that of *commune bonum* the law of the air abandoned the principle of "*l'air est libre*" for that of air sovereignty. Space confronts mankind for the third time with the problem of the legal order applicable to a new medium. The argument for an extensive air sovereignty zone is hardly realistic; only the neutralisation of space can furnish any effective defence. By the laws of God and nature space is *res communes omnium*. The law of the sea and the law of the air developed at times when there was no world organisation to take the lead in formulating and defining them; in this respect we are now more fortunate and the United Nations has taken the lead in declaring space *commune bonum* for all mankind.

Erik Castrén[4] recalls the controversy in the early days of air law between the doctrine of sovereignty and the doctrine of the freedom of the air and notes that while the doctrine of sovereignty prevailed there has been an increasing disposition to question how far it represents a final answer to the question. He envisages demarcating the sovereignty zone from outer space but criticises Cooper's suggestion of a sovereignty zone of thirty miles and a contiguous zone extending up to 300 miles as fixing the lower limit of free space at an excessive height. He suggests that the lower limit of free space should not exceed 200 kilometres and would be better fixed at 50 kilometres on the double ground that the military dangers of permitting the passage of satellites above such a height are outweighed by the prospective advantages to science and that no State can effectively control the activities of another State above such a height; the launching State should however be responsible for any damage and provision should be made by international convention for the prohibition of satellites for military purposes.

José de Yanguas Messia, in an address before the Spanish Real Academia de Ciencias Morales y Politícas[5] compared the attempt to demarcate airspace from outer space to the Bull *Intercoetera* of Pope Alexander VI and suggested that the negotiation of conventions regulating particular activities in space represents a more fruitful approach.

[4] "Situation Juridique de l'Espace Atmosphérique en Droit International", *Hommage d'une Génération de Juristes au Président Basdevant*, 1960, pp. 75–95.
[5] *Aspectos jurídicas y politícas de la utilización del espacio ultraterrestre*, Madrid, 1959.

He regarded such co-operation as particularly important to avoid mutual interference with each other by astronautics and aviation, in respect of telecommunications and for meteorological purposes. He considered that cosmic or extra-terrestrial space is not and cannot be subject to the sovereignty of subjacent States as such space does not, like the atmosphere, accompany the earth in its rotation. He endorsed the view that the celestial bodies are not subject to appropriation or sovereignty and that their exploration and exploitation must be on behalf of the whole of humanity.

R. H. Mankiewicz[6] has made a plea for an international space organisation which, in addition to regulating the use and providing for the inspection of space instrumentalities, would provide certain common facilities, such as extra-terrestrial bases, analogous to the joint support arrangements made through ICAO for financing air navigation services in Greenland and Iceland and the North Atlantic Weather Ships. While rejecting the suggestion that the Chicago Convention and its annexes have any direct application to space instrumentalities, he finds them suggestive concerning matters which should be covered by appropriate space regulations.

[6] "De l'ordre juridique dans l'espace extra-aéronautique", 5 *Annuaire Français de Droit International*, 1959, pp. 103–160.

16

Asian Writers

CERTAIN Japanese studies of space law are available in English in the *Japanese Annual of International Law*.

Professor Yuiohi Takano[1] makes proposals for the free use of outer space, a right of innocent passage for ascending or descending space vehicles, advance notification to and registration with a special international organisation of launchings and flights. This organisation would have certain powers of enquiry and recommendation. Takano envisages that "celestial bodies may be explored and exploited by any State or international organisation in accordance with the principles on the exploration and exploitation thereof to be formulated by the United Nations for the welfare of mankind" and that any State or international organisation which explores and exploits celestial bodies should report to the United Nations on the results of the exploration and exploitation. The United Nations could then make appropriate recommendations to the State or international organisation concerned.

Professor Fumio Ikedo[2] discusses the legal status of planets. He considers that "planets could be occupied and appropriated under existing international law if in the future a State should exercise authority on planets with the intention of acquiring sovereignty rights over them". He does not exclude the possibility of discovery giving rise to a claim to an inchoate title to the Moon, but notes that as the U.S.S.R. has made no such claim on the basis of the Sputniks "we can fairly conclude that nothing has so far been altered in the status of the moon". He considers however that "the rules of occupation in present international

[1] "Legal Status of Outer Space", *The Japanese Annual of International Law*, No. 4, 1960 pp. 42–49.
[2] "The Legal Status of Planets", *ibid*, No. 5, 1961, pp. 25–30.

law are in themselves nothing but historical rules corresponding to the politics and economic demands of the European nations for the acquisition of colonies in the then newly discovered areas of the world and concludes with the plea that "to secure the rule of law in outer space, including celestial bodies, internationalisation of outer space is required".

Among Indian writers, Mr. P. K. Kartha[3] concludes that "while agreement between the United States and the Soviet Union is indispensable, it must be recognised that penetration into outer space is the concern of the international community"; in searching for agreement on the rule of law in outer space we must take account of the present stage of international development; "institutions should be developed, brick by brick, in order to construct eventually a regime of law and order in outer space."

[3] "Some Legal Problems concerning Outer Space," (1963) 3 *Indian Journal of International Law*, 1–43.

17

Latin American Writers

AMONG Latin American writers Haroldo Valladão has been a pioneer. In *Direito Interplanetario e Direito Inter-Gentes Planetarias*,[1] published in 1957, he describes interplanetary law as a new branch of law, analogous to maritime law, air law or atomic law. Like these other branches of the law its scope includes both national and international rules but it also includes interplanetary rules. Interplanetary law is no more concerned with the legal relations among the planets than these other branches of law are concerned with the legal relations among the seas, among air spaces or among atoms; its subject matter is the legal problems presented by the use of interplanetary space. As intelligent life is discovered elsewhere its scope will extend until it becomes a *Jus inter Gentes Planetarum*, but for the immediate future our concern is with interplanetary law which we may distinguish, moreover, from the galactic and extragalactic law which may develop later. This new law is inspired by a universal spirit free from the corrosive acid of national sovereignty. In virtue of it interplanetary space is a *res communis omnium universi* not subject to appropriation and neither planets nor satellites are subject to the acquisition of title on the basis of the outworn law of discovery and conquest.

In *O Direito do Espaço Interplanetario*, 1959,[2] Valladão, restating and expanding his earlier views, pleads for the autonomy of the study of interplanetary law in relation to the study of air law. Interplanetary

---

[1] Separata da *Revista Juridica, da Facultate Nacional de Directo da Universidade do Bresil*, Vol. 15, 1957, pp. 1–32 subsequently published in French in *Festschrift für Walter Schätzel*, pp. 473–494.
[2] Rio de Janeiro 1959; subsequently published in English in *Second Colloquium on the Law of Outer Space, London, 1959, Proceedings*, pp. 156–168.

space he regards as *res communis omnium universi*, a "common good not only for all nations of the Earth, but for all nations of the universe, therefore of other planets and satellites where intelligent beings may exist". The problem is not one of dominion or property but of free use by all men, whether they be terrestrial, selenite or martian. The law of the high seas is not a good model as the high seas are an open field for war. All military activity in space must be forbidden by rules enforced by a police organisation uniting all nations of the solar system. Inter-planetary ships should carry an Earth flag corresponding to their terrestrial nationality. Conquest by occupation was criticised by Francisco de Vitória and is now an outdated principle having no application to planets and satellites. In the light of these considerations Valladão formulated a number of conclusions which were subsequently endorsed by the Inter-American Bar Association.[3]

Among other contributions from Latin America, those of Alvaro Bauzá Araujo,[4] Aldo Armando Cocca,[5] J. Escobar Faría,[6] and Modesto Seara Vasquez[7] have attracted special attention.

Alvaro Bauzá Araujo discusses in turn the origins of astronautic law and its relation to air law, the legal status of space, satellites, spaceships and space stations, the personnel of spaceships and the law applicable to relations with intelligent life in other worlds. His discussion of the position of satellites and spaceships in the law of property, the legal status of space stations and the law applicable there to matters of personal status, crime, tort and insurance, the legal status of the astronaut, and the legal authority of the space captain is particularly full. Bauzá Araujo argues that space law must consist of general principles per-mitting of changes and innovations as advances in astronautics may require. He discusses aerial photography and contends that States are entitled to protection against unsought photography of their strategic dispositions.

Armando Cocca presents interplanetary law as the expression in the

[3] See pp. 164–165, below.
[4] *Hacia un Derecho Astronáutico*, Montevideo, 1957; *Derecho Astronáutico*, Montevideo, 1961.
[5] *Teoría del Derecho Interplanetário*, Buenos Aires, 1957.
[6] *Comentarios ao Transdireito*, São Paulo, 1960.
[7] *Derecho Internacional Cosmico*, Mexico, 1961.

legal order of Einstein's interpretation of space time and relativity, a concept in which the common lawyer may find it difficult to identify any legal content as he understands it. Cocca conceives of interplanetary law as a *jus novum* the only source of which, *stricto sensu*, is "la doctrina" which he reviews in some detail as of 1957. He poses a series of questions relating to the legal status of the astronaut, including questions concerning the effect of deaths, marriages or births in space and the law applicable to contracts concluded and torts or crimes committed in space. He also discusses the establishment of interplanetary stations, which he holds to be legal, and raises, without giving any firm answer to, the question whether there is any general right of use of such stations otherwise than in an emergency.

J. Escobar Faría divides cosmic law into three branches: space law which is concerned with the legal questions arising from human activities in outer space and uninhabited celestial bodies; interplanetary law, which is concerned with the legal and political relations between planets as sovereign States; and metalaw, which is concerned with the legal relationships between physical individuals belonging to different planets. The second two branches are still abstractions but are destined to become realities. Faría envisages the internationalisation of any other uninhabited celestial body explored from Earth.

Seara Vasquez, in addition to discussing the legal status of space and spacecraft, responsibility and control, and sovereignty over celestial bodies, discusses the possibility of legal relationships with any human inhabitants of other celestial bodies, with any intelligent beings not belonging to the human race who may be found there, and with any group of settlers from Earth who might claim to establish an independent State on a celestial body.

Other Latin American writers include Ruben Dario y Badualdo,[8] Victor José Delacio,[9] José Pareja Paz Soldan[10] and Octavio Véjar Vasquez.[11]

The Inter-American Bar Association has adopted a series of resolu-

[8] *La política en la era del espacio*, Managua, 1960.
[9] *Los satélites artificiales ante el Derecho internacional y legislacion nacional*, Caracas, 1958.
[10] *El espacio sideral y las Naciones Unidas*, Medellin, 1960.
[11] *Derecho aeronáutico y Derecho Astronáutico*, Mexico, 1960.

tions concerning space law. These, though somewhat lengthy, contain relatively little detail. They elaborate the general theme that space is a "*res communis omnium universi*, a common *res* for all intelligent creatures of the universe", envisage that activities in space should be conducted under a new flag of the Earth, and that the relations of man with any intelligent beings who may be found elsewhere in the universe should be conducted "in terms of justice and equity".[12]

[12] Resolutions 76, 77 and 78 and the XIth Conference of the Inter-American Bar Association, Miami, Florida.

18

Proposals by International Legal Bodies

STUDIES of space law have been undertaken by a number of international legal bodies, some of which have adopted or may be expected to adopt resolutions or other conclusions containing findings or proposals on the subject. The importance of such resolutions or conclusions naturally varies with their content, the authority and weight of the body adopting them, and the degree of agreement with which they were adopted.

INSTITUTE OF INTERNATIONAL LAW

The Institute of International Law adopted unanimously on September 11, 1963, a resolution concerning the legal régime of outer space[1] which is of special importance by reason of the authority of the Institute and the fact of its having been adopted unanimously. The resolution "recognises the validity" of a series of principles set forth therein and indicates that the Institute "would welcome their inclusion in a generally accepted treaty or declaration governing the legal régime of outer space". The resolution declares that "outer space and the celestial bodies are not subject to any kind of appropriation" but "are free for exploration and use by all States for exclusively peaceful purposes" in conformity with its provisions. It provides that "no space object shall be launched otherwise than under the authority of a State", subsequently so defined as to include an international organisation of States, and that "each State shall ensure that the utilisation of every

---

[1] The full text of the resolution is reproduced in Appendix IX, pp. 416–418, below. For the reports by C. Wilfred Jenks on which the resolution was based and the discussions of the Institute see 1963 *Annuaire de l'Institut de Droit international*, Vol. 50, tome I, pp. 128–496 and tome II, pp. 60–187.

space object launched under its authority complies with the applicable international rules". The resolution contains provisions relating to the registration of space objects, the identification of space objects, jurisdiction over space objects, space telecommunications, the repatriation of astronauts, the return of space objects, the avoidance of space cluttering and contamination, scientific or technological experiments or tests and liability for injury, including loss of life, or damage. It declares that in all matters not provided for therein States are bound by general international law, including the principles of the Charter of the United Nations. In all matters not yet covered by General Assembly resolution or treaty obligation the Institute of International Law resolution may be regarded as the most authoritative available statement of a consensus of view among international lawyers concerning the principles on which the law of space should be based.

INTERNATIONAL LAW ASSOCIATION

The International Law Association at its 49th Conference (Hamburg, 1960) adopted a resolution on "air sovereignty and the legal status of outer space" approving the principle that "outer space and celestial bodies should be utilised only for peaceful purposes to the greatest common profit of all mankind in accordance with the principles of the United Nations Charter" and that "outer space may not be subject to the sovereignty or other exclusive rights of any State", and recommending "the conclusion of an international agreement whereby States would agree not to make claims to sovereignty or other exclusive rights over celestial bodies".

A further discussion at the 50th Conference (Brussels, 1962) did not take the matter substantially further[2]; it was again considered at the 51st Conference held in Tokyo in 1964.

INTERNATIONAL INSTITUTE OF SPACE LAW OF THE INTERNATIONAL ASTRONAUTICAL FEDERATION

The International Institute of Space Law of the International Astronautical Federation established in 1960 a series of working groups to

[2] International Law Association, *Report of the Fiftieth Conference*, Brussels, 1962, pp. 31–100.

deal with the demarcation and legal status of airspace and outer space respectively; the legal definitions and status of space instrumentalities; sovereignty over, the legal status of, and property rights in, celestial bodies; the scope of existing treaties and domestic law concerning airspace and outer space; the regulation of space flight; the role of international organisations and international adjudication in space regulation; space telecommunications; the effect of activities in space on private rights; responsibility for injury or damage resulting from activities in space; the need for new international organisations; and the desirability of international agreements on a wide range of matters. Work is in progress on these matters but no firm conclusions or consensus of view concerning them are on record at the date of writing.[3]

[3] There is a progress report in René H. Mankiewicz, "L'Etat des Doctrines sur le Droit d'Espace extra-aéronautique après le quatrième colloque sur le droit de l'espace" in *Revue Française de Droit Aérien*, 1962, pp. 19–42.

19

General Estimate of the Literature of Space Law

IT is perhaps inevitable that the literature of space law should include some excess of caution on doctrinal, political or military grounds, some excess of fancy, and some balanced realism in which a constructive idealism is tempered by a sense of practicality and timing. It is sometimes suggested that those with the most immediate opportunities and responsibilities in space are most apt to take a cautious and pragmatic view and a comparison of the views expressed in different parts of the world lends some, though far from decisive, support to this suggestion, but while it is arguable that those who have no immediate responsibility escape the compulsion of having to weigh conflicting or competing political, military and scientific considerations of a crucial nature they can for this reason afford to take a longer and broader view of what, subject to the immediate but reasonable requirements of military security, the long range interest of international society may require. A balance between the two approaches is clearly necessary, but while the international lawyer may have to adapt himself to, it is the converse of his true function to make himself the spokesman of, short term political and military reasons for leaving major parts of the law uncertain; where the scientific data necessary for formulating a reasonable legal rule are still unavailable the position is of course quite different, but where the difficulties are political rather than technical, and largely subjective rather than objective, the international lawyer has both a professional and a moral responsibility to devote his skill to a resolute attempt to overcome them.

The resolutions and conclusions adopted by the various international and national bodies which have made special studies are of special interest as expressions of collective and not merely personal views. While there are considerable variations in the proposals made by these various international and national bodies, and in particular important differences in the relative emphasis which they give to different aspects of the problem, most of them nevertheless have three striking features in common.

The general theme that outer space and celestial bodies should be regarded as free for exploration and use by all States in accordance with the Charter of the United Nations and international law, and not subject to national appropriation, tends, though with varying degress of emphasis and completeness, to run through them all.

There is general agreement that matters requiring early action include telecommunications, repatriation of astronauts and return of space objects, and liability for injury, loss of life or damage.

There is a wide measure of agreement that measures to take any element of secrecy or surprise out of activities in space are a major element in ensuring its exclusive dedication to peaceful use.

All three of these preoccupations are reflected in the General Assembly decisions and other steps which are now giving us the elements of a growing body of solid law on the subject.

The first preoccupation runs through virtually all of the literature of space law. Thus there has been widespread agreement among writers on space law that outer space (not necessarily uniformly defined) is not subject to appropriation by any State. While differing in the relative importance which they attach to such varied factors as the basic astronomical facts, the legal nature of space as distinguished from its contents, the impracticability of effective control, the nature of sovereignty, acquiescence in present activities in space, the needs of scientific progress, or the needs of a growing world community, the great majority of writers reach much the same result. The matter has now been placed beyond the pale of reasonable controversy by the unanimous endorsement of the principle by the General Assembly of the United Nations on two successive occasions.

The status of celestial bodies has provoked more divergence of view among writers. These divergences of view have cut across national and regional groupings. American, Soviet and European writers are all to be found in all three of the main schools of thought: the school which holds celestial bodies not subject to national appropriation; the school which holds it premature to attempt to decide the matter until more is known of the probable nature of activities in space; and the school which considers that the possibility of appropriating celestial bodies should be governed by some variant of the principles of discovery, inchoate title, and occupation. As regards this matter also theoretical controversy has been superseded by the unanimous endorsement by the General Assembly of the United Nations on two successive occasions of the principle that celestial bodies are free for exploration and use by all States in accordance with international law and are not subject to national appropriation. The grounds of high international policy for the adoption of this view by the General Assembly are clearly of the utmost cogency and override the considerations which have dominated theoretical controversy on the subject. The principle that the celestial bodies are free for occupation and use by all States in conformity with international law and are not subject to national appropriation is a necessary foundation for taking power politics out of space. The alternative was to leave the matter to be the sport of theoretical controversy until conflicting national interests asserted claims which would make a satisfactory long-term international solution of the problems of space impossible. No claims to sovereignty or any lesser national appropriation of any celestial body were asserted or recognised before the General Assembly acted in the matter. No one was or is constrained to recognise any such claim asserted uni-laterally. The General Assembly, by unanimous decision, has recorded the collective refusal of the Members of the United Nations to recognise any such claim, and has thereby placed the celestial bodies beyond the possibility of national appropriation. In these circumstances the theoretical controversy now belongs to history.

Writers on space law frequently discuss the extent to which maritime or air law analogies are apposite and helpful. Jessup and Taubenfeld on the one hand and Kovalev and Cheprov on the other reach some-what similar conclusions that these analogies are sometimes suggestive but cannot, in view of important physical difference, be decisive, and there we may be content to leave the matter subject to examining it in specific contexts as occasion may require.

Maritime and aviation analogies are particularly suggestive in respect of the status of spacecraft but not necessarily fully applicable. A number of writers envisage that each spacecraft should carry an Earth flag in addition to a national flag. It seems doubtful whether it is necessary or useful to introduce the concept of the spacecraft itself having a nationality.[1]

Concerning the relevance of the Antarctic analogy there has been less agreement. Western writers, notably Jessup and Taubenfeld, while recognising the obvious physical differences and sometimes urging a more direct international control of space than has been found necessary or practicable in the Antarctic, have been inclined to find the analogy stimulating; Soviet writers, notably Korovin, appear to have been more inclined to treat it with scepticism or reserve.

Writers on space law have taken widely divergent views concerning the basis and incidence of liability for injury, loss of life or damage resulting from activities in space. One school of thought has argued that the world as a whole owes so much to space pioneers that, in token of gratitude and by way of part fulfilment of its debt to them, the risks of their undertakings should fall elsewhere, either by letting the loss lie where it falls or by applying the insurance principle through some world fund constituted for the purpose. An opposing (and majority) school of thought accepts the fact that activities in space create novel and unusual dangers against which only those undertaking them can devise and apply adequate precautions, and deduces from the principle that he who engages in an immensely hazardous activity must bear responsibility for the risks he thereby creates the conclusion that there should be absolute or strict liability for injury, loss of life or damage resulting from activities in space. Still another school is inclined to argue that the immediate importance of the problem can be and is exaggerated and that the question can well be left in abeyance until fuller knowledge of all its elements is available. Whatever the theoretical

[1] See p. 236, below.

merits of these different positions may be, practical considerations point towards acceptance of the principle of strict liability and against delay in dealing with the matter. The solution of letting the loss lie where it falls cannot commend itself to any balanced sense of justice. It is not to the launching governments, which are only in a position to launch space objects because they have immense resources which they have chosen to use for the purpose, that the law should give any special consideration. The victim may suffer the most acute hardship, have no resources adequate to make good his loss, and, even assuming that the accident has not destroyed all the evidence of its causes, have no practical means of proving a defect or negligence in the manufacture or operations of the space object. The solution of applying the insurance principle by means of a world fund may well appear more attractive, but the difficulties of organising, financing and administering any such fund would be considerable, and as the major contributors to the fund would presumably be the governments playing major parts in space the practical effect would not differ greatly, except by spreading the burden of the reparation due for particular occurrences, from that of recognising the principle of strict liability. Strict liability places the burden of loss resulting from activities in space where it properly belongs as one of the costs of the venture to be taken into account when deciding whether, to what extent, and under what conditions, to undertake such activities. Recognition of the principle of strict liability is, moreover, a natural extension to activities in space of the principle already accepted in respect of aviation and nuclear tests.

Some of the other questions discussed in the literature of space law have no similar relationship to problems which are both of immediate practical importance and susceptible of early action; it is therefore not surprising that they are not significantly reflected in the emerging law.

Some of the legal controversies which have arisen are of a theoretical rather than a practical character.

Thus there has been much discussion of whether we should speak of cosmic law, interplanetary law, *jus inter gentes planetarium*, metalaw, astronautic law, or space law, and so forth. These various concepts do not, of course, coincide, and much of the discussion concerning their relative advantages and disadvantages is of considerable interest, but the questions at issue are to a substantial extent questions of personal preference. The Institute of International Law, in its 1963 resolution, disposed of the issue by deciding to use the term *droit de l'espace*, without any further qualifying adjective, in French, and the term "law of outer space" in English.[2] The General Assembly of the United Nations has used the terms "outer space" and *espace extra-atmosphérique*.

There has likewise been considerable discussion of the measure in which any legal consequences can reasonably be deduced from the laws of nature and natural phenomena or any firm legal obligations binding upon States from the manner in which they have mutually acquiesced in each other's present activities. Similarly, the discussion of how far anything in the nature of sovereignty may exist in space has a natural tendency to prompt a re-examination of, and an attempt to redefine, the concept of sovereignty itself, an exercise which clearly presents opportunities for widely varying theoretical prepossessions and evaluations of the requirements of sound international policy. Of these questions it is perhaps sufficient to say that it is unnecessary to project into space the innumerable doctrinal controversies of the theory of international law and that our objective should be rather to thread our way among the difficulties presented by differences of a doctrinal nature with a view to assisting in preparing the way for the practical solution of concrete problems.

One of the questions which such an approach will leave unresolved may be of more than doctrinal importance, namely the question of how much firm law can already be said to exist. But as the effect of attempting to define how well-established the law has become is frequently to weaken rather than to strengthen the degree in which a sense of legal obligation already exists, it would seem preferable to leave the determination of the measure in which particular principles or rules have become authoritative in character to be settled as need arises by the practice of States and future treaties and judicial decisions.

There has been some debate on the question how far there are or

[2] *1963 Annuaire de l'Institut de Droit International*, Vol. 50, tome II, p. 99.

can be legal principles prohibiting space contamination. It has been argued that there can be no legal obligation to avoid space contamination as there is no rule of which such contamination is a violation and, it appears to be implied, no beneficiary with a legal interest in the avoidance of such contamination entitling him to claim a right under such a rule. This is not however a valid objection to the suggested obligation as regards either contamination of space or contamination from space. While the legal considerations applicable are somewhat different in the two cases, the general result is much the same. As regards contamination of space, the General Assembly has unanimously declared that outer space and celestial bodies are free for exploration and use by all States in conformity with international law; all States share in this freedom; the rights which exist in space in virtue of this freedom, whatever they may be, are therefore general and all States are legally entitled to claim respect for them. The freedom must, however, be regarded as a freedom to enjoy the use of space and the celestial bodies in their natural state, without avoidable deterioration by contamination due to failure to take reasonable precautions. When the matter is so analysed the alleged difficulty of reducing to a legal obligation the importance of avoiding the contamination of space disappears. As regards contamination from space we are on more familiar ground. The matter is covered by the general obligation not to inflict unlawful harm to one's neighbour common to developed legal systems which is increasingly accepted in contemporary international law[3] and was declared by the Institute of International Law in the preamble to its resolution concerning the utilisation of non-maritime international waters for purposes other than navigation, adopted at Salzburg in 1961, to be one of the "basic general principles governing neighbourly relations".[4]

In the case of at least one of the questions which have been discussed, that of the demarcation of space from airspace, it is still far from clear whether there is or is not any practical problem but all too clear that no satisfactory solution is immediately attainable. Some writers, notably

[3] *Cf.* Jenks, *The Common Law of Mankind*, 1958, pp. 185–163, 293–296 and 362–363.
[4] *1961 Annuaire de l'Institut de Droit International*, Vol. 49, tome II, p. 381.

Cooper, have taken the view that no progress can be made in formulating the law of space until a demarcation of outer space from airspace has been agreed. This view has not commanded general acceptance and has twice been rejected by successive United Nations Committees on the Peaceful Uses of Outer Space. An acceptable demarcation which could be readily agreed would of course have substantial advantages, but any attempt at the present time to agree upon such a demarcation involves a combination of dangers which are partly alternative and partly cumulative. A complete impasse may be reached in view of the widely varying estimates of where the line of demarcation should run (by far the most probable result). If agreement is reached, it may be secured only by conceding prematurely extravagant claims to the extension of national jurisdiction. Alternatively, such agreement may be reached on a basis which further advances in scientific knowledge or technological possibilities show to be inappropriate. A stalemate in an attempt at demarcation might well tend to retard the settlement of problems of immediate practical urgency pending agreement on what may prove to be a theoretical question. Such an attempt, whether successful or unsuccessful, could tend to create a habit of thinking of the problems of space in geographical rather than functional terms, and such an approach would be incompatible with any satisfactory solution of major outstanding problems. For all these reasons it would appear wise to refrain from attempting any demarcation of outer space from airspace designed to be of general validity and to deal with concrete problems as they arise.

Purely legal discussion of the present legal status of military activity in space is equally unlikely to be helpful at the present stage. Throughout the statements of responsible statesmen there runs the theme of the exclusive dedication of space to peaceful purposes. All of the current proposals for general disarmament under international control envisage the demilitarisation of space. In these circumstances, the emphasis placed by some writers on the fact that military activity in space cannot yet be considered to be illegal must be regarded as misplaced. Demilitarisation may be achieved by treaty or by the gradual crystallisation into law of some *modus vivendi* not necessarily originating in a treaty.

To affirm that military activity in space remains legal until such a treaty is concluded may therefore be a grave disservice. On the other hand, specific prohibitions of military activity in space are unlikely to be acceptable in any other form than that of a statement of intention and objective unless they are embodied in a firm treaty obligation and it seems improbable that a treaty on the subject will be generally acceptable unless it is accompanied by adequate guarantees of effective implementation. In these circumstances legal speculation and analysis has little to contribute at this stage.

To these scientific and military questions we may add the questions which are wholly speculative in character, such as the manner in which the relationships of the human race with any forms of intelligent life found elsewhere in space should be initiated and conducted on a basis of law. The objective is appealing but we can leave the manner in which it should be achieved if and when the question arises to be considered at a later stage. We can act boldly in respect of matters which are now ripe for such action only by determining with circumspection the field within which the hour for boldness has now come.

The role of the literature of space law will inevitably change as at least the outlines of the law begin to harden. The purely speculative phase has already passed. McDougal's book may well prove to be its last major landmark. Those who have participated in the pioneer phase can look back upon it with a sense of solid achievement; they have created the intellectual foundation and climate which has made possible the adoption, only six years after the launching of Sputnik I, of the Twelve Tables of the Law of Space, the Declaration of Legal Principles Governing the Activities of States in the Exploration and Use of Outer Space. But the success achieved has changed the nature of the responsibilities and opportunities of the writer upon the law of space. His subject is still, and will long remain, a body of law in the initial phase of its development, but he now has an authoritative point of departure to guide and discipline his future work. The range, effectiveness and constructive nature of his influence will be determined by his willingness to accept the decisions which have now been taken

177

by governments with so impressive a unanimity as the framework within which the independent scholar must in future work, by his grasp of the scientific and technological settling of the problems which pose legal questions, by his awareness of the political (and at times military) context in which their solution must be sought, and by the extent to which his contribution to their solution reflects dynamically the preoccupations, tendencies and growth of contemporary international law. Approaching his responsibility in this spirit the independent scholar must at all times recall that while a beginning has now been made in establishing the rule of law in space, there still remains unanswered the fundamental question of chaos or international control posed by Jessup and Taubenfeld. The world still has a choice between allowing outer space to become subject "to the same power struggle which has in history characterised the demarcation of national territories on the map of the world" and taking time by the forelock by evolving a radical international solution for the problem of the control of space. This choice involves questions of policy on which lawyers as such may have no special professional qualification to speak, but it will nevertheless affect fundamentally the whole future of international law and of the rule of law as such, and indeed the whole future of man, not only in space but equally on Earth. In these circumstances the independent scholar has a continuing responsibility to take as the keynote of all his work the importance for the rule of law of the exclusive dedication of space to peaceful purposes, symbolised and stimulated by the elimination of barriers to the fullest interchange of scientific information and by the fullest possible pooling of space activities on the basis of the widest possible international co-operation, and guaranteed as soon as may be by an effective international control of space taking the form of institutional arrangements devised by a vigour of political imagination corresponding to the magnitude of the challenge. While it is important not to act prematurely in regard to space matters in the absence of fuller knowledge of the probable consequences of various possible courses of action, it is equally necessary to avoid the danger that, by always emphasising the importance of not taking action which might be considered premature, we may forget that developments in space will not wait for us to get our thinking straight about the way in which they should be dealt with and may reach a point at which there is no longer any real possibility of rational control unless effective action is taken without undue delay. It is not the scholar's role to shrink with nervous hesitation from the increasing boldness of practical statesmen.

Part III

THE LAW

Introductory

HAVING surveyed the progress and limitations of scientific co-operation in space, the scope for and beginnings of United Nations action, the tendency to wider participation in space activities by means of regional joint ventures and the likelihood of a measure of private enterprise in space, and having reviewed briefly the already extensive and ever-growing literature of space law, including a number of the proposals formulated by international and national bodies which have devoted themselves to the study of space law, we are now in a position to attempt to give a more systematic account of the solid core of generally accepted principle and practice around which the law is in process of growing.

20

Sources and Form of Space Law

THE sources of space law are to be found in those of international law generally, in "international conventions, whether general or particular, establishing rules expressly recognised by the contesting States", in "international custom, as evidence of a general practice accepted as law", and in "the general principles of law recognised by civilised nations", supplemented by "judicial decisions and the teachings of the most highly qualified publicists of the various nations".[1] Scientific facts and evidence of acquiescence, both of which bulk largely in the literature of space law, should not be regarded as independent sources of legal obligation the significance and weight of which in space law calls for special appraisal, but as important, and in the case of the scientific facts vital, considerations within this accepted framework of legal obligation governing international relations generally.

The forms which space law will ultimately take will be substantially influenced by the nature of any international arrangements which may be evolved for the control of space.

A Space Treaty, similar in general function (but not necessarily in detailed content or in the type and degree of international control and co-operation for which it provides) to the Antarctic Treaty, would have great advantages if there were reasonable assurance of its prompt ratification by the States primarily concerned, but failure to secure agreement upon or ratification of such a treaty would be a grievous setback.

For much of what is required a treaty may not be necessary. General Assembly Resolution No. 1721 (XVI) of December 20, 1961, was in

[1] Article 38 of the Statute of the International Court of Justice.

effect a joint declaration the first part of which settled some of the fundamental principles of the law of space. It afforded a precedent followed by the General Assembly in elaborating further the law of space by the adoption on December 13, 1963, of the Declaration of Legal Principles Governing the Activities of States in the Exploration and Use of Outer Space.[2] Immediately prior to the transmission of the Draft Declaration to the General Assembly by the Committee on the Peaceful Uses of Outer Space, there was a discussion in the Committee in the course of which explanatory statements were made on behalf of delegations concerning the terms of the Declaration and their general attitude towards it.[3] These statements are not to be construed as being necessarily either reservations to the Declaration[4] or an authentic interpretation of its provisions but they are nevertheless an element of importance for its interpretation. Their character is reminiscent of that of the correspondence preceding the signature of the General Treaty for the Renunciation of War, of which it has been said that while the Treaty must doubtless be interpreted in the light of the terms of the correspondence the correspondence must unquestionably be interpreted in the light of the terms of the Treaty. As the terms and effect of the Declaration are clarified by experience on the basis of principle and practice these preliminary exchanges may and probably will lose much of their importance; meanwhile they must be taken into account; as was said by the representative of Canada they "serve as a valuable commentary" on the Declaration.[5]

There was general agreement in the statements made that the principles set forth in the Declaration "do not constitute a closed chapter" (Lachs of Poland, Chairman of the Legal Sub-Committee);[6] that any attempt at a comprehensive codification would not at this stage be appropriate (United States);[7] that the Declaration records "agreement on those legal principles governing the exploration and use of outer space on which there was general accord, leaving for

[2] General Assembly Resolution 1962 (XVIII) of December 13, 1963.
[3] United Nations Document A/5549/Add.1 of November 27, 1963.
[4] See for instance the observations of the representative of Australia at p. 37 and the following exchange with the Reporter.
[5] *Ibid.*, p. 9.

future development those principles on which differences of opinion existed" (Canada);[8] that it "is a broad statement of general legal principles" and "we cannot expect such an instrument to include or to treat in detail everything that all of us would like it to do" (Australia);[9] that it is "but a starting point for the development of the law of outer space" (United Kingdom);[10] that it is "an initial step" incorporating the broad criteria which are to be the guiding lines for activities in outer space which "eventually will be developed further" (Italy);[11] that there must be further evolution "step by step" (India);[12] and that "it is only the very first step, which can and must be followed by other steps" (U.S.S.R.).[13] The French representative, in accepting these views, also described the Declaration as being merely "a declaration of intent"; no other representative expressed this view, which must be regarded as inconsistent with the character of the Declaration which is not a statement of policy or intention but a declaration of legal principles submitted unanimously by the Committee to the General Assembly as representing "the maximum area of agreement possible at this time".[14] The Declaration embodies, as the U.S.S.R. representative said, "whatever was calculated to unite rather than to divide the Members of the United Nations at the present time and at the present stage of the discussion".[15] Its general effect was well described by the Australian representative:

"While in our view a General Assembly Declaration of legal principles cannot itself be creative of legal duties, it is equally not the Australian delegation's view that such a General Assembly Declaration can have no part in the development or creation of international law. It is our view that a Declaration of legal principles by the General Assembly, especially if universally adopted and adhered to in practice, may be valuable evidence of international custom, which in turn is a most important source of law."[16]

It was therefore reasonable to nourish the hope:

"that the conduct enjoined in these principles will become the unvarying practice of all States."

[6] *Ibid.*, p. 4.   [9] *Ibid.*, p. 14.   [12] *Ibid.*, p. 28.   [15] *Ibid.*, p. 33.
[7] *Ibid.*, p. 5.   [10] *Ibid.*, p. 20.   [13] *Ibid.*, p. 32.   [16] *Ibid.*, p. 15.
[8] *Ibid.*, p. 9.   [11] *Ibid.*, p. 22.   [14] *Ibid.*, p. 1.

The authority of the Declaration of Legal Principles may be expected to grow with the passage of years. While it is somewhat less than a treaty is must already be regarded as rather more than a statement of custom. It represents the Twelve Tables of the Law of Space and may well be a precedent for further similar action by the General Assembly as circumstances may require. A convention that the General Assembly should take such action only by general consent, or at least with the concurrence of States taking leading parts in activities in space, might greatly facilitate such a course of development.

There will nevertheless continue to be matters in respect of which unequivocal treaty obligations are desirable. Illustrations are afforded by the matters omitted from the operative provisions of the Declaration of Legal Principles and by matters in respect of which measures to supplement the Declaration by international agreements of a more detailed, precise and binding character are already contemplated. As an illustration of the first type of case we may take the demilitarisation of space; this is a matter in respect of which, by reason of its relationship to general disarmament and the need for certainty concerning the degree of obligation which has been accepted, clear-cut treaty obligations have in general been thought imperative; the only exception thus far has been the General Assembly resolution relating to the placing of weapons of mass destruction in space[17] which is a combination of a statement of intent by the space powers with a recommendation by the General Assembly but does not purport either to state the law or to create an obligation. The second type of case is illustrated by the question of liability for injury, loss of life or damage, in the case of which precision and certainty of obligation are necessary by reason of its relationship to private rights on Earth.

In respect of some matters, such as telecommunications, meteorology, and possible interference with aircraft, the regulation of activities in space has to be integrated with the existing international arrangements for the regulation of activities on Earth. Other matters, including the notification and registration of launchings and spacecraft, mutual assistance, repatriation and return, experiments in space, and space

[17] p. 303, below.

contamination, may at some stage be the subject of international agreements but it may also be possible to deal with them by means of international regulations, standards, or recommended practices, approved either by the General Assembly or by an appropriate technical or scientific body, without invoking the cumbersome mechanism of the law-making treaty; the existing medley of General Assembly resolutions, ITU regulations and COSPAR standards illustrates, without by any means exhausting, the range of possible types of action. Bilateral agreements of widely varying types may well be increasingly important. The existing regional arrangements for joint action are based on formal international agreements, but do not necessarily constitute the only possible legal basis for such joint action. Whenever joint action is undertaken any regulations made by an organisation of States to govern its operations may be of substantial importance in the development of the law. Regulations made by organisations of States or States in the exercise of their jurisdiction over spacecraft, and, pending provision for more direct international administration, over orbital and other extraterrestrial stations may also be important.

Adjudication and arbitration of various types may be expected to play some part in the future development of the law; how significant this part will be as regards matters arising directly between States or between States and international organisations will depend primarily on the progress of international adjudication generally;[18] at some stage it may be desirable to have special arrangements for adjudicating upon private claims arising out of activities in space.

The "teachings of the more highly qualified publicists of the various nations" will also continue to play a part, but the nature of this part will necessarily change as the growth of the law gives it a more definite form and a more settled substance.[19] The influence of legal scholarship on the future of space law will be enhanced if it refrains from entering dogmatically or with partiality into matters which are politically controversial, which continue to be highly speculative on the basis of present scientific knowledge, technological capacity and practical

[18] *Cf.* Jenks, *The Prospects of International Adjudication*, 1964.
[19] *Cf.* pp. 177–179, above.

experience, or which involve technicalities which no legal skill can resolve; it will be most valuable in so far as it succeeds in harmonising the varying but by no means irreconcilable interests reflected in the divergent views which have been expressed on behalf of governments. It is not for scholarship to attempt to determine at this stage when principle has become practice and when practice has become law, but a clear responsibility rests upon all scholars to facilitate rather than to retard the process of such evolution.

21

Demarcation of Space

THE Declaration of Legal Principles makes no attempt to define the term "outer space" or to demarcate outer space from the atmosphere. The controversy among writers concerning the extent to which the question of demarcation is or is not important[1] and the most appropriate basis of demarcation[2] has attracted but little interest among practical men; it seems probable that the matter will continue to be dealt with in so far as it becomes a matter of practical importance in specific contexts to define what is and what is not permissible, and what the exact scope of a particular rule is, rather than in any more general basis.

The only special context in respect of which an agreed definition (without a demarcation) of space already exists is for telecommunication purposes. The Radio Regulations define a space station as a station "located on an object which is beyond, is intended to go beyond, or has been beyond, the major portion of the Earth's atmosphere"[3] and contain a whole series of more detailed definitions relating to space systems, services and stations;[4] they define the term "spacecraft" as including "any type of space vehicle, including an Earth satellite or a deep space probe, whether manned or unmanned"[5] and "deep space" as "space at distances from the Earth equal to or greater than the distance between the Earth and the Moon".[6]

There are implied definitions of scope in certain General Assembly decisions relating to space matters. The provisions of the Declaration of Legal Principles relating to jurisdiction, control, ownership and return of space objects,[7] and liability for damage caused thereby,[8] refer

[1] pp. 107–111 and 175–176, above.
[2] p. 108, above.
[3] Reg. 84AE.
[4] Reg. 84AC to 84BH.
[5] Reg. 84BH.
[6] Reg. 84BA.
[7] Para. 7.
[8] Para. 8.

to objects "launched into outer space". The provisions concerning registration of General Assembly Resolution 1721 (XVI) B of December 20,
1961, refer to objects launched "into orbit or beyond", a provision
which led to some initial difficulty concerning the registration of
launchings failing to go into orbit.[9] General Assembly Resolution
1884 (XVIII) of October 17, 1963, calls on States to refrain from installing weapons of mass destruction "in orbit around the Earth" or installing such weapons "on celestial bodies" or stationing them "in
outer space in any other manner".

The Treaty of Moscow prohibits nuclear tests "in the atmosphere"
or "beyond its limits, including outer space"; no demarcation between
the two was necessary, the provisions applicable in the atmosphere and
beyond its limits being identical. The expression "beyond its limits,
including outer space" is at first glance curious; it may perhaps have
been intended to cover celestial bodies as distinguished from outer
space rather than to reserve the possibility that outer space may not
begin where the atmosphere ends, but however this may be the Treaty
is not drafted with such legal precision that it can be regarded as
settling, or even establishing any presumption concerning, legal matters
beyond its immediate scope as a prohibition of nuclear testing.

In so far as future rules of space law take the form of General Assembly
resolutions, treaty obligations or international regulations they can, so
far as may be necessary, and doubtless will, whenever the matter is of
real practical importance, define their exact scope. It will be important,
when formulating any answer to the question of demarcation which
may be necessary for the purpose of any such definition, to frame it in
such terms that it does not embarrass us in some unexpected context
when we come to deal with an entirely different matter.

If a question of demarcation should become of practical importance
in connection with the interpretation of the Declaration of Legal
Principles, or in any other context in which no agreement concerning
the matters at issue exists, it may become necessary to consider the
question of demarcation on the basis of principle, though preferably
only in relation to the matters immediately at issue. If and as this

[9] p. 222, below.

becomes necessary, the most satisfactory of the various conflicting views may be that which treats the troposphere and stratosphere as airspace and everything beyond as outer space, but a sharp divergence of view concerning both the principle and its application must be expected between those for whom the primary consideration is to secure the greatest possible measure of freedom in space and those for whom the primary consideration is to secure a maximum of national control for security or other reasons.

22

Space as a Common Interest of Mankind

THE Declaration of Legal Principles affirms the general principle that "the exploration and use of outer space shall be carried on for the benefit and in the interests of all mankind".[1] In the Preamble there are further references to "the great prospects opening up before mankind as a result of man's entry into outer space" and "the common interest of all mankind in the progress of the exploration and use of outer space for peaceful purposes" and statements that the General Assembly believes "that the exploration and use of outer space should be for the betterment of mankind and for the benefit of States irrespective of their degree of economic or scientific development", desires "to contribute to broad international co-operation in the scientific as well as in the legal aspects of exploration and use of outer space for peaceful purposes", and believes "that such co-operation will contribute to the development of mutual understanding and to the strengthening of friendly relations between nations and peoples".

During the discussion of the Declaration by the Committee on the Peaceful Uses of Outer Space immediately prior to its transmission to the General Assembly for adoption the Brazilian,[2] Indian,[3] Japanese[4] and Lebanese[5] delegations expressed the view that the operative paragraphs of the Declaration should have contained an unequivocal provision that space may be used only for peaceful purposes. The Institute of International Law resolution does include the limitation "for exclusively peaceful purposes";[6] after some discussion the Institute

---

[1] Para. 1.
[2] United Nations Document A/5549/Add.1 of November 27, 1963, pp. 26–27.
[3] *Ibid.*, p. 28.   [5] *Ibid.*, p. 30.
[4] *Ibid.*, p. 24.   [6] Para. 1.

accepted a suggestion by its reporter[7] that the addition of the words should be agreed unanimously on the understanding that they were necessarily incomplete in the absence of an agreed definition of "peaceful purposes". Governments negotiating through the United Nations, understandably, preferred to state the dedication of space to peaceful purposes as an objective rather than a legal principle pending clarification of the concept of peaceful purposes. The further action taken or projected for the demilitarisation of space, and the questions which remain at issue, are reviewed in the appropriate contexts in later chapters;[8] meanwhile it remains to discuss here the significance of the general principle affirmed by the Declaration that "the exploration and use of outer space shall be carried on for the benefit and in the interests of all mankind".

The principle of the common interest of mankind in space defines the perspective in which the problems of space law are to be resolved; while in itself so general as to lack any clearly defined content, it is important precisely because it is so general. The more specific principles enumerated in the Declaration itself derive from it; freedom of exploration and use on a basis of equality, the impossibility of national appropriation, the concept that space activities are governed by a legal order, the responsibility of States for ensuring that space activities are carried on in conformity therewith, the principles of co-operation and mutual assistance, and the duty to avoid harmful interference with the space activities of others are all natural deductions from the recognition that space is a common interest of mankind. But the scope and vitality of the general principle are not exhausted by the specific applications of it embodied in the later paragraphs of the Declaration. The principle of the common interest of mankind in space is, like the general welfare clause of the Constitution of the United States, a continuing source of authority for new applications of the fundamental concept as further problems come into focus and call for solution on the basis of law. The Declaration was regarded by its authors as essentially a point of departure; innumerable problems not covered directly by its terms will

---

[7] Jenks, *Annuaire de l'Institut de Droit International*, Vol. 50, tome II, p. 104.
[8] Chaps. 60–63, pp. 301–308, below.

inevitably arise; in seeking for a solution of them the preliminary questions whether space is governed by a presumption of interdependence or a presumption of sovereignty,[9] and whether the law applicable in space is a projection of the law of a world community in which the law is in a phase of vigorous growth reflecting that of the community itself or a limited body of rules binding only by specific assent,[10] may be of fundamental importance; the principle of the common interest of mankind in space answers these questions in favour of interdependence and growth.

[9] *Cf.* Jenks, *Law, Freedom and Welfare*, 1963, "Interdependence as the Basic Concept of Contemporary International Law", pp. 71–82.
[10] *Cf.* Jenks, *The Prospects of International Adjudication*, 1964, esp. pp. 258–265, 311–315, 425–427, 544–546, 658–662, and 764–769.

23

Freedom of Exploration and Use

THE Declaration of Legal Principles provides that "outer space and celestial bodies are free for exploration and use by all States on a basis of equality and in accordance with international law".[1] In this respect it repeats the terms of General Assembly Resolution No. 1721 (XVI)A of December 20, 1961,[2] with the addition of the phrase "on a basis of equality".

The freedom of exploration and use must, of course, be understood in the context of the other provisions of the Declaration and of any other agreements or regulations which may be applicable in accordance with international law. The Institute of International Law resolution provides that outer space and the celestial bodies "are free for exploration and use . . ." in accordance with the provisions of the resolution;[3] the same limitation must be regarded as implied in the terms of the Declaration. It follows from the other provisions of the Declaration that the freedom of exploration and use does not include any right of national appropriation "by claim of sovereignty, by means of use or occupation, or by any other means"; that it is subject to the obligation to respect international law including the Charter of the United Nations; that it is accompanied by a correlative responsibility for securing compliance with the provisions of the Declaration; that it is qualified by the principle of co-operation and mutual assistance; that it is limited by the obligation to avoid harmful interference with the

---

[1] Para. 2.

[2] Para. 1 (b); the only other changes are that the term "in conformity with" used in 1961 becomes "in accordance with" in 1962 and that the prohibition of national appropriation becomes in 1963 a separate and more detailed paragraph.

[3] Para. 1.

space activities of others; and that it involves liability for damage done by space objects.

How far, then, does the principle of freedom "for exploration and use by all States on a basis of equality" resolve any of the practical problems which may arise in the course of the exploration and use of space? And, in the first instance, what is the exact connotation of the expression "by all States", of the terms "exploration" and "use", and of the expression "on a basis of equality"?

The provision that outer space and celestial bodies are free for exploration and use "by all States" is a repetition in the Declaration of Legal Principles of an expression used in the 1961 General Assembly resolution. The limitation to "all States" was then regarded as clearly necessary to avoid the enunciation of a right of adventure in space for individuals which would go well beyond anything which would be thought reasonable or desirable even by those who regard private enterprise as having an important contribution to make to developments in space. The limitation was not, it is believed, intended, and cannot be construed, to exclude the freedom of organisations of States to participate in the exploration and use of space; certainly any such construction is untenable in the case of the Declaration in the light of the reference to international organisations later in the text and the observations made by the United Kingdom and other representatives prior to the adoption of the Declaration. From a practical standpoint the matter is of great importance. Only the richest States can participate in activities in space on the basis of their own resources alone. Other States can hope to enjoy the freedom of participation in the exploration and use of outer space and the celestial bodies recognised by the General Assembly resolution only by pooling their resources for this purpose. There are increasing indications that they will do so, of which the European Space Research Organisation and the European Organisation for the Construction and Development of Space Vehicle Launchers[4] may well be only the first examples.

The term "exploration" calls for no exegesis; it clearly includes both exploration by instruments and exploration by man. The term "use"

[4] pp. 74–80, above and 357–374, below.

is less self-explanatory; it does not, as we have seen, include "national appropriation by claim of sovereignty, by means of use or occupation, or by any other means". Nor does freedom of "use"include freedom to misuse; this much is clear from the obligation to have due regard to the interests of other States and to avoid harmful interference with their activities. What is not, and cannot, yet be clear is where the line is to be drawn between use and misuse if some space resource which can be consumed or some deterioration incidental to a legitimate "use" of space or a celestial body is involved. These matters it will be necessary to consider in due course.[5]

The expression "on a basis of equality" is clearly an "open door" provision; how much more does it imply? It poses a dilemma reminiscent of the distinctions between equality before the law (or equal protection of the law), an equality of capacity for rights, and an equality of rights actually acquired which have proved necessary to illuminate, and delimit the scope for the application of, the doctrine of the equality of States in international law.[6] The expression postulates equality of opportunity for States with the economic and technological capacity to take advantage of opportunities in space; it neither can nor does create or give any right to the economic and technological capacity necessary to take advantage of such opportunities by one's own action; how far, and within what limits, does it contemplate any right to equality of enjoyment of the benefits of the exploration and use of space irrespective of equality of economic and technological capacity to participate directly therein? The statement in the Preamble to the Declaration that the exploration and use of outer space should be "for the benefit of States irrespective of their degree of economic or scientific development" and the emphasis placed by the Committee on the Peaceful Uses of Outer Space on international space communications being "available for the use of all countries on a global non-discriminatory basis" make it clear that the concept of "a basis of equality" includes the second as well as the first element.

The "open door" principle presents no special difficulty and is given

---

[5] See pp. 275–282, below.
[6] E. D. Dickinson, *The Equality of States in International Law*, 1920.

more concrete expression in the provision of the following paragraph of the Declaration that outer space and celestial bodies are "not subject to national appropriation".

The equal enjoyment of benefits is a far more difficult matter which can, it is believed, be dealt with only by making provision for the application of the principle in specific contexts by appropriate agreements.

It is in respect of full access to the scientific results of space activities that most progress has been made. Provision for such access is already a commonplace of agreements whereby one State grants another special facilities for its space operations, such as tracking facilities; it is a recognised feature of the United Nations Basic Principles for the Creation and Operation of International Sounding Rocket Launching Facilities and is provided for in the Convention for the Establishment of a European Space Research Organisation and in the Bilateral Space Agreement between the United States and the U.S.S.R. as regards the results of the co-operative programme provided for in that Agreement.

The application of the principle in respect of the use of operational facilities in space is a more complex problem, but the United Nations has already focused attention upon its importance in respect of communication satellites and practical steps for its implementation in the meteorological field have been taken by the United States by making meteorological information from satellites generally available through the World Meteorological Organisation and by a read-out system permitting direct reception from satellites by the use of relatively inexpensive equipment.[7]

The principle clearly does not justify a third State in attempting unilaterally to make use of another State's operational satellites in a manner which may be disruptive of their proper operation, but the extent to which it may be able to take advantage of the services rendered by such satellites without creating any danger of this nature will, as we shall see in due course, vary from one type of satellite to another. It may be possible to make extensive use of meteorological or radio-navigation satellites, or to receive television broadcasts from a communication satellite, without any danger of improper inter-

[7] See pp. 264–265, below.

ference, the only question arising being whether the services rendered by such satellites are offered for general public use or whether any reimbursement is due for services received. If a satellite is used for transmissions or two-way communication the problems which arise are clearly of a different nature analogous to those which have required consideration in many countries in connection with the regulation of public utilities to secure equitable conditions and terms of availability.

24

Space and Celestial Bodies not Subject to

Appropriation

THE Declaration of Legal Principles provides that "outer space and celestial bodies are not subject to national appropriation by claim of sovereignty, by means of use or occupation, or by any other means".[1] It thereby reaffirms in somewhat more detailed terms General Assembly Resolution No. 1721 (XVI)A of December 20, 1961, which specified that "outer space and celestial bodies ... are not subject to national appropriation".[2] In the Institute of International Law Resolution the principle is more widely expressed as being that "outer space and the celestial bodies are not subject to any kind of appropriation".[3]

The general principle that outer space and celestial bodies are not subject to national appropriation can therefore, and indeed must, now be regarded as firmly established. In these circumstances much of the speculation on the subject which was current before these General Assembly decisions were taken must now yield to authority. It is, however, necessary to consider the scope and effect of the principle.

In so doing it is necessary to distinguish outer space and celestial bodies. While the General Assembly has preferred to treat them alike the elements of the problem are not identical in the two cases. Outer space is not subject to appropriation by reason of the facts of nature; while this may be also true of celestial bodies the physical structure and environment of which precludes any human occupation, where such occupation is possible the prohibition of appropriation rests essentially on grounds of international public policy. We must therefore have

---

[1] Para. 3.   [2] Para. 1 (b).   [3] Para. 1.

regard to both natural phenomena and international public policy in construing and applying this provision of the Declaration.

The Declaration of Legal Principles speaks of "national appropriation". The Institute of International Law resolution speaks of "any kind of appropriation". Can the term "national" be regarded as limitative and if so what does it exclude and thereby permit? In the light of the history of territorial acquisitions on Earth,[4] a number of theoretical possibilities may be distinguished. Territory may be appropriated by or on behalf of a State. It may be appropriated by a body in the nature of a Chartered Company, such as the East India Company[5] or the British South Africa Company.[6] It may be appropriated by an adventurer acting on his own account, such as Rajah Brooke of Sarawak.[7] It may be jointly appropriated by a group of closely associated States[8] or a group of potentially unfriendly States desirous of neutralising each other's influence. Conceivably it might be appropriated by the United Nations acting on behalf of the world community as a whole. It is submitted that the prohibition of "national appropriation" contained in the Declaration of Legal Principles forbids all but the last of these possible forms of appropriation. The Declaration itself provides that States bear international responsibility for national activities in space;[9] it follows that what is forbidden to a State is not permitted to a chartered company created by a State or to one of its nationals acting as a private adventurer. The Declaration also makes it clear[10] that its provisions are binding upon all States in respect of their collective as well as their individual acts, even when they act through international organisations; from this it follows that a State cannot escape the prohibition of national appropriation by acting jointly with other States. Only as regards a possible appropriation by the United Nations acting on behalf of the world community as a whole can the matter be regarded as an open one for the future.

---

[4] *Cf.* M. F. Lindley, *The Acquisition and Government of Backward Territory in International Law*, 1926.
[5] *Ibid.*, pp. 94–95.   [6] *Ibid.*, pp. 101–103.   [7] *Ibid.*, pp. 86–88.
[8] *Cf. ibid.*, pp. 119–120 as regards the New Hebrides.
[9] Para. 5; see Chap. 29, below.
[10] Para. 5; Chap. 28, below.

Space and Celestial Bodies not Subject to Appropriation

It is outer space and celestial bodies which the Declaration describes as "not subject to national appropriation"; how do matters stand as regards any natural resources of space or celestial bodies which it may become possible to exploit? The law relating to such resources will be examined in greater detail at a later stage; suffice it to say at this point that outer space and celestial bodies may be found to yield consumable resources which could conceivably be the subject of national appropriation. Such resources may be usable without any exclusive appropriation or usable only by such appropriation. The language of the Declaration does not, it is submitted, prejudice in any way the question how far and in what manner particular resources can be appropriated, the question whether some concession, leave or licence from an appropriate authority should be required for the working of such resources,[11] or the question whether title thereto should be derived from extraction and possession or in some other manner. What is forbidden is the national appropriation of outer space or celestial bodies; the legal régime applicable to any of their natural resources which it may prove possible and profitable to exploit remains for consideration at a later stage in the light of fuller knowledge of what is practicable and probable. Much will depend on the resources which can be utilised and the manner of their utilisation; a frequency or radiation presents quite different problems from a mineral, and we cannot yet judge the probable relative importance in practice of different types of imaginable resource.

[11] I may perhaps refer to my views on the matter as of 1955 as expressed in *The Common Law of Mankind*, 1958, pp. 397–398 and *cf.* as regards Antarctica, pp. 376–378.

25

Space Governed by International Law

THE Declaration of Legal Principles, in addition to specifying that the free exploration and use of outer space and celestial bodies shall be "in accordance with international law",[1] provides that "the activities of States in the exploration and use of outer space shall be carried on in accordance with international law including the Charter of the United Nations, in the interest of maintaining international peace and security and promoting international co-operation and understanding".[2] In General Assembly Resolution 1721 (XVI)A of December 20, 1961, this principle had been stated in the form that "international law, including the Charter of the United Nations, applies to outer space and celestial bodies".[3] So stated, the principle was clearly open to criticism as being anthropocentrically expressed; international law can hardly be regarded as applicable to outer space and celestial bodies as such; what it applies to is activities undertaken there by the subjects of international law, and the principle is correctly stated in this manner in the Declaration of Legal Principles.

During the discussion of the Declaration by the Committee on the Peaceful Uses of Outer Space immediately prior to its transmission to the General Assembly for adoption the French representative commented[4] that the reference to international law was ambiguous. If what was meant was "traditional international law whose principles in matters relating to land, sea and air are well established", that law "could not be applied as it stands in regard to outer space" as was shown

[1] Para. 2; see pp. 195–199, above.
[2] Para. 4.
[3] Para. 1 (a).
[4] United Nations Document A/5549/Add.1 of November 27, 1963, pp. 16–17.

by the inclusion in the Declaration itself of the provision that outer space and celestial bodies are not subject to national appropriation, whereas if the reference was to be regarded as relating "specifically to the law of outer space", and it was in this sense that the French delegation interpreted it, the provisions of such a law were still the subject of study and argument and their enunciation was far from complete. The representative of Brazil also expressed some doubt concerning the "unqualified extension to outer space" of international law.[5]

In a limited sense this observation appears to be valid. There are certain matters in respect of which the law of space is clearly tending to diverge from accepted international law. The outstanding example is the principle that outer space and celestial bodies are not subject to national appropriation, which treats outer space differently from air space and as regards any celestial bodies which may be physically capable of occupation stands in sharp contrast to the traditional law concerning the acquisition of sovereignty over unsettled territory on Earth. Any substantial progress towards the legal demilitarisation of space would, unless it formed an integral part of more comprehensive arrangements for general disarmament, be another illustration of such a major divergence. There must therefore be an implied exception to the principle that international law is applicable to the activities of States in space in respect of matters for which a new rule has been or is in process of being evolved for space on grounds of international public policy as well as for matters in respect of which the facts of space are so different from the facts of Earth as to make some familiar principle or rule inapplicable; this exception clearly includes matters in respect of which the Declaration of Legal Principles states or foreshadows a rule differing from or supplementing existing international law. The relationship between the principle that international law is applicable and the other principles formulated by the Declaration is, it is submitted, well expressed in the corresponding provision of the Institute of International Law resolution which specifies that "in all matters not provided for" in the resolutions, "States are bound by general international law, including the principles of the Charter of the United Nations".[6]

[5] *Ibid.*, p. 27.   [6] Para. 14.

The implied exception is nevertheless an exception, which is limited in scope by reason of its nature as an exception and any overwide interpretation of which is to be deprecated. How much of international law has any practical application in space will of course depend on how much happens in space, but it is important to start from the principle that the activities of States do not cease to be subject to international law when they extend beyond the atmosphere; space is not a legal void; there is a great deal of existing international law immediately applicable to the activities of States in space.

The law governing recourse to force, providing for the peaceful settlement of international disputes and defining the limits of the right of self-defence has an immediate and direct application to space activities. It includes, in addition to the Charter of the United Nations and the Statute of the International Court of Justice (which will be discussed separately in the following chapter), the General Treaty for the Renunciation of War, the Hague Conventions on the Peaceful Settlement of International Disputes, and the customary law on the subject.

In a developing legal system no part of the law is more important than that which governs the development of the law itself. The fundamental concept on which contemporary international law is based, that of interdependence, is the *Leitmotif* of the Declaration of Legal Principles. The overriding and all-pervasive principle of good faith, the binding force of custom, the scope for the application of general principles of law, the general concept of law as a living growth rather than as a body of hard and fast rules in a state of arrested development; all of these have their contribution to make to the basic intellectual structure of the law of space.

The law relating to the conclusion, validity, effect, interpretation and discharge of treaties and other international agreements applies to treaties and agreements covering space matters.

The international law of tort, though in many respects less developed than the law concerning the contractual relations of States, is in process of rapid growth. Much of it is potentially applicable to space activities, and some parts of it, such as the law governing liability for injury and damage and the law of nuisance and negligence, have a direct relationship with the practical application of the provisions of the Declaration of Legal Principles.

The law relating to international adjudication has an important potential application to adjudication relating to space occurrences.

The principle that States remain bound in their space activities by international law is therefore no idly rhetorical affirmation. It has a content the boundaries of which inevitably remain uncertain but which includes a well-defined core of immediate practical importance.

26

The Charter of the United Nations
Applicable in Space

THE Declaration of Legal Principles, when providing that "the activities of States in the exploration and use of outer space shall be carried out in accordance with international law" specifies "including the Charter of the United Nations". There is a similar reference to the international law applicable to outer space and celestial bodies including the Charter in General Assembly Resolution 1721 (XVI)A of December 20, 1961. In the Institute of International Law resolution the corresponding reference to "general international law" is described as including "the principles of the Charter of the United Nations".[1]

As in the case of the reference to international law of which it is a part, the reference to the Charter was expressed in the 1961 resolution in an unhappily anthropocentric form. It is not to outer space and to the celestial bodies as such that the Charter of the United Nations can reasonably be regarded as applicable, but rather to the activities undertaken there by or on behalf of, or under the authority and subject to the responsibility of, the parties to the Charter, whether they act individually or collectively as groups of States or through organisations of which they are members. In the Declaration of Legal Principles the principle is more happily expressed.

The Charter of the United Nations is not earthbound. The principle has been authoritatively proclaimed. What, however, are its practical implications? How much of the Charter has an immediate practical application to activities in space? There appears to have been a wide-

[1] Para. 14.

spread impression that little of the Charter can have any such application. It suffices to read the Charter to demonstrate that this is not so.

The general principles set forth in Article 2 of the Charter are clearly applicable to the space activities of Members. These include the principle that "all members shall settle their international disputes by peaceful means in such a manner that international peace and security, and justice, are not endangered" and the principle that "all Members shall refrain in their international relations from the threat or use of force against the territorial integrity or political independence of any State, or in any other manner inconsistent with the Purposes of the United Nations"; these are fundamental to the rule of law in space no less than on Earth. The principles that "all Members shall give the United Nations every assistance in any action it takes in accordance with" the Charter and "shall refrain from giving assistance to any State against which the United Nations is taking preventive or enforcement action" and that "the Organisation shall ensure that States which are not Members of the United Nations act in accordance with these Principles so far as may be necessary for the maintenance of international law and security" are also potentially applicable to space activities.

The provisions of Chapters VI and VII of the Charter relating to the peaceful settlement of disputes, and to action with respect to threats to the peace, breaches of the peace and acts of aggression, including Article 51 which recognises but limits the "inherent right of individual or collective self-defence if an armed attack occurs", apply to space disputes, and to threats to the peace, breaches of the peace and acts of aggression occurring in space, in the same manner as to disputes and occurrences on Earth.

The provisions of Chapters IX and X of the Charter relating to the co-ordination of the policies and activities of the specialised agencies apply to, and are in fact being applied in respect of, their policies and activities relating to space matters.

Chapter XIV of the Charter, relating to the International Court of Justice, and the Statute of the Court itself, are applicable in respect of disputes and legal questions relating to space matters.

The provisions of Articles 102 and 103 of the Charter, requiring that treaties and international agreements be registered with the United Nations and providing that in the event of any conflict of obligations the provisions of the Charter shall prevail, apply to treaties and agreements relating to space and activities there; Article 102 is already being applied in respect of agreements relating to space activities.

Articles 104 and 105 of the Charter provide that the United Nations as an organisation shall enjoy the legal capacity, privileges and immunities specified therein "in the territory of each of its Members"; there can be no question that the United Nations is entitled to the benefit of these provisions in respect of any space activities which it may undertake in the event of any question relating thereto arising in the territory of one of its Members; it is difficult to see why the position should be less favourable to the United Nations if it becomes possible to conceive of any such question arising outside the territory of any Member in space or on a celestial body; perhaps the answer may be that no such question can arise because any activities undertaken by the United Nations in space or on a celestial body would fall outside the jurisdiction of any of its Members.

There are, on the other hand, certain provisions of the Charter which by reason of their nature and scope would not appear to have any foreseeable application in space.

It is difficult to imagine a reasonable claim that any activity in space is "essentially within the domestic jurisdiction" of any State, within the meaning of Article 2, paragraph 7 of the Charter.

It is difficult to conceive of the membership provisions of the Charter being applicable to extra-terrestrial communities.

The Declaration regarding Non-Self Governing Territories contained in Chapter XI of the Charter and the provisions of Chapter XII establishing an international trusteeship system are not by their nature incapable of extra-terrestrial application, but any such application of them could not be reconciled with the principle that outer space and celestial bodies are not subject to national appropriation "by claim of sovereignty, by means of use or occupation, or by any other means".

27

Responsibility for National Activities in Space

THE Declaration of Legal Principles provides that "States bear international responsibility for national activities in outer space, whether carried on by governmental agencies or by non-governmental entities, and for ensuring that national activities are carried on in conformity with the principles" set forth therein and that "the activities of non-governmental entities in outer space shall require authorisation and continuing supervision by the State concerned".[1] The same principle is expressed somewhat differently in the Institute of International Law resolution which provides that "no space object shall be launched otherwise than under the authority of a State" and that "each State shall ensure that the utilisation of every space object launched under its authority complies with the applicable international rules".[2]

The principle represents a compromise between the conflicting initial positions taken up in the Committee on the Peaceful Uses of Outer Space by the Soviet Union and the United States. The original U.S.S.R. position was that "all activities of any kind pertaining to the exploration and use of outer space shall be carried out solely and exclusively by States"; this position was entirely unacceptable to the United States which had plans for telecommunication satellites to be launched by the Government of the United States but to be made and operated by private enterprise; other Western countries tended to share the United States' view. This divergence of view was so essentially a reflection of contrasted economic and social systems that it would have been unreasonable to expect either view to yield to the other. There are, however, two principles on the basis of which the gap can

---

[1] Para. 5.   [2] Para. 2.

be bridged. The first is that only a State or organisation of States may launch an object into orbit or beyond; the second is that, the launching State or organisation of States remains responsible in all circumstances for whatever it launches. This responsibility of the launching State or organisation of States includes both responsibility for ensuring continuing compliance by the operating body with any applicable international rules and regulations and a direct responsibility of the launching State or organisation of States itself for any injury, loss or damage, subject to whatever right of recovery it may think to reserve to itself under its own law against the operating body. On the basis of these principles a practical reconciliation of the two divergent points of view has proved to be possible. Both principles must be regarded as vital. The launching of objects into orbit and beyond is much too closely related to matters of international peace and security to be a proper field for private enterprise and only by insisting that one or more States must assume the responsibility for every launching can any real responsibility be fastened upon the space operator. The proposed responsibility corresponds to the obligation of parties to the International Telecommunications Convention to take the steps necessary to enforce its provisions upon operating agencies. It accordingly does not involve any new or inherently unacceptable principle for States which, like the United States, envisage private enterprise playing an important part in activities in space.

The modalities of authorisation and supervision may well differ from one type of space activity to another. The Declaration does not indicate how far an authorisation to a non-governmental entity may be of a general or continuing character or should normally be granted specially in respect of each individual launching. Two points emerge clearly: the State cannot devolve its responsibility for assuring that national activities are carried on at all times in conformity with the principles set forth in the Declaration, and it has an obligation of continuing supervision; the régime of authorisation may, it would seem, be of any nature which enables the State to fulfil effectively in respect of the activity in question these two obligations. A general delegation of authority in space matters to a body in the nature of the chartered companies of the early history of overseas exploration, trade and settlement would clearly be incompatible with these continuing obligations of the State.

Any such general delegation of authority to a foreign corporation, chartered in one country with financial resources furnished by private enterprise in another, on the analogy of flag of convenience shipping, would, it is submitted, be inconsistent with the obligations of both the chartering State and the State from which the financial resources were furnished by private enterprise. The chartering State could not reasonably plead that the activities undertaken were not "national" within the meaning of the responsibility for "national activities" provided for in the Declaration and would therefore have an obligation to retain the measure of control necessary to assure continuing compliance and permit continuing supervision. The State from which the financial resources were furnished could not divest itself of its responsibility by contending that activities financed (and probably organised and controlled) by its nationals cease to be "national activities" when chartered by another State. It would not, perhaps, be incompatible with the terms of the Declaration for it to permit its nationals to seek authorisation for space activities from another State, and situations may occur in which this happens, but any such arrangements would not, it is submitted, change the national character of such activities in such a manner as to discharge the State from which the necessary financial and technological resources are provided from its responsibility under the Declaration to ensure continuing compliance and continuing supervision. It may well be that the potential military implications of space activities will afford an adequate safeguard for some time to come against any complications of this kind being allowed to occur.

28

Activities in Space by International Organisations

THE Declaration of Legal Principles provides that "when activities are carried on in space by an international organisation, responsibility for compliance with the principles" set forth in the Declaration "shall be borne by the international organisation and by the States participating in it".[1]

The Institute of International Law resolution states less obliquely that the principles set forth therein "apply to space activities undertaken by States acting individually or collectively or by international organisations" and specifies that references to States contained therein "are to be construed as including a reference to international organisations, it being understood that the States members of an international organisation remain responsible for the space activities of the organisation".[1a] During the discussion of the Declaration of Legal Principles by the Committee on the Peaceful Uses of Outer Space immediately prior to its transmission to the General Assembly for adoption, comments on the position of international organisations under the Declaration were made by the representatives of the United States, the United Kingdom, France, Australia and Canada. The representative of the United States[1b] described the relevant provision as recognising "that States may sometimes conduct activities in space through an international organisation"; when they do so, "both the participating States and the international organisation itself bear responsibility for the activities undertaken" and this responsibility for compliance includes liability for damage; the principle "applies also where outer space activities are carried on by

[1] Para. 5.
[1a] Para. 15.
[1b] United Nations Document A/5349/Add.1 of November 27, 1963, pp. 7–8.

two or more States co-operatively, even if they do not act through a formally established international organisation". The Australian representative regarded the provision as "something in the nature of an interpretative clause applying to the whole of the Declaration".[2] The representative of the United Kingdom[3] concurred with the United States and Australian views that the reference to international organisations contained in the provision "is not limited in its operation to that principle, but is rather related to all the principles" set forth in the Declaration, which the United Kingdom would not regard "as prejudicing in any way the position of international organisations engaged in space activities"; further and more detailed provisions relating to international organisations would be particularly necessary when an agreement on liability was drafted. The French representative considered that paragraph 8, relating to liability, "must be interpreted in the light of the principle" of the responsibility of international organisations for their space activities enunciated in paragraph 5.[4] The Canadian representative regretted the absence of a specific reference to joint responsibility for co-operative activities by States not undertaken through international organisations.[5]

Only the richest and most powerful States can even attempt to "go it alone" in space; there are increasing indications that even they find the strain such as to make some sharing of the costs involved and experience acquired desirable and many of the potential gains from space activities can be secured only by broad based international co-operation. There are therefore major grounds of policy for facilitating participation in space activities through international organisations. Such participation is clearly in the general spirit of the recognition by the Declaration of Legal Principles of the "common interest of all mankind in the progress of the exploration and use of outer space for peaceful purposes", and the desire expressed therein to contribute to "broad international co-operation in the exploration and use of space" and thereby to "the development of mutual understanding" and "the strengthening of friendly

[2] *Ibid.*, p. 13.
[3] *Ibid.*, pp. 18–19.
[4] *Ibid.*, p. 17.
[5] *Ibid.*, p. 11.

relations between nations and peoples"; it constitutes a method of giving effect to the principle that "the exploration and use of outer space shall be carried on for the benefit and in the interests of all mankind".[6] Co-operative arrangements relating to space activities are becoming increasingly important in practice.[7]

It is still far from clear exactly how such co-operative arrangements will work when translated into practical application; some of them may prove to be primarily devices for reducing the overhead costs of activities in space which leave to individual States the operational responsibility for particular activities; others of them may involve collective activities the responsibility for which rests collectively with an international organisation of States. Activities of the second type may also prove to be desirable and possible as a means of depoliticising certain major advances in the exploration and use of space. In these circumstances it is of vital importance, both for the purpose of securing a reasonable distribution and balance of effective participation in activities in space (which may prove to be an increasingly important factor in maintaining a reasonable distribution and balance of political power on earth) and for the purpose of facilitating pooled action designed to depoliticise new developments, that the law of space should be so formulated as to treat international organisations of States and States alike for most purposes. There may be some respects in which for special reasons they should be treated differently, but space law should not start from an assumption comparable to the underlying assumption of the International Civil Aviation Convention that all aircraft are nationally operated. That assumption is increasingly inappropriate and inconvenient in respect of aviation and has no proper place in space law. This conclusion is submitted on the basis of the existing and probable facts concerning the respective contributions to activities in space of international organisations and States. It is not based on any ideological preconception that spacecraft must be identified with the Earth as a whole rather than with any particular nation or upon any assumption that a comprehensive international control of space has either been achieved or is probable. It implies nothing more than the recognition

[6] Para. 1.   [7] See pp. 74–86, above.

that some activities in space are likely to be undertaken by organisations of States rather than by individual States and that this probability must be reflected in the formulation of the law.

This general approach has a number of applications.

It implies, as we have already seen, that the principle that outer space and celestial bodies are free for exploration and use "by all States" does not exclude, but includes, freedom for exploration and use by international organisations.[8]

It implies that whatever arrangements may be developed for the registration of space objects should permit of international as well as national registration.[9]

It implies a most guarded approach to any suggestion that the concept of "nationality" should be applied to spacecraft.[10]

It implies a need for careful examination of the problems involved in the development of space activities subject to international rather than national jurisdiction and control.

It implies that the responsibility for securing compliance with the principles set forth in the Declaration, and such other international arrangements as may be applicable, may rest upon an international organisation.

It implies, as was emphasised during the discussion preceding the adoption of the Declaration, that liability for a space vehicle accident may rest upon an international organisation.[11]

It is only in respect of responsibility for compliance that the Declaration defines specifically the position of international organisations. It provides that "when activities are carried on in outer space by an international organisation, responsibility for compliance with the principles set forth in this Declaration shall be borne by the international organisation and by the States participating in it".[12] This is perhaps a happier formula than that used in the Institute of International Law resolution that "the States members of an international organisation remain responsible for the space activities of the organisation", but it is not believed that there is any difference of substantive meaning between the

---

[8] p. 196, above.   [9] pp. 223–224, below.   [10] p. 236, below.
[11] pp. 284–285, below.   [12] Para. 3.

two formulations of the principle. Neither formula implies that international organisations are to be regarded as States, or as being equivalent to States, for any other purposes; neither formula involves any expression of view on the general question of the extent to which States may be responsible for the acts of international organisations of which they are members. The matter is dealt with only in the special context of a case in respect of which it is generally agreed that international organisations of States and States should be treated alike, but in which it is reasonable that third parties should not lose any rights against the States participating in action in space by reason of the States participating in such action having acted through an international organisation. General questions relating to the status of international organisations in international law are therefore not prejudiced in any way.

29

Co-operation and Mutual Assistance in Space

THE Declaration of Legal Principles affirms the general principle that "in the exploration and use of outer space, States shall be guided by the principle of co-operation and mutual assistance and shall conduct all their activities in outer space with due regard for the corresponding interests of other States".[1] This principle is enunciated not as a moral or political maxim but as a legal principle. Some of its implications are spelled out more fully in the Declaration. The Declaration itself links directly to this principle the obligation of appropriate international consultation before proceeding with any activity or experiment liable to cause potentially harmful interference with the activities of other States in the peaceful exploration and use of outer space. The same principle underlies the concept of freedom "for exploration and use by all States on a basis of equality",[2] the obligation of assuring that national and international activities are carried out in accordance with the provisions of the Declaration,[3] and the provisions of the Declaration relating to the return of space objects,[4] liability for damage,[5] and assistance to and repatriation of astronauts.[6] It also lies at the root of the mutual obligations of States in respect of telecommunications,[7] space cluttering,[8] and contamination of and from space. How much wider an application the principle may prove to have remains to be determined by experience.

[1] Para. 6.
[2] Chapter 23, above.
[3] Chaps. 27 and 28, above.
[4] Chap. 38, below.
[5] Chap. 52, below.
[6] Chap. 39, below.
[7] Chap. 40, below.
[8] Chap. 52, below.

30

Notification and Registration of Launchings

THE original rules governing the notification of launchings were IGY rules embodied in the *IGY Manual of Rockets and Satellites*[1] which, though neither legally binding nor fully effective, provided a framework for international co-operation. These rules were revised for continuing use by COSPAR in May 1962 and reissued as the *COSPAR Guide to Rocket and Satellite Information and Data Exchange*, accompanied by *Unified Synoptic Codes for Rapid Communication of Satellite Orbital Data*.[2] While not technically constituting a legal obligation, these arrangements are the *de facto* basis of the international interchange among scientists of space data. They are supplemented but not replaced by General Assembly Resolution 1721 (XVI) of December 20, 1961, which requests the Committee on the Peaceful Uses of Outer Space, in co-operation with the Secretary-General, "to provide for the exchange of such information relating to outer space activities as Governments may supply on a voluntary basis, supplementing but not duplicating existing technical and scientific interchanges".[3]

The successive proposals for the demilitarisation of space submitted to the Ten Nation and Eighteen Nation Disarmament Committees during the period from 1960 to 1962[4] have provided for advance notification of launchings and pre-launch inspections but no obligation of this nature has been accepted. Notification therefore continues to be a matter of recognised good practice and not of legal obligation. The *COSPAR Guide* deals guardedly with the question of advance notification and there is no provision for pre-launch inspection.

[1] See pp. 31–32, above and *Annals of the International Geophysical Year*, Vol. VI, pp. 465–472.　　　　[2] *COSPAR Information Bulletin*, No. 9, July 1962, pp. 4–42.
[3] Para. 3 (b).　　　　　　　　　　　　　　[4] pp. 46–51, above.

The COSPAR rules are nevertheless important as the basis of the international interchange of space data. Their importance is implicitly recognised by General Assembly Resolution 1721 (XVI) of December 20, 1961, which specifies that the exchange of information through the United Nations Committee on the Peaceful Uses of Outer Space should supplement but not duplicate "existing scientific and technical exchanges".

The *COSPAR Guide*[5] specifies that "in view of the scientific value to be obtained by the maximum participation of scientists throughout the world in space research programmes, technical information will be provided to COSPAR for distribution to COSPAR adherents well in advance of launch in at least those cases where such participation is feasible;" particulars of the pre-launch information desired are indicated; it will be observed that these provisions concerning pre-launch information are expressed as a *desideratum* rather than as a requirement. Within a few hours after successful launching of a satellite or space probe, an abbreviated launching announcement suitable for brief radio broadcast and further specified details are to be distributed in plain language by Spacewarn (a network of Satellite Regional Warning Centres for rapid communication of satellite information with centres at Darmstadt, Moscow, Slough, Tokyo and Washington); this information is also to be distributed promptly by regularly used channels of public information. All satellites and space probes which have a lifetime of at least ninety minutes and which require a designation for scientific purposes are to be numbered as indicated in the Guide. Orbital elements, including specified particulars of indicated accuracies, are to be distributed periodically by the launching station via Spacewarn and supplemented by the direct supply of station predictions from compiling centres to the appropriate stations. Special arrangements are envisaged between launching authorities and specialised stations which can achieve useful results in tracking deep space probes. Descriptive experimental information is to be furnished to COSPAR within a few weeks after launching; reports of experimental results, including an adequate

[5] Extracts from the text of the *Guide* are reproduced in Appendix VIII, pp. 393–402, below.

description of the instrumentation involved, are to be published in scientific literature of general availability beginning as soon as possible after each launching, and thereafter promptly as they become available. Information and data are exchanged through World Data Centres for Rockets and Satellites at Washington, Moscow and Slough.

The *COSPAR Guide* is accompanied by Unified Synoptic Codes for rapid communication of satellite orbital data.[6] These specify the format of Spacewarn messages, give models of launching announcements, contain codes for the communication of modified orbital elements for prediction purposes (SATOR), of the ephemeris for optical observations at individual stations (SATAT) and of reports of tracking observations (SATEV), and list code numbers of optical tracking stations.

Without constituting legal obligations, the provisions of the *COSPAR Guide* establish the framework of scientific co-operation in space.

Whereas the *COSPAR Guide* provides for notification, the United Nations, approaching the problem in legal rather than scientific terms, has provided for registration. There is no provision in the Declaration of Legal Principles requiring in terms either registration by the launching state in a national register or registration by it with an international body, but General Assembly Resolution 1721 (XVI) B of December 20, 1961, "calls upon states launching objects into orbit or beyond to furnish information promptly to the Committee on the Peaceful Uses of Outer Space through the Secretary General for the registration of launchings"[7] and "requests the Secretary General to maintain a public registry of the information" so furnished.[8] The Secretary General has maintained such a register since March 7, 1962. In communicating to the Secretary General on behalf of the United States information to open the registry, Ambassador Adlai Stevenson wrote that "the establishment of such a registry marks another step forward in the direction of open and orderly conduct of outer space activities".[9] The existence of such a register is indeed of crucial importance. The first step towards any effective legal regulation of happenings in space is the

[6] *COSPAR Information Bulletin*, No. 9, July 1962, pp. 15–42.
[7] Para. 1.
[8] Para. 2.
[9] United Nations Document A/AC.105/Inf.1 of March 7, 1962.

existence of some authentic record of what and who is presumed to be there. Apart from being an important element in military security, such a record is the necessary point of departure for determining jurisdiction over spacecraft and extra-terrestrial stations, establishing responsibility for space operations, maintaining orderly space telecommunications, applying rules for mutual assistance and for the repatriation of astronauts and return of space objects, and imputing liability for injury, loss or damage or for space contamination. The General Assembly resolution, while requesting the Secretary-General to maintain a public registry, does not attempt to define classes of objects which should be, or need not be, registered, to give any further precision to the concept that particulars shall be furnished "promptly", or to specify the particulars which should accompany registrations. Questions have already arisen in regard to the types of launching which should be registered and the amount of information which should be given. The United States originally registered only information "concerning objects launched into sustained orbit or beyond";[10] subsequently it modified its practice by supplying information concerning space vehicles which had achieved orbit but were no longer in orbit when the information was supplied and space vehicles which had failed to achieve orbit.[11] There is no uniformity between the information registered by the United States and that registered by the U.S.S.R. The United States normally furnishes for objects in orbit particulars of the international designation, the launch vehicle, the satellite category, the date of launch, the nodal period, the inclination in degrees and the apogee and perigee in kilometres; these particulars are now furnished as of the 15th and last day of each month. The U.S.S.R. normally registers information consisting of the number, name and purpose of each space object, with the date of launching, the perigee and apogee in kilometres and the inclination in degrees;[12] there is no fixed periodicity in the supply of the information. One can conceive that there might well be further variations of practice with an increase in the number of States furnishing

[10] A/AC.105/INF.1 of March 7, 1962.
[11] A/AC.105/INF.7 of June 1, 1962.
[12] A/AC.105/INF.2 of March 24, 1962

information for registration. Such a situation, in which it is left to States to give such details as they think fit of objects they have launched into orbit or beyond, can hardly be regarded as satisfactory. It would seem logical that if provision is made for the registration of objects launched into orbit or beyond, agreement should be reached on the details to be given. The Institute of International Law resolution provides that "every launching of a space object shall be registered by the State under the authority of which the launching took place with the United Nations or a special body to be created" and that "the registration shall be effected promptly and with particulars to be agreed". Such an obligation to give agreed particulars when registering a launching would not, of course, imply any obligation to give advance notification of launchings, as the existence of such an obligation involves other issues closely related to the control of armaments. Registration regulations covering these matters would therefore appear to be desirable. Despite obvious differences in their nature they might be similar in legal form to the Treaty Registration Regulations adopted by the General Assembly in pursuance of Article 102 of the Charter on December 14, 1946.[13] As rules governing the registry they would derive their authority from adoption of a General Assembly resolution; such a resolution could not, of course, place upon States an obligation equivalent to Article 102 of the Charter, but it could recommend States to comply with the regulations and, if such a recommendation proved inadequate, negotiations could subsequently be undertaken for the conclusion of an international agreement embodying firm obligations in the matter. Like the Treaty Registration Regulations, the proposed Launching Registration Regulations should apply to international organisations of States as well as to States but without any distinction between "registration" and "filing and recording".

The responsibility for registration should clearly rest in the first instance with the launching State or organisation of States primarily because the responsibility derives from the fact of launching but also for the practical reason that only the launching State or organisation of States is likely to be able to furnish promptly the particulars which

[13] *United Nations Treaty Series*, Vo. I, pp. 20–30.

should accompany registration. It is, however, desirable that the register should be as complete as possible, and some provision for adding to it, with whatever particulars may be available, information from other sources concerning space objects found to be in orbit or beyond which have not been registered by the launching State or organisation of States would also appear to be desirable.

The need for further consideration of the question of registration was recognised when the Declaration of Legal Principles was adopted. During the discussion of the Declaration by the Committee on the Peaceful Uses of Outer Space immediately prior to its transmission to the General Assembly for adoption the representative of the United Kingdom pointed out[14] that, while the provision of the Declaration relating to jurisdiction and control over space objects refers to "the State on whose registry an object launched into outer space is carried",[15] the Declaration itself "does not make any provision for registration" and gave this as an illustration of the range of matters which "will subsequently need to be considered in much more detail". While registration with the United Nations had already been provided for by General Assembly Resolution 1721 (XVI)B of December 20, 1961, there is no corresponding international provision for national registration. The existence of a system of national registry is, however, presumed by the reference in the Declaration to jurisdiction and control over space objects being retained by "the State on whose registry an object launched into outer space is carried".[16]

These general provisions concerning notification and registration may be expected to be supplemented by special arrangements relating to launchings in particular areas.[17]

[14] United Nations Document A/5549/Add.1 of November 27, 1963, p. 19.
[15] Para. 7.
[16] Para. 7.
[17] See Chap. 33, below.

3 I

Marks and Signals of Identification

THE Declaration of Legal Principles does not contain any provision that space objects shall bear marks and use signals of identification; the only clause bearing upon the subject is the provision that, when space objects or component parts thereof are found beyond the limits of the State of registry, that State "shall furnish identifying data upon request prior to return".[1] The Institute of International Law resolution provides that "every space object shall bear marks of identification showing its origin and use call signals making it possible to identify the State under the authority of which the launching took place",[2] the primary purpose of a mark being to facilitate the identification of a space object on its return to earth, whereas the call signal is designed to facilitate identification while in orbit or flight.

Such a rule is, of course, practicable only if the term "space object" is reasonably defined; it would be unreasonable to expect an identifying mark on a component part or fragment not intended to be detached from the space object or on débris. Reasonably understood, such a provision appears desirable. The matter may have been of limited importance while only two States have had the launching capacity necessary to place objects in orbit and beyond; during this phase each of these States has been able to presume that any space object not launched by it was launched by the other, and space objects launched by either have been readily identifiable as of its own manufacture; mistaken identification by third parties has been possible but no mistake of identity was likely as between space powers. This situation will inevitably change as launching capacity and facilities are more widely distributed and space

---

[1] Para. 7.   [2] Para. 4.

objects of the same manufacture, or including components of the same manufacture, are launched by or on behalf of different States. The identification of space objects may then become a real problem. Ships, aircraft and motor vehicles are all required by international practice and regulations to bear identifying marks and ships and aircraft to use identifying signals in defined circumstances; a similar requirement in respect of space objects is both reasonable and necessary.

32

Sounding Rocket Facilities

———————————

EXPERIMENTS with high altitude sounding rockets were the starting
point of space programmes. They continue to be important in the most
advanced space programmes as a source of information concerning
levels of the atmosphere above the ceiling for balloons and below the
height at which satellites can orbit; they still constitute the whole or the
greater part of the immediate space programmes of the majority of
countries having such programmes; and they are possible only within a
limited radius from points where appropriate facilities exist. It is therefore not surprising that the creation and operation of international
sounding rocket launching facilities should have been one of the first
questions to be considered by the Scientific and Technical Sub-Committee of the United Nations Committee on the Peaceful Uses of
Outer Space.[1] The principles governing United Nations sponsorship of
such facilities formulated by the Committee are therefore important
both in themselves and as an indication of some of the conditions which
may be applicable to any more ambitious launching facilities which
may subsequently be placed under United Nations sponsorship or
control.

The Committee on the Peaceful Uses of Outer Space envisaged a
"broad Charter" for the creation and operation of international sounding rocket launching facilities on the lines of the following basic
principles:

"(i) Each sounding rocket launching facility would be the responsibility
of the country ('Host State') within whose territory the facility is
located.

[1] pp. 58–59, above.

(ii) A launching site would be recognised as an international facility if the United Nations Committee on the Peaceful Uses of Outer Space, on considering each case, so recommends, and if the facility conforms to the principles established.

(iii) The sounding rocket launching facility would be used only for peaceful scientific experiments.

(iv) The facilities recommended at the site would be indicated by the United Nations Committee on the Peaceful Uses of Outer Space with such advice as it may deem useful.

(v) The Host State would be responsible for making working agreements with user nations for the provision, through voluntary agreements, of funds or equipment, or both, for the required facilities.

(vi) Operating costs would be apportioned to the users on an equitable basis.

(vii) Complete information about all facilities and experiments at the site would be available to scientists and technicians of all Member States. The latter would have the right to inspect these, subject, of course, to safety and operational requirements.

(viii) Results obtained from experiments would be made available through publication in scientific periodicals openly available to all.

(ix) The objectives and the tentative schedules of the experiments to be conducted at an international launching site must be previously announced to the United Nations Committee on the Peaceful Uses of Outer Space, COSPAR, and users.

(x) For launchings conducted at the facility, data on the experiments, schedules and firings would be reported by host and user States both to the United Nations Committee on the Peaceful Uses of Outer Space and to COSPAR.

(xi) The Host State would report periodically to the United Nations Committee on the Peaceful Uses of Outer Space on the operations and use of the sounding rocket launching facility. Continued United Nations sponsorship of the facility would depend upon annual endorsement by the Committee.

(xii) An advisory panel composed of scientific representatives of the user States shall be associated with the launching facility to advise on the implementation and scheduling of projects proposed by scientists and on training programmes.

(xiii) The Host State would be responsible for management and operation of the range, including matters of range safety, scheduling, staffing, housekeeping, and basic transportation at the site.

These "basic principles" were endorsed by the General Assembly by resolution 1802 (XVIII) of December 14, 1962. Stripped of technicalities they involve five major points: management and operation are the responsibility of the host State; facilities are to be used only for peaceful scientific experiments; operating costs are to be equitably apportioned among users; the scientific results are to be openly available to all; objectives and tentative schedules are to be previously announced. United Nations sponsorship of a facility involves co-operative arrangements in which the host State, user States, an advisory panel of scientific representatives of user States and the United Nations Committee on the Peaceful Uses of Outer Space all play defined parts; continued United Nations sponsorship depends upon annual endorsement by the Committee. In course of time the "basic principles" may be expected to be supplemented by such special agreements both between the United Nations and host States and between host States and user States as may be required.

The first United Nations-sponsored facility is in process of establishment at Thumba, South India, and a second is projected at Natal, Brazil.

33

Launching and Recovery Facilities

Where the launching and recovery of space objects is undertaken in circumstances involving the use on any significant scale, of the territory, territorial waters or airspace of another state an agreement providing for launching and recovery facilities will generally be desirable.

Launching and recovery facility agreements may be concluded between two or more States, between one or more States and one or more international organisations, or between one or more States and/ or one or more international organisations and one or more satellite operating companies.

A relatively simple type of agreement between States is represented by the agreements between the United States and the United Kingdom in respect of the Bahamas and the Turk and Caicos Islands[1] concerning the Flight Testing Range of the Bahamas Long-Range Proving Ground. As amended to include flights of space objects[2] these agreements grant the Government of the United States the right to "launch, fly and land" such objects; the contracting Governments are to take all reasonable precautions against possible dangers and damage resulting from operations under the Agreement; the rights granted are not to be "exercised unreasonably or so as to interfere with or to prejudice the safety of navigation, aviation, or communication within the Flight Testing Range" but "in a spirit of good neighbourliness between the Governments concerned", the details of their practical application being "arranged by friendly co-operation". Provisions of this nature represent the minimum content of such an agreement which may also con-

[1] pp. 82–83, above.
[2] In 1959.

tain provisions concerning[3] the sites and facilities to be provided, rights of way, telecommunications, jurisdictional arrangements, security and other matters.

Arrangements for launching facilities at Woomera, Australia, have been negotiated between the European Launcher Development Organisation, the Governments of the Members thereof, and the Government of Australia.

The United States Communications Satellite Act[4] of 1962 envisages the purchase by the Communications Satellite Corporation of launching and related services from the United States Government; provision for these will presumably be made by some appropriate form of agreement.

More complex types of launching and recovery facility agreements may therefore be expected to be developed as the number of parties involved increases and the range of satellite and deep space operations extends. One of the questions which may be increasingly dealt with in such agreements is that of the respective responsibilities and rights of indemnification against each other of the launcher and any State, international organisation or company on behalf of which the satellite is launched. When a space object is to be launched on behalf of a non-governmental entity there will presumably be included in such an agreement the conditions and guarantees necessary to enable the State or international organisation responsible to fulfil its obligation under paragraph 5 of the Declaration of Legal Principles to assure compliance with the principles set forth in the Declaration and exercise continuing supervision.

[3] Concerning the other provisions of the Agreements see pp. 82–83, above.
[4] pp. 88–91, above.

34

Passage through Airspace

THOUGH there appears to be no authoritative pronouncement on the subject, the right of passage through airspace *en route* to or from outer space must be presumed on grounds of general principle to be subject to the consent of the subjacent State.

Where the question is likely to arise with any frequency a passage agreement, granting the right of passage and containing any necessary provisions concerning the advance notification of launchings and of expected re-entry arrangements, will presumably be concluded between the States immediately concerned. If a joint control of the upper airspace, such as Eurocontrol, is applicable to the airspace of one of the parties, the control authority will be a necessary party to any such passage agreement. Questions of demarcation could conceivably arise in connection with the negotiation of passage agreements, but it would seem undesirable to conclude such agreements, which have a quite limited purpose, in terms liable to prejudice wider questions.

Passage through the airspace of another State without its consent, whether deliberate or resulting from miscalculation or misfire, would appear to constitute a violation of the territorial sovereignty of that State within the meaning of the principle stated by the International Court of Justice in the *Corfu Channel (Merits) Case* that "respect for territorial sovereignty is an essential foundation of international relations".[1] There would, however, appear, likewise on grounds of general principle, to be an exception for cases of proved *force majeure* on re-entry from space; planned re-entry on the territory of a foreign State would not qualify as *force majeure* for the purpose of the exception.

[1] [1949] I.C.J., 35.

We must not, however, overlook the possibility that the present law relating to passage through airspace may prove to be a phase of development rather than definitive. As I have ventured to say elsewhere the principle of the sovereignty of each State over the airspace above its territory "may become increasingly unreal as greater use is made of the upper airspace" and "the present law relating to sovereignty over airspace, while well established at the present time, may be regarded by future generations much as we regard the claims to maritime sovereignty which were more or less successfully asserted for several hundreds of years before Grotius and Bynkershoeck established the principle of the freedom of the seas".[1]

[1] *The Common Law of Mankind*, 1958, p. 389.

35

Tracking

SPACE objects are tracked visually, optically and by radar and radio and infra-red systems; tracking may be limited to keeping track of the whereabouts of the space object; it may include telemetry read-out of data from the space object.

As every State has a legitimate interest in knowing what is in space, every State is entitled to track all objects in space as fully as the resources at its disposal allow; the right to track includes that of receiving, but not that of triggering, telemetry read-out.

The curvature and rotation of the earth and the geographical distribution of the territories of launching States and of the land masses of the Earth make it impossible for any State to track continuously any space object with the exception of a satellite in stationary orbit at an altitude of 22,300 miles; a continuous telemetric record can be received through one station only by the use of memory devices which transmit on telecommand. International co-operation in tracking and the reception of telemetry read-out is therefore a matter of the utmost practical importance. Such co-operation involves three elements, the availability of orbital information to tracking facilities, the availability of such facilities, and the co-operation of such facilities in the exchange of information.

The general obligation of States to be guided in their space activities by the principle of co-operation and mutual assistance[1] does not involve a firm obligation of co-operation in any particular arrangements for the tracking of space objects but suggests the desirability of appropriate measures of co-operation in tracking.

[1] Para. 6 of the Declaration of Legal Principles.

The existing arrangements for the purpose comprise arrangements for the exchange of information and data through COSPAR, direct arrangements between launching authorities and specialised stations designed for or, as in the case of Jodrell Bank, capable of, tracking, and agreements between governments relating to the establishment and operation of tracking stations. The registration with the United Nations of objects launched into orbit and beyond and the registration with ITU of space radio stations also have some bearing on the matter.

The *COSPAR Guide to Rocket and Satellite Information* provides for the rapid communication through the Spacewarn network or directly of the information required for tracking, including launching announcements and particulars of orbital elements,[2] and of tracking observations.

Agreements relating to the establishment and operation of tracking stations have been concluded by the United States with a number of countries, including the United Kingdom;[3] they provide for varying relationships between the United States and the other country concerned in the degree of responsibility assumed by each for the installation and maintenance of the station. A provision for the exchange between the parties of the scientific data acquired through the operation of a tracking station is a normal feature of such agreements; the United States–United Kingdom agreement provides that such data shall be exchanged "promptly and in their entirety".

The United Nations Registry of Space Objects contains certain orbital information, but this is of a somewhat general character. The ITU Radio Regulations, as amended in 1963, require the communication to the International Frequency Registration Board and publication of orbital information concerning space radio stations.[4]

[2] pp. 395–397, above.　　[3] pp. 83–85, above and 375–378, below.
[4] p. 338, below.

36

Jurisdiction Over Objects Launched

THE Declaration of Legal Principles provides that "the State on whose registry an object launched into space is carried shall retain jurisdiction and control over such object, and any personnel thereon, while in outer space".[1] This, as we have seen,[2] is the only reference in the Declaration to space objects being carried on the register of a State and further clarification of the position in cases in which there may be doubt which State is responsible and entitled to jurisdiction and control will be necessary.

It seems doubtful whether it is necessary to introduce for this purpose the concept of the space object having a nationality, but if the concept were to be used it would be necessary to have an equivalent concept to define the status of space objects on the register of an international organisation of States. Neither maritime law nor aviation law has yet accommodated itself to the need for an international flag[3] and international registration for internationally-operated vessels and aircraft; it would be an obvious mistake to use the old mould for the development of space law. All that appears to be necessary is that every space object should be registered and that on the basis of such registration responsibility for it should rest with a determined State or international organisation of States having jurisdiction and control over it.

A space object may of course have an existence quite distinct from that of the original launching mechanism and there may in such cases be a question on whose register the object should be carried. The

---

[1] Para. 7.
[2] p. 224, above.
[3] Art. 7 of the 1958 Geneva Convention on the High Seas is perhaps the first swallow but not yet proof of springtime.

Declaration of Legal Principles leaves this question unresolved. The Institute of International Law resolution accepts the principle that it is preferable, at least at the present stage, to regard the launching authority as remaining responsible for space objects launched by it, leaving the launching authority and the authority operating the space object to work out between themselves some arrangement whereby the latter will indemnify the former if the former has to bear the responsibility for some activity of the space object.

Pending some further clarification of the matter we may assume that the State concerned has been identified and proceed on the basis of this assumption to consider what is included in the "jurisdiction and control" which, in accordance with the Declaration of Legal Principles, it retains.

The first question which arises is whether there are any preliminary conditions to be fulfilled before the State of registry can claim jurisdiction and control. The Institute of International Law resolution specifies that "every space object launched in accordance with the foregoing provisions shall remain subject to the jurisdiction of the State under the authority of which it was launched",[4] the "foregoing provisions" include requirements concerning compliance with the applicable international rules, prompt registration with the United Nations or a special body to be created, and the use of marks and signals of identification. The Declaration of Legal Principles does not specify any such conditions to be fulfilled by the claimant to jurisdiction and control.

There is clearly an advantage of simplicity and certainty in refraining from imposing any such conditions. A space object which complies with the applicable international rules today may, as the result of some defect of operation, cease to comply with them tomorrow. There will always be an interval between launching and registration and it may be an arguable matter whether the registration has been "prompt" within the meaning of the requirement. Whether identifying marks have been used will not be known until the object has been recovered and it may fail to transmit an identifying signal by reason of a failure of equipment or power. On balance, therefore, the unqualified rule

[4] Para. 5.

stated by the Declaration of Legal Principles appears to be preferable as a point of departure to the more cautious formation of the Institute of International Law resolution. It is, however, a point of departure which will call for some qualification as the law develops.

The "jurisdiction and control" of the State on whose registry the space object is carried clearly implies that no other State is entitled to interfere, by electronic or other means, with its normal operation. The only general principle in the matter which would appear to be workable is that no State is entitled to telecommand, divert or destroy space objects not subject to its jurisdiction, except by agreement, for good cause in circumstances brooking no delay for further consultation, or for good cause after failure to secure agreement by consultation.

The "jurisdiction and control" of the State on whose registry the space object is carried also clearly includes the applicability to the space object, and occurrences thereon, of the law of the State of registry, in the same manner in which occurrences on board a ship are governed by the law of the flag. Disciplinary authority is vested in the captain of a spacecraft in the same manner in which it is vested in the master of a vessel or the pilot of an aircraft.

There would appear to be two main limitations on the jurisdiction over a space object of the State on the registry of which it is carried.

The space object may enter the territorial jurisdiction (including the airspace within the territorial jurisdiction) of another State either while remaining operational or in distress. While within such jurisdiction it would appear to be subject to the local law with a probable exception (the scope of which remains to be defined) for matters internal to the space object.

More difficult problems are presented by the question of the extent to which and manner in which States may for good cause interfere, by electronic or other means, with the activities in space of other States (or possibly organisations of States) for the purpose of self-protection against interference from space with matters within their territorial jurisdiction or for any other reason. What constitutes good cause for such interference it will not be easy to define, and any clear agreement on the matter seems improbable until substantial progress has been made in dealing with the problem of the demilitarisation of space. Pending agreement on the matter only the most extraordinary emergency would justify interference which, prima facie, would be a violation of the provision that the State of registry retains jurisdiction and control; any such interference should, it is submitted, be reported immediately to the Security Council with particulars of the circumstances alleged to justify it.

The Declaration of Legal Principles deals on the same footing with jurisdiction and control over space objects and jurisdiction and control over any personnel thereon. The Institute of International Law resolution deals separately with jurisdiction over persons in connection with space installations;[5] it does not refer to personnel on any space object which is not regarded as a space installation.

[5] Para. 6.

37

Ownership of Objects Launched

THE Declaration of Legal Principles provides that "ownership of objects launched into outer space, and of their component parts, is not affected by their passage through outer space or by their return to the Earth".[1] This principle establishes that neither the launching of a space object nor its return to Earth within the jurisdiction of another State makes it a derelict on the ground that the launcher has lost ownership by losing control.

The principle does not appear to imply that a space object can never become a derelict and thereby subject to appropriation by a third party. One can conceive of circumstances in which the only reasonable course would be to regard the space object as having become derelict, for instance if the launcher has disclaimed any interest in it, or has made no attempt to recover it over a long period of time. But whatever the effect of disclaimer of interest or prescription may be, passage through space and return to Earth outside the control of the launcher does not in itself affect the ownership of the space object. A space object or component part thereof launched from one country and recovered in another therefore remains the property of the launcher; similarly, such an object placed in orbit or in space does not thereby become derelict.

The principle does not preclude the owner from transferring the ownership of a space object while it is in space; nor has it any bearing on the question whether anything in the nature of real property can be acquired on a celestial body.[2]

[1] Para. 7.
[2] See Chap. 57, below.

38

Return of Space Objects

THE Declaration of Legal Principles provides that objects launched into outer space, and component parts thereof, "found beyond the limits of the State of registry" shall "be returned to that State, which shall furnish identifying data upon request prior to return".[1] During the discussion of the Declaration by the Committee on the Peaceful Uses of Outer Space immediately prior to its transmission to the General Assembly for adoption, the United States representative emphasised that this provision, like the other parts of the draft, "is a broad statement of general principles" which "does not seek to cover every conceivable situation" and "does not contain details for precise application"; these would require further study and elaboration in subsequent instruments.[2] The Japanese representative took the view that the obligation to return a space object or component part thereof landing on the territory of a non-launching State was reasonable only if prior registration or notification had been given of the launching of that object together with adequate information about it.[3] General Assembly Resolution 1963 (XVIII) of December 13, 1963, requests the Committee on the Peaceful Uses of Outer Space to arrange as a matter of priority for the prompt preparation of a draft international agreement on the return of space vehicles. Such an agreement is also envisaged by the Institute of International Law resolution which provides that "appropriate measures shall be agreed upon for the return to the State under the authority of which the launching took place of space objects the launching of which

[1] Para. 7.
[2] United Nations Document A/5549/Add.1 of November 27, 1963, p. 8.
[3] *Ibid.*, p. 25.

241

has been officially notified, which bear identification marks showing their origin, and which on return to Earth have come into the possession of another State".[4]

The Legal Sub-Committee of the Committee on the Peaceful Uses of Outer Space reached tentative agreement in October 1964 on certain provisions concerning the return of space objects.[5] These specify that a contracting party which receives information or discovers that a space object or any component part thereof has landed in territory under the jurisdiction of the contracting party, or on the high seas or in any other place not under the jurisdiction of any State shall do its utmost immediately to notify the State which announced the launching and shall immediately notify the Secretary-General of the United Nations. They lay down special rules concerning space objects of a hazardous or deleterious nature: a contracting party which finds that a space object or any part thereof discovered in territory under its jurisdiction or recovered by it elsewhere is of a hazardous or deleterious nature may so notify the State which announced the launching, which shall thereupon take prompt and effective steps, under the direction and control of the contracting party, to recover the object or part thereof and to remove it from territory under the jurisdiction of the contracting party or otherwise render it harmless; if a space object or any part thereof which has landed on territory under the jurisdiction of a contracting party may to the knowledge of the State which announced the launching be of a hazardous or deleterious nature, the State which announced the launching shall immediately so notify the contracting party and, if the contracting party so requests, shall take prompt and effective steps under its direction and control to recover the object or part thereof and to remove it from territory under the jurisdiction of the contracting party or otherwise render it harmless. The agreed provisions also deal with the provision of identifying data and co-operation in recovery and return operations. The State which announced the launching of a space object and has requested its return shall, if requested by the contracting party which has discovered the

---

[4] Para. 9.
[5] For the text see Appendix XII below.

object or any part thereof in territory under its jurisdiction or has recovered the object or part elsewhere, furnish identifying data to the contracting party. If a contracting party considers that the assistance of the State which announced the launching of the space object concerned would contribute substantially to the effectiveness of recovery or return operations carried out by it in territory under its jurisdiction, it shall request the State which announced the launching to co-operate with it with a view to the effective conduct of such operations, under the direction and control of that contracting party.

As of October 1964 no agreement had been reached concerning the extent of the obligation to return space objects, any conditions limiting the obligation, the existence or otherwise of a lien for damage caused, the reimbursement of expenses incurred, or the modalities of return of a space object launched by an international organisation.

The conclusion of the international agreement envisaged by the General Assembly therefore remains in abeyance pending the outcome of further negotiation on these matters.

Pending such an agreement, and in respect of States not parties thereto, the position is, it is submitted, as follows:

The obligation to return space objects exists independently of the agreement which is envisaged to define its extent and modalities. It flows from the principle stated unconditionally by the Declaration that "ownership of objects launched into outer space and of their component parts, is not affected by their passage through outer space or by their return to Earth".

The condition that the State requesting return must furnish identifying data is likewise independent of any agreement specifying the data to be furnished. The Declaration requires such data to be furnished when the request is made, whereas the Institute of International Law resolution limits the obligation of return to space objects bearing identifying marks; this should, it is submitted, be regarded as the normal case, but other identifying data should be acceptable in respect of component parts or fragments not intended to be detached and in respect of débris.

The Declaration does not specify that the obligation is one of prompt

243

return, but this may be implied subject to the term being reasonably understood.

Liability for the expense of return, and for any expenses of retrieval prior to return, should clearly fall upon the State requesting return of the space object.

It is submitted that a lien on whatever has returned from space for any injury, loss or damage which it has caused should also be recognised. Governments may be reluctant to return a space object in respect of which a claim for injury, loss or damage is known to be pending or probable until the claim has been settled or abandoned, or liability in respect of any damages awarded in respect thereof accepted, and a recognised principle governing the matter is therefore desirable.

One can assume that governments will in practice learn what they can from space objects which come into their possession; to minimise the probability of controversy in the matter it would seem desirable to acknowledge a right of inspection prior to return subject to the right being exercised promptly and in such a manner as to avoid destroying the value of scientific data or deterioration of valuable equipment.

Greater difficulty arises in respect of a space object which has been used for a purpose regarded by the State into whose possession it comes as illegal. The proposal on the subject made by the U.S.S.R. to the Committee on the Peaceful Uses of Outer Space contained a provision that "space vehicles aboard which devices have been discovered for the collection of intelligence information in the territory of another State shall not be returned". At this point the question of the return of space objects for peaceful and scientific purposes tends to merge into that of the demilitarisation of space. It would seem undesirable that progress in the one field should remain impossible pending progress in the other. The proposed rule would hardly be appropriate in respect of space devices designed to record and diffuse intelligence information as part of an agreed international plan for mutual protection against surprise attack, the discontinuance of nuclear weapon tests, the demilitarisation of space, or general and controlled disarmament. On the other hand, it is hardly realistic to expect one of two States the political relations between which are strained to accept an obligation to return to the other devices for the collection of intelligence information. Even if the devices are no longer the bearers of such information there are certain limitations to the measure of mutual co-operation which governments can enforce upon interests and opinion averse to or sceptical of such co-operation. The obligation to return space objects should therefore be regarded as being without prejudice to the separate consideration in an appropriate context of military and intelligence matters, but with the distinct understanding that space objects launched in pursuance of co-operative telecommunication, meteorological or other plans are not regarded as military.

39

Assistance to and Repatriation of Astronauts

THE Declaration of Legal Principles formulates three principles concerning astronauts. States are to regard astronauts as envoys of mankind in outer space. States are to render astronauts all possible assistance in the event of accident, distress or emergency landing on the territory of a foreign State or on the high seas. Astronauts who make such a landing are to be safely and promptly returned to the State of registry of their space vehicle.[1] The Institute of International Law resolution provides that States shall take appropriate measures for mutual assistance among astronauts, mutual assistance among States on behalf of astronauts in need of assistance, and prompt repatriation of astronauts after any emergency landing or rescue.[2]

The implications of the concept, expressed in the Declaration as a "legal principle", that "States shall regard astronauts as envoys of mankind in outer space" are not immediately apparent and will call for elucidation by experience. Three of the terms used in this expression may require further clarification; astronauts are described as "envoys", as envoys "of mankind", and as envoys of mankind "in outer space". The term "envoy" has been used in international law with meanings as varied as a diplomatic envoy and a bearer of a flag of truce; it therefore has little precise content but such content as it has always includes an element of inviolability; how much more it includes would appear to depend on the status and mission of the envoy and all the attendant circumstances. Presumably an "envoy of mankind" can act as such only on behalf of mankind; he cannot therefore, in his capacity as an "envoy of mankind", exercise the public authority of a particular State on its

[1] Para. 9.   [2] Para. 8.

behalf, by any symbolical taking of possession as an assertion of a claim of sovereignty (in any case prohibited elsewhere in the Declaration[3]) or in any similar way; what measure of authority he may exercise on behalf of a particular State, in relation to other astronauts from that State or otherwise, while remaining an "envoy of mankind", remains to be determined. Nor is it clear how much of the status of "envoy of mankind in outer space" has any continuing legal effect after the return of the astronaut to Earth; perhaps it is to be regarded as conferring on him the personal inviolability of an envoy in the event of his falling into hostile hands, but presumably only if he has not forfeited the status of "envoy of mankind" by conduct alien thereto. The whole matter will require consideration in more concrete terms before any generally agreed meaning can be given to the concept; meanwhile it doubtless has value as a reinforcement of the general principle that the exploration and use of outer space is a common interest of mankind, a principle from which important practical consequences may flow.

The question of assistance to astronauts stands on a quite different footing; it may at any time be a matter of immediate practical urgency and General Assembly Resolution 1963 (XVIII) of December 13, 1963, requests the Committee on the Peaceful Uses of Outer Space to arrange as a matter of priority for the prompt preparation of a draft international agreement on such assistance.

The Legal Sub-Committee of the Committee on the Peaceful Uses of Outer Space reached tentative agreement in October 1964 on provisions concerning the notification of accident and assistance in the territory of a contracting party.[4] These specify that each contracting party which receives information or discovers that the personnel of a spacecraft of another State have suffered accident or are experiencing conditions of distress or that they have made an emergency landing in territory under the jurisdiction of the contracting party, on the high seas, or in any other place not under the jurisdiction of any State, shall do its utmost immediately to notify the State which announced the launching, and shall immediately notify the Secretary-General of the United Nations. They provide that, if as a result of accident, distress or

[3] Para. 3.   [4] For the text agreed see Appendix XII below.

247

emergency landing, personnel of a spacecraft are in territory under the jurisdiction of a contracting party, it shall immediately take all possible steps, within the limits of the means at its disposal, to rescue the personnel and to render them the necessary assistance, and that it shall keep the State which announced the launching, and the Secretary-General of the United Nations, informed of the steps so taken and of their result; the assistance to be furnished when necessary by the contracting party to the personnel of a spacecraft of another State shall in no way differ from the assistance which it would furnish to its own personnel; if the contracting party considers that the assistance of the State which announced the launching of the spacecraft concerned would contribute substantially to the effectiveness of its search and rescue operations, it shall request the State which announced the launching to co-operate with it with a view to the effective conduct of such operations, under the direction and control of that contracting party.

As of October 1964 no agreement had been reached concerning the inclusion in the proposed agreement of certain general obligations, the return of space personnel, assistance outside the territory of a contracting State, or the application of the agreement to launchings by international organisations.

The conclusion of the international agreement envisaged by the General Assembly therefore remains in abeyance pending the outcome of further negotiation on these matters.

Pending such an agreement, and in respect of States not becoming parties thereto, the position is, it is submitted, as follows.

Assistance to astronauts who may be in distress by reason of accident, mistake or other unforeseen eventuality clearly constitutes an obligation of humanity which should be regarded as binding by all civilised States which are in a position to render appropriate assistance. The duty of such assistance affirmed by the Declaration of Legal Principles cannot be regarded as conditional upon subsequent agreement concerning its modalities.

The measure of the duty is defined by the Declaration as "all possible assistance". The duty clearly always includes the immediate notification to the launching State of all available information; if no direct channel of official communication exists for political reasons this element in the duty could presumably be discharged by notification through the United Nations or the International Committee of the Red Cross. What further assistance the duty includes will clearly depend on circumstances and the means of assistance at the disposal of the State concerned.

A State giving assistance would appear to be entitled to reimbursement of expenses incurred. While it is true that the Safety of Life at Sea Convention and the Search and Rescue Annex to the International Civil Aviation Convention do not provide for the reimbursement of expenses incurred for saving human life at sea or in the event of accident to an aircraft, the expenses involved in the rescue of astronauts may be of such an altogether different order of magnitude as to render the analogy of rescue operations in virtue of the Safety of Life at Sea Convention or the Search and Rescue Annex an inappropriate one.

The obligation of safe and prompt return of the astronaut who has made an emergency landing to the State of registry of his space vehicle is stated in the Declaration unconditionally and this appears to be a wise rule. If there is any question at issue concerning the nature of the activities in which he has been engaged it is better that it should be dealt with directly between the States concerned rather than that controversy should be embittered and the probability of an amicable and generally acceptable settlement reduced by the personal detention of the astronaut. If the astronaut has been personally guilty of some outrageous conduct which makes it inappropriate or unwise to give him full personal freedom arrangements analogous to extradition can be made for transferring him to the custody of the launching State; except in any such case it will normally suffice to make appropriate repatriation arrangements in consultation with a diplomatic or consular representative of the State of registry of the space vehicle, who will presumably accept financial responsibility.

The Declaration does not deal with any obligation of assistance to astronauts in distress which may rest directly upon other astronauts, aircraft, or ships at sea.

It does not, for instance, embody an obligation of mutual assistance among astronauts, comparable to the obligation placed on the master of a ship by the Safety of Life at Sea Convention[5] to proceed with all speed to the assistance of the persons in distress on receiving a wireless distress signal from any other ship. The omission is understandable as space activities and technology had not when the United Nations discussions were initiated reached the point at which astronauts can in practice render each other mutual assistance in space, but such a possibility can no longer be regarded as remote and provision should therefore be made for a contingency which may arise as soon as a number of manned expeditions with some measure of freedom of movement are in space simultaneously. The Institute of International Law Resolution envisages States taking "appropriate measures for mutual assistance among astronauts" and the concept of astronauts as "envoys of mankind" clearly implies that each State should give its astronauts a directive to extend to all other astronauts the mutual assistance which they would give to colleagues among their own compatriots. In space there can be "neither East nor West, border nor breed nor birth"; the obligation of mutual assistance binds all, "though they come from the ends of the Earth".

Still less remote is the possibility that an astronaut may, on return to Earth, be in distress on the high seas or in some inaccessible mountain, desert or jungle area. At some appropriate stage a comprehensive agreement providing for mutual assistance by ships, aircraft and spacecraft will probably be desirable. Meanwhile, it would seem reasonable to regard ships as having the same responsibilities when an astronaut is known or believed to be in distress at sea as they have when another ship is in distress and aircraft as having the same responsibilities towards astronauts in distress as they have when another aircraft is in distress, the provisions of the Safety of Life at Sea Convention and of the Search and Rescue Annex of the International Civil Aviation Convention being regarded as applicable in principle pending their formal amendment and any necessary adaptation of their terms.

[5] Regulation 10 of Chap. V of the Regulations annexed to the 1948 Convention, 164 United Nations Treaty Series, p. 332.

40

Space Telecommunications

THE Declaration of Legal Principles omits, presumably as superfluous, any statement of the general principle that space telecommunications must be conducted in accordance with the International Telecommunication Convention and Regulations. The principle is, however, implied in General Assembly Resolution 1721 (XVI)D of December 20, 1961, requesting the International Telecommunication Union to take appropriate action in respect of space telecommunications, while the Institute of International Law resolution states specifically that "all States shall ensure that space telecommunications comply with the regulations of the International Telecommunication Union".[1] The importance of the principle can hardly be overestimated. Telecommunications are the nervous system of all activities in space. Without them no guidance, little tracking, no reception of scientific data from orbit or beyond, no contact with the astronaut and no telecommanding are possible. But the radiospectrum available for these purposes, which are in competition with the multitude of other purposes for which it is required, is limited, and the strictest economy is therefore necessary in its management. Space telecommunications cannot be dealt with separately from telecommunications generally because of this crucial fact that all telecommunications are in competition for use of the limited radiospectrum available. Even if there were to be a special agency for space matters it could no more regulate space telecommunications outside the framework of the International Telecommunication Convention than ICAO or IMCO can regulate telecommunications with aircraft or shipping outside that framework. The General Assembly of the United Nations has,

[1] Para. 7.

moreover, recognised that the economical management of the available radiospectrum and the reconciliation of the needs of space communications with competing claims is a matter for the International Telecommunication Union. In these circumstances, there is no practicable alternative to the general principle that space telecommunications shall be conducted in accordance with the International Telecommunication Union regulations. Without this principle there is a clear and present danger of a degree of anarchy which would paralyse all useful activity in space. The principle includes an obligation to comply with the regulations of the International Telecommunications Union in respect of both (*a*) the allocation, recording and use of radio frequencies for operational Earth satellite systems and space research purposes (including the associated telemetry, command and control) and (*b*) the technical characteristics and operation of Earth satellite systems and the space research service, including the identification and cessation of radio emissions from satellites and other space vehicles.

It is sometimes suggested that, as one of the guarantees of the demilitarisation of space which are desirable and as a means of making effective the principle that activities in space should be conducted in "the common interest of all mankind", transmissions from objects launched into orbit or beyond should be in clear and not in code. Expressed in this form the suggestion is based on a misunderstanding of the technicalities of space telecommunication. A large proportion of the transmissions from unmanned space objects are instrumental readings which are neither in clear nor in the commonly accepted sense in code but are understandable only to those who have full information concerning the experiments the results of which are recorded by such readings; failing such information, what is received consists of unintelligible electrical impulses. Provision has been made in a number of contexts for the results of space experiments being generally available. In the field of meteorology, in particular, provision is being made for "readouts" to be in a form suitable for direct reception with equipment available at a minimal cost. On the same principle steps may be taken to make the data received from various types of satellite generally available by direct reception or through world data centres. It is in this sense and in this manner that effect can be given to the suggestion that transmissions from space should be in clear.

The ITU Radio Regulations, as amended in 1963,[2] now constitute the elements of a space telecommunications code. The Radio Regulations contain the detailed definitions necessary for the operation of space systems, services and stations including definitions of Earth and space stations, of communication-satellite, space research, broadcasting-satellite radio-navigation-satellite and meteorological-satellite systems, of Earth and space stations in such systems, and of space telemetry, telecommand and tracking. Some of the definitions, such as that of a "space station" as one "located on an object which is beyond, is intended to go beyond, or has been beyond, the major portion of the Earth's atmosphere"[3] and that of "deep space" as "space at distances from the Earth equal to or greater than the distance between the Earth and the Moon",[4] while adopted and authoritative only for telecommunication purposes, are relevant to wider problems and controversies. The Regulations also assign symbols to the various types of station.

The Table of Frequency Allocations embodied in the Radio Regulations, as amended in 1963, allocates frequencies for satellites identification, telemetry and tracking, space research, meteorological satellites, radio-navigation satellites, communications satellites and radio astronomy. Certain frequency bands are to be shared between terrestrial services and space services and sites and frequencies for terrestrial and Earth stations operating in such bands are to be selected having regard to the recommendations of the International Consultative Committee for Radiocommunications of ITU (the CCIR) with respect to geographical separation of such stations from each other.

The Radio Regulations, as amended, contain specifications concerning the technical characteristics of Earth and space stations.[5] They prescribe power limits and a minimum angle of elevation (both designed to protect other services from interference) for Earth stations in the communications satellite service and power flux density limits at the

[2] pp. 69–70, above.
[3] Reg. 84AE; and see p. 189, above.
[4] Reg. 84BA.
[5] Reg. 470 F to 470 U.

Earth's surface for emissions or reflections from communication satellite space stations and for emissions from meteorological space stations. They require space stations to "be made capable of ceasing radio emissions by the use of appropriate devices that will ensure definite cessation of emissions",[6] a footnote indicating that "appropriate devices" includes "battery life timing devices, ground command, etc".[7] Call signs for stations in the space service are recommended to consist of two letters followed by two or three digits.[8]

Frequency assignments in the space and radio astronomy services are to be notified and recorded in the master international frequency register of frequency assignments; before notifying or bringing into use any frequency assignments to an Earth station, whether for transmitting or receiving, in a shared band, the administration concerned is to effect co-ordination of the assignment with any other administration whose territory lies wholly or partly within co-ordination distance as determined by procedures indicated in a Recommendation annexed to the Regulations; the International Frequency Registration Board is granted certain powers of co-ordination in the matter. The information to be contained in notices to the Board relating to stations in the space and radio-astronomy services is specified; the specified information includes, for both Earth and space stations, the "operating administration or company". ITU is required to issue and keep up to date a list of stations in the space service and in the radio-astronomy service; the information to be contained in the list is separately specified for Earth and space stations in the communication, meteorological, radio-navigation and space research services respectively and for radio-astronomy stations, with particulars of frequency, class of emission and power for transmissions and frequency and class of emission for receptions.

The technical regulation of space telecommunications, as distinguished from action concerning the political, economic and social aspects of the control and operation of space telecommunications for communication and other purposes, is therefore relatively well advanced.

[6] Reg. 470 V.   [7] See also pp. 280–281, below.
[8] Reg. 773 A § 21A.

41

Communication Satellites

THE ITU Regulations deal with space telecommunications in general; communications satellites present special problems which require separate treatment. There is no reference to these problems in the Declaration of Legal Principles but during the discussion of the Declaration by the Committee on the Peaceful Uses of Outer Space immediately prior to its transmission to the General Assembly for adoption the representative of Brazil expressed the view that it should have indicated "a reference to some international scrutiny of global satellite communication".[1] General Assembly resolution 1802 (XVII) of December 14, 1962, emphasised "the importance of international co-operation to achieve effective satellite communications which will be available on a world-wide basis" and the Committee on the Peaceful Uses of Outer Space reiterated in 1963 that "international space communications should be available for the use of all countries, on a global non-discriminatory basis". The measures necessary to this end remain to be taken, but meanwhile important steps towards co-operation in global satellite communications have been initiated.

The problems which arise differ in respect of passive and active communications satellites.

The passive satellite typified by the United States Echo series,[2] is a reflector; Echo is an inflated balloon from which messages are reflected back to Earth. The Bilateral Space Agreement between the United States and the U.S.S.R. of June 8, 1962,[3] as implemented by the First

---

[1] United Nations Document A/5549/Add.1 of November 27, 1963, p. 27.

[2] Orbiting dipoles, discussed at pp. 35–36, above, are also a type of reflector satellite, but the questions which have arisen in connection with them relate essentially to the legality of an experiment having a deteriorating effect on natural environment.

[3] p. 86, above, and pp. 378–392, below.

Memorandum of Understanding of March 20–May 24, 1963,[4] provides for joint participation in passive communications experiments using a large reflector satellite, Echo II, to be launched by the United States. The agreement indicates the intended characteristics and orbit of the satellite, specifies the frequencies and route to be used for the experiments, and envisages possible further experiments; it involves the use of United Kingdom facilities at Jodrell Bank (and possibly at Goonhilly Downs) on the basis of arrangements to be made with the United Kingdom by the United States. One objective of the experiments is to test the feasibility of direct communication between the United States and the U.S.S.R. The United States is to provide orbital information and the U.S.S.R. tracking data. Observational data are to be promptly exchanged and to "be made generally available to the scientific and technical community" and "information about the equipment used for the experiments" is to be "exchanged to the extent necessary for the interpretation of these data". The Agreement provides that "after the completion of preliminary national tests, negotiations will be continued to discuss the possibility of joint experiments of mutual interest with active communications satellites".

Failing such an agreement, questions may arise in regard to the use of a reflector satellite by States other than the launching State. The use of the moon or the ionosphere as a reflector is free to all; what is the position in respect of a reflector satellite? Being a reflector it is available to many users at the same time, and may be available for use by other users at times when it is out of range of possible use by the launcher. Subject to compliance with the ITU regulations relating to frequencies and the avoidance of interference, such use would not appear to be inconsistent with the "jurisdiction and control" retained by the "State on whose registry an object launched into outer space is carried in accordance with the Declaration of Legal Principles or with the obligation to conduct all space activities with due regard for the corresponding interests of other States"[5]; it would, however, involve the use of an expensive and valuable property without the consent of the owner and the Declaration of Legal Principles provides that ownership of an object

4 United Nations Document A/5482 of August 20, 1963.   5 Para. 7.

launched into space is not affected by its passage through outer space. Whatever the strict legal position may be, the normal courtesies of international intercourse would appear to require a State proposing to use as a reflector a satellite launched by another State to seek the consent of the launching State; it is difficult to believe that such consent would be unreasonably refused; one may hope that it would normally be granted unless the proposed use was liable to interfere with already approved uses. If the amount of use by States other than the launcher became considerable, some accepted international rules governing such use might become necessary. If such use developed on a commercial scale, the question of reimbursement of the value of reflector service might arise. If, as may well be the case, passive satellite systems become important for limited capacity services precisely because of their availability to a large number of users and their inherent simplicity, some combination of rules governing their use, technical standards to facilitate use, and provision for financing on an agreed basis, will presumably be evolved.

Active communications satellites pose quite different problems. These are of varied types, but the main distinction is between low altitude systems (using satellites in orbit at distances of from 3,000 to 6,000 miles from the Earth which are available for communication between any two points only while within line of sight from these points) and high altitude systems (using satellites placed in a 24 hour synchronous orbit at an altitude of 22,300 miles which therefore remain stationary with respect to any point on the Earth's surface and can accordingly provide a 24 hour serve). Active satellites contain electronic components, notably a receiver for signals from the ground, a transmitter to amplify these signals and rebroadcast them back to the ground, the power supplies necessary to operate these components, and, in the case of high altitude satellites, velocity and altitude control systems. Any interference with a satellite of this nature without the concurrence of the launching or operating State would be both inconsistent with the provision of the Declaration of Legal Principles[6] that "the State on whose registry an object launched into outer space is carried shall retain

[6] Para. 7.

jurisdiction and control over such object" and an unauthorised use of a valuable property and would therefore, except in the cases of *force majeure* identified in our discussion of jurisdiction and control,[7] be a wrongful act.

Bilateral agreements concerning intercontinental testing of active communications satellites have been concluded by the United States, notably with the United Kingdom and France;[8] they designate co-operating agencies which are to make all the necessary technical arrangements.

The ITU Regulations, as we have seen,[9] allocate frequencies for communications satellites (for Earth to satellite and satellite to Earth communications) and specify power limits and minimum angles of elevation for Earth stations and power flux density limits for space stations.

Arrangements for a global commercial communications satellite system have now been embodied in an agreement establishing interim arrangements for such a system opened for signature by governments in Washington on August 19, 1964, and an accompanying Special Agreement of even date the parties to which may be either governments or communications entities.[10]

The Agreement establishing interim arrangements sets forth certain basic principles in a preamble. These are that "a single global commercial communications satellite system" should be established "as part of an improved global communications network which will provide expanded telecommunications services to all areas of the world and which will contribute to world peace and understanding"; that "the most efficient and economical service possible consistent with the best and most equitable use of the radiospectrum" should be provided "through the most advanced technology available, for the benefit of all nations of the world"; and that "satellite communications should be organised in such a way as to permit all States to have access to the global system and those States so wishing to invest in the system with consequent participation in the design, development,

[7] Chap. 36, pp. 238–239, above.   [8] p. 85, above.
[9] p. 253, above.   [10] Appendix V, pp. 339–356, below.

construction (including the provision of equipment), establishment, maintenance, operation and ownership of the system."

The parties to the Agreement are to co-operate to provide, in accordance with the principles, "for the design, development, construction, establishment, maintenance and operation of the space segment of" a global communications satellite system.[11] Each party is either to sign or designate a communications entity, public or private, to sign the Special Agreement establishing interim arrangements.[12] Administrations and communications carriers are to negotiate traffic agreements.[13] The space segment is to be owned in undivided shares by the signatories to the Special Agreement in proportion to their respective contributions to the costs.[14] An Interim Communications Satellite Committee of representatives of the parties to the Special Agreement is to administer the two agreements.[15] No earth station is to be permitted to use the space segment unless it has been approved by this Committee.[16] Pursuant to the general policies of the Committee and in accordance with specific determinations made by it, the United States Communications Satellite Corporation is to "act as the manager in the design, development, construction, establishment, operation and maintenance of the space segment".[17] These arrangements and the possibility of establishing a permanent international organisation are to be reconsidered when the system becomes operational with a view to definitive arrangements coming into force not later than 1 January 1970; these definite arrangements are to be open to all States Members of the International Telecommunication Union or their designated entities, are to safeguard the investment made by signatories to the Special Agreement, and are to be such that all parties to the definitive arrangements may have an opportunity of contributing to the determination of general policy.[18] In considering contracts and in exercising its other responsibilities, the Committee and the Corporation as manager are to be guided by the need to design, develop and procure the best equipment and services at the best price; when

[11] Art. I.
[12] Art. II (*a*).
[13] Art. II (*b*).
[14] Art. III.
[15] Arts. IV, V and VI.
[16] Art. VII.
[17] Art. VIII.
[18] Art. IX.

proposals or tenders are comparable they are to seek to ensure that contracts are so distributed that equipment is designed, developed and procured in the States whose Governments are parties to the Agreement in approximate proportion to the respective quotas of their corresponding signatories to the Special Agreement.[19]

The Special Agreement sets out in detail the arrangements for financing the system,[20] for the approval of applications by earth stations to use the space segment,[21] for the allotment of satellite utilisation,[22] for the charges in respect of satellite utilisation,[23] and for the placing of contracts.[24] It provides that each applicant for approval of an earth station "shall be responsible for making equitable and non-discriminatory arrangements for the use of the earth station by all signatories or duly authorised communications entities intended to be served by the earth station individually or jointly with other earth stations";[25] that the Committee and the Corporation shall take, to the extent specified, appropriate steps to secure the availability to signatories of inventions technical data and information;[26] and that neither the Corporation as signatory or manager, nor any other signatory as such, shall be liable to any other signatory for loss or damage sustained by reason of a failure or breakdown of a satellite at or after launching or a failure by breakdown of any other portion of the space segment.[27] Provision for an impartial tribunal to decide legal disputes "in accordance with general principles of law" is to be made by a Supplementary Agreement.[28]

[19] Art. X.
[21] Arts. 7 and 8.
[23] Art. 9.
[25] Art. 8 (*a*).
[27] Art. 13.

[20] Arts. 3–6.
[22] Art. 8.
[24] Art. 10.
[26] Arts. 10 (*f*)–(*h*) and 12 (*g*).
[28] Art. 14.

42

Space Broadcasting

SPACE broadcasting as a legal problem has attracted attention hitherto in its political rather than its technical aspect. The ITU Radio Regulations, as amended in 1963, define a "broadcasting satellite service" as "a space service in which signals transmitted or retransmitted by space stations, or transmitted by reflection from objects in orbit around the Earth, are intended for direct reception by the general public",[1] but do not otherwise distinguish between a broadcasting service and the varied types of satellite service (including communication, radio-navigation and meteorological services) which may broadcast.

On the political plane the question has attracted attention of a different order.

The Preamble to the Declaration of Legal Principles recalls General Assembly Resolution 110 (II) of November 3, 1947, "which condemned propaganda designed or likely to promote or encourage any threat to the peace, breach of the peace, or act of aggression" and indicates that the General Assembly considers "that the aforementioned resolution is applicable to outer space". The inclusion of this provision in the Preamble was a compromise between the original Soviet view that the Declaration should include a provision that "the use of outer space for propagating war, national or racial hatred or enmity between nations" is prohibited and the original United States view that the inclusion of such a provision in a Declaration of Legal Principles Governing the Activities of States in the Exploration and Use of Outer Space would be inappropriate. While the compromise reached appears to have been generally acceptable, the representative of Brazil expressed,

[1] Reg. 84AP.

during the discussion of the Declaration by the Committee on the Peaceful Uses of Outer Space immediately prior to its transmission to the General Assembly for adoption the view that the operative part of the Declaration should have incorporated "a ban on the utilisation of a communication system based on satellites for purposes of encouraging national, racial or class rivalries".[2] A suggestion for a provision in these terms inevitably raises questions which have already arisen in other contexts concerning the extent to which governments should interfere with the freedom of information *media* for the purpose of preventing what others may regard as objectionable propaganda; this complication does not, however, arise in respect of government-sponsored broadcasts. There is, moreover, in respect of government-sponsored and private broadcasts alike, a potential real problem for the handling of which some appropriate form of international action may be desirable,[3] though it is difficult to see in what respects space propaganda constitutes a different or more urgent problem than other forms of international propaganda; even its wider potential range and relative freedom from interference do not at present give it a greater immediate impact in view of the special equipment still necessary for the reception of space broadcasts. The 1947 Resolution, which the Declaration of Legal Principles declares applicable to outer space, avoids the form of a prohibition any breach of which involves punitive measures; it expresses its prohibitory clause in the form of a condemnation of all forms of propaganda "designed or likely to provoke or encourage any threat to the peace, breach of the peace or act of aggression", and shifts the main emphasis to a more positive note in the form of a request to the government of each Member to take appropriate steps, within its constitutional limits, "to promote, by all the means of propaganda and publicity available to them, friendly relations among nations based on the Purposes and Principles of the Charter", and "to encourage the dissemination of all information designed to give expression to the undoubted desire of all peoples for peace". While placing the accent upon this positive approach

---

[2] United Nations Document A/5549/Add.1 of November 27, 1963, p. 27.
[3] *Cf.* L. John Martin, *International Propaganda: Its Legal and Diplomatic Control*, 1958; Arthur Larson and John B. Whitton, *Propaganda: Towards Disarmament in the War of Words*, 1964.

there still remains scope for a recognised international code of conduct governing space broadcasting, preferably administered by some independent body of a professional character.

43

Meteorological Satellites

No problem has arisen concerning the legality of meteorological observation satellites, primarily no doubt because of the large measure of international co-operation already achieved in the matter on the basis of the resolutions of the General Assembly through the World Meteorological Organisation[1] and carried a stage further by the Bilateral Space Agreement between the United States and the U.S.S.R.[2] There is therefore little hard law concerning meteorological satellites, but the developments which have occurred or are taking place are rapidly giving a specific content in the meteorological field to the concept of the equal availability to all States "of the benefits of the exploration and use of space".

Thus, a World Weather Watch based on the interchange of information through world data centres at Washington, Moscow and a place to be chosen in the Southern Hemisphere is being developed through the World Meteorological Organisation.

Arrangements have been made through the World Meteorological Organisation for world-wide distribution by radio in coded and facsimile form of analyses of photographic data obtained from United States Tiros satellites, the necessary information for the utilisation of such data being available in a *Technical Note on the Reduction and Use of Data Obtained by Tiros Meteorological Satellites* issued by WMO.

WMO is also making available technical details of the Automatic Picture Transmission System developed by the United States, a relatively Inexpensive device likely to make it possible for any country to receive certain data directly from meteorological satellites.

[1] See. pp. 64–67, above. [2] p. 86, above.

The ITU Radio Regulations, as amended in 1963, allocate frequency bands for meteorological satellites and specify the technical requirements to be complied with by meteorological satellite space stations and the particulars concerning meteorological satellite Earth and space stations to be furnished to and published by ITU.

The Bilateral Space Agreement between the United States and the U.S.S.R. of June 8, 1962,[3] as implemented by the First Memorandum of Understanding of March 20 and May 24, 1963,[4] provides for a co-ordinated meteorological satellite programme. Data is to be exchanged within six hours of observation time so that it will be useful in weather analysis and forecasting; cloud photographs are to be exchanged, the accuracy of location, brightness levels and field of view to be attained being specified. There is also to be an exchange of techniques of interpretation and analysis. A regular full-time link, allowing simultaneous transmission of facsimile telegraphy information in both directions, is to be established; the technical arrangements for the sections of the link from Washington to Berlin are to be made by the United States and those for the sector from Berlin to Moscow by the U.S.S.R., the cost of the whole line being shared equally; use of the line by other countries on a receiver-only basis to obtain data for their own use is to be welcomed subject to their making a proportional contribution to the total expenses of the link. Launchings of weather satellites are to be co-ordinated by arrangements for mutually agreeable launching schedules. In all joint activities the pertinent recommendations of the World Meteorological Organisation are to be given due consideration.

Substantial steps have therefore been taken in the meteorological field towards implementing through appropriate agreements the principles of making equally available "to all States" the benefits of the exploration and use of space; they are an apposite illustration of the manner in which the principle can be progressively implemented by measures appropriate to different types of space activity.

[3] p. 86, above.
[4] United Nations Document A/5482 of August 26, 1963.

44

Geodetic and Magnetic Survey Satellites

GEODETIC and magnetic survey satellites are designed to give more accurate information concerning the size, shape and magnetic field of the Earth; such information gives us more accurate knowledge than was previously available and makes possible the determination with greater accuracy in intercontinental distances, a matter which may be of military as well as of scientific importance.

The legality of such surveys by satellites does not appear to have been questioned or to be open to question. The knowledge secured by such a survey may be of military value in the same sense in which all basic scientific knowledge may be of military value but the making of a geodetic or magnetic survey by satellites is in itself a peaceful use of space, the value of such a survey depends on its world-wide character, and accordingly no State is entitled to regard such a survey of its own area by satellite as an illegal or unfriendly act.

The Bilateral Space Agreement between the United States and the U.S.S.R. of June 8, 1962,[1] as implemented by the First Memorandum of Understanding of March 20–May 24, 1963,[2] provides for a co-operative effort to map the Earth's magnetic field by the use of United States and U.S.S.R. satellites during the International Year of the Quiet Sun. Satellite orbits are to be selected, and the times of launchings determined, by the satellite launching country, taking account of specified considerations. The Memorandum embodies agreed desiderata concerning the lifetime of satellites, the use of magnetometers, and measures to be taken with a view to working out a common method of making time

[1] p. 86, above.
[2] United Nations Document A/5482 of August 26, 1963.

variation corrections. It provides for the exchange of satellite magnetic measurements and of comparable amounts of data from magnetic surveys of other types and for the communication of the resulting scientific data to the International Council of Scientific Unions. This provision for communication to ICSU reflects the general principle that the results of space research should be available for the use of all "on a basis of equality".

45

Navigational Satellites

NAVIGATION by satellite techniques are designed to combine accuracy equalling or surpassing optical celestial navigation with the all-weather performance of radio navigation; they enable any observer with the appropriate electronic equipment and information to determine his position from radio observations of the satellite. Navigational satellite systems are potentially of great importance for shipping, navigation and spacecraft,[1] but in the developmental phase military interest in such systems has predominated; the United States, for instance, has assigned to the Navy responsibility for the development of the Transit satellite; It is therefore not surprising that no arrangements have yet been evolved to facilitate general use of navigational satellite systems "on a basis of equality". Only as regards the telecommunication requirements for such systems has progress been made in giving legal form to the measures of co-operation which may be desirable for the purpose. The ITU Radio Regulations, as amended in 1963, define a radio–navigation satellite service as a service using space stations on Earth satellites for the purpose of radio-navigation, including, in certain cases, transmission or re-transmission of supplementary information necessary for the operation of the radio-navigation system. The Regulations allocate certain frequencies for radio-navigation satellites as well as for radio-navigation generally and for aeronautical radio-navigation. The assignment of a frequency within an allocated band to an individual radio-navigation space station has to be notified to the International Frequency Registration Board with particulars of the station for inclusion in the

[1] See, for instance, Vice-Admiral John T. Hayward, Deputy Chief of Naval Operations (Development) U.S. Navy, "Space Technology for World Navigation", in Simon Ramo, *Peacetime Uses of Outer Space*, 1961, pp. 55–84.

published list of Stations in the Space Service and the Radio-astronomy Service. The particulars to be given for radio-navigation satellite space systems include the orbital information necessary for use of the satellite, namely angle of inclination of the orbit, period of the object in space, altitude of apogee and perigee, and, in the case of a stationary satellite, the mean geographical longitude of the projection of the satellite's position on the surface of the Earth, together with particulars of any special channelling arrangements for telegraphy, telephony and other types of communication as appropriate, and any special methods of modulation.

One can conceive that there will ultimately be a network of agreements providing for the maintenance of navigational satellites analogous to the agreements now existing concerning loran services and other radio-navigational aids. Such agreements are not, however, indispensable to permit of the legal use of a navigational satellite by a third party. Such a satellite is akin to a lighthouse or radio beacon rather than to a communications satellite. The use of a navigational satellite consists of making radio observations of the satellite by receiving signals from it; there is therefore no element of interference with the operation of the satellite or unauthorised use of another's property involved, comparable to the use as a reflector of a passive communications satellite; the satellite can, so to speak, be used without being used by anyone with the necessary equipment and information; by its nature the launcher makes it available as a public service to everyone with the equipment and information necessary to make use of it.

46

Observatory Satellites

THE placing in orbit and operation of an observatory satellite for purposes of astronomical research does not in itself pose any special legal problem.

Such satellites would be peculiarly appropriate for co-operative international action with a view to making a reality of the principle that "outer space and celestial bodies are free for exploration and use by all States on a basis of equality". CERN (the European Council for Nuclear Research) may afford a prototype for such action, possibly sponsored jointly by the United States, the U.S.S.R., the European Space Research Organisation, and the European Launcher Development Organisation. Such an arrangement might be an important safeguard against the danger of questions arising concerning the possible use of such a satellite for military purposes.

47

Manned Orbital Stations

THE establishment of manned orbital stations now appears to be within the range of early possibilities; the United States, for instance, has announced plans for a manned orbital space laboratory. The Declaration of Legal Principles is silent on the subject, but the Institute of International Law Resolution provides that "the State establishing a space installation is required to ensure good order and safety at the installation" and that "subject to any subsequent international agreement, persons using, and occurrences at, any space installation are subject to the jurisdiction of the State having established the installation".[1] Both of these rules may be regarded as almost self-evident. The obligation to ensure good order and safety is implicit in the provisions of the Declaration of Legal Principles, notably in the obligation to assure that national activities are carried on in conformity with the principles set forth in the Declaration,[2] in the obligation to conduct space activities with "due regard for the corresponding rights of other States",[3] and in the liability for damage[4] recognised by the Declaration. The attribution of jurisdiction over a space station, and persons and occurrences there, to the State establishing the station represents the application to the specific case of a space station of the principle expressed in the Declaration in general terms that "the State on whose registry an object launched into outer space is carried shall retain jurisdiction and control over such object, and any personnel thereon, while in outer space".[5]

There has been some discussion in the literature of the possible application to orbital stations of the principle of freedom of use by all

[1] Para. 6.
[2] Para. 4.
[3] Para. 6.
[4] Para. 8.
[5] Para. 7.

271

States on a basis of equality,[6] but this presupposes a type of orbital station which is not immediately in prospect and the suggested right of non-discriminatory access must therefore be regarded as a speculative possibility at the present stage.

[6] Para. 2; and see p. 164, above.

48

Manned Stations on Celestial Bodies

THE Declaration of Legal Principles makes no attempt to anticipate the problems which will be found when manned stations are established on celestial bodies. The paragraph of the Institute of International Law Resolution providing that "the State establishing a space installation is required to ensure good order and safety at the installation" and, subject to any subsequent international agreement, has jurisdiction there, applies to manned stations on celestial bodies no less than to manned orbital stations.

Manned stations on celestial bodies do not yet exist, but their establishment would appear to be not only probable but essential if man succeeds in remaining continuously in space for any extended period for any purpose other than a long exploratory voyage during which he does not leave his spacecraft. Such stations have been envisaged not merely by imaginative writers but by responsible scientists and technologists and plans for them are in preparation by industrial research units. The legal status of such stations presents a problem distinct from that of the legal status of space, of celestial bodies, spacecraft or even manned orbital stations, and there is still no authoritative pronouncement in a General Assembly Resolution concerning the problem. As Jessup and Taubenfeld have pointed out, the principle that national sovereignties shall not extend into space does not in itself provide a solution for the problems of government, perhaps quite simple at the outset but increasingly complex as new developments occur, which the existence of such stations will create. "When man develops the necessary capabilities there will arise questions of occupation, use and exploration of resources by human beings whether or not in government service, the control of such persons, their comings and goings, and their mutual relationships". The principle of no national appropriation already unanimously accepted by the General Assembly, embodied in the Declaration of Legal Principles, and fundamental to the attainment of the common interest of mankind that space shall be used exclusively for peaceful purposes, will be viable on a permanent basis only if these problems are satisfactorily solved. The history of territorial annexations on Earth shows decisively that there is no greater stimulus to annexation, often despite the initial considered policy of the annexor, than the existence of a political void. Some form of direct international administration of manned stations on celestial bodies under the auspices of the United Nations, would appear to be the ideal solution and might be an essential element of any agreed plan for the permanent demilitarisation of space. In so far as such stations were established by international organisations of States rather than by States the problem would be greatly simplified. In so far as such stations may be established by individual States it will be necessary to have some practical arrangements which, without impairing by gradual erosion the principle that neither outer space nor the celestial bodies are subject to national appropriation and while providing for an appropriate measure of international supervision, recognise that the State establishing the station has, by reason of its responsibility to ensure good order and safety there, jurisdiction over persons using and occurrences at the station to the extent necessary to enable it to discharge that responsibility.

The experience acquired in the application of the provisions of the Antarctic Treaty relating to the exercise of jurisdiction may throw some further light on the problem.

49

Exploitation of Space Resources

THE Declaration of Legal Principles contains no specific provision relating to any exploitation of space resources which may become possible but some of its general provisions are relevant, notably the provision that outer space and celestial bodies are free for exploration and use by all "on a basis of equality"[1] and the provision that space activities shall be conducted "with due regard for the corresponding interests of other States".[2] The prohibition of "national appropriation"[3] must be regarded as applying to outer space and celestial bodies as such, rather than to their resources.[4] The régime applicable to any exploitable resources of outer space and celestial bodies therefore remains to be determined. Distinctions may well be necessary between use which is by its nature exclusive and use which can be shared simultaneously, use which involves the resource used being consumed and use which leaves it available for further use, use which involves some transformation or deterioration and use which has no such effect. It is difficult to elaborate the matter in any precise detail until it is known what can be used and how. In respect of consumable resources it may be necessary or desirable to recognise that title thereto can be acquired by extraction or use, but it may be desirable to require some kind of United Nations concession, leave or licence for the working of such resources, both to eliminate any uncertainty of title or international disagreement in the matter and to permit of any measures which may be desirable to avoid waste or contamination and to provide for resource conservation.

[1] Para. 2.
[2] Para. 6.
[3] Para. 3.
[4] Chap. 24, p. 202, above.

50

Space Experiments

THE Declaration of Legal Principles affirms, as we have seen,[1] the general principle that "in the exploration and use of outer space States shall be guided by the principle of co-operation and mutual assistance and shall conduct all their activities in outer space with due regard for the corresponding interests of other States". It links to this general principle two more specific provisions concerning potentially harmful space activities or experiments. The first of these provisions postulates an obligation for States undertaking such activities or experiments; it provides that "if a State has reason to believe that an outer space activity or experiment planned by it or its nationals would cause potentially harmful interference with activities of other States in the peaceful exploration and use of outer space it shall undertake appropriate international consultations before proceeding with any such activity or experiment". The second provision claims a right for other States; it specifies that "a State which has reason to believe that an outer space activity or experiment planned by another State would cause potentially harmful interference with activities in the peaceful exploration and use of outer space may request consultation concerning the activity or experiment."

These provisions were a compromise between an original U.S.S.R. proposal to provide in the Declaration that "any measures that might in any way hinder the exploration or use of outer space for peaceful purposes by other countries may be implemented only after prior discussion of and agreement upon such measures between the countries concerned" and the unwillingness of other countries to grant anything in the nature of a veto upon their space experiments.

[1] Chap. 29, above.

During the discussion of the Declaration by the Committee on the Peaceful Uses of Outer Space immediately prior to its transmission to the General Assembly for adoption a number of comments were made on the provisions adopted. The representative of the United States described them as "a statement of principle" which "does not specify the manner in which consultations are to be held"; the United States regarded the COSPAR Consultative Group as "an appropriate forum for consultation" but "in a statement of general principles it would be inappropriate to specify one particular mode exclusively and for all time".[2] The Canadian representative regretted that there was no specific request to States to undertake consultation if an experiment planned by a State or its nationals "might involve a risk of modifying the natural environment of the Earth in a manner likely to be prejudicial to the well-being of human life or the interests of another State;" he was "confident that any State considering an experiment which would have these consequences would spontaneously undertake consultation" and understood that "it is considered that any experiment which would affect the Earth's environment would also interfere with activities of other States in outer space, so that States planning an experiment would for this latter reason be under an obligation to consult internationally"; he therefore accepted the principle as drafted as sufficient but trusted that, when it proved possible to elaborate it, the omission would be rectified by specifying "that States had an obligation to consult in the event that an experiment were being planned which might have the effect of influencing the Earth's environment".[3] The Brazilian representative would have preferred the system of consultation provided for to be made "more binding and more precise".[4]

The Declaration requires consultation; it does not require agreement; and it does not, apart from the general principle that States are to conduct their space activities "with due regard for the corresponding interests of other States", formulate any principles to serve as the basis of such consultation or define in any way the legal consequences of action following failure to reach agreement in the course of such consul-

[2] United Nations Document A/5549/Add.1 of November 27, 1963, p. 7.
[3] *Ibid.*, p. 10.   [4] *Ibid.*, p. 27.

tation. The law on the subject must therefore be regarded as being still in the earliest phase of its development.

The Institute of International Law Resolution states the general principle involved in more comprehensive language but is equally tentative concerning the appropriate remedy. It declares that "scientific or technological experiments or tests in space which may involve a risk of modifying the natural environment of the Earth, of any of the celestial bodies or in space in a manner liable to be prejudicial to the future of scientific investigation and experiment, the well-being of human life or the interests of another State, necessarily affect directly the interests of the whole international community" and that "appropriate international arrangements" should be made "to forestall such risk".[5] The Institute resolution deals specifically with risks prejudicial to the well-being of human life or the interests of another State; these were, it will be recalled, the points not specifically mentioned in the Declaration of Legal Principles which the Canadian representative, in regretting the omission of any specific mention of them, assumed to be covered by its general terms.

The COSPAR Consultative Group on Potentially Harmful Effects of Space Experiments[6] has a mandate from COSPAR to examine or provide for the examination of the possible results of experiments.

While consultations concerning potentially harmful space experiments, conducted through COSPAR or otherwise, will presumably consist primarily of the objective evaluation of the relevant scientific evidence and weighing of any conflicting scientific considerations, due weight should be attached in the course of such consultations to such fundamental principles of law as *alterum non laedere, nemo judex in re sua, audi alteram partem,* the maintenance *litis pendente* of the existing rights of the parties, *ubi injuria ibi jus,* and absolute liability for dangerous activities.

More elaborate procedural arrangements,[7] involving a firmer degree of legal obligation, may well prove desirable as progress is made in the matter. Meanwhile, disregard of the outcome of such consultations

[5] Para. 12.   [6] pp. 34–36 above, and pp. 402–415, below.
[7] See, for instance, the suggestions recapitulated at pp. 148–150, above.

would appear to constitute a degree of recklessness placing on the State concerned full responsibility for all of the consequences of its action in so far as these can be remedied by restoration of the preceding state of affairs or an award of damages.

51

Space Cluttering and Contamination

THE Declaration of Legal Principles contains no special provisions relating to space cluttering and contamination; it formulates the general principle that States "shall conduct all their activites in outer space with due regard to the corresponding interests of other States" and provides for consultation concerning potentially harmful activities and experiments[1] but does not attempt to formulate an obligation to avoid space cluttering and contamination on more general terms. The Institute of International Law resolution contains two paragraphs on the subject, one relating to cluttering and the other to contamination.

The paragraph concerning cluttering provides that "the State under the authority of which a space object takes place shall ensure that every such object is, so far as practicable, fitted with a suitable device permitting the launcher to recover it on the termination of its useful life or if recovery is not feasible as a minimum to silence radio transmission therefrom and eliminate its other effects". Unlimited in absorptive capacity as space may appear to be, it is most undesirable that there should remain in orbit around the Earth, the Moon or the nearer planets for indefinite periods of time, substantial numbers of space objects the useful lives of which have ended. Apart from any danger there may be of collision with new and active space instrumentalities, "dead hardware", as it has been called, may interfere in other ways with current activities in space. It is particularly important that radio emissions from space vehicles should not continue when they have ceased to serve a useful purpose. The radiospectrum available for space communications requires highly economical management to secure

Para. 6; Chap. 50, above.

satisfactory results and there is nothing to spare which one can afford to waste on hangovers from space instrumentalities with long life transmitting equipment powered by solar batteries or otherwise. The practical problems of space cluttering are not, however, limited to the risk of collision (which may remain negligible for a long time) and the cluttering of the radiospectrum. It also has an important bearing on the close relationship between a full knowledge of what is in space and what it is doing there and the problem of military security. The existence of clear rules requiring objects launched into orbit or beyond to be fitted with instruments permitting their recovery or destruction at the end of their useful lives in order to avoid space being cluttered with derelicts the continued observation of which places an impossible burden on the ground tracking networks may therefore be of political and military as well as of practical and scientific importance. No provision requiring space objects to be fitted so far as practicable with a recovery device has as yet been adopted. A provision concerning the silencing of radio transmission has now been included in the ITU Radio Regulations, as amended in 1963, which provide that "space stations shall be made capable of causing radio transmissions by the use of appropriate devices that will ensure definite cessation of emissions".[2]

The paragraph concerning contamination provides that "the State under the authority of which the launching takes place shall ensure that appropriate precautions are taken against biological, radiological or chemical contamination of or from outer space or celestial bodies" and that "international co-operation in respect of the matter should be arranged".[3] This also is a matter of potentially capital importance. inter-planetary communication would involve the artificial dissemination of terrestial life to new habitants and expose the Earth to a hazard of contamination by foreign organisms.[4] Proposed precautions for the sterilisation of space vehicles were formulated in 1959 by the Committee on the Exploration of Extraterrestial Space of the International

[2] Para. 10 (2) Reg. 470 V1.24; a footnote gives as illustrations of "appropriate devices" battery life, timing devices and ground command.
[3] Para. 11.
[4] *Cf.* Joshua Lederberg, "Exobiology: Experimental Approaches to Life Beyond the Earth" in L. U. Berkner and Hugh Odishaw, *Science and Space*, 1961, pp. 407–425, and Sir Bernard Lovell, *The Exploration of Outer Space*, 1962, pp. 78–80

Council of Scientific Unions,[5] now superseded by COSPAR, and are, it is understood, applied by both the United States and the U.S.S.R. authorities.

COSPAR in 1964[6] accepted as tentatively recommended interim objectives a sterilisation level such that the probability of a single viable organism aboard any spacecraft intended for planetary landing or atmospheric penetration would be less than 1×10^{-4}, and a probability limit for accidental planetary impact by unsterilised fly-by or orbiting spacecraft of 3×10^{-5} or less, and envisaged the convening of an international conference on biological sterilisation and sterility testing techniques at any time and place and in co-operation with any other scientific organisations it may deem appropriate, provided it can be assured in advance of substantial participation in the conference by scientists of both the major deep space probe launching authorities.

It may at some stage become desirable, if manned space travel becomes of significant proportions, to include certain provisions on the subject in the International Sanitary Regulations administered by the World Health Organisation.

[5] ICSU Review, Vol. 1 (1959), p. 100; *Nature*, Vol. 183 (1959), p. 925.
[6] See Appendix VIII, pp. 410–414, below.

52

Liability for Space Vehicle Accidents

THE Declaration of Legal Principles provides that "each State which launches or procures the launching of an object into outer space, and each State from whose territory or facility an object is launched, is internationally liable for damage done to a foreign State or its natural or juridical persons by such object or its component parts on the Earth, in air space, or in outer space".[1] During the discussion of the Declaration by the Committee on the Peaceful Uses of Outer Space, immediately prior to its transmission to the General Assembly for adoption, the United States representative pointed out that "the details of the application" of the provisions relating to liability "will need to be spelled out in an appropriate international agreement",[2] and the United Kingdom representative said that paragraph 8 "is in very broad terms and will need considerable amplification when a detailed agreement concerning liability for space vehicle accidents comes to be drafted" as its application "might well give rise to certain difficulties unless, as we are certain is intended, it is in due course implemented by other bilateral and multilateral agreements".[3] Australia, as a lender of launching facilities, expressed a special view.[4] The Australian delegation accepted the principle "that each State which launches or procures the launching of an object into outer space is internationally liable for damage done by such object" but considered it "not so obvious" that "a State which has simply lent its territory or facility for the launching of an object by

---

[1] Para. 8.
[2] United Nations Document A/5549/Add.1 of November 27, 1963, p. 8.
[3] *Ibid.*, p. 19.
[4] *Ibid.*, pp. 12–13.

another State should bear international liability"; in such a case there were "arguments for the 'lending' State not bearing any international responsibility for subsequent damage", but Australia would nevertheless "accept the proposition that some liability may properly rest with the 'lending' State, though in that case the primary responsibility would be on the State or States launching or procuring the launching of the object"; paragraph 8 was acceptable "because it does not preclude that position and because it does not prejudice the right of a 'lending' State to enter into agreements with the 'launching' or 'procuring' States on the division of liability". The details would "need to be articulated in an appropriate international agreement, without, of course, prejudicing the right of States to make in the meantime specific bilateral or multi-lateral indemnity agreements if that should be thought necessary".[5] The United States, United Kingdom, Australian and French representatives[6] all made clear their view that the Declaration recognises the liability of international organisations, as well as of States participating in them, for damage caused by space activities in which international organisations engage.

A number of questions of detail concerning the extent and nature of liability requiring further consideration were mentioned by the Australian representative. Should it be without fault? Should damages be limited in size? Does the word "damage" cover, as may be presumed, personal injury, loss of life and property damage?

The Institute of International Law resolution provides that "the State under the authority of which the launching of a space object has taken place shall be liable, irrespective of fault, for any injury, including loss of life, or damage that may result", that "modalities of application of this principle may be determined by special convention", and that "any limitation of the amount of the reparation due shall be determined in the same manner";[7] it defines the term "State" as including international organisations "it being understood that the States members of an international organisation remain responsible for the space activities

[5] *Ibid.*, pp. 8, 13, 17 and 19.
[6] *Ibid.*, p, 14.
[7] Para. 13.

of the organisation". The main points of difference are that the Institute resolution places liability unequivocally upon the launching State or international organisation rather than upon the State procuring the launching or permitting launching from its territory or facility (leaving any question of indemnification to be settled between those concerned), that it specifies that liability is irrespective of fault, and that it envisages liability being unlimited unless a limitation is agreed by special convention.

General Assembly Resolution of December 13, 1963, requests the Committee on the Peaceful Uses of Outer Space to arrange for the prompt preparation of a draft international agreement on liability for damage caused by objects launched into outer space.

As of October 1964 the Legal Sub-Committee of the Committee still had before it three different proposals for such an agreement submitted respectively by the United States, Belgium and Hungary.[8] The questions at issue included the scope of the agreement and of any exemptions therefrom; the exclusion of claims for damage caused to nationals of the launching State and damage caused on its territory; the respective liabilities of a State launching or procuring the launching of an object and a State whose territory or facility is used in such launching by an international organisation; the nature of liability where more than one party is liable; the extent of any exceptions to the principle of absolute liability and extent of liability for damage in outer space; the extent to which the national law of the injured person is relevant for the purpose of determining the relationship of cause and effect between the damage and the outer space activity or determining the extent of the liability; the limitation of liability in amount; the payment of compensation in a convertible currency; time-limits for the presentation of claims; whether there should be any obligation to pursue local remedies and the effect of the pursuit of remedies available in the liable State or under other international agreements. These are difficult and intricate questions and the negotiation of the agreement concerning them envisaged by the General Assembly may therefore take some time.

[8] For the texts of these see Appendix XII below.

Pending the conclusion of any such agreement, and in relation to States not parties thereto, it will remain necessary to consider the matter as on of general principle on the basis of the Declaration of Legal Principles; the terms of the Declaration being so general, the Institute of International Law resolution is of value as a contribution to the elucidation of the questions of principle involved.

The liability clearly includes liability for any injury, including loss of life, or damage that may result from the space vehicle accident. The English translation of the Institute of International Law resolution uses the expression "injury, including loss of life, or damage" as a translation of the French term "dommages" and this is, it is submitted, both a correct rendering and a correct statement of the principle involved.

Liability should be, in principle, irrespective of fault. Whatever theoretical controversies there may be in the matter,[9] only the principle of liability irrespective of fault places the burden of loss resulting from activities in space where it properly belongs as one of the costs of the venture to be taken into account when deciding whether, to what extent, and under what conditions, to undertake such activities; it is, moreover, a natural extension to activities in space of the principle already accepted in respect of aviation and nuclear accident.

Certain exceptions to the principle nevertheless seem legitimate and desirable.

While no proof of fault by the launcher or operator should be required, it is proper to have regard in determining the reparation due to any failure by the claimant to show reasonable care. We may take by way of example an extreme illustration; an aircraft flying near a launching site without warning or at a time when a launching has been announced or may be reasonably expected, fails to show reasonable care.

Secondly, a distinction seems necessary between injury, loss of life, or damage occurring on the ground or at sea and injury, loss of life, or damage occurring in space. Persons on the ground or at sea must be regarded as pursuing their normal avocations; they cannot be presumed to have accepted the risks of activities in space; the same principle applies in respect of property on the ground or at sea. Persons and

[9] Concerning the views of writers on the subject see pp. 172–173, above.

property in space share in the risks of activities in space and the principle of strict liability is therefore inapplicable in respect of them. The most appropriate principle to apply in space would appear to be one of equitable apportionment of the loss, taking into account any evidence concerning relative degrees of fault or lack of reasonable care which may be available. The position regarding injury, loss of life or damage in the air represents an intermediate case, which has generally been regarded as more akin to that of occurrences on the ground or at sea than to that of occurrences in space but may call for further consideration in view of the imminence of supersonic flight, the risks of which may be comparable to those of activities in space.

The submission of an international claim in respect of injury, loss of life or damage resulting from activities in space should not be subject to any condition of prior exhaustion of any local remedies that may be available. The whole concept of the prior exhaustion of local remedies has no real application to happenings beyond the normal range of local remedies; activities in space are of this nature. If injury or damage arising from the activities in space of Laputa occurs to a Laputan national there may be no recourse beyond any local remedy which may be applicable; if such injury or damage occurs in Laputan territory, waters or air space to a national of Lilliput or Brobdingnag the *rationale* of the local remedies rule applies; but if it occurs in the territory, waters or air space of Lilliput or Brobdingnag there is no good reason for requiring recourse to a local remedy in Laputa and little prospect of securing satisfaction by taking proceedings against Laputa in Lilliput or Brobdingnag; if it occurs on the high seas there is no possibility of taking proceedings *in rem* against the vessel responsible wherever it can be found; and if it occurs in space there is, unless and until some full fledged machinery of government develops there, no conceivable local remedy to exhaust. The practical importance of the matter is well illustrated by the fact that the U.S.A. proposal concerning liability for space vehicle accident submitted to the United Nations Legal Sub-Committee in 1962 specifically envisages that a claim may be presented internationally "without regard to the prior exhaustion of any local remedies that may be available".

The most difficult of the questions pending is that of the incidence of liability in cases in which more than one State has some measure of responsibility as launching State, State procuring the launching, or State from whose territory or facility the object is launched, or in which an international organisation is involved; until this question has been resolved in a generally acceptable manner it may be anticipated that the States concerned will make a practice of dealing with it in launching facility agreements. Thus the Interim Agreement of May 6, 1964, between Australia, the United Kingdom and the European Organisation for the Development and Construction of Space Vehicle Launchers[10] concerning ELDO firings contains provisions on the subject. ELDO is to indemnify the Commonwealth of Australia and the United Kingdom against any loss or damage suffered by the Commonwealth or the United Kingdom and against any liability of any kind in respect of claims against the commonwealth or the United Kingdom, their respective servants or agents for loss, damage or injury that occurs in any place, whether within or outside Australia arising howsoever out of any activity carried out on behalf of the Organisation in Australia;[11] there is no obligation to indemnify if the loss, damage or injury resulted from any failure of the Australian or the United Kingdom departments concerned to exercise any of the responsibilities attributed to them by the Agreement. Claims against the Commonwealth or the United Kingdom may be settled by them for amounts not exceeding £10,000 Australian or £8,000 sterling, subject to consultation with the Organisation if a question of principle is involved; settlements in excess of these amounts are not to be effected by Australia or the United Kingdom except after consultation with and the concurrence of the Organisation; the Commonwealth and the United Kingdom have the conduct of any judicial proceedings instituted against them in their own courts and may, if satisfied that it is just and reasonable to do so, admit liability; they are to inform the Organisation of any pending proceedings.[12] Disputes between the parties to the Agreement are to be referred to an Arbitration Tribunal provided for therein.[13]

[10] Appendix VI, pp. 368–374, below.
[11] Art. 6.
[12] Arts. 7 and 8.
[13] Art. 9.

The parties to a joint undertaking may, on the other hand, without attempting to define their respective liabilities to third parties, waive in advance possible claims against each other. Thus the Special Agreement for a Global Commercial Communications Satellite system provides that neither the United States Communications Satellite Corporation as signatory of the Agreement or manager of the space segment, nor any other signatory as such, shall be liable to any other signatory for loss or damage sustained by reason of a failure or breakdown of a satellite at or after launching or a failure or breakdown of any other portion of the space segment.[14]

[14] Art. 13, p. 355, below.

53

Torts other than Damage by Space Vehicles

DAMAGE by a space vehicle is not the only kind of tort which may be committed in or from space. Other possible types of space tort may include damage to space installations, failure to maintain space installations in a safe condition, conversion, trespass, nuisance or negligence in space resulting in injury or damage in space or on Earth, and, assuming any substantial number of persons to be in space simultaneously, such personal torts as assault and defamation. Neither the Declaration of Legal Principles nor the Institute of International Law resolution affords us any guidance for the future development of the law on this subject.

Any such tort committed in space but taking effect on Earth, on the surface or in territorial airspace, would appear to be governed, subject to the general rules of international law and of any applicable international agreements, by the law of the jurisdiction within which it takes effect.

A tort taking effect in space, when attributable to a space object or committed in a spacecraft, at a manned orbital station, or at a manned station on a celestial body, would clearly be governed by the law of the jurisdiction to which the space object, spacecraft or station is subject.

A tort consisting of action taken on earth but taking effect in space would appear to be governed by the law applicable to any space object, spacecraft or orbital or celestial body station where it takes effect, subject to the possible substitution of the law of the place where the tort was committed if there was no reasonable ground for anticipating its point of impact in space.

Any other tort taking effect in space would appear to be governed by the general principles of law recognised by civilised nations.

Jurisdiction on Earth in respect of space torts would presumably be determined by the law of the *lex fori* relating to foreign torts; in England it would be governed by the principle that the alleged wrong must be actionable if committed in England and not justifiable by the law applicable thereto in space as determined on the basis of the foregoing principles.

Jurisdiction in space in respect of space torts must remain a speculative matter until a later stage of development.

54

Crime

THE commission of a crime in space is clearly a possibility. However carefully the first generation of astronauts may be chosen, a point will some day be reached at which human weakness betrays itself in space as well as on Earth. And before that point is reached space law may have to concern itself with the consequences of crime on Earth.

The Declaration of Legal Principles provides that States shall be guided in the exploration and use of outer space "by the principle of co-operation and mutual assistance" and shall "conduct all their activities in outer space with due regard for the corresponding interests of other States". The general obligation of co-operation and mutual assistance must be regarded as including co-operation and mutual assistance in criminal matters. It would be inconsistent with this obligation for a State to allow its space facilities to be used by a criminal or suspect to escape by way of space from trial or punishment on Earth. Extradition treaties and measures of judicial co-operation in criminal matters should, it is submitted, be regarded as applicable in respect of offences committed in space.

What, however, is the law applicable to crimes committed in space and how far has international law anything to say concerning the question of jurisdiction to deal with such crimes?

Acts of violence in space by an irresponsible adventurer should, it is submitted, be treated as piracy. While piracy was originally a concept of maritime law, the better view would appear to be that piracy *jure gentium* is not exclusively a maritime offence. Hall found its essence to be "acts of violence done upon the ocean or unappropriated lands, or within the territory of the State through descent from the sea, by a

body of men acting independently of any politically organised society".[1]
The Harvard Research in International Law specifically included in its
definition of piracy acts "committed in a place not within the territorial jurisdiction of any State" which are "connected with an attack
on or from the sea or in or from the air"[2] and commented that while
"the pirate of tradition attacked on or from the sea" the possibility of
similar attacks in or from the air cannot now be regarded "as too slight
or too remote for consideration". *In re Piracy Jure Gentium* decided only
that "actual robbery is not an essential element in the crime of piracy
jure gentium and that a frustrated attempt to commit piratical robbery is
equally piracy *jure gentium*"[3] but the Judicial Committee of the Privy
Council pointed out in the report delivered by Lord Sankey that "a
body of international law is growing up with regard to aerial warfare
and aerial transport of which Sir Charles Hedges in 1696 could have
had no possible idea"[4] and said that "a careful examination of the
subject shows a gradual widening of the earlier definition of piracy to
bring it from time to time more in consonance with situations either
not thought of or not in existence when the older juris-consultants were
expressing their opinion".[5] It is therefore submitted that acts which
would be piracy if committed at sea are piracy if committed in space
and are, accordingly, punishable by the law of nations by any State.

In respect of other offences we must take as our point of departure
the provision of the Declaration of Legal Principles that the State on
whose registry an object launched into outer space is carried "shall
retain jurisdiction and control over such objects, and any personnel
thereon, while in outer space".[6] The Institute of International Law
resolution contains a similar provision that "subject to any subsequent
international agreement, persons using, and occurrences at, any space
installation are subject to the jurisdiction of the State having established
the installation".[7] It is therefore clear that if a crime is committed in a
spacecraft or other "object launched into outer space" the law of the

---

[1] Hall, *International Law*, 8th ed. by Pearce Higgins, 1924, p. 314.
[2] Harvard Law School, *Research in International Law, Drafts of Conventions Prepared for the Codification of International Law*, Pt. IV, Piracy, 1932, pp. 768–822.
[3] (1934) A.C. 586–600.   [4] p. 593.   [5] p. 600,
[6] Para. 7.   [7] Para. 6.

State of registry is applicable and it has jurisdiction in the matter, but the principle also appears to be of wider application. Any personnel on an object launched into outer space appear to remain subject to the law and jurisdiction of the State of registry while they remain in outer space; the Institute of International Law resolution covers the point clearly in respect of "persons using, and occurrences at, any space installation"; the Declaration of Legal Principles appears to cover any crime committed while the person remains in outer space. While criminal law is generally regarded as being in principle territorial in its application and outer space and the celestial bodies are not subject to national appropriation by claim of sovereignty or otherwise, it is clearly important to avoid a vacuum in the application of criminal law in space; the principle that the law and jurisdiction of the State of registry of the spacecraft by which the offender entered space are applicable affords a convenient solution of the dilemma.

There remains the question whether the law and jurisdiction of the State of registry of the spacecraft or space station where the offence occurred or, if it occurred elsewhere in space, of the spacecraft by which the offender entered space, are exclusive. There are two cases in which they are clearly not.

A space offender remains subject, in respect of offences committed in space, to the law and courts of his own country in so far as that law so provides in respect of the offence charged.

A crime committed in space may take effect on earth within the territorial jurisdiction of a State; in such a case the State where the crime takes effect is entitled to take jurisdiction of the matter and apply its own law.

How far a State may also take jurisdiction of offences committed against one of its nationals by a foreigner must be regarded as being, in the light of the decision of the Court of International Justice in the *Lotus Case*[8] and the widespread criticism thereof,[9] as doubtful; the recognition by the Declaration of Legal Principles of the jurisdiction of the State of registry appears to create a presumption against the applicability of the *Lotus* precedent to space crimes.

[8] 1927 P.C.I.J., Series A, No. 10.
[9] *Cf.* Jenks, *The Prospects of International Adjudication*, 1964, pp. 240–245.

55

Contract

THE term "space contract", as currently used, relates primarily to contracts for space equipment made between parties on earth and governed by the proper law of the contract in the same manner as any other contract for the supply of equipment.

One can, however, conceive of a variety of possible types of contract which would be space contracts in a more distinctive sense.

A contract for personal services in space concluded on Earth would appear to be on the same footing as any other contract for personal services to be rendered outside the jurisdiction where it is conducted; it would be governed on earth by the proper law determined on the basis of the intention of the parties.

Any other contract relating to matters in space concluded on Earth would presumably be governed on Earth by the law applicable in virtue of the rules of private international law of the *forum* where the question arose: for certain classes of such contracts agreed rules will probably be gradually evolved.

A contract concluded in space would presumably be regarded on Earth as governed by the law determined by the will of the parties or the law with which the contract had the most substantial connection.

How any question relating to the law applicable to a contract which might arise in space should be determined is a matter for later consideration.

56

Salvage

THE question of salvage may arise in connection with,[1] or separately from, that of the return to the launcher of space objects which have returned to Earth. One can conceive of salvage operations arising out of space activities being undertaken on earth (at sea, in the airspace or on land), in outer space, or on a celestial body. The matter presents considerable difficulty as only in respect of maritime salvage are well established rules generally recognised.[1]

Salvage at sea arising out of space activities may perhaps be regarded as being, pending agreement on any special rules on the subject, governed by maritime law, though even this cannot be regarded as certain as the maritime law of salvage does not apply, except by special agreement or enactment, to aircraft salvaged at sea; in all other respects further clarification of the position is clearly necessary. The maritime rule, which is that salvage is due for services rendered to a vessel in danger or distress, the amount due being calculated on the basis of the actual services rendered by the salvors, may well commend itself for application in outer space and on celestial bodies.

A comprehensive sea-air-space salvage agreement for salvage operations at sea, by land, or in the atmosphere, and a space salvage agreement for such salvage operations as may become practicable in outer space and on celestial bodies, may well be desirable.

[1] See, for instance, as regards salvage of aircraft, McNair, *Law of the Air*, 3rd ed. by Kerr and Evans, 1964, p. 331 *et seq.*

57

Property Transactions

IF property transactions should take place in space it would seem appropriate to regard them as governed by the law with which the transaction has the most substantial connection. If anything in the nature of real property rights at a space station on a celestial body were to be recognised, the law applicable there would presumably govern them as *lex situs*. Any recognition of real property rights beyond the limits of such a station would, unless a system of concessions, leases or licenses from the United Nations had been established, raise a major question of policy concerning the basis of authority to confer or recognise such rights.

58

Personal Status

_____

THE time may not be far distant when events affecting personal status take place in space.

A man may at any time die in space and his death in space would have legal consequences, but until anything in the nature of a permanent settlement exists in space these consequences would occur primarily on earth. The law governing any presumption of death would be that applicable in the jurisdiction where the question arose, while the law governing inheritance would be determined by the personal law of the deceased, subject to compliance with the fiscal and any other requirements of any jurisdiction where assets are located. Complications would begin to occur if the deceased left any assets in space as the question of the law applicable there to their distribution, or applicable to their distribution on the repatriation of such assets to earth, would then arise.

There is no present reason for supposing that marriages or births in space will occur sufficiently soon to give any immediate character to such questions as the law governing marital capacity or formal validity in respect of marriages in space or the nationality of children born in space.

As regards all such questions it must suffice to say that any matters of personal status which may be relevant in space must be regarded as governed by the personal law of the person concerned; the elaboration of any more detailed treatment of particular questions must await experience.

59

Corporate Personality for Space Purposes

JOINT action in space matters is already of significant, and appears destined to be of increasing, importance; it may prove desirable that some of the instrumentalities entrusted with the conduct of such activities should be constituted as corporate bodies. This may pose the question whether a space corporation can be created by some appropriate type of international action without recourse to incorporation under any particular municipal legal system.

Jessup and Taubenfeld have envisaged the establishment of a Cosmic Development Corporation "reflecting the interests and contributions of all nations in its composition" and entrusted with wide responsibilities, including, in the "early period where no large population were involved", the provisions of "governmental services in outlying areas, as did the great trading companies of the age of discovery on Earth".[1] A body of this importance and scope would presumably be created by treaty as an international organisation or by decision of the General Assembly as an organ of the United Nations.

In the early stages, however, space corporations might be designed primarily to discharge specific limited functions comparable in organisation and importance to the European Company for the Financing of Railway Equipment, the Free Port of Trieste, or the former Whangpu Conservancy Board, rather than to the International Bank for Reconstruction and Development or the International Civil Aviation Organisation. It is not, it is submitted, necessary in order to give such a corporation a distinctively international character to have it created by treaty or to resort to the device of multiple incorporation in a number

---

[1] *Controls for Outer Space and the Antarctic Analogy*, 1959, p. 282.

of countries; there appears to be no reason why the United Nations should not, by General Assembly action or in some other appropriate way, assume by general agreement authority to charter space corporations and to regulate their activities. Everything must have a beginning at some time and the absence of any directly applicable precedent is not a valid argument against the legitimacy and desirability of something which is inherently reasonable and involves no interference with any existing rights or jurisdiction; there is no good reason why the United Nations should not exercise on behalf of the world community as a whole the right to create new corporate persons which each of its Members concedes to all other Members. The corporate personality of international organisations created by treaty was regarded as a novelty until it was firmly established by the specific provisions which became a matter of common form in the constitutions of international organisations drafted in the nineteen forties and by the decision of the International Court of Justice in the *Reparation for Injuries Case;*[2] a comparable but further development may be imminent in respect of space corporations created directly by the action of international organisations.

[2] 1949 I.C.J. 174.

60

Demilitarisation of Space

GENERAL Assembly Resolution 1148 (XII) of November 14, 1957, called, in a resolution relating to disarmament, for "the joint study of an inspection system designed to ensure that the sending of objects through outer space should be exclusively for peaceful and scientific purposes".[1] General Assembly Resolution 1348 (XIII) of December 13, 1958, reaffirmed the exclusive dedication of space to peaceful purposes but again stated it as an aim rather than as an accomplished reality, primarily by means of a recital in the Preamble "that it is the common aim that outer space should be used for peaceful purposes only". Successive proposals for the demilitarisation of space submitted to the Ten Nation and Eighteen Nation Disarmament Committees during the period from 1960 to 1962[2] envisaged such measures as prohibition of placing weapons of mass destruction in orbit or stationing them in outer space, advance notification of launchings, and prelaunch inspection. None of these proposals has materialised into an accepted treaty.

The Treaty Banning Nuclear Weapon Tests in the Atmosphere, in Outer Space and Underwater, signed at Moscow on August 5, 1962, on behalf of the United States of America, the United Kingdom and the U.S.S.R., and signed subsequently on behalf of more than one hundred countries, represents the first step towards the demilitarisation of space by treaty. Each of the parties to the Moscow Treaty "undertakes to prohibit, to prevent, and not to carry out any nuclear weapon test explosion, or any other nuclear explosion, at any place under its jurisdiction or control" (a) in the atmosphere, (b) beyond its limits, including outer space, or (c) underwater, including territorial waters, or

---

[1] Para. 1. (f).   [2] pp. 46–51, above.

high seas, or (d) in any other environment if such explosion causes radio-active débris to be present outside the territorial limits of the State under whose jurisdiction or control such explosion is conducted; this last provision is stated to be without prejudice to the conclusion of a treaty resulting in the permanent banning of all nuclear test explosions, including such explositions underground.[3] Each of the parties "undertakes furthermore to refrain from causing, encouraging or in any way participating in, the carrying out of any nuclear weapon test explosion, or any other nuclear explosion, anywhere which would take place in any of the environments described, or have the effect referred to" in the Treaty.[4] The Treaty may be amended by a majority of votes of all the parties to the Treaty including the votes of all the original parties; amendments "enter into force for all parties upon the deposit of instruments of ratification by a majority of all the parties, including the instruments of ratification of all of the Original Parties".[5] The Treaty is "of unlimited duration" but provides that "each Party shall in exercising its national sovereignty have the right to withdraw from the Treaty if it decides that extraordinary events, related to the subject matter of this Treaty, have jeopardised the supreme interests of its country" and that "it shall give notice of such withdrawal to all other Parties to the Treaty three months in advance".[6]

The withdrawal clause of the Treaty, though understandable, is most unhappily expressed. The right of withdrawal conferred by the Treaty is not an attribute of sovereignty but a right which the specific terms of the Treaty permit each party to exercise in its discretion if satisfied that extraordinary events related to the subject matter of the Treaty have jeopardised its supreme interests. As the International Court has affirmed and reaffirmed[7] the conclusion of treaty engagements is not a violation or surrender but an exercise of sovereignty; it is of great importance that reference to sovereignty in the withdrawal clause of the Treaty of Moscow should not become a precedent which would tend to undermine this position.

Questions may also arise concerning the effect of the Treaty in

[3] Art. 1. (1).   [4] Art. 1 (2).   [5] Art. 2.   [6] Art. 4.
[7] *Cf.* Jenks, *The Prospects of International Adjudication*, 1964, pp. 498–500.

relation to States which are not parties to it, particularly France and China which have declined to sign. The possibility that the treaty may at some stage come to be regarded as having been so widely accepted that it must be considered binding on signatories and non-signatories alike, in much the same manner in which the provision of the Declaration of Paris of 1856 that privateering is and remains abolished, though never formally accepted by the United States, came to be regarded as a statement of customary law, cannot be lightly dismissed.[8]

General Assembly Resolution 1884 (XVIII) of October 17, 1963, welcomes "expressions by the U.S.S.R. and the United States of their intention not to station in outer space any objects carrying nuclear weapons or other kinds of weapons of mass destruction" and solemnly calls upon all States "to refrain from placing in orbit around the Earth any objects carrying nuclear weapons or any other kinds of weapons of mass destruction, installing such weapons on celestial bodies, or stationing such weapons in outer space in any other manner". This resolution does not purport to state the existing law or to create any new obligation; it welcomes certain statements of intention by the U.S.S.R. and the United States and solemnly calls upon all States to act in the same manner. During the discussion of the Declaration of Legal Principles Governing the Activities of States in the Exploration and Use of Outer Space which took place in the Committee on the Peaceful Uses of Outer Space immediately prior to its transmission to the General Assembly for adoption the representatives of Austria and India expressed regret that the Declaration contains no provision prohibiting the stationing of weapons in orbit[9] but no such provision was included. It would nevertheless be a grave mistake to underestimate or belittle the importance of General Assembly Resolution 1884 (XVIII). A State repudiating such a statement of intention or failing to respond to such a solemn appeal would assume a responsibility equivalent to the violation of a legal obligation. Such conduct would put the whole world on its guard; its political consequences would be far-reaching but it might

[8] *Cf.* R. F. Roxburgh, *International Conventions and Third States*, 1917, pp. 91–94; *The Marie Glaeser* (1914), p. 218–233.
[9] United Nations Document A/5549/Add.1 of November 27, 1963, pp. 21 and 28.

also have legal effects; in the event of a deterioration of the international situation resulting in hostilities, it might well create a presumption of aggression. The resolution may also come to be regarded as a statement of accepted usage and such usage may, in course of time, and perhaps within a relatively brief period of time, be recognised to have acquired the force of customary law.

The Declaration of Legal Principles contains nothing relating directly and specifically to the demilitarisation of space, but the references in the Preamble to "peaceful purposes", the principle that "the exploration and use of outer space shall be carried on for the benefit and in the interests of all mankind", the principle that space activities "shall be carried on in accordance with international law, including the Charter of the United Nations, in the interest of maintaining international peace and security and promoting international co-operation and understanding", the "principle of co-operation and mutual assistance" by which States are to be guided in the exploration and use of outer space, and the principle that astronauts are "envoys of mankind", all have a significant bearing on the matter. Further provisions relating to the demilitarisation of space may be expected to be included in any general disarmament treaty which may be negotiated; meanwhile a number of problems arise in connection with the determination of what are, and what are not, peaceful purposes.

61

Intelligence Satellites

THE legality or illegality of intelligence satellites has been a matter of acute controversy and was one of the points of disagreement which for a time delayed all progress in the consideration of the proposed Declaration of Legal Principles. The Declaration is silent on the subject; so also is the Institute of International Law resolution. The text of a proposed Declaration originally submitted by the U.S.S.R. contained a provision that "the use of artificial satellites for the collection of intelligence information in the territory of a foreign State is incompatible with the objectives of mankind in its conquest of outer space"; the inclusion of such a provision in the text of the Declaration was not acceptable to the United States and other Western States. The suggested text did not, it will be observed, propose to declare that the use of intelligence satellites is illegal; it proposed to declare their use incompatible with the objectives of mankind in its conquest of outer space. The United States acknowledges that it uses such satellites; the U.S.S.R. practice in the matter has not been publicly announced in any similar manner. Intelligence activities by reason of their nature cannot claim any special clothing of positive legality; whether they are positively illegal depends on their purpose and the manner in which they are conducted; in general, they are not illegal by international law but are, when carried on within the territory of a State, subject to heavy municipal law penalties. In these circumstances the question does not admit of a direct answer; all that can be said with confidence is that no agreement exists on any special rule governing the use of intelligence satellites and that the use of such satellites is therefore governed by the general rules of international law relating to intelligence activities. A more satisfactory solution for the problem is unlikely to be forthcoming until some agreed international plan for mutual protection against surprise attack, including provision for the exchange through the United Nations of intelligence information available from satellite data, has become generally effective.[1]

[1] See also as regards the return of space objects used for intelligence purposes Chap. 38, pp. 244–245, above and, as regards the repatriation of astronauts engaged on intelligence work, Chap. 39, p. 249, *Cf*, also Roland J. Stanger (editor), *Essays on Espionage and International Law*, 1963.

62

Nuclear Test Detection Satellites

THE Draft Treaty submitted to the Conference on the Discontinuance of Nuclear Weapon Tests by the United Kingdom and United States Delegations on April 18, 1961, provided for a system of detection of high altitude tests based on the use of satellites.[1] No provision for anything of this nature is made in the Moscow Treaty, but the United States has announced that it has placed in orbit satellites for this purpose. While one may regret that it has not been possible to establish such a detection system on a co-operative basis, there can be no question concerning the legality of action for the purpose taken by any of the parties to the Treaty. Such action is a normal incident of the right of every party to the Treaty to satisfy itself that the provisions of the Treaty are being scrupulously observed.

[1] pp. 51–52, above.

63

Missile Warning Satellites

THE use in outer space of a missile warning satellite, equipped only to warn and not to retaliate, is not inconsistent with the expressions of intention and recommendation not to station weapons of mass destruction in outer space contained in General Assembly Resolution 1884 (XVIII) of October 17, 1963. The use of such satellites falls clearly within the right of self-defence as defined and limited by Article 51 of the Charter of the United Nations. Co-operative arrangements among friendly powers concerning missile warning satellites may be expected to be of increasing importance and may form the subject of bilateral or plurilateral agreements.

64

Settlement of Disputes

THE Declaration of Legal Principles provides that space activities shall be carried on "in accordance with international law, including the Charter of the United Nations".[1] The provisions and procedures of the Charter, and of international law generally, relating to the settlement of disputes are therefore applicable to disputes arising out of space activities. Some of the more important implications of this position may be stated briefly as follows.

The principles stated in the Charter that all Members of the United Nations "shall settle their international disputes by peaceful means in such a manner that international peace and security, and justice, are not endangered" and that "all Members shall refrain in their international relations from the threat or use of force against the territorial integrity or political independence of any State, or in any other manner inconsistent with the purposes of the United Nations" are applicable to space disputes; while the threat or use of force against the space activities of another State may not necessarily always constitute a threat or use of force against the territorial integrity or political independence of that State (though in certain cases it would do so by reason of its probable effects) such a threat or use of force would be "inconsistent with the purposes of the United Nations" which in virtue of the Charter itself include the development of "friendly relations among nations based on respect for the principle of equal rights" and may now be regarded as having been more fully expressed in respect of space matters by the Declaration of Legal Principles.

The obligation under Article 33 of the Charter of "the parties to any

[1] Para. 4.

309

dispute the continuance of which is likely to endanger the maintenance of peace and security" to "seek a solution by negotiation, enquiry, mediation, conciliation, arbitration, judicial settlement, resort to regional agencies or arrangements, or other peaceful means of their own choice" applies to space disputes between States, and the powers and procedures of the Security Council and the General Assembly with respect to the pacific settlement of disputes and threats to the peace, breaches of the peace, and acts of aggression apply to such disputes.

The jurisdiction of the International Court of Justice as defined by the Statute of the Court, and the compulsory jurisdiction of the Court as between States having accepted the Optional Clause or bound by other instruments conferring compulsory jurisdiction on the Court,[2] apply to space disputes between States; legal questions relating to activities in space may be referred to the Court for an advisory opinion by the General Assembly or the Security Council, or, in respect of questions arising within the scope of their activities, by the other organs of the United Nations and specialised agencies which have been authorised by the General Assembly to request advisory opinions.[3]

Other obligations of peaceful settlement, such as the provisions of bilateral arbitration and conciliation treaties, are potentially applicable to space disputes; these may include the compromissary clauses of any law-making treaties which are by their terms, or must be regarded by reason of their nature as being, applicable to space.

In general, therefore, the settlement of space disputes is subject to the provisions and procedures governing the settlement of international disputes generally. The procedures for peaceful settlement in force between the parties concerned, whatever they may be and whatever combination of enquiry, conciliation, aribtration and reference to judicial settlement they may comprise, are applicable. What is chiefly important in the matter is that there should be arrangements reasonably appropriate to ensure that such disputes are settled and do not remain the subject of a continuing stalemate prejudicial to the further development of international co-operation in space matters.

[2] *Cf.* Jenks, *The Prospects of International Adjudication*, 1964, pp. 13–118.
[3] *Cf.* Jenks, *op. cit.*, pp. 193–208.

We must naturally consider from this angle whether the normal procedures of peaceful settlement can and should be supplemented in respect of disputes arising out of space activities. The problems which make progress in the matter difficult are a reflection of those which have become familiar in connection with the peaceful settlement of international disputes generally. One would like to carry into the new world of activities in space the principle of the general applicability of the compulsory jurisdiction of the International Court of Justice, but the political obstacles to the general acceptance of compulsory jurisdiction are no less applicable to activities in space than to activities on Earth and one can sense a not unnatural reluctance to leave to judicial determination some of the larger questions of policy relating to the legal status of space and the celestial bodies. In these circumstances a more cautious and hybrid approach, consisting partly of reliance on existing obligations and procedures of peaceful settlement with their recognised limitations and partly on special measures for certain defined and limited classes of dispute arising out of space activities, appears to be desirable.

There are three types of space dispute for which special measures do appear desirable.

Disputed questions of fact relating to activities in space may present special difficulties of verification and the establishment by the United Nations of appropriate arrangements for the prompt and impartial investigation of any such questions in a competent manner might render a service of great value.

Disputes relating to liability for space vehicle accidents may call for special treatment by reason of both the human and financial considerations involved. The recognition of such liability is of little practical value unless accompanied by a reasonably expeditious and effective procedure for the recovery of the reparation due. Such a procedure presupposes an agreed international forum, where governmental immunity is not a bar to action and preferably (as envisaged in the United States proposal to the United Nations Committee on the Peaceful Uses of Outer Space) where the local remedies rule is inapplicable. Where the proceedings are between States the International Court of

Justice would be an appropriate forum; the Court could, if desirable, have recourse in such cases to the powers conferred by its Statute to form chambers to deal with particular categories of cases[4] and to appoint assessors.[5] If the responsibility rested upon an international organisation of States within the United Nations system it might be practicable to have recourse to the advisory jurisdiction of the Court; it would not be possible under the Statute of the Court as at present in force to initiate contentious proceedings before the Court in a case one of the parties to which was an international organisation, and a case involving an international organisation outside the United Nations system could be referred for an advisory opinion only through a United Nations body.[6] Nor would it be possible under the Statute to give an injured party other than a State any direct access to the Court as plaintiff, or to give an operating company engaged in activities in space a *locus standi* in the Court as either plaintiff or defendant. It might therefore be necessary or wise to envisage the possibility of certain cases being referred to special arbitral tribunals, possibly constituted in accordance with the United Nations Model Rules on Arbitral Procedure adapted as necessary to the fact that one of the parties is not a State.

When any substantial number of people come to be in space, a space magistracy with a jurisdiction comparable to that of a magistrate's court, and possibly entrusted in the first instance to officers in charge of a space station, may be required; the experience gained in the application of the Antarctic Treaty may alternatively prove to be suggestive in the matter.

Apart from any measures which may prove possible as regards these special types of cases, it is clearly desirable that future general and bilateral treaties relating to space matters should, whenever practicable, make provision for the impartial determination of any disputes relating to other interpretation or application which it has not been possible to settle by negotiation.[7]

---

[4] Art. 26.
[5] Art. 32.
[6] *Cf.* Jenks, *The Prospects of International Adjudication,* 1964, pp. 219–220.
[7] For illustrations of such provisions, see pp. 355–356, 359, 366–367, 373–374, 456–457, 459 and 462, below.

65

Some Considerations Affecting Further Developments

It is of paramount importance that the future development of space law should be shaped and moulded by a continuing partnership of bold statesmanship, imaginative legal vision, and thorough grasp of the scientific and technological factors involved.

Modern society is confronted by no more crucial problem than that of ensuring that scientific and technological developments and gadgetry remain the servant and do not become the master of man. Thinkers and writers, philosophers and playwrights have been preoccupied and at times almost obsessed by the problem for a generation. Capek, Kafka and Ionesco have taught us all to shudder in contemplation of robots coming to life, of science and technology as the thumbscrews and rack of an inhuman statecraft, and of human compassion and human dignity metamorphosised into the ways of the rhinoceros. We lawyers, as is our wont, have been less sensitive to the problem. Only recently have we become sufficiently aware that the impact of an ever more dynamic science and technology upon society confronts us, as lawyers no less than as citizens, with a wide range of new and urgent problems. Only now are international lawyers beginning to be conscious that nuclear energy and activities in space are adding new dimensions to the constant interaction of law, science and politics.

Gagarin and Glenn are the Christopher Columbus and Vasco da Gama of our day, and the riddle of the hidden side of the moon has become for our children what the search for the north-west passage was for the Elizabethans or the mystery of the sources of the Nile for the Victorians. The age following the great maritime discoveries of the sixteenth century bequeathed to us the freedom of the seas; the generation following the opening up of Africa gave us the principle that the development of the resources of the world for the benefit of all its peoples is a sacred trust of civilisation. The evolution of law and politics, while lagging well behind the supersonic speed now attained by the progress of science and technology, has nevertheless developed in our time a momentum unprecedented in previous experience. Less than seven years have elapsed since the launching of the first sputnik and we already have the makings of the common law of space.

With the unanimous adoption by the General Assembly of the Declaration of Legal Principles space law has passed from the speculative phase in which it was essentially a body of general but, by their very nature, debatable propositions formulated by legal writers, and has come to consist of a body of principles and rules recognised by States and international organisations.

To attempt to predict the course or rate of further development would be hazardous in the extreme, but we can at least attempt to distinguish some of the broad considerations of policy which will call for continuing attention.

It will remain essential to hold a balance between too fast and too slow. This has been from the outset the central dilemma of space law – to establish firmly the common interest of mankind in space and the rule of law in space before *de facto* situations have crystallised too far to permit of any bold international initiative, while avoiding crystallising the law prematurely before enough is known of the facts to which it will apply. Hitherto, this balance has been well held, but the problem is a continuing one which will confront us through successive stages in the development of the law.

A similar balance must be held between what is appropriate for regulation by law and what is best left to understandings among scientists. In certain fields, such as that of what precautions should be taken against contamination of or from space, this may in the near future become an immediate and key issue.

There is an obvious danger that space law, by reason of its novelty and the knowledge of advanced technology necessary for dealing with some of its more technical aspects, will become a speciality at much too early a stage of its development. In respect of such matters as space telecommunications and space contamination highly specialised knowledge and skills are indispensable, but it is of vital importance that the general principles of space law should reflect fully contemporary tendencies in general international law and the law of international organisation. We cannot afford to imprison the development of space law in concepts and prejudices derived from an earlier stage in the development of international law in which responsible international lawyers no longer believe. The cloven hoof of sovereignty and sterile semantics of inductive positivism have no place in space law.

Another danger which must be watched with special care during the formative stages of the development of the law is that States which are at present space powers may be apt to think of themselves too exclusively as space powers rather than as States which may some day be affected by the space activities of others, while States which are not at present space powers may be too apt to think of themselves as potential victims of the activities in space of others rather than as potential participants in such activities. These instinctive attitudes do not necessarily reflect the long-term interests of the States of either group. Only when they come to terms with each other will we be able to deal satisfactorily with the details of such matters as liability for damage.

Space activities have caught the imagination of international lawyers, as they have caught that of the public generally, by their dramatic quality. Man's love of adventure has never been intoxicated by quite so strong a wine as the sense that man is no longer earthbound. Neither the Poles nor Everest could quite compare with this supreme challenge. But activities in space are only one facet of the complex problems which scientific and technological progress poses today for international law, and the law of space is only one branch of the law governing the impact of scientific and technological progress upon international society. In developing it we must never lose sight of its place in a larger whole.

In like manner, man's activities in space are a projection of his life on earth. It is for this reason that the suggestion sometimes made that responsibility for international action in respect of space matters should be concentrated in a special agency for the purpose is so lacking in realism. Space telecommunications are by their nature a part of tele-communications generally, the demilitarisation of space cannot be divorced from the general problem of disarmament, and the problem of law and order in space is but a new phase of the perennial problem of peace on earth and goodwill among men. The problems of space must therefore be tackled and mastered within the general framework of the Charter of the United Nations.

If, without losing sight of these broad issues of policy, we apply ourselves with patience to the task of resolving the successive problems which the development of space activities presents, the solid progress already made since the launching of the first sputnik may prove to have been a memorable turning-point in man's long endeavour to seek peace and pursue it.

DECLARATION OF LEGAL PRINCIPLES GOVERNING THE ACTIVITIES OF STATES IN THE EXPLORATION AND USE OF OUTER SPACE

Unanimously adopted by the General Assembly of the United Nations on December 13, 1963[1]

The General Assembly

Inspired by the great prospects opening up before mankind as a result of man's entry into outer space,

Recognising the common interest of all mankind in the progress of the exploration and use of outer space for peaceful purposes,

Believing that the exploration and use of outer space should be carried on for the betterment of mankind and for the benefit of States irrespective of their degree of economic or scientific development,

Desiring to contribute to broad international co-operation in the scientific as well as in the legal aspects of exploration and use of outer space for peaceful purposes,

Believing that such co-operation will contribute to the development of mutual understanding and to the strengthening of friendly relations between nations and peoples,

Recalling its resolution 110 (II) of November 3, 1947, which condemned propaganda designed or likely to provoke or encourage any threat to the peace, breach of the peace, or act of aggression, and considering that the aforementioned resolution is applicable to outer space,

Taking into consideration its resolutions 1721 (XVI) of December 20, 1961, and 1802 (XVII) of December 14, 1962, adopted unanimously by the States Members of the United Nations,

Solemnly declares that in the exploration and use of outer space States should be guided by the following principles:

1. The exploration and use of outer space shall be carried on for the benefit and in the interests of all mankind.

2. Outer space and celestial bodies are free for exploration and use by all States on a basis of equality and in accordance with international law.

3. Outer space and celestial bodies are not subject to national appropriation

[1] Resolution 1962 (XVIII).

317

by claim of sovereignty, by means of use or occupation, or by any other means.

4. The activities of States in the exploration and use of outer space shall be carried on in accordance with international law, including the Charter of the United Nations, in the interest of maintaining international peace and security and promoting international co-operation and understanding.

5. States bear international responsibility for national activities in outer space, whether carried on by governmental agencies or by non-governmental entities, and for assuring that national activities are carried on in conformity with the principles set forth in the present Declaration. The activities of non-governmental entities in outer space shall require authorisation and continuing supervision by the State concerned. When activities are carried on in outer space by an international organisation, responsibility for compliance with the principles set forth in this Declaration shall be borne by the international organisation and by the States participating in it.

6. In the exploration and use of outer space, States shall be guided by the principle of co-operation and mutual assistance and shall conduct all their activities in outer space with due regard for the corresponding interests of other States. If a State has reason to believe that an outer space activity or experiment planned by it or its nationals would cause potentially harmful interference with activities of other States in the peaceful exploration and use of outer space, it shall undertake appropriate international consultations before proceeding with any such activity or experiment. A State which has reason to believe that an outer space activity or experiment planned by another State would cause potentially harmful interference with activities in the peaceful exploration and use of outer space may request consultation concerning the activity or experiment.

7. The State on whose registry an object launched into outer space is carried shall retain jurisdiction and control over such object, and any personnel thereon, while in outer space. Ownership of objects launched into outer space, and of their component parts, is not affected by their passage through outer space or by their return to the Earth. Such objects or component parts found beyond the limits of the State or registry shall be returned to that State, which shall furnish identifying data upon request prior to return.

8. Each State which launches or procures the launching of an object into outer space, and each State from whose territory or facility an object is launched, is internationally liable for damage to a foreign State or to its natural or juridical persons by such object or its component parts on the Earth, in air space, or in outer space.

9. States shall regard astronauts as envoys of mankind in outer space, and

shall render to them all possible assistance in the event of accident, distress, or emergency landing on the territory of a foreign State or on the high seas. Astronauts who make such a landing shall be safely and promptly returned to the State of registry of their space vehicle.

1280th Plenary Meeting
December 13, 1963

EXTRACTS FROM OTHER GENERAL ASSEMBLY RESOLUTIONS

RESOLUTION 1148 (XII) OF NOVEMBER 14, 1957

The General Assembly

Recalling its resolution 808 (IX) of November 4, 1954,

Emphasising the urgency of decreasing the danger of war and improving the prospects of a durable peace through achieving international agreement on reduction, limitation and open inspection of armaments and armed forces,

Welcoming the narrowing of differences which has resulted from the extensive negotiations in the Sub-Committee of the Disarmament Commission,

Believing that immediate, carefully measured steps can be taken for partial measures of disarmament and that such steps will facilitate further measures of disarmament,

1. *Urges* that the States concerned, and particularly those which are members of the Sub-Committee of the Disarmament Commission, give priority to reach a disarmament agreement which, upon its entry into force, will provide for the following:

* * *

(f) The joint study of an inspection system designed to ensure that the sending of objects through outer space shall be exclusively for peaceful and scientific purposes;

* * *

RESOLUTION 1721 (XVI) OF DECEMBER 20, 1961

International co-operation in the peaceful uses of outer space

A

The General Assembly

Recognising the common interest of mankind in furthering the peaceful uses of outer space and the urgent need to strengthen international co-operation in this important field,

Believing that the exploration and use of outer space should be only for the betterment of mankind and to the benefit of States irrespective of the stage of their economic or scientific development,

1. *Commends* to States for their guidance in the exploration and use of outer space the following principles:

(a) International law, including the Charter of the United Nations, applies to outer space and celestial bodies;

(b) Outer space and celestial bodies are free for exploration and use by all States in conformity with international law and are not subject to national appropriation;

2. *Invites* the Committee on the Peaceful Uses of Outer Space to study and report on the legal problems which may arise from the exploration and use of outer space.

1085*th Plenary Meeting*
December 20, 1961

B

The General Assembly

Believing that the United Nations should provide a focal point for international co-operation in the peaceful exploration and use of outer space,

1. *Calls upon* States launching objects into orbit or beyond to furnish information promptly to the Committee on the Peaceful Uses of Outer Space, through the Secretary-General, for the registration of launchings;

2. *Requests* the Secretary-General to maintain a public registry of the information furnished in accordance with paragraph 1 above;

3. *Requests* the Committee on the Peaceful Uses of Outer Space, in co-operation with the Secretary-General and making full use of the functions and resources of the Secretariat:

(a) To maintain close contact with governmental and non-governmental organisations concerned with outer space matters;

(b) To provide for the exchange of such information relating to outer space activities as Governments may supply on a voluntary basis, supplementing but not duplicating existing technical and scientific exchanges;

(c) To assist in the study of measures for the promotion of international co-operation in outer space activities;

4. *Further* requests the Committee on the Peaceful Uses of Outer Space to report to the General Assembly on the arrangements undertaken for the performance of those functions and on such developments relating to the peaceful uses of outer space as it considers significant.

1085*th Plenary Meeting*
December 20, 1961

Appendix

C

The General Assembly

Noting with gratification the marked progress for meteorological science and technology opened up by the advances in outer space,

Convinced of the world-wide benefits to be derived from international co-operation in weather research and analysis,

1. *Recommends* to all Member States and to the World Meteorological Organisation and other appropriate specialised agencies the early and comprehensive study, in the light of developments in outer space, of measures:

(a) To advance the state of atmospheric science and technology so as to provide greater knowledge of basic physical forces affecting climate and the possibility of large-scale weather modification;

(b) To develop existing weather forecasting capabilities and to help Member States make effective use of such capabilities through regional meteorological centres;

2. *Requests* the World Meteorological Organisation, consulting as appropriate with the United Nations Educational, Scientific and Cultural Organisation and other specialised agencies and governmental and non-governmental organisations, such as the International Council of Scientific Unions, to submit a report to the Governments of its Member States and to the Economic and Social Council at its thirty-fourth session regarding appropriate organisational and financial arrangements to achieve those ends, with a view to their further consideration by the General Assembly at its seventeenth session;

3. *Requests* the Committee on the Peaceful Uses of Outer Space, as it deems appropriate, to review that report and submit its comments and recommendations to the Economic and Social Council and to the General Assembly.

1085th Plenary Meeting
December 20, 1961

D

The General Assembly

Believing that communication by means of satellites should be available to the nations of the world as soon as practicable on a global and non-discrimatory basis,

Convinced of the need to prepare the way for the establishment of effective operational satellite communication,

1. *Notes with satisfaction* that the International Telecommunication Union

plans to call a special conference in 1963 to make allocations of radio frequency bands for outer space activities;

2. *Recommends* that the International Telecommunication Union consider at that conference those aspects of space communication in which international co-operation will be required;

3. *Notes* the potential importance of communication satellites for use by the United Nations and its principal organs and specialised agencies for both operational and informational requirements;

4. *Invites* the Special Fund and the Expanded Programme of Technical Assistance, in consultation with the International Telecommunication Union, to give sympathetic consideration to requests from Member States for technical and other assistance for the survey of their communication needs and for the development of their domestic communication facilities, so that they may make effective use of space communication;

5. *Requests* the International Telecommunication Union, consulting as appropriate with Member States, the United Nations Educational, Scientific and Cultural Organisation and other specialised agencies and governmental and non-governmental organisations, such as the Committee on Space Research of the International Council of Scientific Unions, to submit a report on the implementation of these proposals to the Economic and Social Council as its thirty-fourth session and to the General Assembly at its seventeenth session;

6. *Requests* the Committee on the Peaceful Uses of Outer Space, as it deems appropriate, to review that report and submit its comments and recommendations to the Economic and Social Council and to the General Assembly.

1085th Plenary Meeting
December 20, 1961

*　　*　　*

RESOLUTION 1802 (XVII) OF DECEMBER 14, 1962

International co-operation in the peaceful uses of outer space

The General Assembly

Recalling its resolution 1721 (XVI) of December 20, 1961, on international co-operation in the peaceful uses of outer space,

Believing that the activities of States in the exploration and use of outer space should be carried out in conformity with international law, including the Charter of the United Nations, in the interest of friendly relations among nations,

Appendix

Stressing the necessity of the progressive development of international law pertaining to the further elaboration of basic legal principles governing the activities of States in the exploration and use of outer space and to liability for space vehicle accidents and to assistance to and return of astronauts and space vehicles and to other legal problems,

Bearing in mind that the application of scientific and technological advances in outer space, particularly in the fields of meteorology and communications, can bring great advantages to mankind and contribute to the economic and social progress of the developing countries as envisaged in the United Nations Development Decade programme,

Having considered the report submitted by the Committee on the Peaceful Uses of Outer Space in response to resolution 1721 (XVI).

* * *

II

1. *Endorses* the recommendations set forth in the report of the Committee on the Peaceful Uses of Outer Space concerning the exchange of information;

2. *Notes with appreciation* that a number of Member States have already, on a voluntary basis, provided information on their national space programmes, and urges other States and regional and international organisations to do so;

3. *Urges* all Member States and appropriate specialised agencies to give whole-hearted and effective support to the international programmes mentioned in the report and already under way, including the International Year of the Quiet Sun and the World Magnetic Survey;

4. *Notes* that the Committee on the Peaceful Uses of Outer Space considers that the creation and use of sounding rocket launching facilities under United Nations sponsorship would contribute to the achievement of the objectives of resolution 1721 (XVI) by furthering international collaboration in space research and the advancement of human knowledge, and by providing opportunity for valuable practical training for interested users;

5. *Notes* the recommendation that Member States should consider the establishment under United Nations sponsorship of a sounding rocket facility, or facilities, on the geomagnetic equator, in time for the International Year of the Quiet Sun;

6. *Endorses* the basic principles suggested by the Committee on the Peaceful Uses of Outer Space for the operation of such facilities under United Nations sponsorship;

7. *Affirms* that such facilities, when established and operated in accordance

with these principles, shall, at the request of the host Member State, be eligible for United Nations sponsorship;

III

1. *Notes with appreciation* the prompt initial response of the World Meteorological Organisation to the request of the General Assembly, as embodied in resolution 1721 C (XVI), that it report on a programme to advance atmospheric science research and to develop improved weather forecasting capabilities in the light of developments in outer space;

2. *Calls upon* Member States to strengthen weather forecasting services and to encourage their scientific communities to co-operate in the expansion of atmospheric science research;

3. *Recommends* that the World Meteorological Organisation, in consultation with other United Nation agencies and governmental and nongovernmental organisations, should develop in greater detail its plan for an expanded programme to strengthen meteorological services and research, placing particular emphasis on the use of meteorological satellites and on the expansion of training and educational opportunities in these fields;

4. *Invites* the International Council of Scientific Unions through its member unions and national academies to develop an expanded programme of atmospheric science research which will complement the programmes fostered by the World Meteorological Organisation;

5. *Invites* United Nations agencies concerned with the granting of technical and financial assistance, in consultation with the World Meteorological Organisation, to give sympathetic consideration to requests from Member States for technical and financial assistance to supplement their own resources for these activities, including the improvement of meteorological networks;

6. *Requests* the World Meteorological Organisation, following its Congress in April 1963, to report to the Committee on the Peaceful Uses of Outer Space, and to the Economic and Social Council at its thirty-sixth session, on steps taken relating to these activities;

IV

1. *Notes with appreciation* the prompt initial response of the International Telecommunication Union to the request of the General Assembly, as embodied in resolution 1721 D (XVI), that it report on those aspects of space communications in which international co-operation will be required;

2. *Believes* that communication by satellite offers great benefits to mankind, as it will permit the expansion of radio, telephone and television transmissions,

including the broadcast of United Nations activities, thus facilitating contact among the peoples of the world;

3. *Emphasises* the importance of international co-operation to achieve effective satellite communications which will be available on a world-wide basis;

4. *Observes* that the Secretary-General of the International Telecommunication Union has invited Member States to submit information on:

(a) Technical progress and developments in space telecommunications;

(b) Subjects which they regard as appropriate for international co-operation in order to achieve the objectives set forth in resolution 1721 D (XVI);

(c) Which of those subjects, if any, should be included in the agenda of the Extraordinary Administrative Radio Conference to be held in October 1963;

5. *Notes* that the Secretary-General of the International Telecommunication Union, in the light of the replies, will report on these questions to the next meeting of its Administrative Council in March 1963 in order that the Council may complete the agenda for this Conference;

6. *Considers* it of the utmost importance that this Conference make allocations of radio frequency bands sufficient to meet expected outer space needs;

7. *Requests* the International Telecommunication Union to report to the Committee on the Peaceful Uses of Outer Space, and to the Economic and Social Council at its thirty-sixth session, on progress made relating to its outer space activities.

1192nd *Plenary Meeting*
December 14, 1962

RESOLUTION 1884 (XVIII) OF OCTOBER 17, 1963

Question of general and complete disarmament

The General Assembly

Recalling its resolution 1721 A (XVI) of December 20, 1961, in which it expressed the belief that the exploration and use of outer space should be only for the betterment of mankind,

Determined to take steps to prevent the spread of the arms race to outer space,

1. *Welcomes* the expressions by the Union of Soviet Socialist Republics and the United States of America of their intention not to station in outer

space any objects carrying nuclear weapons or other kinds of weapons of mass destruction;

2. *Solemnly calls upon* all States:

(a) To refrain from placing in orbit around the Earth any objects carrying nuclear weapons or any other kinds of weapons of mass destruction, installing such weapons on celestial bodies, or stationing such weapons in outer space in any other manner;

(b) To refrain from causing, encouraging or in any way participating in the conduct of the foregoing activities.

1244th Plenary Meeting
October 17, 1963

TREATY BANNING NUCLEAR WEAPONS TESTS IN THE ATMOSPHERE, IN OUTER SPACE AND UNDER WATER

The Governments of the United States of America, the United Kingdom of Great Britain and Northern Ireland, and the Union of Soviet Socialist Republics, hereinafter referred to as the "Original Parties",

Proclaiming as their principal aim the speediest possible achievement of an agreement on general and complete disarmament under strict international control in accordance with the objectives of the United Nations which would put an end to the armaments race and eliminate the incentive to the production and testing of all kinds of weapons, including nuclear weapons,

Seeking to achieve the discontinuance of all test explosions of nuclear weapons for all time, determined to continue negotiations to this end, and desiring to put an end to the contamination of man's environment by radioactive substances,

Have agreed as follows:

ARTICLE I

1. Each of the Parties to this Treaty undertakes to prohibit, to prevent, and not to carry out any nuclear weapon test explosion, or any other nuclear explosion, at any place under its jurisdiction or control:

(a) in the atmosphere; beyond its limits, including outer space; or underwater, including territorial waters or high seas; or

(b) in any other environment if such explosion causes radioactive debris to be present outside the territorial limits of the State under whose jurisdiction or control such explosion is conducted. It is understood in this connection that the provisions of this subparagraph are without prejudice to the conclusion of a treaty resulting in the permanent banning of all nuclear test explosions, including all such explosions underground, the conclusion of which, as the Parties have stated in the Preamble to this Treaty, they seek to achieve.

2. Each of the Parties to this Treaty undertakes furthermore to refrain from causing, encouraging, or in any way participating in, the carrying out of any nuclear weapon test explosion, or any other nuclear explosion, any-

where which would take place in any of the environments described, or have the effect referred to, in paragraph 1 of this Article.

ARTICLE II

1. Any Party may propose amendments to this Treaty. The text of any proposed amendment shall be submitted to the Depositary Governments which shall circulate it to all Parties to this Treaty. Thereafter, if requested to do so by one-third or more of the Parties, the Depositary Governments shall convene a conference, to which they shall invite all the Parties, to consider such amendment.

2. Any amendment to this Treaty must be approved by a majority of the votes of all the Parties to this Treaty, including the votes of all of the Original Parties. The amendment shall enter into force for all Parties upon the deposit of instruments of ratification by a majority of all the Parties, including the instruments of ratification of all of the Original Parties.

ARTICLE III

1. This Treaty shall be open to all States for signature. Any State which does not sign this Treaty before its entry into force in accordance with paragraph 3 of this Article may accede to it at any time.

2. This Treaty shall be subject to ratification by signatory States. Instruments of ratification and instruments of accession shall be deposited with the Governments of the Original Parties – the United States of America, the United Kingdom of Great Britain and Northern Ireland, and the Union of Soviet Socialist Republics – which are hereby designated the Depositary Governments.

3. This Treaty shall enter into force after its ratification by all the Original Parties and the deposit of their instruments of ratification.

4. For States whose instruments of ratification or accession are deposited subsequent to the entry into force of this Treaty, it shall enter into force on the date of the deposit of their instruments of ratification or accession.

5. The Depositary Governments shall promptly inform all signatory and acceding States of the date of each signature, the date of deposit of each instrument of ratification of and accession to this Treaty, the date of its entry into force, and the date of receipt of any requests for conferences or other notices.

6. This Treaty shall be registered by the Depositary Governments pursuant to Article 102 of the Charter of the United Nations.

Article IV

This Treaty shall be of unlimited duration.

Each Party shall in exercising its national sovereignty have the right to withdraw from the treaty if it decides that extraordinary events, related to the subject matter of this Treaty, have jeopardised the supreme interests of its country. It shall give notice of such withdrawal to all other Parties to the Treaty three months in advance.

Article V

This Treaty, of which the English and Russian texts are equally authentic, shall be deposited in the archives of the Depositary Governments. Duly certified copies of this Treaty shall be transmitted by the Depositary Governments to the Governments of the signatory and acceding States.

IN WITNESS WHEREOF the undersigned, duly authorised, have signed this Treaty.

DONE in triplicate at the city of Moscow the fifth day of August, one thousand nine hundred and sixty-three.

For the Government of the United States of America: DEAN RUSK.

For the Government of the United Kingdom of Great Britain and Northern Ireland: HOME.

For the Government of the Union of Soviet Socialist Republics: A. GROMYKO.

EXTRACTS FROM I.T.U. REGULATIONS

DEFINITIONS RELATING TO SPACE TELECOMMUNICATION

SECTION IIA. *Space Systems, Services and Stations.*

84 AC Space Service

A radiocommunication service:
— between Earth stations and space stations,
— or between space stations,
— or between Earth stations when the signals are re-transmitted by space stations, or transmitted by reflection from objects in space, excluding reflection or scattering by the ionosphere or within the Earth's atmosphere.

84 AD Earth Station

A station in the space service located either on the Earth's surface, including on board a ship, or on board an aircraft.

84 AE Space Station

A station in the space service located on an object which is beyond, is intended to go beyond, or has been beyond, the major portion of the Earth's atmosphere.

84 AF Space System

Any group of co-operating Earth and space stations, providing a given space service and which, in certain cases, may use objects in space for the reflection of the radiocommunication signals.

84 AG Communication-Satellite Service

A space service:
— between Earth stations, when using active or passive satellites for the exchange of communications of the fixed or mobile service, or
— between an Earth station and stations on active satellites for the exchange of communications of the mobile service, with a view to their re-transmission to or from stations in the mobile service.

84 AH Communication-Satellite Earth Station

An Earth station in the communication-satellite service.

331

84 AI Communication-Satellite Space Station

A space station in the communication-satellite service, on an Earth satellite.

84 AJ Active Satellite

An Earth satellite carrying a station intended to transmit or re-transmit radiocommunication signals.

84 AK Passive Satellite

An Earth satellite intended to transmit radiocommunication signals by reflection.

84 AL Satellite System

Any group of co-operating stations providing a given space service and including one or more active or passive satellites.

84 AM Space Research Service

A space service in which spacecraft or other objects in space are used for scientific or technological research purposes.

84 AN Space Research Earth Station

An Earth station in the space research service.

84 AO Space Research Space Station

A space station in the space research service.

84 AP Broadcasting-Satellite Service

A space service in which signals transmitted or re-transmitted by reflection from objects in orbit around the Earth, are intended for direct reception by the general public.

84 AQ Radionavigation-Satellite Service

A service using space stations on Earth satellites for the purpose of radionavigation, including, in certain cases, transmission or re-transmission of supplementary information necessary for the operation of the radionavigation system.

84 AR Radionavigation-Satellite Earth Station

An Earth station in the radionavigation-satellite service.

84 AS Radionavigation-Satellite Space Station

A space station in the radionavigation-satellite service, on an Earth satellite.

84 AT Meteorological-Satellite Service

A space service in which the results of meteorological observations, made by instruments on Earth satellites, are transmitted to Earth stations by space stations on these satellites.

84 AU Meteorological-Satellite Earth Station
An Earth station in the meteorological-satellite service.

84 AV Meteorological-Satellite Space Station
A space station in the meteorological-satellite service, on an Earth satellite.

84 AW Space Telemetering
The use of telemetering for the transmission from a space station of results of measurements made in a spacecraft, including those relating to the functioning of the spacecraft.

84 AX Maintenance Space Telemetering
Space telemetering relating exclusively to the electrical and mechanical condition of a spacecraft and its equipment together with the condition of the environment of the spacecraft.

84 AY Space Telecommand
The use of radiocommunication for the transmission of signals to a space station to initiate, modify or terminate functions of the equipment on a space object, including the space station.

84 AZ Space Tracking
Determination of the orbit, velocity or instantaneous position of an object in space by means of radiodetermination, excluding primary radar, for the purpose of following the movement of the object.

SECTION IIB. *Space, Orbits and Types of Objects in Space.*

84 BA Deep Space
Space at distances from the Earth equal to or greater than the distance between the Earth and the Moon.

84 BB Orbit
The path in space described by the centre of mass of a satellite or other object in space.

84 BC Angle of Inclination of an Orbit
The acute angle between the plane containing an orbit and the plane of the Earth's equator.

84 BD Period of an Object in Space
The time elapsing between two consecutive passages of an object in space through the same point on its closed orbit.

84 BE Altitude of the Apogee
Altitude above the surface of the Earth of the point on a closed orbit where a satellite is at its maximum distance from the centre of the Earth.

333

84 BF Altitude of the Perigree

Altitude above the surface of the Earth of the point on a closed orbit where a satellite is at its minimum distance from the centre of the Earth.

84 BG Stationary Satellite

A satellite, the circular orbit of which lies in the plane of the Earth's equator and which turns about the polar axis of the Earth in the same direction and with the same period as those of the Earth's rotation.

84 BH Spacecraft

Any type of space vehicle, including an Earth satellite or a deep-space probe, whether manned or unmanned.

FREQUENCY ALLOCATIONS

The Table of Frequency Allocations allocates frequencies for the various types of space service.

REGULATIONS GOVERNING THE TECHNICAL CHARACTERISTICS
OF SPACE SERVICES

SECTION VIII. *Space Services sharing Frequency Bands with Terrestrial Services between 1 Gc/s and 10 Gc/s.*

Choice of Sites and Frequencies

470E § 20. Sites and frequencies for Earth stations, operating in frequency bands shared with equal rights between terrestrial and space services, shall be selected having regard to the relevant recommendations of the CCIR with respect to geographical separation from terrestrial stations.

Power Limits

470F § 21. (1) Earth Stations in the Communication-Satellite Service.

470G (2) The mean effective radiated power transmitted by an Earth station in any direction in the horizontal plane[1] shall not exceed +55dbW in any 4 kc/s band, except that it may be increased subject to the provisions of 470H or 470I. However, in no case shall it exceed a value of +65dbW in any 4 kc/s band.

---

[1] For the purpose of this Regulation, the effective radiated power transmitted in the horizontal plane shall be taken to mean the effective radiated power actually transmitted towards the horizon, reduced by the site-shielding factor that may be applicable. The value of this site-shielding factor shall be determined as indicated in section 5 of the Annex to Recommendation No. 1A.

334

470H   (3) In any direction where the distance from an Earth station to the boundary of the territory of another administration exceeds 400 km, the limit of +55dbW in any 4 kc/s band may be increased in that direction by 2 db for each 100 km in excess of 400 km.

470I   (4) The limit of +55dbW in any 4 kc/s band may be exceeded by agreement between the administrations concerned or affected.

470J   (5) The limits given in 470G apply in the following frequency bands allocated to transmission by Earth stations in the communication-satellite service, where these are shared with equal rights with the fixed or mobile service:

         4400–4700 Mc/s
         5800–5850 Mc/s (for the countries mentioned in 390)
         5850–5925 Mc/s (Regions 1 and 3)
         5925–6425 Mc/s
         7900–8400 Mc/s

Minimum Angle of Elevation

470K   § 22. (1) Earth Stations in the Communication-Satellite Service.

470L   (2) Earth station antennas shall not be employed for transmission at elevation angles less than 3 degrees, measured from the horizontal plane to the central axis of the main lobe, except when agreed to by the administrations concerned or affected.

470M   (3) The limit given in 470L applies in the following frequency bands allocated to transmission by Earth stations in the communication-satellite service, where these are shared with equal rights with the fixed or mobile service:

         4400–4700 Mc/s
         5800–5850 Mc/s (for the countries mentioned in 390)
         5850–5925 Mc/s (Regions 1 and 3)
         5925–6425 Mc/s
         7250–7750 Mc/s
         7900–8400 Mc/s

Power Flux Density Limits

470N   § 23. (1) Communication-Satellite Space Stations.

470O   (a) The total power flux density at the Earth's surface, produced by an emission from a communication-satellite space station, or reflected from a passive communication-satellite, where wide-deviation frequency (or phase) modulation is used, shall in no case exceed $-130\,\text{db}\,\text{W}/\text{m}^2$ for all angles of arrival. In addition, such signals shall if necessary be continuously modulated by a suitable waveform, so that the power flux density shall in no case exceed $-149\,\text{db}\,\text{W}/\text{m}^2$ in any 4 kc/s band for all angles of arrival.

470P   (b) The power flux density at the Earth's surface, produced by an emission from a communication-satellite space station, or reflected from a passive communication-satellite, where modulation other than wide-deviation frequency (or phase) modulation is used, shall in no case exceed $-152\,\text{db}\,\text{W}/\text{m}^2$ in any 4 kc/s band for all angles of arrival.

470Q   (c) The limits given in 470O and 470P apply in the following frequency bands allocated to transmission by space stations in the communication-satellite service, where these are shared with equal rights with the fixed or mobile services:

    3400–4200 Mc/s
    7250–7750 Mc/s

470R   (2) Meteorological-Satellite Space Stations.[2]

470S   (a) The power flux density at the Earth's surface, produced by an emission from a meteorological-satellite space station, where wide-deviation frequency (or phase) modulation is used, shall in no case exceed $-130\,\text{db}\,\text{W}/\text{m}^2$ for all angles of arrival. In addition, such signals shall if necessary be continuously modulated by a suitable waveform, so that the power flux density shall in no case exceed $-149\,\text{db}\,\text{W}/\text{m}^2$ in any 4 kc/s band for all angles of arrival.

470T   (b) The power flux density at the Earth's surface, produced by an emission from a meteorological-satellite space station, where modulation other than wide-deviation frequency (or phase) modulation is used, shall in no case exceed $-152\,\text{db}\,\text{W}/\text{m}^2$ in any 4 kc/s band for all angles of arrival.

[2] In view of the absence of any CCIR Recommendations relative to sharing between the meteorological-satellite service and other services, power flux density levels applicable to communication-satellite space stations are extended to meteorological-satellite space stations.

470U   (c) The limits given in 470S and 470T apply in the following frequency bands allocated to transmissions by space stations in the meteorological-satellite service, shared with equal rights with the fixed or mobile service:

1660–1670 Mc/s

1690–1700 Mc/s

7200–7250 Mc/s

7300–7750 Mc/s

The limits given in 470S and 470T also apply in the band 1770–1790 Mc/s although the meteorological-satellite service is a secondary service in this band.

SECTION IX. *Space Services.*

Cessation of Emissions

470V   § 24. Space stations shall be made capable of ceasing radio emission by the use of appropriate devices[3] that will ensure definite cessation of emissions.

Harmful Interference by Space Stations

695   § 3. In order to avoid interference:

— locations of transmitting stations and, where the nature of the service permits, locations of receiving stations shall be selected with particular care;

— radiation in and reception from unnecessary directions shall be minimised, where the nature of the service permits, by taking the maximum practical advantage of the properties of directional antennae;

— the choice and use of transmitters and receivers shall be in accordance with the provisions of Article 12;

— space stations shall be fitted with appropriate devices to quickly terminate their radio emissions whenever required to do so under the provisions of these Regulations.

711A   8A. When the service rendered by an Earth station suffers interference, the administration having jurisdiction of the receiving station experiencing the interference may also approach directly the administration having jurisdiction over the interfering station.

711B   8B. When cases of harmful interference occur as a result of emissions from space stations, the administrations concerned shall, upon request from the administration having jurisdiction over the station ex-

---

[3] Battery life, timing devices, ground command, etc.

periencing the interference, furnish current ephemeral data necessary to allow calculation of the positions of the space station.

Identification of Space Stations

735.I 1. In the present state of the technique, it is recognised nevertheless that the transmission of identifying signals for certain radio systems (*e.g.*, radio-determination, radio relay systems and space systems) is not always possible.

737A 2A. In the event that the transmission of identification signals by a space station is not possible, that station shall be identified by specifying the angle of inclination of the orbit, the period of the object in space and the altitudes of apogee and perigree of the space station in kilometres. In the case of a space station on board a stationary satellite, the mean geographical longitude of the projection of the satellite's position on the surface of the Earth shall be specified. (See Appendix 1A.)

Stations in the Space Service

773A 21A. When call signs for stations in the space service are employed, it is recommended that they consist of:
— two letters followed by two or three digits (other than the digits 0 and 1 in cases where they immediately follow a letter). (See also No. 737A.)

Particulars of the information to be notified to the International Frequency Registration Board in respect of stations in the space and radioastronomy services are specified in Appendix 1A to the Regulations.

ARRANGEMENTS FOR A GLOBAL COMMERCIAL COMMUNICATIONS SATELLITE SYSTEM

AGREEMENT ESTABLISHING INTERIM ARRANGEMENTS FOR A GLOBAL COMMERCIAL COMMUNICATIONS SATELLITE SYSTEM

(Opened for signature at Washington, August 19, 1964)

The Governments signatory to this Agreement,

Recalling the principle set forth in Resolution No. 1721 (XVI) of the General Assembly of the United Nations that communications by means of satellites should be available to the nations of the world as soon as practicable on a global and non-discriminatory basis;

Desiring to establish a single global commercial communications satellite system as part of an improved global communications network which will provide expanded telecommunications services to all areas of the world and which will contribute to world peace and understanding;

Determined, to this end, to provide, through the most advanced technology available, for the benefit of all nations of the world, the most efficient and economical service possible consistent with the best and most equitable use of the radio spectrum;

Believing that satellite communications should be organised in such a way as to permit all States to have access to the global system and those States so wishing to invest in the system with consequent participation in the design, development, construction (including the provision of equipment), establishment, maintenance, operation and ownership of the system;

Believing that it is desirable to conclude interim arrangements providing for the establishment of a single global commercial communications satellite system at the earliest practicable date, pending the working out of definitive arrangements for the organisation of such a system;

Agree as follows:

ARTICLE I

(a) The Parties to this Agreement shall co-operate to provide, in accordance with the principles set forth in the Preamble to this Agreement, for the design, development, construction, establishment, maintenance and operation of the space segment of the global commercial communications satellite system, to include

   (i) an experimental and operational phase in which it is proposed to use one or more satellites to be placed in synchronous orbit in 1965;

   (ii) succeeding phases employing satellites, of types to be determined, with the objective of achieving basic global coverage in the latter part of 1967; and

   (iii) such improvements and extensions thereof as the Committee established by Article IV of this Agreement may decide subject to the provisions of Article VI of this Agreement.

(b) In this Agreement,

   (i) the term "space segment" comprises the communications satellites and the tracking, control, command and related facilities and equipment required to support the operation of the communications satellites;

   (ii) the terms "design" and "development" include research.

ARTICLE II

(a) Each Party either shall sign or shall designate a communications entity, public or private, to sign the Special Agreement which is to be concluded further to this Agreement and which is to be opened for signature at the same time as this Agreement. Relations between any such designated entity and the Party which has designated it shall be governed by the applicable domestic law.

(b) The Parties to this Agreement contemplate that administrations and communications carriers will, subject to the requirements of their applicable domestic law, negotiate and enter directly into such traffic agreements as may be appropriate with respect to their use of channels of communication provided by the system to be established under this Agreement, services to be furnished to the public, facilities, divisions of revenues and related business arrangements.

ARTICLE III

The space segment shall be owned in undivided shares by the signatories to the Special Agreement in proportion to their respective contributions to the costs of the design, development, construction and establishment of the space segment.

ARTICLE IV

(a) An Interim Communications Satellite Committee, hereinafter referred to as "the Committee", is hereby established to give effect to the co-operation provided for by Article I of this Agreement. The Committee shall have responsibility for the design, development, construction, establishment, maintenance and operation of the space segment of the system and, in particular, shall exercise the functions and have the powers set forth in this Agreement and in the Special Agreement.

(b) The Committee shall be composed as follows: one representative from each of the signatories to the Special Agreement whose quota is not less than 1.5 per cent, and one representative from any two or more signatories to the Special Agreement where combined quotas total not less than 1.5 per cent and which have agreed to be so represented.

(c) In the performance of its financial functions under this Agreement and under the Special Agreement the Committee shall be assisted by an advisory sub-committee on finance. This sub-committee shall be established by the Committee as soon as the Committee becomes operative.

(d) The Committee may establish such other advisory sub-committees as it thinks fit.

(e) No signatory or group of signatories to the Special Agreement shall be deprived of representation on the Committee because of any reduction pursuant to Article XII (c) of this Agreement.

(f) In this Agreement, the term "quota", in relation to a signatory to the Special Agreement, means the percentage set forth opposite its name in the Annex to the Special Agreement as modified pursuant to this Agreement and the Special Agreement.

Article V

(a) Each signatory to the Special Agreement, or group of signatories to the Special Agreement, represented on the Committee shall have a number of votes equal to its quota, or to their combined quotas, as the case may be.

(b) A quorum for any meeting of the Committee shall consist of representatives having, in total, a number of votes exceeding the vote of the representative with the largest vote by not less than 8.5.

(c) The Committee shall endeavour to act unanimously; however, if it fails to reach agreement it shall take decisions by a majority of the votes cast, except that, with respect to the following matters, and subject to paragraphs (d) and (e) of this Article, any decision must have the concurrence of representatives whose total votes exceed the vote of the representative with the largest vote by not less than 12.5:

(i) choice of type or types of space segment to be established;
(ii) establishment of general standards for approval of Earth stations for access to the space segment;

(iii) approval of budgets by major categories;

(iv) adjustment of accounts pursuant to Article 4 (c) of the Special Agreement;

(v) establishment of the rate of charge per unit of satellite utilisation pursuant to Article 9 (a) of the Special Agreement;

(vi) decisions on additional contributions pursuant to Article VI (b) of this Agreement;

(vii) approval of the placing of contracts pursuant to Article 10 (c) of the Special Agreement;

(viii) approval of matters relating to satellite launchings pursuant to Article 10 (d) of the Special Agreement;

(ix) approval of quotas pursuant to Article XII (a) (ii) of this Agreement;

(x) determination of financial conditions of accession pursuant to Article XII (b) of this Agreement;

(xi) decisions relating to withdrawal pursuant to Article XI (a) and (b) of this Agreement and Article 4 (d) of the Special Agreement;

(xii) recommendation of amendments pursuant to Article 15 of the Special Agreement;

(xiii) adoption of the rules of procedure of the Committee and the advisory sub-committees;

(xiv) approval of appropriate compensation to the Corporation for its performance of services as manager pursuant to Articles 5 (c) and 9 (b) of the Special Agreement.

(d) If the Committee, upon the expiration of sixty days following the date when such matter has been proposed for decision, shall not have taken a decision pursuant to paragraph (c) (i) of this Article on the type of space segment to be established to achieve the objective stated in paragraph (a) (ii) of Article I of this Agreement, a decision on such matter may thereafter be taken by the concurring votes of representatives whose total votes exceed the vote of the representative with the largest vote by not less than 8.5.

(e) If the Committee, upon the expiration of sixty days following the date when such matter has been proposed for decision, shall not have approved

(i) any particular budget category pursuant to paragraph (c) (iii) of this Article

(ii) the placing of any particular contract pursuant to paragraph (c) (vii) of this Article or

(iii) any particular matter relating to satellite launchings, pursuant to paragraph (c) (viii) of this Article

relating to achievement of the objectives stated in paragraphs (a) (i) and (a) (ii) of Article I of this Agreement, a decision on such matter may thereafter be taken by the concurring votes of representatives whose total votes exceed the vote of the representative with the largest vote by not less than 8.5.

Article VI

(a) The contributions of the signatories to the Special Agreement towards the costs of the design, development, construction and establishment of the space segment during the interim arrangements shall be based upon an estimate of U.S. $200,000,000 for such costs. Each signatory to the Special Agreement shall pay its quota of such costs in accordance with the provisions of the Special Agreement.

(b) The Committee shall determine whether contributions are required during the interim arrangements in excess of the U.S. $200,000,000 estimate and, if so, in what amounts. If the additional contributions required during the interim arrangements would result in total contributions exceeding U.S. $300,000,000, a special conference of the signatories to the Special Agreement shall be convened to consider the matter and recommend appropriate action before decisions are taken by the Committee. The conference shall determine its own procedure.

(c) Each signatory to the Special Agreement may assume the obligation to pay all or part of its quota of any such additional contributions, but no signatory to the Special Agreement shall be required to do so. To the extent that such obligation is not assumed by any signatory to the Special Agreement, it may be assumed by the remaining signatories to the Special Agreement in the proportion that their respective quotas bear to each other or as they may otherwise agree. However, if a signatory to the Special Agreement, which is a member of a group of signatories formed in order to appoint jointly a representative on the Committee pursuant to Article IV (b) of this Agreement, does not assume the obligation to pay such additional contributions, the remaining signatories of that group may assume that obligation in whole or in part to the extent that these remaining signatories may agree. The quotas of the signatories to the Special Agreement shall be adjusted accordingly.

Article VII

In order to ensure the most effective utilisation of the space segment in accordance with the principles set forth in the Preamble to this Agreement, no earth station shall be permitted to utilise the space segment unless it has been approved by the Committee pursuant to Article 7 of the Special Agreement.

Appendix

Article VIII

The Communications Satellite Corporation, incorporated under the laws of the District of Columbia (herein referred to as the Corporation) shall, pursuant to general policies of the Committee and in accordance with specific determinations which may be made by the Committee, act as the manager in the design, development, construction, establishment, operation and maintenance of the space segment.

Article IX

(a) Having regard to the programme outlined in Article I of this Agreement, within one year after the initial global system becomes operational and in any case not later than January 1, 1969, the Committee shall render a report to each Party to this Agreement containing the Committee's recommendations concerning the definitive arrangements for an international global system which shall supersede the interim arrangements established by this Agreement. This report, which shall be fully representative of all shades of opinion, shall consider, among other things, whether the interim arrangements should be continued on a permanent basis or whether a permanent international organisation with a General Conference and an international administrative and technical staff should be established.

(b) Regardless of the form of the definitive arrangements,
 (i) their aims shall be consonant with the principles set forth in the Preamble to this Agreement;
 (ii) they shall, like this Agreement, be open to all States members of the International Telecommunication Union or their designated entities;
 (iii) they shall safeguard the investment made by signatories to the Special Agreement; and
 (iv) they shall be such that all parties to the definitive arrangements may have an opportunity of contributing to the determination of general policy.

(c) The report of the Committee shall be considered at an international conference, at which duly designated communications entities may also participate, to be convened by the Government of the United States of America for that purpose within three months following submission of the report. The Parties to this Agreement shall seek to ensure that the definitive arrangements will be established at the earliest practicable date, with a view to their entry into force by January 1, 1970.

Article X

In considering contracts and in exercising its other responsibilities, the Committee and the Corporation as manager shall be guided by the need to design, develop and procure the best equipment and services at the best price for the most efficient conduct and operation of the space segment. When proposals or tenders are determined to be comparable in terms of quality, c.i.f. price and timely performance, the Committee and the Corporation as manager shall also seek to ensure that contracts are so distributed that equipment is designed, developed and procured in the States whose Governments are Parties to this Agreement in approximate proportion to the respective quotas of their corresponding signatories to the Special Agreement; provided that such design, development and procurement are not contrary to the joint interests of the Parties to this Agreement and the signatories to the Special Agreement. The Committee and the Corporation as manager shall also seek to ensure that the foregoing principles are applied with respect to major subcontracts to the extent that this can be accomplished without impairing the responsibility of the prime contractor for the performance of work under the contract.

ARTICLE XI

(a) Any Party may withdraw from this Agreement, and this Agreement shall cease to be in force for that Party three months after that Party shall have notified the Government of the United States of America of its intention to withdraw and the latter shall inform the other Parties accordingly. In the event of such withdrawal, the corresponding signatory to the Special Agreement shall pay all sums already due under the Special Agreement, together with a sum which shall be agreed between that signatory and the Committee in respect of costs which will result in the future from contracts concluded prior to notification of withdrawal. If agreement has not been reached within three months after notification of withdrawal, the Committee shall make a final determination of the sums which shall be paid by that signatory.

(b) Not less than three months after the rights of a signatory to the Special Agreement have been suspended pursuant to Article 4 (d) of the Special Agreement, and if that signatory has not meanwhile paid all sums due, the Committee, having taken into account any statement by that signatory or the corresponding Party, may decide that the Party in question is deemed to have withdrawn from this Agreement; this Agreement shall thereupon cease to be in force for that Party.

(c) Withdrawal by a Party from this Agreement shall automatically effect withdrawal from the Special Agreement by the corresponding signatory to the Special Agreement, but the obligation to make payments under paragraph (a) of the Article or under Article 4 (d) of the Special Agreement shall not be affected by such withdrawal.

(d) Upon any withdrawal under paragraph (a) or (b) of this Article, the Committee, to the extent required to account for the quota of the withdrawing signatory to the Special Agreement, shall increase the quotas of the remaining signatories to the Special Agreement in proportion to their respective quotas or as they may otherwise agree. However, if the signatory to the Special Agreement corresponding to the withdrawing Party was at the time of withdrawal a member of a group of signatories formed in order to appoint jointly a representative on the Committee pursuant to Article IV (b) of this Agreement, the quota of the signatory in question shall be distributed by increasing the quotas of the remaining signatories of that group to the extent that those remaining signatories may agree.

(e) Withdrawal by any Party may also take place if, at the request of the Party concerned, the Committee approves the transfer of the rights and obligations of that Party and the corresponding signatory to the Special Agreement under this Agreement and the Special Agreement to another Party and its corresponding signatory to the Special Agreement. Such transferee or transferees need not have been Parties to the Agreement or signatories to the Special Agreement prior to the time of such transfer.

ARTICLE XII

(a) This Agreement shall be open at Washington for six months from August 19, 1964 for signature:
  (i) by the Government of any State which is listed by name in the Annex to the Special Agreement when it is first opened for signature, and
  (ii) by the Government of any other State which is a member of the International Telecommunication Union, subject to approval by the Committee of the quota of that Government or its designated communications entity, public or private. On such approval and entry into force or provisional application, the name of that State and the name of its corresponding signatory to the Special Agreement, and its quota are deemed to be inserted in the Annex to the Special Agreement.

(b) The Government of any State which is a member of the International Telecommunication Union may accede to this Agreement after it is closed for signature upon such financial conditions as the Committee shall determine. On such accession, the name of that State and the name of its corresponding signatory to the Special Agreement, and its quota are deemed to be inserted in the Annex to the Special Agreement.

(c) The quotas of the signatories to the Special Agreement shall be reduced pro rata as necessary to accommodate additional signatories to the Special

Agreement, provided that the combined original quotas of all signatories to the Special Agreement other than the signatories listed in the Annex to the Special Agreement when this Agreement is first opened for signature shall not exceed 17 per cent.

(d) This Agreement shall enter into force on the date upon which it has been signed without reservation as to approval, or has been approved after such reservation, by two or more Governments. Subsequently it shall enter into force in respect of each signatory Government on signature or, if it signs subject to a reservation as to approval, on approval by it.

(e) Any Government which signs this Agreement subject to a reservation as to approval may, so long as this Agreement is open for signature, declare that it applies this Agreement provisionally and shall thereupon be considered a Party to this Agreement. Such provisional application shall terminate

(i) upon approval of this Agreement by that Government, or

(ii) upon withdrawal by that Government in accordance with Article XI of this Agreement.

(f) Notwithstanding anything contained in this Article, this Agreement shall not enter into force for any Government nor be applied provisionally by any Government until that Government or its corresponding signatory shall have signed the Special Agreement.

(g) If at the expiration of a period of nine months from the date when it is first opened for signature this Agreement has not entered into force for or has not been provisionally applied by the Government of a State which has signed it in accordance with paragraph (a) (i) of this Article, the signature shall be considered of no effect and the name of that State and of its corresponding signatory to the Special Agreement, and its quota shall be deemed to be deleted from the Annex to the Special Agreement; the quotas of the signatories to the Special Agreement shall accordingly be increased pro rata. If this Agreement has not entered into force for or has not been provisionally applied by the Government of a State which has signed it in accordance with paragraph (a) (ii) of this Article within a period of nine months from the date when it is first opened for signature, the signature shall be considered of no effect.

(h) The corresponding signatory to the Special Agreement of any Government which has signed this Agreement subject to a reservation as to approval, and which has not provisionally applied it, may appoint an observer to the Committee in the same manner as that signatory could have been represented in accordance with Article IV (b) of this Agreement if that Government had approved this Agreement. Any such observer, who shall have the right to speak but not to vote, may attend the Committee only during a period of nine months from the date when this Agreement is first opened for signature.

(i) No reservation may be made to this Agreement except as provided in this Article.

ARTICLE XIII

(a) Notifications of approval or of provisional application and instruments of accession shall be deposited with the Government of the United States of America.

(b) The Government of the United States of America shall notify all signatory and acceding States of signatures, reservations of approval, deposits of notifications of approval or of provisional application, deposits of instruments of accession and notifications of withdrawals from this Agreement.

ARTICLE XIV

Upon entry into force of this Agreement, the Government of the United States of America shall register it with the Secretary-General of the United Nations in accordance with Article 102 of the Charter of the United Nations.

ARTICLE XV

This Agreement shall remain in effect until the entry into force of the definitive arrangements referred to in Article IX of this Agreement.

SPECIAL AGREEMENT

(Opened for signature at Washington, August 19, 1964)

Whereas certain Governments have become Parties to an Agreement Establishing Interim Arrangements for a Global Commercial Communications Satellite System; and

Whereas those Governments have undertaken therein to sign or to designate a communications entity to sign this Special Agreement;

The signatories to this Special Agreement hereby agree as follows:

ARTICLE I

In this Special Agreement:

(a) "The Agreement" means the Agreement Establishing Interim Arrangements for a Global Commercial Communications Satellite System opened for signature on August 19, 1964, at Washington;

(b) "The Committee" means the Interim Communications Satellite Committee established by Article IV of the Agreement;

(c) "The Corporation" means the Communications Satellite Corporation incorporated under the laws of the District of Columbia pursuant to the

Communications Satellite Act of 1962 of the United States of America;

(d) "Design" and "development" include research;

(e) "Quota", in relation to a signatory, means the percentage set forth opposite its name in the Annex to this Special Agreement as modified pursuant to the Agreement and this Special Agreement;

(f) "Signatory" means a Government or a communications entity which has signed this Special Agreement and in respect of which it is in force;

(g) "The space segment" means the space segment defined in Article I (b) (i) of the Agreement.

ARTICLE 2

Each signatory undertakes to fulfill the obligations placed upon it by the Agreement and thereby obtains the rights provided therein.

ARTICLE 3

Each signatory undertakes to contribute a percentage of the costs of the design, development, construction and establishment of the space segment equal to its quota.

ARTICLE 4

(a) During a period of nine months from the date when the Agreement is first opened for signature, each signatory shall, within four weeks from the date of entry into force of this Special Agreement for that signatory, make a payment on account to the Corporation, in United States dollars, or in currency freely convertible into United States dollars, of a percentage equal to its quota of the expenditure which the Corporation has incurred for the design, development, construction and establishment of the space segment prior to the date when the Agreement is first opened for signature, and, according to estimates established by the Corporation at that date, is to incur for those purposes within six months after that date, together with its proportionate share of any additional contribution required pursuant to paragraph (b) of this Article, and appropriate interest on all such amounts. Each signatory shall pay the remainder of its contribution pursuant to Article 3 of this Special Agreement in accordance with paragraph (b) of this Article.

(b) The Corporation shall submit to the Committee estimates of the time phasing of payments required pursuant to Article 3 of this Special Agreement. The Committee shall call on the signatories to make their respective proportionate payments in order to enable obligations to be met as they become due. Payments shall be made to the Corporation by each signatory in United States dollars or in currency freely convertible into United States dollars, and in such amounts that, accounting on a cumulative basis, the sums paid by the signatories are in proportion to their respective quotas. Where a signatory other than the Corporation incurs obligations pursuant to authorisation by the Committee, the Committee shall cause payments to be made to that signatory.

(c) Accounts for expenditure referred to in paragraphs (a) and (b) of this Article shall be subject to review by the Committee and shall be subject to such adjustment as the Committee may decide.

(d) Each signatory shall pay the amount due from it under paragraph (b) of this Article on the date designated by the Committee. Interest at the rate of six per cent per annum shall be added to any amount unpaid after that date. If the signatory has not made a payment within three months of its becoming due, the rights of the signatory under the Agreement and this Special Agreement shall be suspended. If, after such suspension, the Committee decides, pursuant to Article XI (b) of the Agreement, that the defaulting signatory is deemed to have withdrawn from this Special Agreement, the Committee shall then make a binding determination of the sums already due together with a sum to be paid in respect of the costs which will result in the future from contracts concluded while that signatory was a party. Such withdrawal shall not, however, affect the obligation of the signatory concerned to pay sums due under this Special Agreement, whether falling due before it ceased to be a party or payable in accordance with the aforesaid determination of the Committee.

Article 5

The following shall be included as part of the costs of the design, development, construction and establishment of the space segment to be shared by the signatories in proportion to their respective quotas:

(a) The direct and indirect costs for the design, development, construction and establishment of the space segment incurred by the Corporation prior to the date when the Agreement is first opened for signature;

(b) All direct and indirect costs for the design, development, construction and establishment of the space segment incurred by the Corporation or pursuant to authorisation by the Committee by any other signatory on behalf of the signatories to this Special Agreement subsequent to the date when the Agreement is first opened for signature;

(c) All direct and indirect costs incurred by the Corporation which are allocable to its performance of services as manager in the design, development, construction and establishment of the space segment and appropriate compensation to the Corporation, as may be agreed between the Corporation and the Committee, for such services.

ARTICLE 6

The following shall not form part of the costs to be shared by the signatories:

(a) Taxes on the net income of any of the signatories;

(b) Design and development expenditure on launchers and launching facilities except expenditure incurred for the adaptation of launchers and launching facilities in connection with the design, development, construction and establishment of the space segment;

(c) The costs of the representatives of the signatories on the Committee and on its advisory sub-committees and the staffs of those representatives except in so far as the Committee may otherwise determine.

ARTICLE 7

(a) In considering whether an Earth station should be permitted to utilise the space segment, the Committee shall take into account the technical characteristics of the station, the technical limitations on multiple access to satellites due to the existing state of the art, the effect of geographical distribution of Earth stations on the efficiency of the services to be provided by the system, the recommended standards of the International Telegraph and Telephone Consultative Committee and the International Radio Consultative Committee of the International Telecommunication Union, and such general standards as the Committee may establish. Failure by the Committee to establish general standards shall not of itself preclude the Committee from considering or acting upon any application for approval of an Earth station to utilise the space segment.

(b) Any application for approval of an Earth station to utilise the space segment shall be submitted to the Committee by the signatory to this Special Agreement in whose area the earth station is or will be located or, with respect to other areas, by a duly authorised communications entity. Each such application shall be submitted either individually or jointly on behalf of all signatories and duly authorised communications entities intending to utilise the space segment by means of the Earth station which is the subject of the application.

(c) Any application for approval of an Earth station located in the territory of a State whose Government is party to the Agreement which is to be owned or operated by an organisation or organisations other than the corresponding signatory shall be made by that signatory.

ARTICLE 8

(a) Each applicant for approval of an earth station pursuant to Article 7 of this Special Agreement shall be responsible for making equitable and non-discriminatory arrangements for the use of the Earth station by all signatories or duly authorised communications entities intended to be served by the Earth station individually or jointly with other Earth stations.

(b) To the extent feasible the Committee shall allot to the respective signatory or duly authorised communications entity, for use by each Earth station which has been approved pursuant to Article 7 of this Special Agreement, an amount of satellite utilisation appropriate to satisfy the total communications capability requested on behalf of all signatories and duly authorised communications entities to be served by such Earth station.

(c) In making allotments of satellite utilisation the Committee shall give due consideration to the quotas of the signatories to be served by each Earth station.

ARTICLE 9

(a) The Committee shall specify the unit of satellite utilisation and from time to time shall establish the rate of charge per unit at a level which, as a general rule, shall be sufficient, on the basis of the estimated total use of the space segment, to cover amortisation of the capital cost of the space segment, an adequate compensation for use of capital, and the estimated operating, maintenance and administration costs of the space segment.

(b) In establishing the unit rate of charge pursuant to paragraph (a) of this Article, the Committee shall include in the estimated operating, maintenance and administration costs of the space segment the estimated direct and indirect costs of the Corporation which are allocable to its performance of services as manager in the operation and maintenance of the space segment and appropriate compensation to the Corporation, as may be agreed between the Corporation and the Committee, for such services.

(c) The Committee shall arrange for the payment of charges for allotments of satellite utilisation to be made quarterly to the Corporation. The charges shall be computed in United States dollars and paid in United States dollars or in currency freely convertible into United States dollars.

(d) The components of the unit rate of charge representing amortisation and compensation for the use of capital shall be credited to the signatories in proportion to their respective quotas. In the interests of avoiding unnecessary transfers of funds between signatories, and of keeping to a minimum the funds held by the Corporation on behalf of the signatories, the Committee shall make suitable arrangements for funds representing these components to be retained by signatories where appropriate or, if collected, to be distributed among the signatories in such a way that the credits established for signatories are discharged.

(e) The other components of the unit rate of charge shall be applied to meet all operating, maintenance, and administration costs, and to establish such reserves as the Committee may determine to be necessary. After providing for such costs and reserves, any balance remaining shall be distributed by the Corporation, in United States dollars, or in currency freely convertible into United States dollars, among the signatories in proportion to their respective quotas; but if insufficient funds remain to meet the operating, maintenance and administration costs, the signatories shall pay to the Corporation, in proportion to their respective quotas, such amounts as may be determined by the Committee to be required to meet the deficiency.

(f) The Committee shall institute appropriate sanctions in cases where payments pursuant to this Article shall have been in default for three months or longer.

ARTICLE 10

(a) All contracts placed by the Corporation or by any other signatory pursuant to authorisation by the Committee relating to design, development and procurement of equipment for the space segment shall, except as otherwise provided by the Committee, be based on responses to appropriate requests for quotations or invitations to tender from among persons and organisations qualified to perform the work under the proposed contract whose names are furnished to the Committee by the signatories.

(b) For contracts which exceed U.S. $125,000 the issue by the Corporation of requests for quotations or invitations to tender shall be in accordance with such conditions as the Committee may determine. The Corporation shall keep the Committee fully informed of decisions taken relating to such contracts.

(c) The Corporation shall consult the Committee before issuing requests for proposals and invitations to tender for contracts for design, development and procurement of equipment for the space segment which are expected to exceed U.S. $500,000. If, as a result of its evaluation of responses to such requests or invitations, the Corporation desires that a contract be placed which exceeds U.S. $500,000, it shall submit its evaluation and recommendations to the Committee. The approval of the Committee shall be required before each such contract is placed either by the Corporation as manager or by any other signatory pursuant to authorisation by the Committee.

(d) The Committee shall approve the programme for the launching of satellites and for associated services, the launch source and the contracting arrangements.

(e) Except as otherwise directed by the Committee, and subject to paragraphs (c) and (d) of this Article, all contractors shall be selected by the Corporation and all contracts shall be in the name of and be executed and administered by the Corporation as manager.

(f) Except as otherwise determined by the Committee, all contracts and sub-contracts placed for design, development and procurement of equipment for the space segment shall contain appropriate provisions to the effect that all inventions, technical data and information arising directly from any work performed under such contracts (except inventions, technical data and information pertaining to launchers and launchings) shall be disclosed to the Committee and may be used only in the design, development, manufacture and use of equipment and components for the space segment established under the present interim arrangements or under any definitive arrangements which may succeed these interim arrangements, without payment of royalties, by each signatory or any person in the jurisdiction of a signatory or the Government which has designated that signatory.

(g) Except as it may otherwise determine, the Committee shall endeavour to have included in all contracts placed for design and development appropriate provisions which will ensure that inventions, technical data and information owned by the contractor and its sub-contractors which are directly incorporated in work performed under such contracts, may be used on fair and reasonable terms by each signatory or any person in the jurisdiction of a signatory or the Government which has designated that signatory, provided that such use is necessary, and to the extent that it is necessary to use such inventions, technical data and information for the exercise of the right to use under paragraph (f) of this Article.

(h) The provisions of this Article shall not be held to apply to contracts for design, development, construction and establishment of the space segment to which the Corporation is a party on the date when the Agreement is first opened for signature. Subject to the provisions of Article 4 (c) of this Agreement, all such contracts shall be recognised by the Committee as continuing obligations for budgetary purposes.

ARTICLE II

Each signatory shall keep such books, records, vouchers and accounts of of all costs for which it is authorised to be reimbursed under this Special Agreement with respect to the design, development, construction, establishment, maintenance and operation of the space segment as may be appropriate and shall at all reasonable times make them available for inspection by members of the Committee.

ARTICLE 12

In addition to functions stated elsewhere in this Special Agreement, the Corporation, as manager pursuant to Article VIII of the Agreement, shall:

(a) prepare and submit to the Committee the annual programmes and budgets;

(b) recommend to the Committee the type or types of space segment to be established;

(c) plan, conduct, arrange for and co-operate in studies, design work and development for improvement of the space segment;

(d) operate and maintain the space segment;

(e) furnish to the Committee such information as may be required by any representative on the Committee to enable him to discharge his responsibilities as a representative;

(f) arrange for technicians, selected by the Committee with the concurrence of the Corporation from among persons nominated by signatories, to participate in the assessment of designs and of specifications for equipment for the space segment;

(g) use its best efforts to arrange for inventions, technical data and information arising directly from any jointly financed work performed under contracts placed before the date on which the Agreement is opened for signature to be disclosed to each signatory and to be made available for use free of charge in the design, development, manufacture and use of equipment and components for the space segment by each signatory or any person in the jurisdiction of the signatory or the Government which has designated that signatory.

ARTICLE 13

Neither the Corporation as signatory or manager, nor any other signatory as such, shall be liable to any other signatory for loss or damage sustained by reason of a failure or breakdown of a satellite at or after launching or a failure or breakdown of any other portion of the space segment.

ARTICLE 14

Arrangements shall be made whereby all legal disputes arising in connection with this Special Agreement or in connection with the rights and obligations of signatories can, if not otherwise settled, be submitted to the decision of an impartial tribunal, to be established in accordance with such arrangements, which would decide such questions in accordance with general principles of law. To this end, a group of legal experts appointed by the signatories and by the prospective signatories listed in the Annex to this

Agreement when it is first opened for signature shall recommend a draft of a Supplementary Agreement containing such arrangements; the signatories shall, after considering that draft, conclude a Supplementary Agreement for such arrangements within a period of three months from the date when the Agreement is first opened for signature. The Supplementary Agreement shall be binding on all those who subsequently become signatories to this Special Agreement.

ARTICLE 15

Any proposed amendment to this Special Agreement shall first be submitted to the Committee. If recommended by the Committee for adoption, it shall enter into force for all signatories when notifications of approval have been deposited with the Government of the United States of America by two-thirds of the signatories, provided that no amendment may impose upon any signatory any additional financial obligation without its consent.

ARTICLE 16

This Special Agreement shall enter into force for each signatory on the day of signature, provided that the Agreement shall have entered into force for or shall have been provisionally applied by the Government which is or has designated the signatory in question; it shall continue in force for as long as the Agreement continues in force.

EXTRACTS FROM REGIONAL AGREEMENTS

CONVENTION FOR THE ESTABLISHMENT OF A EUROPEAN SPACE RESEARCH ORGANISATION

June 14, 1962

THE STATES parties to this Convention,

DESIRING to establish European collaboration, exclusively for peaceful purposes, in the field of space research,

CONSIDERING the proposals submitted by the Preparatory Commission established by the Agreement opened for signature at Meyrin (Switzerland) on the first of December, 1960.

HAVE AGREED as follows:

*   *   *

ARTICLE II

Purpose

The purpose of the Organisation shall be to provide for, and to promote, collaboration among European States in space research and technology, exclusively for peaceful purposes.

ARTICLE III

Information and Data

1. The scientific results of experiments carried out with the assistance of the Organisation shall be published or otherwise made generally available. After prior use by the scientists responsible for the experiments, the reduced data resulting from such experiments shall be the property of the Organisation.

2. Subject to patent rights, the technical results of the Organisation's activities shall normally be published or otherwise made generally available.

3. Member States shall facilitate the exchange of scientific and technical information, provided that a Member State shall not be required to communicate information obtained outside the Organisation if it considers that such communication would be contrary to the interests of its security, or to its own agreement with a third party, or that it would violate the conditions under which this information had been obtained.

ARTICLE IV
Exchange of Persons

Member States shall facilitate the exchange of persons concerned with space research and technology, provided that this shall not affect the application to any person of their laws and regulations relating to entry into, residence in, or departure from, their territories.

ARTICLE V
Programme and Activities

In order to fulfil its purpose the Organisation shall carry out a programme of scientific research and related technological activities. It may in particular:

(a) design and construct sounding rocket payloads, satellites and space probes, carrying instruments provided by Member States or by the Organisation itself;

(b) procure launching vehicles and arrange for their launching;

(c) provide means for the reception, collection, reduction and analysis of data;

(d) support research and development as required for its programme;

(e) promote and provide for contacts between scientists and engineers, their interchange and advanced training;

(f) disseminate information among Member States;

(g) co-operate with research institutions in the Member States and assist in the co-ordination of their efforts;

(h) make contractual arrangements for the use of launching ranges for rockets and satellites and other facilities available in Member or other States.

ARTICLE VI
Facilities

The Organisation may establish and operate the facilities necessary for its programme. In order to meet its initial requirements, it shall establish and operate:

(a) a European Space Technology Centre to undertake or arrange for the activities referred to under Article V(a) and to promote and take part in advanced technological research and specific studies related to space research;

(b) near the Centre referred to under sub-paragraph (a) above, a research laboratory to undertake joint research programmes on the minimum scale deemed necessary by the Council, referred to in Article X, to complete or complement the scientific studies carried out in the Member States;

(c) sounding rocket launching facilities;

(d) a Data Centre and tracking, telemetry and telecommand stations equipped with the apparatus necessary to fulfil the tasks referred to in Article V(c).

ARTICLE VII
Launchings

1. The programme of the Organisation shall provide for the launching of:
(a) sounding rockets;
(b) small satellites in near Earth orbits and small space probes;
(c) large satellites and large space probes;
2. The number of launchings shall be decided by the Council with a view to providing reasonable opportunities for scientifically valuable experiments, devised by Member States or by the Organisation itself, to be carried out.

ARTICLE VIII
Special Projects

If, outside the agreed programme but within the scope of the Organisation, one or more Member States engage in a project in connection with which the Council decides, by a two-thirds majority of all Member States, to make available the assistance of the Organisation or the use of its facilities, the resulting cost to the Organisation shall be refunded to the Organisation by the State or States concerned.

*   *   *

ARTICLE XIII
Co-operation

The Organisation may, by a unanimous decision of the Council, co-operate with other international organisations and institutions and with Governments, organisations and institutions of non-Member States.

*   *   *

ARTICLE XVI
Disputes

Any dispute concerning the interpretation or application of this Convention, which is not settled by the good offices of the Council, shall be submitted to the International Court of Justice, unless the Member States concerned agree on some other mode of settlement.

*   *   *

Appendix

Article XIX
Dissolution

1. The Organisation shall be dissolved if at any time there are less than five Member States. It may be dissolved at any time by agreement between the Member States.

2. In the event of dissolution the Council shall appoint a liquidation authority which will negotiate with the States on the territories of which the Headquarters and the Establishments of the Organisation are at that time. The legal personality of the Organisation shall subsist for the purposes of the liquidation.

3. Any surplus shall be distributed among those States, which are members of the Organisation at the time of the dissolution, in proportion to the contributions actually made by them from the dates of their becoming parties to this Convention. In the event of a deficit, this shall be met by the same States in proportion to their contributions as assessed for the financial year then current.

Convention for the Establishment of a European Organisation for the Development and Construction of Space Vehicle Launchers
March 29, 1962

THE STATES parties to this Convention:

Conscious of the role which space activities are destined to play in the progress of science and technology;

Convinced that a common effort undertaken without delay holds the best promise of achievements in keeping with the creative capacities of their countries;

Desiring to harmonise their policies in space matters with a view to common action for peaceful purposes;

Having decided to co-operate in the development of space vehicle launchers and to study their scientific and commercial application;

Have agreed as follows:

* * *

Article 2
Aims

1. The Organisation shall have as its aim the development and construction of space vehicle launchers and their equipment suitable for practical applications and for supply to eventual users.

2. The Organisation shall concern itself only with peaceful applications of such launchers and equipment.

3. The results of the work of the Organisation shall be freely accessible to Member States, in accordance with the provisions of this Convention.

4. The Organisation shall seek to promote the co-ordinated development of techniques relevant to its activity in the Member States and shall assist Member States, on request, to make use of the techniques used or developed in the course of its work.

*   *   *

ARTICLE 4
Participation in Programmes

1. The States parties to this Convention shall participate in the initial programme described in Article 16.

2. Further programmes shall be decided by the Council.

3. Subject to the provisions of Article 18 (3), every Member State shall be obliged to contribute financially to further programmes, unless it formally declares itself as not interested and therefore does not participate in them.

ARTICLE 5
Facilities

1. The Organisation shall use, to the fullest extent practicable any facilities available to Member States.

2. The Organisation may, if necessary, establish additional facilities.

3. Any Member State participating in a programme of the Organisation shall be entitled to use for any peaceful purpose of its own, facilities that have been established by it in the course of that programme subject to the approval having first been obtained of the State within whose jurisdiction the facilities are situated and on conditions agreed with that State and, in the case of facilities established by the Organisation, with the Organisation. The Member State which makes facilities available to the Organisation shall retain the right to use those facilities freely and by priority, with due regard to the contractual arrangements between that State and the Organisation.

4. Any arrangement between the Organisation and a Member State for the creation of facilities on the territory of that State shall provide for the circumstances which would arise should that State cease to be a Member of the Organisation.

Appendix

ARTICLE 6
Distribution of Work and Placing of Contracts

1. Within the framework of the decisions of the Council on the distribution of work in accordance with the provisions of Article 14 (2) (f) and within the budgetary provisions made by the Council, whenever the Government of the Member State to which work is allotted so desires, contracts for carrying out the initial programme shall be placed by that Government according to its usual procedures or such other procedures as may be adopted by a unanimous decision of the Council. Such contracts shall be carried out at the expense of the Organisation.

2. Contracts may also be placed directly by the Organisation in agreement with the Government of the State in the territory of which the work is to be carried out.

3. The Council shall determine the adequate distribution of work on the further programmes of the Organisation in the light of technical and economic criteria.

4. The Council shall determine the rules by which contracts for carrying out work on such further programmes shall be placed.

ARTICLE 7
Access to Work of the Organisation

Member States which contribute to the cost of a programme of the Organisation shall have the right to designate to the Organisation a limited number of individuals:

(a) to participate in the work on that programme proceeding in the governmental establishments of other Member States, including the firing trials at Woomera, Australia;

(b) to participate in the work on that programme proceeding in non-governmental organisations, subject to the agreement of such organisations;

Provided in either case that the number and qualifications of such individuals, including their qualifications in the matter of security, and the conditions of such participation are approved by the Government of the Member State within whose jurisdiction such establishments and organisations are located. Such approval shall not be unreasonably withheld.

ARTICLE 8
Exchange of Information

1. While this Convention remains in force:

(a) there shall be made available to the Organisation and to any Member State which participates in the initial programme:

(i) all technical information arising from work relevant to the initial programme of the Organisation done for the development of "Blue Streak" or done on the French rocket to be used as the second stage and which has been carried out before the entry into force of this Convention and

(ii) all technical information arising from work done directly by the Organisation or under contracts placed as part of the Organisation's initial programme;

(b) there shall be made available to the Organisation and to any Member State which contributes to the cost of the further programmes of the Organisation all technical information arising from work done either directly by the Organisation or under contracts placed for such programmes;

(c) the term "technical information" includes inventions covered by patents or other forms of legal protection. In the contracts concluded with a view to carrying out the programmes of the Organisation, in accordance with Article 6, the Organisation or the Member States shall insert clauses allowing the free disclosure and the use referred to in this Article, except when otherwise authorised by the Secretary-General;

(d) the Organisation may use such information or cause such information to be used for the carrying out of its programmes without payment;

(e) Member States;

(i) may use such information for any purposes of their own without payment and

(ii) may make the information available to persons, whether individuals, companies or organisations under their jurisdiction to use for their own purposes within the field of space technology provided such persons are resident in the territory of the Member State making the information available. The conditions under which such technical information arising under contracts placed as part of the programmes of the Organisation may be used by such persons for purposes not within the field of space technology shall be determined in a Protocol to be concluded among all Member States.

In either case, subject to the provisions of sub-paragraph (f), the information shall only be used within and shall not be transferred beyond the territory of the Member State making the information available on the territory of another Member State. When disclosing such information to persons under their jurisdiction Member States shall impose a restriction by contract or otherwise on the disclosure of that information to any other individual, company or organisation;

(f) even after dissolution of the Organisation, Member States may not disclose such information to a non–Member State or to a Member State which has not taken part in a particular programme or to persons other than those referred to in sub-paragraph (e) (ii) above, except that by unanimous decision of the Council:

(i) such restriction shall not apply to the disclosure of information by Member States or persons as defined in sub-paragraph (e) (ii) above, under reciprocal agreements for the exchange of information in the interests of the Organisation;

(ii) information may in certain circumstances be used in or transferred to non–Member States or non-participating Member States;

(g) technical information incorporated in a space vehicle launcher arising outside contracts placed as part of any of the Organisation's programmes, or arising outside the work referred to in sub-paragraph (a) (i) above, done on the development of "Blue Streak" or the French rocket to be used as the second stage, shall not be made available to Member States without the consent of the persons who own that information.

2 (a) Information and matter which originate from or are made use of within the scope of the activities of the Organisation, the unauthorised disclosure of which may endanger the security interests of a Member State shall be protected accordingly. The Council shall establish by unanimous decision regulations to ensure a common minimum standard of protection for such information and matter.

(b) Member States shall take all appropriate measures to protect the information and matter referred to in the preceding sub-paragraph and to give effect to the regulations established by the Council.

ARTICLE 9
Acquisition and Production of Jointly Developed Equipment by Member States

Each Member State which has contributed to the cost of a programme of the Organisation shall have the right to procure, for any peaceful purpose of its own, the launchers and equipment jointly developed under such programme or any part thereof. For this purpose, each Member State shall have the right to call upon the Organisation, or any other Member State in the territory of which such launchers and equipment is or has been in production, to sell such launchers and equipment or to use its best endeavours by means of the framing of the contracts to enable such launchers and equipment to be procured from non-governmental organisations in its own territory. In either case, Governments shall use their best endeavours to ensure that the cost is calculated on the same basis as the cost of procurement by the Organisation or by the Member State in the territory of which such equipment is produced and shall ensure that contracts placed with non-governmental organisations contain clauses to that effect.

ARTICLE 10
Commercial Exploitation

Member States which propose to exploit commercially, either alone or in conjunction with non-Member States, a space vehicle launcher jointly developed under a programme of the Organisation shall give to all Member States which have contributed to the cost of that programme an opportunity to participate in such exploitation on reasonable terms.

ARTICLE 11
Delivery to Third Parties

The conditions for delivery to States which are not Members of the Organisation, or to international organisations, of launchers and equipment developed by the Organisation shall be decided by the Council in accordance with the provisions of Article 14 of this Convention.

ARTICLE 12
Co-operation with Other States or Organisations

1. The Organisation may co-operate with any Government or body pursuing purposes analogous to its own. To this end and in accordance with the provisions of Article 14 (3) (d) (i), the Council may conclude with a non-Member State, a union of States or an international organisation, agreements containing reciprocal rights and obligations, common action and special procedures.

2. In the event of the creation of a European organisation for collaboration in the field of space research referred to in the Agreement setting up a Preparatory Commission to study the possibilities of European collaboration in the field of space research, signed at Meyrin on December 1, 1960, the closest possible co-operation shall be maintained between the two organisations. To this end, the Council shall formally suggest to the European Space Research Organisation the establishment of a joint co-ordinating committee to consider matters of joint concern including the desirability of a merger between the two organisations.

3. The Council shall transmit an annual report on its activities for the information of the Council of Europe.

*   *   *

ARTICLE 16
Initial programme and Study of Further Programmes

1. The Organisation shall undertake as its initial programme the design, development and construction of a space vehicle launcher using as its first stage the rocket "Blue Streak" and with a French rocket as its second stage. The design and development of the other parts of the system and of a first series of satellite test vehicles shall be carried out under such arrangements as the Council may decide in so far as no other decisions have been taken as recorded in the Protocol annexed to this Convention.

2. In the initial programme, the development firings of the first stage and of the complete launcher shall be conducted at Woomera, Australia. The development firings of the second and third stages shall be carried out wherever economic and technical conditions are most favourable.

3. When the Organisation comes into existence, it shall continue the study of future possiblities and the need for launchers and ranges. This study shall include experimental research. After a period of two years a report on the study shall be presented to the Council. The Council shall then consider what new programme it would be desirable to undertake and also the orientation of the initial programme, having regard to the progress already obtained and the state of the art.

4. The initial programme shall be financed in accordance with the provisions of the Financial Protocol annexed to this Convention. This Protocol also includes the amount of the budget which will be allocated to the study mentioned in paragraph 3 of this Article during the first two years.

5. If it is decided to undertake a further programme, the sum expended on the study mentioned in paragraph 3 of this Article shall then be reimbursed to the initial programme and divided accordingly.

ARTICLE 17
Operations in Member States

Subject to the provisions of this Convention, all operations in connection with a programme of the Organisation shall be carried out in accordance with conditions agreed with the Member State within whose jurisdiction the operations take place.

ARTICLE 22
Disputes

1. In the event of any dispute between two or more States, Members of the Organisation or former Members, or between one of more of them and

the Organisation, concerning the interpretation or the application of this Convention, not being settled by the good offices of the Council, an Arbitral Tribunal shall be set up at the request of one of the parties, unless the parties agree on some other mode of peaceful settlement.

2. Each of the parties to the dispute shall appoint a member of the Tribunal within a period of two months from the date of receipt of the request from the other party. If several Member States or former States of the Organisation are co-plaintiffs or co-defendants, such States shall agree upon a joint member. The members so appointed shall agree on the choice of a chairman for the Arbitral Tribunal, who shall be a national of a Member State other than the States parties to the dispute. If all the Member States are parties to the dispute, the chairman of the Arbitral Tribunal may not be a national of a Member State or of a former Member State of the Organisation, but a national of a State which is a Member of the Council of Europe. If, within the period of two months referred to above, one of the parties has not appointed the member of the Arbitral Tribunal for whose nomination it is responsible, or if, within a period of two months from the date of nomination of all the members of the Arbitral Tribunal, the latter have not agreed upon the appointment of a chairman, the President of the Court of Justice of the European Communities shall make such appointments at the request of any one of the parties.

3. The decision of the Arbitral Tribunal shall be by a majority vote. Their decisions shall be binding on the parties to the dispute. Each party shall be responsible for the expenses incurred by its member of the Arbitral Tribunal as well as for those of its representation in the proceedings before the Tribunal. In addition, unless the Tribunal decides otherwise, the parties to the dispute shall share equally in the expenses incurred by the chairman of the Arbitral Tribunal and in the other expenses. In all other respects, the Arbitral Tribunal shall determine its own rules of procedure.

*   *   *

ARTICLE 25
Dissolution

The Organisation may be dissolved at any time by agreement between the Member States. Subject to any agreement which may be made between Member States at the time of dissolution, the State in the territory of which the seat of the Organisation is at that time established shall in conjunction with the Organisation be responsible for liquidation of the Organisation and for the disposal on behalf of the Organisation of any property of the Organisation situated in the territory of Member States, and the surplus shall be distributed among those States which are Members of the Organisation at the time of the dissolution, in proportion to the contributions made by them from the dates of their becoming parties to this Convention. In the event of a deficit, this shall be met by such Member States in the same proportions as those in which their contributions have been assessed for the financial year then current.

INTERIM AGREEMENT BETWEEN AUSTRALIA, UNITED KINGDOM OF GREAT BRITAIN AND NORTHERN IRELAND, AND THE EUROPEAN ORGANISATION FOR THE DEVELOPMENT AND CONSTRUCTION OF SPACE VEHICLE LAUNCHERS FOR THE CONDUCT OF THE PHASE I FIRING OF THE INITIAL PROGRAMME OF THE ORGANISATION

May 6, 1964

The Government of the Commonwealth of Australia (hereinafter called "the Commonwealth"),
The Government of the United Kingdom of Great Britain and Northern Ireland (hereinafter called "the United Kingdom"),
and
The European Organisation for the Development and Construction of Space Vehicle Launchers (hereinafter called "the Organisation"),
CONSIDERING that certain firings in relation to the initial programme defined in Article 16 of the Convention for the establishment of a European Organisation for the Development and Construction of Space Vehicle Launchers, opened for signature at London from March 29 to April 30, 1962, shall be conducted in Australia soon after the entry into force of said Convention, and that final agreement has not yet been reached regarding the conditions under which firings shall be conducted in Australia;

AND CONSIDERING that it is provided in Article 17 of the Convention that subject to the provisions of the Convention all operations in connection with a programme of the Organisation shall be carried out in accordance with conditions agreed with the Member State within whose jurisdiction the operations take place;

AND CONSIDERING that it has been agreed that the conditions for the carrying out of operations in Australia during such time as is required for the final agreement to be concluded will be provided by an interim agreement;

HAVE AGREED AS FOLLOWS:

ARTICLE I

Scope of the Interim Agreement

This Interim Agreement shall apply to the operations of the Organisation within Australia until the entry into force of a final agreement entered into in respect of those operations as provided in Article 17 of the Convention or until the completion of firings of the first stage alone from Woomera on behalf of the Organisation by the Department of Supply of the Government of the Commonwealth (hereinafter called "the Department") and the Ministry of Aviation of the United Kingdom (hereinafter called "the Ministry") whichever first occurs.

ARTICLE 2

Firings Procedure

1. As far as is practicable firings will be planned and conducted in accordance with the established practices and procedures of the Department.

2. Further specifications relating to the planning and procedures for the conduct of the firings will be introduced by agreement between the Department and the Ministry.

ARTICLE 3

Functions of the Ministry on behalf of the Organisation

The Ministry shall be responsible for the provision of:

(a) a general statement of the overall requirements of the Organisation in terms acceptable to the Department;

(b) (i) specifications covering the requirements for each firing;

(ii) advice of the information required by the Organisation from the Department in respect of each firing;

(c) such further technical information as is required by the Department including that required by the procedures referred to in Article 2 (1) above;

(d) complete test vehicles with appropriate checkout and monitoring and other equipment as agreed with the Department;

(e) personnel to perform and accept responsibility for the preparation of the test vehicles and for all other activities as agreed with the Department and not vested in it by the terms of Article 4 hereunder;

(f) range user equipment as agreed with the Department, including its installation, operation and maintenance;

(g) training of personnel of the Department to the extent that the parties agree is necessary for firings;

(h) assistance to the Department in obtaining equipment which is necessary for the firings and which the Department cannot readily obtain;

(i) equipment necessary for firings which cannot be obtained by the Department.

ARTICLE 4
Functions of the Department on behalf of the Organisation

Subject to funds being made available in advance* the Department shall be responsible for the provision, general range management and operational co-ordination of all areas and facilities associated with firings within Australia, and, subject as aforesaid and without affecting the generality of the foregoing shall be responsible for:

(a) (i) the provision and allocation of areas and buildings to be used in connection with the firings of test vehicles;

    (ii) the construction of additional, and the modification of existing site facilities as required by the Organisation pursuant to paragraphs (a) and (b) of Article 3;

(b) the overall management and operation of the Woomera Range;

(c) the provision as agreed with the Ministry of transport for test vehicles and associated equipment between the point of entry into Australia and the point of use;

(d) provision of such items of Range equipment as are agreed with the Ministry;

(e) provision as agreed with the Ministry of the propellants required for test vehicles and the loading thereof into test vehicles, including provision of the necessary equipment, except for that covered by Article 3 (f) above;

(f) the supply of the information required by the Organisation in respect of each firing.

ARTICLE 5
Safety

The Department will, in its responsibilities:

(a) decide the location of any facility having regard particularly to the requirement for safe distances where explosive or fire risks are involved;

(b) determine the periods when potentially hazardous conditions exist and regulate the movement of personnel, the occupation and use of facilities in such circumstances;

(c) lay down the protective measures which are necessary to safeguard against recognised hazards;

(d) regulate hours of working in potentially hazardous environments;

* in amounts mutually determined by the Department and the Organisation.

(e) have freedom of access to all facilities in order to observe the safety of procedures and practices therein;

(f) prescribe the safety requirements in relation to the design and use of all systems involving the use of explosives, liquid propellants and other dangerous materials;

(g) reject any system involving the use of explosives, liquid propellants or other dangerous material which does not meet requirements prescribed, or agreed with the Ministry;

(h) stop any operation, including firing sequences, when the department judges that a dangerous situation is developing, or that continuation of the operation may cause a dangerous situation to develop;

(i) reject any proposal involving the launching of a test vehicle in any direction until the ability of the test vehicle or any of its stages to perform as planned has been accepted by the Commonwealth;

(j) determine the criteria relative to the inflight safety of the test vehicle, having regard to the safety of life and property within or bordering the flight zones, and to terminate any flight when the Department considers that the criteria cannot be met.

ARTICLE 6
Indemnity

1. The Organisation shall indemnify the Commonwealth and the United Kingdom:

(a) against any loss or damage suffered by the Commonwealth or by the United Kingdom, and

(b) against liability of any kind in respect of claims against the Commonwealth or the United Kingdom, their respective servants or agents for loss, damage or injury that occurs in any place, whether within or outside Australia arising howsoever out of any activity carried out by or on behalf of the Organisation in Australia.

2. The Indemnity to the Commonwealth provided for by paragraph 1 of this Article shall not apply if the loss, damage or injury resulted from any failure of the Department to exercise any of the responsibilities referred to in Articles 4 and 5 of this Agreement.

3. The Indemnity to the United Kingdom provided for by paragraph 1 of this Article shall not apply if the loss, damage or injury resulted from any failure of the Ministry to exercise any of the responsibilities referred to in Article 3 of this Agreement.

4. When the Department or the Ministry has bona fide taken action to carry out the responsibilities assigned to it by virtue of Articles 3, 4 or 5 of

this Agreement the act or omission of a servant or agent of the Commonwealth or of the United Kingdom which directly brings about direct or indirect loss, damage or injury will not be considered as a failure by the Department or by the Ministry as the case may be, to exercise its responsibilities.

Any amount recovered by the Commonwealth or the United Kingdom in respect of an act or omission of a servant or agent of the Commonwealth or the United Kingdom which results in loss, damage or injury shall be taken into account in ascertaining the amount payable by the Organisation to the Commonwealth or the United Kingdom under this Article in respect of the loss, damage or injury.

5. The provisions of paragraph 1 of this Article apply even if the activity from which the loss, damage or injury arises, may have occurred between November 1, 1961, and the date of signature of this Agreement.

ARTICLE 7
Claims against the Commonwealth

1. A claim against the Commonwealth for loss, damage or injury may be settled by the Commonwealth at any time for any amount not exceeding ten thousand Australian pounds (£A10,000); however, the Organisation shall be consulted if it appears to the Commonwealth that a question of principle is involved. A settlement in excess of the amount shall not be effected by the Commonwealth except after consultation with and with the concurrence of the Organisation.

2. The Commonwealth, without prejudice to the exercise of its rights under paragraph 1 of this Article, shall have the conduct of any judicial proceedings instituted and carried on against it in Australia for the purpose of establishing that the Commonwealth is liable for any loss, damage or injury as aforesaid and may, if at any time it is satisfied that it is just and reasonable that it should do so, admit liability for the loss, damage or injury. The Commonwealth will inform the Organisation of any proceedings which are pending.

ARTICLE 8
Claims against the United Kingdom

1. A claim against the United Kingdom for loss, damage or injury may be settled by the United Kingdom at any time for any amount not exceeding eight thousand pounds sterling (£8,000); however the Organisation shall be consulted if it appears to the United Kingdom that a question of principle is involved. A settlement in excess of that amount shall not be effected by the

United Kingdom except after consultation with and with the concurrence of the Organisation.

2. The United Kingdom without prejudice to the exercise of its rights under paragraph 1 of this Article, shall have the conduct of any judicial proceedings instituted and carried on against it in the United Kingdom for the purpose of establishing that the United Kingdom is liable for any loss, damage or injury as aforesaid and may, if at any time it is satisfied that it is just and reasonable that it should do so, admit liability for the loss, damage or injury. The United Kingdom will inform the Organisation of any proceedings which are pending.

ARTICLE 9
Disputes

Any dispute between the parties to this Agreement:

(a) as to whether the loss, damage or injury arose out of any activity carried out by or on behalf of the Organisation in Australia;

(b) as to whether the loss, damage or injury resulted from any failure of the Department or of the Ministry to exercise any of the responsibilities referred to in Articles 3, 4 and 5 of this Agreement;

(c) concerning the amount payable by the Organisation for loss or damage suffered by the Commonwealth or the United Kingdom shall be settled in accordance with the procedures laid down in Article 10 of the present Agreement.

ARTICLE 10
International Arbitration

1. If a party to this Agreement intends to submit a dispute to arbitration it shall notify the Secretary General who shall forthwith inform each Member State of such notification.

2. No appeal shall lie against the award of the Arbitration Tribunal, which shall be final; it shall be binding on the parties. In case of dispute concerning the import or scope of the award, it shall be incumbent upon the Arbitration Tribunal to interpret it on request by either party.

3. The Arbitration Tribunal shall consist of three members, one arbitrator nominated by the State or States, party to the arbitration, one arbitrator nominated by the Organisation and a third arbitrator who shall be the chairman, nominated by the said two arbitrators.

4. The arbitrators shall be nominated from a panel comprising no more than six arbitrators appointed by each of the Commonwealth and the United Kingdom and six arbitrators appointed by the Organisation.

5. If, within three months from the date of the notification referred to in paragraph 1 of this Article, either party fails to make the nomination referred to in paragraph 3 of this Article, the choice of the arbitrator shall, on request of the other party, be made by the President of the International Court of Justice from the persons comprised in the said panel. This shall also apply, when so requested by either party, if within one month from the date of appointment of the second arbitrator, the first two arbitrators are unable to agree on the nomination of the third arbitrator. However, a national of the State applying for arbitration may not be chosen to fill the post of the arbitrator whose appointment devolves on the Organisation, nor may a person comprised in the panel and appointed by the Organisation be chosen to fill the post of an arbitrator whose appointment devolves on the State which is the claimant. Nor may a person of either of these categories be chosen as Chairman of the Tribunal.

6. The Council shall establish the procedure to be followed in the Arbitration Tribunal.

ARTICLE 11

Entry into Force

This Agreement shall enter into force on the date of signature.

APPENDIX VII

EXTRACTS FROM BILATERAL AGREEMENTS

EXTRACT FROM EXCHANGE OF NOTES CONSTITUTING AN AGREEMENT
BETWEEN THE UNITED STATES OF AMERICA AND THE UNITED
KINGDOM OF GREAT BRITAIN AND NORTHERN IRELAND RELATING TO
THE ESTABLISHMENT AND OPERATION OF TRACKING STATIONS
WITHIN THE UNITED KINGDOM

January 20, 1961

(1) Each Government shall designate an agency or agencies which shall be responsible for carrying out the programme. For the Government of the United States, this shall be the National Aeronautics and Space Administration and for the Government of the United Kingdom this shall be such agencies as that Government may from time to time designate through the normal diplomatic channels. The agency designated by the Government of the United States and the agency or agencies designated by the Government of the United Kingdom are hereinafter respectively referred to as a "Co-operating Agency".

(2) (a) The programme shall include the establishment of a Tracking Station at an agreed site at Windfield, Windsor, Berkshire, England and such other stations at other locations as may from time to time be agreed upon by the two Governments.

(b) The Government of the United Kingdom shall provide the site for the station at Windfield at no cost to the Government of the United States.

(3) The Government of the United Kingdom shall upon request of a Co-operating Agency investigate any interference to radio reception at the station or stations which may be due to electrical apparatus, and shall take all reasonable steps to secure the removal of the interference.

(4) (a) All radio operations by the stations or station shall be conducted so as not to interfere with the services provided by installations in the United Kingdom or in neighbouring territories, and shall comply at all times with the provisions of the International Telecommunication Convention.[1]

(b) All frequencies to be used at the station or stations shall be subject to approval in advance by the appropriate United Kingdom authorities. So far

[1] United States of America: *Treaties and Other International Act Series 3266.*

375

as is possible, these frequencies shall be in such frequency bands as may be allocated for use in space research in the International Radio Regulations annexed to the International Telecommunication Convention.

(c) The Government of the United Kingdom shall be responsible for notifying the International Telecommunication Union of the frequencies used at the station or stations. The Government of the United States shall at all times convey promptly to the Government of the United Kingdom, through the Co-operating Agencies, all the information needed to enable that Government to fulfil this obligation.

(5) In connection with each station to be established and operated under the programme, the Co-operating Agencies shall agree, subject to the grant of any wireless telegraphy license required under the law in force in the United Kingdom, upon arrangements with respect to the duration of use of the station, the responsibility for and financing of the construction, installation, equipping, maintenance, and operation of the station, and other details relating to the establishment and operation of the station.

(6) Each Co-operating Agency shall provide to the other, from the data acquired through the operation of each station, such reduced scientific data as the other Agency may request for scientific studies it may wish to carry out. The results of all such studies shall be made available promptly and in their entirety to both Co-operating Agencies.

(7) Each station established may be used for independent scientific activities of the Government of the United Kingdom or of a United Kingdom Co-operating Agency, it being understood that such activities shall be conducted so as not to conflict with schedules of operations agreed between the two Governments or between the Co-operating Agencies and that any additional operating costs resulting from such independent activities shall be borne by the Government of the United Kingdom or by the United Kingdom Co-operating Agency concerned unless otherwise agreed.

(8) (a) The Government of the United Kingdom shall, upon request, take the necessary steps to facilitate the admission into the United Kingdom of materials, equipment, supplies, goods and other items of property owned by the Government of the United States and brought into the United Kingdom for the purpose of this Agreement.

(b) No customs duties shall be charged on the importation into the United Kingdom of materials, equipment, supplies, goods and other items of property in connection with this Agreement provided that such materials, equipment, supplies, goods and other items of property are and continue to be the property of, and are imported by, the Government of the United States.

(9) (a) Title to any property provided by the Government of the United States for use in connection with each station shall remain in the Government of the United States until that Government sells or otherwise disposes of such property, notwithstanding that it is affixed to the land or to any structure on it. Such property of the Government of the United States at each station may be removed from the United Kingdom by the Government of the United States at any time, free of taxes and other charges. The Government of the United States shall arrange for the removal of such property from the site of the station when that site is no longer required for the purposes of this Agreement.

(b) If the Government of the United States should desire to dispose of all or part of the property to which it holds title within the United Kingdom for the purposes of this Agreement, the two Governments shall consult beforehand on arrangements therefor.

(10) (a) The Government of the United Kingdom shall take the necessary steps to facilitate, subject to the normal laws and regulations governing the admission of foreign nationals to the United Kingdom, the admission into the United Kingdom of such United States personnel as may be assigned by the Co-operating Agency of the Government of the United States to visit or participate in the co-operative activities provided for under this Agreement, due regard being paid to the principle that United States personnel shall only be employed where no suitably qualified British subjects are available.

(b) Subject to such conditions as the Government of the United Kingdom may deem necessary, personal and household effects of United States personnel assigned to a station under the programme by the Co-operating Agency of the Government of the United States may be brought into the United Kingdom at the time of the owner's first arrival and removed from the United Kingdom on the termination of his assignment free of all taxes and duties. Such effects shall not be sold or otherwise disposed of within the United Kingdom except under conditions approved by the Government of the United Kingdom.

(c) For the purposes of this paragraph, the expression "United States personnel" means persons not normally resident in the United Kingdom who are employees of or under contract with the Government of the United States, or with a United States contractor engaged by that Government, in connection with the establishment and operation of the station, except that sub-paragraph (b) of this paragraph shall apply only to employees of the Government of the United States.

(11) The programme of co-operation set forth in this Agreement shall,

subject to the availability of funds, remain in effect for a period of five years and may thereafter be extended for such additional period and on such terms as may be agreed in writing between the two Governments. Nevertheless, either Government may terminate this Agreement by giving ninety days' notice in writing to the other Government.

BILATERAL SPACE AGREEMENT OF JUNE 8, 1962 BETWEEN THE ACADEMY OF SCIENCES OF THE U.S.S.R. AND THE NATIONAL AERONAUTICS AND SPACE ADMINISTRATION OF THE UNITED STATES

Introduction

Following the exchange of views between Nikita S. Khrushchev, Chairman of the Council of Ministers of the Union of Soviet Socialist Republics, and John F. Kennedy, President of the United States of America, regarding co-operation in the exploration and use of space for peaceful purposes, the U.S.S.R. and U.S. representatives designated for the purpose have discussed in some detail the possibilities of co-operation in meteorology, a world geomagnetic survey, and satellite telecommunications.

In the field of meteorology, it is important that the two satellite launching nations contribute their capabilities toward the establishment of a global weather satellite system for the benefit of other nations.

The compilation of a map of the magnetic field of the Earth with the aid of satellites is extremely important both for the further successful exploration of space and for advancing the science of Earth magnetism.

Telecommunications by means of satellites is expected to lead to a considerable improvement of communications facilities all over the world and can be a most important contribution to the extension of contacts and friendship among nations. Communication satellites can also be used for domestic needs within a single country.

The U.S.S.R. and U.S. representatives have arrived at the following understanding which they agree to refer to their governments for consideration.

Meteorology

It is agreed that this programme falls naturally into two stages, an experimental and an operational one.

The first stage will extend approximately from the present time through 1963–64 during the development of experimental weather satellites by both the U.S.S.R. and the U.S.

In this first stage, the two countries will arrange for the establishment of communication links adequate for the transfer, from each to the other, of the data gathered by each nation from its own experimental meteorological satellites. These communication links would connect the World Weather Centers at Moscow and Washington. A Joint Working Group of technical experts will meet in October 1962 to decide upon suitable communication links to be established with due regard to the sharing of costs and the interests of other nations.

The Joint Working Group will also establish the criteria for the two-way transfer of satellite data over such links, with the understanding that such transfers will include selected cloud-cover pictures, especially related to storms, vortices, fronts, and the generation of these phenomena, with geographical co-ordinates provided for all pictures selected, together with nephanalyses based upon the data as a whole. The Joint Working Group will agree upon a date for initiating the two-way transfer of such data, designating this date with due regard for the readiness of the communication links and the readiness of the U.S.S.R. and the U.S. to provide data of approximately equivalent interest. Data should be exchanged as quickly as possible. The same communication links would be used to exchange weather charts, diagrams, vertical cross-sections, and the material required for solving the problems of world weather, including the extension of prediction periods. Co-ordinated research efforts should be directed toward these goals.

The second stage of the meteorological satellite programme will begin approximately in 1964–65 and will apply to the co-ordinated launchings by the two nations of a system of operational weather satellites. In order to prepare adequately and in a timely fashion for such co-ordinated launchings, a second Joint Working Group will meet in March 1963 to determine mutually agreeable launching schedules for the operational satellites, the numbers of such satellites, their orbits, and the comparability (to the degree desirable) of the characteristics of their sensors and the data to be obtained.

These discussions as to satellite characteristics, numbers, and orbits shall be made with due consideration of recommendations of the World Meteorological Organization (WMO) with regard to the objectives of weather-data acquisition by satellites for both operations and research.

The two-way transfer of data during the second stage shall be determined by the two nations and shall be made on a real-time basis. This transfer and the wider dissemination of such data to other nations will proceed with full consideration of the recommendations and procedures of the World Meteorological Organization (WMO). Nephanalyses, pictures of cloud cover, and processed data on radiation fluxes will be exchanged mutually.

Appendix

World Geomagnetic Survey

It was agreed to be useful to arrange for a joint effort in this field by the co-ordinated launching of two artificial Earth satellites equipped with magneto-meters during the period of the International Year of the Quiet Sun. These two satellites will be launched, one by the U.S.S.R. and the other by the U.S., on different mutually agreed orbits. The period before the International Year of the Quiet Sun will be used by both parties (the U.S.S.R. and the U.S.) to continue magnetic measurements in space in accordance with national work programmes, with mutual exchange of processed data of the magnetic measurements.

The representatives of the U.S.S.R. and the U.S. agreed that it would be desirable to establish a Joint Working Group, consisting of U.S.S.R. and U.S. specialists, for preliminary consideration of the scientific and technical aspects of the compilation of a map of the magnetic field of the Earth with the aid of artificial Earth satellites. In particular, the Joint Working Group is to make recommendations on the shape of the orbits, their angle of inclination to the equator, the period during which the satellites are to be operated, the necessary accuracy of measurements, the type of magnometers to be used on the satellites, the methods of processing and analyzing the data obtained, the methods of correcting them, and so on.

Conducting its work, the Joint Working Group will take into consideration any possible recommendations on this question of the Scientific and Technical Subcommittee of the UN Committee on the Peaceful Uses of Outer Space.

The parties agreed that it would be desirable for the members of this Joint Working Group to be appointed by each side as soon as technically possible to begin work on the problems placed before the group, by correspondence and by subsequent meetings, if necessary.

The parties recognized that data obtained in Earth magnetic observatories were of particularly great importance for the successful compilation of a map of the magnetic field of the Earth with the aid of the artificial Earth satellites. They therefore agreed to make efforts to arrange, through World Data Centers A and B, for a prompt exchange of standard magnetograms from Earth observatories, and to arrange that these magnetograms contain all the data required for their use for analyzing the data acquired by satellites. Each side agreed to use its influence with non-governmental organizations (such as the International Committee on Geophysics (CIG), the Committee on Space Research (COSPAR), and others) to expedite the transmission to World Data Centers A and B of the necessary Earth magnetic data from third countries co-operating with the U.S.S.R. and U.S.

Satellite Telecommunications

Recognizing the role of the International Telecommunication Union and the importance of the establishment of bilateral co-operation between the U.S.S.R. and the U.S. in the exploration and peaceful uses of outer space, we submit the following recommendations:

In 1962–63 the U.S.S.R. and the U.S. agree to co-operate in experiments on communication by means of the U.S. satellite "Echo A-12".

We agree to give further consideration to the possibilities of co-operation in joint experiments using active satellites that may be launched by either nation in the future, including the mutual exchange of information on the results of such experiments, and to resume discussions of these possibilities at our next series of meetings.

Among the problems which should be discussed at the following meetings is that of the preparation for working out with other nations of a project for an experimental global system of space communications with due regard to the recommendations of the ITU.

Conclusion

The recommendations proposed at the present stage of the bilateral discussions by the representatives of the U.S.S.R. and the U.S. have a preliminary character and will be presented by both parties to their governments through appropriate agencies for final consideration. If either of the two parties finds it necessary to make any corrections, additions, or deletions in the text of the prepared documents, then all of these changes should be made within the period of two months from this date by correspondence, which will be sent to the following address in Moscow:

Academy of Sciences of the U.S.S.R.
Leninsk: Prospekt 14
Moscow
U.S.S.R.

and to the following address in Washington:

National Aeronautics and Space Administration
Attention: Dr. Hugh L. Dryden
400 Maryland Avenue, S.W.
Washington 25, D.C., U.S.A.

Geneva, June 8, 1962.

Appendix

First Memorandum of Understanding to Implement the
Bilateral Space Agreement of June 8, 1962 Between the
Academy of Sciences of the U.S.S.R. and the National
Aeronautics and Space Administration of the
United States

I. *Preamble*

The purpose of the present Memorandum of Understanding is to begin the implementation of the sections of the bilateral space agreement of June 8, 1962, dealing with a co-ordinated meteorological satellite programme, world magnetic survey using satellites, and a passive communication satellite experiment. It also provides for future discussions by the scientists of both countries of scientific results obtained from deep space probes (Mariner II and Mars I).

II. *Co-ordinated Meteorological Satellite Programme*

A. Exchange of Meteorological Satellite Data

The bilateral space agreement of June 8, 1962, provided that the exchange of meteorological satellite data between Moscow and Washington be of approximately equivalent interest to the two countries.

The following sections describe the data to be exchanged. It is agreed that, in general, the data exchange is to be completed within six hours of the observation time so that it will be useful in weather analysis and forecasting.

In all of the joint activities relating to meteorological satellites and exchange of meteorological data, the pertinent recommendations of the World Meteorological Organization shall be given due consideration.

1. *Cloud Photographs*
(a) Selection of Photographs
   Cloud photographs will be exchanged; the selection of those to be transmitted will be based on the following criteria:
1. Areas of the Earth having few conventional observations.
2. Pictures along active international air routes, particularly oceanic.
3. Pictures containing patterns of meteorological significance such as fronts, vortices, cloud bands and streets.
(b) Accuracy of Location
1. Positions of identifiable cloud elements in the pictures will be located with an accuracy of about 200 km. Where landmarks are available, this accuracy should be about 100 km. It is expected that this accuracy will be improved later.
2. The pictures will include latitude and longitude grids at 2° intervals.

(c) Brightness Levels
1. At the satellite receiving stations, six to ten brightness (gray) levels[1] will be contained in the pictures.
2. The pictures as received at the end of the communications link will contain five to six brightness levels, if possible.
3. To aid in the interpretation of cloud images, copies of some of the original pictures transmitted over the link will be mailed to the other country.
(d) Resolution
1. The ground resolution provided by the pictures initially will be about 2.5 km and are expected to improve to about 1 km.
(e) Field of View
1. The minimum field of view, on the Earth's surface, of each picture will be about 1,000 km on a side.

2. *Nephanalyses*
(a) Nephanalyses will be transmitted for all pictures received by the meteorological satellites.
(b) Whether possible, format, representation, and map projections will follow World Meteorological Organization recommendations.
(c) Polar stereographic projection will be used, except in equatorial areas where Mercator projection will be used.
(d) A map scale 1 : 20,000,000 or 1 : 15,000,000 will be used as convenient to the transmitting country.

3. *Other Satellite Observations*
As satellite observation techniques are developed to the point where they provide new useful information for weather forecasting, the data obtained will be considered for inclusion in this exchange programme.

B. Exchange of Techniques and Results of Scientific Research

To assist in making maximum use of the satellite data in weather analysis and forecasting, there will be an exchange, on a basis of mutual interest, of techniques of interpretation and analysis.

It is also desirable to exchange scientific literature and data for research purposes, and to organize co-operative symposia.

C. Exchange of Conventional Meteorological Data

The establishment of a facsimile quality communications link between Washington and Moscow for the exchange of satellite data provides an opportunity, when it is not being used for the transmission of satellite data,

---

[1] Brightness levels should be clearly distinguished by eye, such as the ratio of the intensities of adjacent steps being equal to the square root of two.

for the exchange of related data obtained by conventional means of observations, and related maps, which will allow for improved correlation between satellite and conventional observations. Each country will indicate which of these data, available in the other, it wishes to receive and determine the priority of transmission. Some details of the exchange of the conventional data are given in an appendix and others are expected to be clarified, as they arise, by an appropriate working group.

D. Establishment of Communication Link

With the understanding that the regular exchange of meteorological data obtained from meteorological satellites will commence in the beginning of the second half of 1964, NASA and the Academy of Sciences of the U.S.S.R. consider it desirable in the beginning of the first half of 1964, to start the occasional exchange of conventional meteorological data and experimental satellite data and for this purpose to establish the communication link between Moscow and Washington provided in the agreement of June 8, 1962.

1. Characteristics of the Communication Link

The communication link shall be arranged on a four-wire basis, for full-time use, allowing simultaneous transmission of facsimile telegraphy information in both directions. Technical parameters of the communication link shall conform to the CCITT series T recommendations.

The link shall be equipped for non-simultaneous voice use to allow technical and meteorological co-ordination as necessary.

2. Characteristics of Terminal Equipment

Terminal equipment used for transmission of weather maps and charts shall conform with WMO recommendation 10.6.17/I – "Standardization of International Meteorological Transmissions by Facsimile – Equipment Characteristics". The preferred index of co-operation will be 576. The drum speed shall be 60, 90, or 120 rpm, depending upon the results of the technical tests.

Additional requirements for the terminal equipment for transmitting information obtained from meteorological satellites shall be determined during 1963. Each party shall provide and operate its own terminal equipment.

3. Routing of Communication Link

The circuit for the link shall be routed Washington – New York – London or Paris – Berlin – Poland – Moscow, assuming first that adequate facilities (circuits) are available over this route and second, that tests prove this routing to be technically acceptable to both NASA and the Academy of Sciences of the U.S.S.R. Technical arrangements for those sections of the link from Washington to Berlin shall be made by NASA. Technical arrangements for those sections of the link from Berlin to Moscow shall be made by the Academy of Sciences of the U.S.S.R.

Joint technical tests of the communication link along the selected route shall be conducted during January 1964, and after this the communication link will be put into regular operation.

4. Cost of the Communication Link

NASA and the Academy of Sciences of the U.S.S.R. shall, within one month, agree upon a suitable mechanism for the handling of charges over the centre link in such a way as to provide for equal sharing of cost of the whole line by the two parties.

5. Reception of Meteorological Data by Weather Services of Other Countries

The desire of Weather Services of other countries to bridge the line on a receive-only basis in order to obtain meteorological data for their own use will be welcomed with the condition that each such Weather Service will make a proportional contribution to the total expenses of the communication link.

6. Co-ordination

NASA and the Academy of Sciences of the U.S.S.R. shall, within 60 days, designate representatives for continuing direct technical co-ordination of details concerning this link.

E. Co-ordinated Launchings of Weather Satellites

The Bilateral Space Agreement of June 8, 1962, provided, among other things, for the co-ordinated launching of operational weather satellites. It is considered desirable to initiate co-ordinated launchings of weather satellites towards the end of the experimental period in order to gain experience with such co-ordination and to provide for more frequent receipt and exchange of data of both experimental and operational value.

The Academy of Sciences of the U.S.S.R. and NASA therefore agree to convene a suitable Joint Working Group by the end of 1963, so that arrangements may be made, consistent with the provisions of the June 8, 1962 agreement, for mutually agreeable launching schedules.

III. *Arrangements for Passive Communications Satellite Experiments*

A. General

The National Aeronautics and Space Administration and the Academy of Sciences of the U.S.S.R. agree to participate jointly in passive communica-

385

tions experiments using a large reflector satellite, Echo II (referred to as Echo A-12 in the agreement of June 8, 1962), which NASA is expected to launch prior to the middle of 1964.

B. Satellite Characteristics

The satellite to be used in these experiments shall be approximately 44 meters in diameter and shall be constructed of a material having a radio wave reflectivity of 98 per cent. It will carry two telementry transmitters (approximately 136 mc/s) to be used as tracking aids. The intended orbit will be inclined about 82° to the equator and will be roughly circular at an altitude of 1,290 km.

C. Frequencies and Route

Communications experiments shall be carried out at frequencies of approximately 162 mc/s between the U.S.S.R. (Zemenki Observatory, Gorky State University) and the United Kingdom (Jodrell Bank Observatory, University of Manchester).

In view of the technical desirability of carrying out communication experiments with a passive satellite using higher frequencies, NASA and the Academy of Sciences of the U.S.S.R. shall consider, within three months following the date of this agreement, the possibility of extending these tests into the microwave region of the radio frequency spectrum. The possibility of arranging radar and optical observations of the Echo II satellite sphere during the period of its inflation and thereafter shall be considered within the same period.

D. Arrangements

The Academy of Sciences of the U.S.S.R. shall make necessary arrangements for use of the Gorky State University facilities. NASA shall make necessary arrangements for the use of the facilities of the University of Manchester at Jodrell Bank. Within sixty days NASA and the Academy of Sciences of the U.S.S.R. shall appoint representatives to begin and carry on continuing technical co-ordination with respect to the experiments at approximately 162 mc/s. NASA will request the appointment of a corresponding technical representative of the University of Manchester.

In case the question of suing higher frequencies for carrying out the passive satellite experiments is settled positively, NASA shall arrange, through the General Post Office of the United Kingdom, for the use of the Goonhilly Downs Station and shall request that technical representatives also be appointed by the General Post Office. The technical representatives for NASA and the Academy of Sciences of the U.S.S.R., referred to in the preceding paragraph, shall also serve to carry on continuing technical co-ordination for these experiments or other representatives may be named for this purpose.

It is understood that there will be no mutual money reimbursements between NASA and the Academy of Sciences of the U.S.S.R. for the use of any facilities.

E. Orbital Information

NASA shall provide a prediction of the expected initial orbital elements at least two months prior to launching of the satellite. Actual orbital elements based on tracking information will be supplied for the duration of the experimental period, at intervals of approximately once per week, or as necessary for adequate pointing of the communication antennas. The Academy of Sciences of the U.S.S.R. shall provide tracking data on orbits that are visible in the U.S.S.R. but not in the U.S.A. in a form to be mutually agreed on by the technical representatives.

F. Planned Types of Transmission

The passive Echo II satellite experiments shall basically consist of measurements of the quality of transmission over the circuit between the U.S.S.R. and the U.K. for the following kinds of transmissions:

(a) Unmodulated carrier.
(b) Single frequency modulation.
(c) Telegraphy.
(d) Facsimile and voice if feasible.

It shall also be an objective of these experiments to test the feasibility of direct communication between the U.S. and the U.S.S.R. using the Echo II satellite as a part of the link. For this purpose NASA will arrange for the part of the link from the U.S. to the U.K.

G. Exchange of Observational Data

The results of the experiments and observations shall be promptly exchanged between NASA and the Academy of Sciences of the U.S.S.R., and be made generally available to the scientific and technical community. Information about the equipment used for the experiments shall be exchanged to the extent necessary for the interpretation of these data.

H. Future Plans

NASA and the Academy of Sciences of the U.S.S.R. will continue experimental research with active communications satellites under their national programmes; after the completion of preliminary national tests, negotiations will be continued to discuss the possibility of joint experiments of mutual interest with active communications satellites.

387

Appendix

IV. *Magnetic Field Survey Through the use of Artificial Satellites*

1. Objectives

It shall be the aim of the co-operative effort at this stage to produce a mapping of the Earth's magnetic field by using U.S. and U.S.S.R. satellites flow during the International Year of the Quiet Sun (IQSY).

2. Satellite Orbits

The forms of orbits, their altitudes and inclination to the equator will be selected by the satellite-launching country, in accordance with the objective of the experiment. It is agreed that the accuracy of determining space and time co-ordinates for the separate magnetic measurements on the satellite be such that after necessary processing by the satellite-launching country the magnetic data would not contain errors greater than plus or minus 10 gammas.

3. Times of Satellite Launchings

The times of satellite launchings will be determined by the satellite-launching country and will take place during the IQSY. It is recommended that launchings take place in 1965 since one may expect, in 1965, that the ground-based magnetic observatory programmes of all countries participating in the IQSY will be in full operation.

4. Lifetime of Satellites

It is agreed that the lifetime of each satellite be such that the minimum density of magnetic measurements from each satellite correspond to no less than one per 200 kilometer square on the Earth's surface.

5. Satellite Apparatus

It is agreed that absolute magnetometers of various types be used, such as optical pumping and proton precession magnetometers. It is recommended that the sensitive elements of magnetometers be located on the satellites in such a way as to minimize the effects of magnetic fields from the spacecraft.

6. Time Variation Corrections

With a view towards the desirability of working out a common method of introducing time variation corrections into the results of observations from satellites, it is agreed that each side conduct research in this direction and exchange results with the other side. The following possibilities should be considered:

    (a) comparison of satellite magnetic measurements taken at different times but corresponding to the same region of space within a diameter of 10–20 kilometers;

(b) comparison between experimental data obtained from satellites with those from ground-based magnetic observatories.

For the compilation of a magnetic map it is agreed that the results of satellite measurements made on magnetically quiet days be utilized.

In connection with the above, an exchange is recommended between the Academy of Sciences of the U.S.S.R. and the NASA of the U.S.A., namely: microfilm copies of magnetograms and tables of hourly averages of magnetic elements. In addition, copies of magnetograms shall be accompanied by data on the preliminary base line values, scale values, temperature coefficients, and types of instruments.

It is agreed that these data be exchanged no later than three months after the month of observation from the following observatories:

U.S.S.R.	U.S.A.
Yakutsk	Sitka
Sverdlovsk	College
Irkutsk	Fredericksburg
Odessa	Tucson
Tashkent	San Juan
	Guam

It is agreed that the final base line values be exchanged on a quarterly basis.

7. Exchange of Satellite Magnetic Measurements

It is agreed to exchange results of magnetic measurements from satellites in the form of scientific articles or reports containing information on the satellite equipment, the data, its accuracy, methods of processing, introduced corrections, and estimates of the accuracy achieved judged necessary by the authors of the experiment.

It is agreed that each side if necessary will furnish by mail to the other side any additional data which may help to clarify the questions which arise in the use of the data received by exchange to remove the difficulties in utilization of those data.

8. Exchange of Data from Magnetic Surveys of Other Types

It is agreed to exchange comparable amounts of data from magnetic surveys which may be necessary for the compilation of a magnetic map and which are made without using satellites (ground, sea, aerial surveys) in the form of maps or of reports with attachments giving the results of surveys in tabular form, indicating co-ordinates and the times to which these data refer.

9. International Co-operation

It is agreed that appropriate organizations under the International Council of Scientific Unions, including the International Union of Geodesy and Geophysics and COSPAR, concerned with the Worked Magnetic Survey be kept informed of the proposed joint U.S.–U.S.S.R. contributions to the World Magnetic Survey and of analysis of the results. Scientific data resulting from this work which is suitable for storage and dissemination through the World Data Centers will be supplied in a timely way.

V. *Other Questions of Co-operation*

Representatives of the Academy of Sciences of the U.S.S.R. and NASA consider it to be useful for further progress in the space sciences to exchange scientific data received as a result of the launching in the U.S.S.R. of an automatic space station towards the planet of Mars and the launching in the U.S.A. of a space station towards the planet of Venus. For this purpose it is desirable to conduct meetings of scientists of the two countries to discuss the results of those experiments in outer space. The preliminary discussion of these questions will be held during the next meeting of COSPAR in June 1963 in Warsaw. Additional meetings may be arranged at a later date, dependent on progress in analyzing the data received from "Mars I" and "Mariner II" by the scientists of both countries.

VI. *Effective Date*

The recommendations proposed in the present document have a preliminary character and will be presented by both parties to the Academy of Sciences of the U.S.S.R. and the National Aeronautics and Space Administration of the U.S. for final consideration. If either of the two parties finds it necessary to make any corrections, additions, or deletions in the text of the prepared documents, then all of these changes should be made in the shortest possible time after the conclusion of discussions concerning the conduct of a world magnetic survey by means of artificial satellites, by correspondence, which will be sent to the following address in Moscow:

> Academy of Sciences of the U.S.S.R.
> Leninski Prospekt 14
> Moscow
> U.S.S.R.

and to the following address in Washington:

> National Aeronautics and Space Administration
> Attention: Dr. Hugh L. Dryden
> 400 Maryland Avenue, S.W.
> Washington 25, D.C.
> U.S.A.

If in this final consideration there is failure to agree on any of the three major areas, the recommendations in the other major areas will continue in effect.

APPENDIX TO MEMORANDUM OF UNDERSTANDING

Exchange of Conventional Meteorological Data

A. Types of Conventional Data

1. *Computer Processed and Checked Upper Air Data*

(a) It is not anticipated that all conventional data would be processed and transmitted but rather the data for a few selected upper air levels that are particularly significant for analysis and forecasting. Criteria for the extent of this kind of data exchange would be based on the following:

1. Limited to these stations from which the original upper air reports are received within three to four hours at Moscow or Washington. (This amounts to a "Regional" collection.)
2. Original reports will be subjected to rapid computer processing in order to eliminate and/or correct erroneous reports and to arrange the data in a convenient and systematic form for transmission.
3. The upper air levels useful for numerical weather prediction are 1000 mb, 850 mb, 700 mb, 500mb, 300 mb, and 200 mb.
4. At the levels indicated above, the following data will be transmitted: temperature, geopotential height, dew point and wind.
5. The areas and network of stations for which the data are to be transmitted will be determined later.

2. *Conventional Weather Charts*

Charts prepared by objective numerical techniques in graphical form should receive priority for exchange on the communications link. The types of charts that would contribute to improved world weather analyses and predictions are:

(a) Northern Hemispheric analyses of the 1000 mb and several upper air levels such as the 500 mb, 300 mb, and 200 mb levels.

(b) Northern Hemispheric predictions for 24 hours with the possibility of extending the period of forecast to 72 hours in the future, for 500, 300 and 200 mb.

(c) It is desirable in the future to exchange extended period forecasts of five days or longer and a selection of the important working charts or diagrams that may be used in generating these forecasts.

(d) In order to co-ordinate satellite and conventional observations associated with important weather developments, available detailed analyses and satellite photographs for specific areas will be transmitted on request as soon as possible.

3. *Timing and Frequency of Exchanges*

To be of maximum operational value, all information should be submitted as early as practical.

Suggested items are:

(a) Processed upper air data within 4–5 hours of observation (twice per day).

(b) Analyses within 6 hours of observation (twice per day).

(c) Prognoses within 6–9 hours of observation (twice per day).

4. *Map Scales and Projections*

(a) Polar stereographic projections will be used for all chart exchanges.

(b) Analysis and prognostic charts having a scale of 1 : 30 million or 1 : 40 million will be used.

(c) Special charts exchanged on request would be on scales most convenient for the transmitting country.

COSPAR STANDARDS

COSPAR GUIDE TO ROCKET AND SATELLITE INFORMATION AND DATA EXCHANGE

As part of the fundamental international planning for the programme of the International Geophysical Year, World Data Centers were established to collect data from the numerous and wide-spread IGY observational programmes and to make such data readily available to interested scientists for an indefinite period of time. By the beginning of the IGY, three WDC's had been established: WDC-A, divided by discipline among eleven institutions in the United States; WDC-B, in three institutions in the U.S.S.R.; and WDC-C, in twenty-one institutions located in eight nations of Western Europe, in Australia, and in Japan. Included in each of these WDC's was a subcentre for rocket and satellite data: in Washington, in Moscow, and in Slough, England.

The final IGY data-interchange agreements were published in Volume VII of the IGY *Annals*, and applied specifically to data taken during the IGY period (July 1957–December 1958); subsequently these agreements were extended to cover the International Geophysical Co-operation – 1959. Thereafter, responsibility for rocket and satellite data centres was assumed by the Committee on Space Research (COSPAR), which decided that the data-interchange agreements of the IGY–IGC period should be continued. Subsequently, at its Fourth Meeting in Florence in April 1961, COSPAR resolved to undertake a revision of the IGY Guide to Rocket and Satellite Data Centers. The revised Guide, which follows, was adopted by COSPAR at its Fifth Meeting, Washington, D.C., May 1962.

WDC's endeavour to collect and maintain rocket and satellite data and unpublished reports in a form which can be readily handled and interpreted by scientists other than the experimenter. Accordingly, WDC's do not normally house raw, or even calibrated, data but rather analyzed data, usually in the form of published reports containing sampled calibrated data. If a scientist requires original data, or the complete calibrated data, they should be obtained by him directly from the experimenter. By consulting the catalogue of data held in a WDC, the scientist can apprise himself of the material that it holds, and should know that he can obtain copies of this material from the WDC at cost, or if it is not practicable to copy the material, he can consult it at the WDC.

1. *Sounding Rockets*[1]

1. 1 Launching Information

After each successful launching the responsible institution will, within four (4) weeks, complete and forward a Report of Sounding Rocket Launching (Appendix I) to each World Data Center for Rockets and Satellites (WDC), or, alternatively, three (3) copies to one WDC to permit distribution to the others.

1. 2 Report of Results

As soon as possible after the performance of an experiment in which significant data are obtained, a full scientific report of the experiment, including an adequate description of the instrumentation involved, will be published in scientific literature of general availability. Publication within one (1) year is desirable, but in any event should occur no later than three (3) years after the experiment. Two (2) copies of the published report will be sent to each WDC or, alternatively, six (6) copies to one WDC to permit distribution to the others.

Data supporting the conclusions of the report will be included in the body or appendix of the published report, or in an interim report, available upon request and referenced in the published report, or, if this procedure is not practicable, will be sent to WDC's in tabulated form.

Original (raw) data and the complete, calibrated data will not normally be deposited in the WDC's; however, such data will be retained by the experimenter. The calibrated data and, where appropriate, the original data will be made available for use by other scientists upon request one (1) year or more after performance of the experiment. Raw data are original records on film, magnetic tape, paper, etc. Calibrated data are data to which calibrations have been applied to give values of the physical quantities measured in the experiment. Analysed data are sampled calibrated data or the results of computations on calibrated data.

---

[1] The following provisions apply primarily to *experimental* rocket flights, in which new kinds of observations are being made. In cases where numbers of rockets are fired to obtain *more coutine* or *synoptir* data, the procedures for data exchange will need to be modified from those already specified. The procedure for data exchange, being compatible in each case with the aims and restrictions of the co-ordinated synoptic rocket experiments, will be left to the COSPAR Panel on Synoptic Rocket Soundings.

2. *Satellites and Space Probes*

2. 1 Pre-Launch Information

In view of the scientific value to be obtained by the maximum participation of scientists throughout the world in space research programmes, technical information will be provided to COSPAR for distribution to COSPAR adherents well in advance of launch in at least those cases where such participation is feasible. (See also 2. 8, *Descriptive Experimental Information.*) As appropriate for such participation, this information will include a description of the experiments; approximate date of launch, planned orbit, and expected lifetime; frequencies, power output, mode of transmission, and other information needed for tracking or telemetry read-out; and, when appropriate, telemetry codes and calibrations by which to reduce the data to usable form. (It is recognized that it is often not possible to distribute telemetry codes and calibrations in useful form until tested against data received; the traditional prerogatives of the experimenter must also be recognized.) As a matter of courtesy, the recipients of such advance information will leave public announcement to the launching nation.

2. 2 Launching Announcements

Within a few hours after successful launching of a satellite or space probe (cosmic rocket), the following information will be distributed via SPACE-WARN (with a copy direct by cable to the Secretariat of COSPAR):

The data and time of launch; date, time, and co-ordinates of injection into orbit, approximate apogee, perigee, orbital period, and angle of inclination of the orbit (for satellites); geocentric or heliocentric co-ordinates at a specific date and time, and expected approximate flight path (for space probes); radio-transmitter frequencies, approximate power, and mode of transmission, size, shape, reflectivity, and weight of the satellite or probe and other significant objects placed in orbit; other information which will facilitate observations or the subsequent computations of orbital predictions; and a brief description of experiments.

This information will also be distributed promptly by regularly used channels of public information.

The message distributed via SPACEWARN will be in plain language and will be composed of two parts: first, an abbreviated launching announcement suitable for brief radio broadcast, and, second, further details as required above.

2. 3 Designation

Beginning January 1, 1963, all satellites and space probes which have a lifetime of at least 90 minutes and which require a designation for scientific purposes, will be numbered as follows: the first satellite in 1963 is 1963–1, the second is 1963–2, etc. Where more than one component exists, the order of classification will be by alphabetical suffix A, B, C, etc., where A refers to the component carrying the principal scientific payload; B, C, etc., as needed are used first for any subsidiary payloads, and then for inert components in order of maximum brightness during the early life of the satellite. Thus, a satellite component which under the old designation scheme would have been known as 1963 β2, under the new scheme will be known as 1963 2B. (In case the number of components or objects of a satellite launching is large, the following convention will be used: the letters I and O will always be skipped; the 25th object or component will be designated AA, the 26th AB, etc., the 49th BA, etc., etc.) The designations will be tentatively assigned in the launching announcement, a copy of which is sent to the COSPAR Secretariat (see section 2. 2) which will then be responsible for making the final assignment according to the Universal Time of the launching, and for promulgating this information in the COSPAR *Information Bulletin*; the Secretariat will send telegraphic notice of any error to the originator of the launching announcement, who will promptly distribute a correction via SPACEWARN.

The Greek-letter designation system in effect prior to 1963 will be retained for satellites and space probes launched from 1957 through 1962.

2. 4 Orbital Elements

Orbital elements, in SATOR code, will be distributed periodically by the launching nation via SPACEWARN. The elements to be supplied will include the following or their equivalent, with at least the accuracies indicated:

(i) the inclination of the plane and the longitude of the node to an accuracy of ..th degree;

(ii) the period of the orbit to an accuracy of $\frac{1}{10}$th second;

(iii) the eccentricity of the orbit accurate to 4 decimal places;

(iv) the argument of the perigee to an accuracy consistent with that of the other elements, depending on eccentricity;

(v) the epoch to an accuracy of 1 second.

The elements will be provided on a current basis, as long as the experiment is active, as frequently as is required to permit observations based upon the accuracies indicated.

2. 5 Station Predictions

It is considered that current orbital elements with rates of change, such as given in the SATOR code, are the most convenient present method for efficiently distributing orbital information for large numbers of tracking and observing stations. At the same time, it is recognized that station predictions are valuable if they can be supplied and distributed more promptly than orbital elements. In general, any station predictions provided will go directly from computing centres to the appropriate stations, utilizing the SPACE-WARN network only under special arrangement.

2. 6 Acquisition Data for Space Probes

Inasmuch as only specialized stations can achieve useful results in tracking deep space probes, it is expected that private arrangements will be made between the launching authorities and such stations for the rapid transmission of acquisition data. However, the provisions above concerning pre-launch and launching information also apply to space probes because of the wide-spread interest in such information on the part of the scientific community generally.

2. 7 Precise Orbits

Precision positional observations, orbital elements, and ephemerides (*i.e.*, tables of subsatellite positions and heights at specific times), which are of great scientific interest and value to research workers in various fields, together with estimates of their accuracy, will be deposited as soon as possible in the WDC's.

2. 8 Descriptive Experimental Information

In addition to the reports listed in 2. 1, *Pre-Launch Information*, and 2. 2, *Launching Announcements*, reports describing the experiments and instruments in greater detail will be sent to COSPAR within a few weeks after launching for distribution to COSPAR adherents and publication in the *Bulletin*. Even when such material has been published in the national press, an authoritative version will also be supplied to the COSPAR Secretariat for distribution to COSPAR adherents and publication in the *Bulletin*.

2. 9 Report of Results

Reports of experimental results, including an adequate description of the instrumentation involved, will be published in scientific literature of general availability beginning as soon as possible after each launching, and thereafter promptly as they become available. Publication within one (1) year after the end of the experiment is desirable, but in any event should occur within three (3) years. Two (2) copies of all reports are to be provided to each WDC, or, alternatively, six (6) copies to one WDC to permit distribution to the others.

Original (raw) data, whether film records of optical observations or primary records of radio observations and telemetered signals, and the complete, calibrated data will not normally be deposited in the WDC's; however, such data will be retained by the experimenter. The reduced data and, where appropriate, the original data, will be made available for use by other scientists upon request one (1) year or more after completion of the experiment. Raw data are original records on film, magnetic tape, paper, etc. Calibrated data are data to which calibrations have been applied to give values of the physical quantities measured in the experiment. Analyzed data are sampled calibrated data or the results of computations on calibrated data.

3. *National Reports and Bibliographies*

3. 1 National Reports

Each national member of COSPAR will, during the annual meeting of COSPAR, present a report summarizing its national space programme, including an over-all review of launchings and new scientific results of the preceding year, research projects under way, and plans for future experiments and activities.

3. 2 Bibliographies

Each national member of COSPAR will prepare a bibliography of reports and papers in the space sciences published in its country during the preceding year, such bibliography to be appended to its annual report to COSPAR and also deposited with each WDC.

4. *World Data Centers for Rockets and Satellites*

4. 1 Addresses

World Data Center A for Rockets and Satellites
National Academy of Sciences
2101 Constitution Avenue, N.W.
Washington 25, D.C.

World Data Center B for Rockets and Satellites
Soviet Geophysical Committee
Academy of Sciences of the U.S.S.R.
Molodezhnaya 3
Moscow B–296, U.S.S.R.

World Data Center C for Rockets and Satellites
Radio Research Station
Ditton Park, Slough, Bucks., England.

4. 2 Exchange of Information and Data

Investigators will provide at least two (2) copies of reports or reprints to each WDC at the address listed above, or, alternatively, six (6) copies to one WDC to permit distribution to the others; the number of copies of other material, *e.g.*, reports of sounding rocket launchings, precise orbits, tabulated data, etc. – should be at least one (1) or three (3), respectively. Each WDC will provide, upon receipt, and on a free-exchange basis, copies of all incoming data to the other WDC's for Rockets and Satellites which have not already received them.

Requests for data held by WDC's will be satisfied within three (3) months, and the fee charged, if any, will not exceed the cost of copying and postage.

Rocket and Satellite WDC's will also pass data which concern other disciplines to the WDC's in those disciplines.

4. 3 Catalogues

Each WDC will prepare and circulate to other WDC's and to COSPAR, every six (6) months a complete catalogue of materials received in the previous six (6) months. The semi-annual catalogues will be accumulated every two years, beginning with the period January 1, 1960, to December 31, 1961, the catalogue for which will be submitted to COSPAR by March 1, 1962.

5. Communications

5. 1 SPACEWARN Network

The SPACEWARN net for rapid communication of satellite information consists of four Satellite Regional Warning Centers (SRWC), located as follows (telegraphic addresses are given in parentheses):

Western Pacific
Radio Research Laboratories
Kokubunji Tokyo, Japan
(DEMPA KOKUBUNJI)

Western Europe
Fernmeldetechnisches Zentralamt der Bundespost
Rheinstrasse 110
Darmstadt, German Federal Republic
(IONOSPHARE DARMSTADT)
and
Radio Research Station
Ditton Park, Slough, Bucks., England
(RADSEARCH SLOUGH)

Eurasia
Astronomicheskiy Soviet
Akademii Nauk
Bol'shaya Gruzinskaya
dom 10, Moscow, U.S.S.R.
    and
Soviet Geophysical Committee
Academy of Sciences of the U.S.S.R.
Molodezhnaya 3
Moscow B–296, U.S.S.R.
(MOSCOW COSMOS COPY MGG)

Western Hemisphere
North Atlantic Radio Warning Service
Box 178
Fort Belvoir, Virginia, U.S.A.
(AGIWARN WASHINGTON)

Associate centres, which handle some satellite message traffic, are located at Nederhorst den Berg, Netherlands, and at Sydney and Salisbury, Australia.

The main types of messages transmitted by SPACEWARN are launching announcements and current orbital elements. The messages go from one continent to another by telegram, and further distribution to national centres and individual laboratories is accomplished by the most effective rapid means available.

5. 2 Identification of SPACEWARN Messages

SPACEWARN messages will begin with the word SPACEWARN, followed by, in the code established for this purpose, identification of the SRWC of origin, identification of message type, and serial number of the message in the specified category.

5. 3 National Contact for SPACEWARN

Each national member of COSPAR will specify a national contact for SPACEWARN, whose responsibilities are (i) to ascertain and communicate to the appropriate SRWC the addresses of centres, stations, or individual scientists in his country requiring messages of centres, stations, or individual scientists in his country requiring messages and information of the categories handled by SPACEWARN; (ii) to determine what, if any, changes or improvements are necessary to assure effective communications and coverage within his area; and (iii) to make appropriate recommendations to the COSPAR correspondent for SPACEWARN.

5. 4 Launching Announcements

Launching announcements will be sent in plain language without delay by the SRWC of origin to the other SRWC's; distribution within each region will proceed immediately in accordance with regional plans.

5. 5 Current Orbital Elements

Current orbital elements, as made available by computing centres, will be distributed by the SRWC of origin to the other SRWC's at a regular time of day; distribution within each region will be carried out at a regular time of day, in accordance with regional plans. Orbital elements should be appended to a regular daily solar geophysical data message whenever convenient.

5. 6 Supplementary Regional Broadcasts

At several centres there are daily broadcasts of satellite information of general applicability and interest, including abbreviated plain-language launching announcements and current orbital elements in plain language or in SATOR code. Current details of these broadcasts, which supplement the activities of the SRWC's, appear in the COSPAR *Information Bulletin*.

5. 7 Reports of Tracking Observations

In general, tracking observations will be sent directly from the tracking station to the computing centre of the launching agency, either by telegram or by air-letter, as appropriate. Tracking observations may be sent under special circumstances via SRWC's for forwarding by telegram, if unique or urgent, or by air-letter, as deemed appropriate.

5. 8 Special Messages

Launching agencies may provide special information or requests of general interest for distribution over the SPACEWARN network by telegram or air-letter, as appropriate.

5. 9 Codes

In accordance with Resolution 28 of the Fourth COSPAR Meeting, Florence, 1961, synoptic codes such as those used for reporting tracking observations have been revised and unified (see Part II – Unified Synoptic Codes). National SPACEWARN contacts are urged to arrange for the adoption of such revised and unified codes by stations and centres in their countries so that there will be uniformity in the forms of messages communicated to and from centres.

5. 10 Communication Costs

It is understood that costs of communications among SRWC's will be borne by the SRWC of origin of the message. Arrangements regarding the costs of distribution within each region will be made between the SRWC and the recipient.

COSPAR REPORT AND RESOLUTIONS CONCERNING THE POTENTIALLY HARMFUL EFFECTS OF SPACE EXPERIMENTS

REPORT TO THE EXECUTIVE COUNCIL OF COSPAR OF THE COSPAR CONSULTATIVE GROUP ON POTENTIALLY HARMFUL EFFECTS OF SPACE EXPERIMENTS

(Florence, May 1964)

1. The Consultative Group was formed in January 1963 with the following composition: V. Sarabhai (Chairman), C. G. Heden, H. C. van de Hulst, W. W. Kellogg, G. A. Ratcliffe, G. A. Savenko, V. V. Vitkevitch.

2. The Group was created in response to the following resolution of the Executive Council of COSPAR:

"In order to carry out the responsibility for careful, objective, quantitative studies of space experiments with potentially undesirable effects on scientific activities and observations, which COSPAR has accepted in response to ICSU resolution 10 (1961) (COSPAR Doc./62/11), the Executive Council decides to establish a Consultative Group on Potentially Harmful Effects of Space Experiments, to consists of not more than six broadly competent scientists having among them specialized knowledge of Astronomy, Radiation Physics and Chemistry, Communications, Meteorite Penetration and Microbiology, to be named by the President of COSPAR.

"It is expected that this Consultative Group will act as a focal point in ICSU for consideration of all questions regarding potentially harmful effects of space experiments on scientific activities and observations, and that in this capacity it would (1) examine in a preliminary way all questions relating to possibly harmful effects of proposed space experiments, including but not restricted to questions referred to it by any of the ICSU Unions; (2) determine whether or not any serious possibility of harmful effects would indeed result from the proposed experiment; (3) in consultation with appropriate Unions, appoint and arrange for convening an ad hoc Working Group or Groups to study any expected effects which are considered to be potentially harmful, such Working Group or Groups to include competent scientists in the appropriate specialised disciplines; (4) receive and consider conclusions or recommendations of these ad hoc Working Groups in a timely manner; and (5) prepare final recommendations to the COSPAR Executive Council for its further action.

"Positive or negative recommendations or studies considered appropriate by the Council for dissemination would then be made available to all COSPAR adherents, the ICSU Bureau, the appropriate Unions of ICSU, and to appropriate bodies of the United Nations or its specialized agencies."

3. The Group has met in: Paris—March 1963, Warsaw—June 1963, Geneva—February 1964 and Florence—May 1964.

In a preliminary report submitted by COSPAR at Warsaw in June 1963, it was stated that the Group was initially concerning itself with the following topics: (a) Pollution of the Upper Atmosphere, (b) Orbiting Dipoles, (c) Contamination of the Moon and Planets. The present report gives the current status of the studies on each topic. Appendices incorporate statements by the Group on those topics for which the Group feels it is appropriate to do so at the present time.

4. The Group has approached its task broadly as follows. It has discussed and attempted to identify the scientific questions involved in each problem by studying existing literature. Where the literature has been available in widely scattered sources, as in the problem of contamination of planets, the Group has arranged for a compilation of the literature to facilitate its evaluation.

At times an individual member of the Group has critically examined current scientific information and prepared his own report which has been used for stimulating further comments and discussions.

The Group has then consulted individual scientists and scientific groups. Where discrepancies or divergent opinions have emerged, the Group has attempted to bring together the specialists concerned in order to resolve differences if possible, or at least to evolve a consensus and a clarification for further studies.

In attempting quantitative evaluation of potentially harmful effects the Group has thus relied heavily on assistance of scientists and scientific organisations.

5. The present status of the studies can be summarised as follows:

(a) *Pollution of the Upper Atmosphere*

A statement by the Group is enclosed as Annex 1. It gives an evaluation of likely consequences to environmental conditions of the firing of a relatively large number of super rockets per year and of the extensive use of chemical tracers in the upper atmosphere. It also indicates the uncertainties in our present knowledge, and the need for further quantitative studies.

Appendix

(b) *Orbiting Dipoles*

A statement by the Group is enclosed as Annex 2. It represents agreed views of leading specialists in the field providing a basis for quantitative evaluation of the consequences of a dipole belt of given characteristics of radio and optical astronomy.

(c) *Contamination of the Moon and Planets*

The Group decided at its meeting in February 1964 that a statement as reproduced in Annex 3 be immediately communicated to COSPAR on behalf of the Group. This points out the extreme importance of undertaking, for the time being, only fly-by missions for the study of Mars.

Following the compilation of available literature on the subject, a Panel of the following specialists has met in Florence during the COSPAR Symposium in May 1964.

Members

Prof. A. Brown, Dept. of Biology, Univ. of Pennsylvania.
Prof. A. Dollfus, Astrophysics Section, Paris Observatory.
Prof. M. Florkin, Biochemical Laboratory, University of Liège.
Dr. L. Hall, Bioscience Programmes NASA.
Acad. A.A. Imshenetskii, Inst. of Microbiology, U.S.S.R. Academy of Sciences.
Prof. C. Sagan, Harvard College Observatory (Rapporteur).
Dr. P. H. A. Sneath, British Medical Research Council.
—Additional Russian member (not present).
Prof. C. G. Heden (Convenor).

The Panel has discussed the standards of sterilisation which can be recommended for the protection of possible life on Mars. Its report is enclosed in Annex 4.

The Group has considered the report of the Panel and in relation to its statement contained in Annex 3 invites special attention to remarks concerning the danger of contamination through accidental landings of fly-by missions and the definitive steps suggested to reduce this danger.

The Group urges continued efforts for the improvement of sterilisation techniques and full sharing of information concerning procedures designed to achieve spacecraft with the required level of sterility.

The Group recommends early action to declare Mars a biological preserve to ensure that in the exploration of this planet, considerations of biological research receive priority over others.

The Group recommends the proposal for convening an international conference in early 1965 to consider the technology of sterilisation and sterilisation testing.

6. In concluding the present report, the Group wishes to thank the scientists and scientific organisations who have made possible the studies which have been undertaken.

*Statement on Upper Atmospheric Pollution by Rocket Exhaust
and Chemical Injection Experiments
by the COSPAR Consultative Group
on
Potentially Harmful Effects of Space Experiments*

(Florence, May 16, 1964)

1. Interest and concern about the possible effects of space experiments, particularly those involving large rockets or the repeated injection of metallic vapours, on the composition and structure of the Earth's atmosphere had been occasionally expressed before COSPAR decided to set up its Consultative Group on Potentially Harmful Effects of Space Experiments (May 1962). A request to COSPAR by the ICSU Executive Board in October 1962 (Resolution EB XIV 27) suggested a study of this topic. However, the publicity given to a report (part of a series) on rocket pollution of the upper atmosphere by J. Pressman, W. Reidy, and W. Lank (Institute of Aerospace Science, January 1963) created a certain amount of public concern. Hence, this problem was selected at once by the Consultative Group as deserving further study.

2. The COSPAR Consultative Group has been instructed by its Charter "to arrange for careful quantitative studies" of the problems referred to it, in order that the conclusions of such studies may be available to all concerned. The arrangements in the present case were as follows: Copies of the Pressman report were obtained and W. W. Kellogg, a member of the Consultative Group, was asked to prepare an independent report, reviewing the general question in as quantitative a way as possible. The two reports, which arrived in part at rather different conclusions, were then submitted to a number of experts in the world with a request for criticism and comments. The comments received from twenty experts in six countries (Belgium, Germany, India, Netherlands, United Kingdom, U.S.A.) were reviewed at a meeting of the Consultative Group in February 1964. A second version of Kellogg's report, taking these comments into account, will be published in an inter-

national scientific journal and reprints will be available from the COSPAR Secretariat.

3. While there was not absolute unanimity in the views of the experts who volunteered comments, the following is believed by the Consultative Group to be a fair consensus of the situation as it is now understood.

There are a variety of ways in which man can alter the conditions in the upper atmosphere, and the degree of such alteration can obviously vary over a wide range. Some such effects are merely detectable, and are probably not "potentially harmful", while there are other changes that cause interference with future experiments or that can be considered as harmful in other ways. In order to discuss the vastly different effects that could be caused by injections of chemicals into the upper atmosphere, it has been convenient to distinguish between four classes of effects which are:

(a) a harmless, short-term and localised alteration of the upper atmosphere that can be readily observed at the ground;

(b) a long-term and world-wide alteration of the observable characteristics of the upper atmosphere, but one which causes no identifiable interference or harmful effect;

(c) an extensive alteration of the upper atmosphere that interferes with scientific experiments or other human activities;

(d) an atmospheric alteration that affects man's environment.

4. It appears that there are many instances where (a) has occurred. For example, local effects of the passage of a large rocket through the upper atmosphere can be observed visually, especially at twilight when it may leave a bright trail, and perturbations of the ionosphere by large rockets, detectable by radio means, have been observed repeatedly; none of these more or less localised phenomena have been judged as "harmful". On the other hand (b) has not occurred, with the possible exception of the reported instances where the lithium content of the upper atmosphere may have been affected on a world-wide basis for a few months in 1962 by man-made injections. There has not been an instance of (c) as far as chemical injections are concerned, but the world-wide background of some radioactive tracers (tritium, carbon-14, etc.) has been charged by repeated injections, and this has interfered with certain studies of circulation and exchange rates between regions of the atmosphere. Case (d) has not occurred, and seems most unlikely. The reasons for this opinion are outlined in part in the next paragraphs.

5. In order for the atmosphere to be so changed that the environment of life is affected—case (d)—the pollution of the upper atmosphere would surely have to be very extensive, and so we must distinguish between long-term and short-term pollutants, and concentrate on the former. If at a certain

injection rate a pollutant builds up a concentration exceeding a specified value in a relevant region, we refer to it as a long-term pollutant. It is obvious that the specified limiting value must differ with different pollutants, and also for the same pollutant with reference to different effects.

A world-wide, long-term change of the background concentration of some atmospheric constituent that would be just detectable might be 10 per cent or less for a relatively well mixed and permanent gas (*e.g.* CO_2, CH_4), and it might be by a factor of two or three for constituents that vary a great deal naturally (*e.g.* H_2O, NO, Li). Considering what would be involved in causing a change of the composition of the upper atmosphere above 60 or 70 km., the region above the stratosphere, it is necessary to know what the rate of depletion of a given substance is due to mixing and dissociation (by sunlight and chemical reactions), and also what its natural concentration is. These are only known very approximately, but it seems that on the order of 10^5 to 10^6 *tons per year* of water vapour or nitric oxide would have to be injected above 60 km. to double the amounts of these gases world-wide, and about the same tonnage would be required to add 10 per cent to the carbon dioxide content. (This corresponds approximately to an annual launching of 10^3 to 10^4 Saturn-type rockets, or of the type of Soviet rocket used to put the second Soviet cosmonaut into orbit.) On the other hand, only 2×10^3 to 10^4 *kilograms per year* of atomic sodium would have to be injected above 60 km. to double this constituent, and only a few tens of kilograms of lithium annually would be expected to double its background concentration. These last figures are within the capability of man now, and may (as mentioned above) have already been achieved temporarily in the case of lithium. The larger figures for nitric oxide, carbon dioxide, and water vapour, the main combustion products of rocket fuels, seem unattainable in the foreseeable future.

The Consultative Group is aware of the various dire consequences of contamination that have been cited in certain public pronouncements, and has examined them as far as present knowledge would permit. (Examples of these are: the removal of the ozone layer, thereby permitting far ultraviolet sunlight through to the ground; the removal of the free electrons in the ionosphere by introducing an electron "getter" in large quantities; changing the temperature of the atmosphere by changing the water vapour or carbon dioxide content, etc.) We are unable to identify and physical processes which would produce these consequences. Although it is always possible that there might be other undesirable effects which have not been anticipated, this seems unlikely.

6. The present study, which is based on information in the open literature,

while providing some comfort as regards climatological changes which may be induced by the rocket gases in the foreseeable future, indicates the need for early experimental and theoretical studies dealing with the following problems:

(a) the evaluation of exchange times between the various regions of the upper atmosphere, especially between 60 and 100 km., where current estimates of diffusion rates differ by two orders of magnitude in extreme cases and by an order of magnitude generally;

(b) the short-term local and zonal effects of rocket contamination;

(c) possible catalytic effects which might trigger chemical and photo-chemical processes as yet unanticipated;

(d) radiation balance in the upper atmosphere and the effects on it of changes in composition there.

In view of the importance of developing a sound scientific capability for accurate predictions of the effects of future space operations and experiments which may involve injecting larger amounts of materials with different chemical and physical characteristics, the Consultative Group suggests that COSPAR urges scientists, particularly those of nations which are active in space exploration with large rockets, to undertake serious quantitative studies which could provide answers to some of these questions in the near future.

7. The present study does not include three contingencies of possible significance to the pollution of the upper atmosphere and which may be realised in the next few years. These are:

(a) the use of nuclear powered rockets and nuclear reactors in satellites;

(b) the extensive use of high-flying supersonic transport aircraft;

(c) the extensive use of completely disintegrating meteorological rockets.

It is intended that the Consultative Group will examine these contingencies in a preliminary way during the next year, and will arrange for more detailed studies if warranted.

ANNEX 2

Statement on Belts of Orbiting Dipoles
by
The COSPAR Consultative Group on Potentially Harmful
Effects of Space Experiments
(Florence, May 16, 1964)

Belts of orbiting dipoles (needles) have been proposed for the use of a telecommunication system between stations at the earth's surface. Two experiments to create a test belt of this nature have come to our knowledge.

The first launched October 1961, did not dispense separate needles; the second, launched May 12, 1963, went as planned. The first announcement of this plan, about August 1960, created grave concern about the possible interference to be expected in optical astronomy by scattered sunlight and in radio astronomy by scattered signals from radio stations on the earth. The calculation of this interference by a specified belt contains no major uncertain factors. It was soon ascertained that the effects of the specified belt would be hardly measurable and would not cause harmful interference. This has been confirmed by the observations of the actual test belt.

In view of initial uncertainties about the life time and in view of the expressed fear that frequent launchings or far denser belts might be proposed, the problem was held under review by several committees of experts. The most important ones, the "West Ford Committee" of the International Astronomical Union and the "Ad hoc West Ford Committee" of the Space Science Board of the National Academy of Sciences of the U.S.A., have now produced their reports with identical conclusions.

The COSPAR Consultative Group on Potentially Harmful Effects of Space Experiments has frequently consulted with members of both committees and is in concurrence with their conclusions. It feels no need, therefore, to repeat these conclusions in detail. The observations and calculations have been published in scientific journals.

As an illustration of the *optical* effects, we may mention that the scattered sunlight received from the test belt a week after launch was a factor 10 below the brightness of faintest measured parts of galaxies, the study of which forms one of the basic means by which present-day astronomy penetrates the problems of the universe. This margin gets wider as the belt spreads in time.

The possible interference to *radio* astronomy has been newly evaluated by FINDLAY and RYLE with a view to the types of radiotelescopes that may come into operation within ten years. Interference equal to one tenth of the effective limit of detection would be produced with a single 10 kW transmitter illuminating part of a belt with a dipole density five to ten times that of the sixty-day West Ford belt.

Experience has shown that there are reasonably good procedures for calculating in advance the effects of any belts.

The numbers quoted above by way of illustration show that the test belt constituted no interference. However, adding a factor 10 would be significant and a factor 100 might be detrimental to much advanced research in astronomy.

The Consultative Group recommends that any future experiments with this general character be given the benefit of a thorough evaluation by the international scientific community and notably by the International Astronomical Union in order to check in advance their harmlessness to other scientific research.

ANNEX 3

Statement by the Consultative Group on Potentially Harmful
Effects of Space Experiments
concerning
The Contamination of Planets
(Geneva, 1964)

"The COSPAR Consultative Group on Potentially Harmful Effects of Space Experiments has considered presently available scientific evaluations of the likely consequences of the biological contamination of Mars. There is consensus of opinion among scientific workers of the extreme importance of not jeopardising the value of information that can be gained from studies of this planet about many crucial problems of biology and the evolution of life. Realising that the technology of sterilisation has many practical problems, the Group is endeavouring to establish through consultation with competent biologists the limits of permissible contamination of objects that may land on Mars. The Group moreover recommends that early discussions be held between specialists of launching nations to discuss techniques of sterilisation and problems of technology involved in launching sterilised payloads. In the meantime, the Group urges these nations who presently have capability of attempting the exploration of Mars, to take steps to organise only fly-by missions for the time being."

ANNEX 4

Report of the Panel on Standards for Space Probe Sterilisation

At the Florence meeting of COSPAR, the Panel on Standards for Space Probe Sterilisation considered data and expressions of expert opinion from a variety of sources. The following statements represent a synthesis of the views of the members of the Panel; it is suggested that they be made the basis of a position paper by COSPAR.

We reaffirm the conviction that exobiology should be a primary objective of activities in the space sciences. This view is justified for the following reasons:

1. The detection and subsequent investigation of extra-terrestrial life has profound scientific significance.

2. Studies in planetary biology must, in large part, be completed before contamination is effected by unsterilised devices used in physical or geophysical investigations. The successful performance of physical experiments is primarily unaffected by previous biological experiments; because of contamination, the converse may be false.

3. A study of the prebiological chemistry of a planet which proves to be sterile would nevertheless be of major biological significance.

We *believe* that space probe sterilisation and trajectory control of fly-by spacecraft are essential until further information gives strong indication that such standards could be relaxed without jeopardising planetary studies. This policy is justified for the following reasons:

1. A search for extra-terrestrial life is essentially a search for materials with the properties of the known organisms on the planet Earth. Therefore all life-detection experiments will be capable of detecting viable terrestrial contaminants. Consequently the introduction of such contaminants (for example, by inadequate spacecraft sterilisation) would render it impossible to decide whether positive results of a life-detection experiment are significant or spurious.

2. Aside from such interference with remote life-detection experiments, biological contamination of a planet may lead to undesirable alterations of the planetary environment from the standpoints of both exobiology and physical studies of planetary surfaces. If the proliferation of terrestrial contaminants—at some time after their introduction—is *not* excluded, the extensive changes in the planetary environment which are possible as a consequence *could* inhibit or destroy our opportunity to

(a) identify and investigate the indigenous biota,

(b) understand the ecological interactions of the original indigenous biota, and

(c) investigate the prebiological chemistry of a planet which proves to be sterile.

It is difficult to estimate adequately the period of time which would pass before such undesirable consequences occur. As a simple example of heuristic interest we note that a single viable organism deposited in an environment in which it slowly grows (general time, thirty days) would in the course of eight years produce a population of 10^{27} organisms, a number equal approximately to the bacterial population of the Earth. The calculation assumes zero death rate, and no interaction between indigenous planetary organisms and exogenous terrestrial contaminants.

We *believe* that the scientific desirability of sterility control is absolute; but the degree of sterilisation required must be based on our judgments of the risks acceptable so planetary exploration will not be impossibly difficult. The probability that a single viable organism is aboard any space vehicle intended for planetary impact can then be computed as the solution of a waiting time problem in probability theory. Adopting values for the acceptable risk during approximately a decade of planetary exploration by landing vehicles, and for the biological and spacecraft reliability parameters involved—values which we consider conservative—we conclude that

1. the probability that a single viable organism be aboard any vehicle intended for planetary landing must be less than 1×10^{-4} and that

2. the probability of accidental planetary impact by an unsterilised fly-by or orbiter must be less than 3×10^{-5} during the interval terminating at the end of the initial period of planetary exploration by landing vehicles (approximately one decade).

We appreciate the considerable technical difficulties involved in realising these probabilities in practice, but we consider that they are attainable by known means. The probabilities also apply to contamination by spacecraft propulsion and attitude-control systems. The probability of contamination by accidental impact of fly-bys and orbiters can be minimised by

1. initial trajectory control,

2. initial spacecraft sterilisation, or by

3. inclusion of programmed or commanded terminal precautionary systems for assuming non-intercept trajectories or for initiating destruction sterilisation.

The probabilities given above are obviously subject to future revision as our knowledge of planetary environments, microbial ecology, and spacecraft design improves.

We *feel* that while our recommendations apply immediately to fly-by, orbitor and lander missions planned for Mars, the same recommendation should apply to any planet which on the basis of current information, cannot *firmly* be excluded as a possible abode of extra-terrestrial life. The standards of space vehicle sterilisation are, we believe, unrelated to the probability of indigenous life on the planet in question; except in the limiting case that indigenous life and the proliferation of terrestrial contaminants can both be firmly excluded. While there is a sizeable probability that the surface temperatures of Venus are too high for either indigenous or exogenous organisms, this conclusion is based on indirect lines of argument. Also, we cannot entirely exclude the possibility of biological contamination of the clouds of Venus. Until unambiguous astronomical information is available, we recommend that Martian standards of sterility control should also apply to Venus. In the case of the Moon, the surface conditions are rigorous enough to reliably exclude biological contamination of the surface. We cannot exclude the possibility that conditions several tens of metres below the lunar surface will permit microbial replication. Such depths, however, are unlikely to be reached unintentionally during lunar landings. Accordingly, we recommend such less rigorous sterilisation techniques as biocleanroom assembly and terminal gaseous sterilisation of all spacecraft intended for lunar landings; but rigorous sterilisation of drills designed for lunar subsurface boring. Our information about the conditions on other planets is insufficient to form a basis for definitive recommendations at this time.

To encourage broader consideration of the diverse means which can be employed to meet these recommended standards of sterility, it is suggested that an international conference be sponsored by COSPAR, possibly in co-operation with one or more other appropriate international scientific groups, to consider the technology of sterilisation, and sterilisation testing. To implement this suggestion, it will be necessary for COSPAR to endorse the proposed conference and to supply a budget for bringing it about. It is suggested further that the conference be held as soon as feasible, preferably in early 1965.

RESOLUTION ADOPTED BY THE EXECUTIVE COUNCIL OF COSPAR
IN ITS MEETING OF MAY 20TH, 1964, FLORENCE

COSPAR notes with appreciation and interest the extensive work done by the Consultative Group on Potentially Harmful Effects of Space Experiments as expressed by the Group in its report and annexes.

COSPAR

1. *Instructs* its Secretariat to make this Report and annexes available to ICSU, the adhering bodies of COSPAR and other interested parties;

2. *Welcomes* the encouraging conclusions of the Consultative Group that harmful contamination of the upper atmosphere on a long-term global basis is unlikely on present and expected scale of firings of super rockets and the release of experimental seeding. COSPAR urges its adhering organisations to report any major new experiments which may produce harmful contamination. Moreover, it urges them to encourage these scientists to continue studies of the following matters:

(a) evaluation of exchange times between the various regions of the upper atmosphere, especially between 60 and 100 km.,

(b) short and long term local and zonal effects of rocket contamination in the upper atmosphere,

(c) the possibility of any catalytic effects which might trigger chemical and photochemical processes in the upper atmosphere, and

(d) radiation balance in the upper atmosphere and its dependence on changes in composition there.

3. *Welcomes* the conclusion of the Consultative Group that no interference to optical and/or radio astronomy has resulted from the belt of orbiting dipoles launched in May 1963, and recommends to its Members that any proposals for future experiments of this sort also be given the benefit of thorough evaluation by the scientific community and notably by the International Astronomical Union, in order to check in advance their harmlessness to other scientific research.

4. *Affirms* that the search for extra-terrestrial life is an important objective of space research, that the planet Mars may offer the only feasible opportunity to conduct this search during the foreseeable future, that contamination of this planet would make such a search far more difficult and possibly even prevent for all time an unequivocal result, that all practical steps should be taken to ensure that Mars be not biologically contaminated until such time as this search can have been satisfactorily carried out, and that co-operation in proper scheduling of experiments and in use of adequate spacecraft sterilisation techniques is required on the part of all deep space probe launching authorities to avoid such contamination;

5. *Accepts*, as tentatively recommended interim objectives, a sterilisation level such that the probability of a single viable organism aboard any spacecraft intended for planetary landing or atmospheric penetration would be less than 1×10^{-4}, and a probability limit for accidental planetary impact by unsterilised fly-by or orbiting spacecraft of 3×10^{-5} or less;

6. *Calls* attention to the opinion of its Consultative Group that although less rigorous sterilisation techniques are required for lunar landings, because the lunar surface conditions would almost certainly exclude microbal replication, it is desirable that drills designed for deep lunar subsurface boring should be very carefully sterilised to avoid contamination of regions below the surface where a more favourable environment might exist;

7. *Calls* on its members that are concerned with planetary probes to urge the vehicle construction and launching authorities in their countries to try to achieve these sterilisation objectives and especially to forego the launching of planetary atmospheric entry and lander vehicles until such time as the above-mentioned level of sterility can be achieved with a high degree of certainty;

8. *Requests* its members concerned with planetary probes to report to COSPAR any disagreement or objections they may have to use of these

tentative objectives or to any other aspects of Annex IV of the Consultative Group Report, and *expresses* the hope that the Consultative Group will arrange continued studies in the area of biological contamination of the Moon and planets, taking into account any such reports or comments as may be received; and finally,

9. *Authorises* the Consultative Group in consultation with the Chairman of Working Group V to arrange for the convening of an international conference on biological sterilisation and sterility testing techniques at any time and place and in co-operation with any other scientific organisations it may deem appropriate, provided it can be assured in advance of substantial participation in the conference by scientists of both the major deep space probe launching authorities.

INSTITUTE OF INTERNATIONAL LAW

RESOLUTION ON THE LEGAL RÉGIME OF OUTER SPACE

adopted unanimously at Brussels on September 11, 1963

The Institute of International Law

Considering that the legal régime of the exploration and utilisation of outer space and celestial bodies should be inspired by a spirit of universality;

Acknowledging the common interest of mankind in the exclusive dedication of outer space to peaceful purposes in accordance with the Charter of the United Nations;

Noting the resolutions on international co-operation in the peaceful uses of outer space adopted unanimously by the General Assembly of the United Nations on December 20, 1961, and December 14, 1962, and the Treaty Banning Nuclear Weapon Tests in the Atmosphere, in Outer Space and Under Water signed at Moscow on August 6, 1963;

Having regard to the urgency of international regulation of the matter in view of the rapidity of scientific and technical progress;

Recognises the validity of the following principles and would welcome their inclusion in a generally accepted treaty or declaration governing the legal régime of outer space:

1. Outer space and the celestial bodies are not subject to any kind of appropriation; they are free for exploration and use by all States for exclusively peaceful purposes in conformity with the following provisions.

2. No space object shall be launched otherwise than under the authority of a State. Each State shall ensure that the utilisation of every space object launched under its authority complies with the applicable international rules.

3. Every launching of a space object shall be registered by the State under the authority of which the launching took place with the United Nations or a special body to be created; the registration shall be effected promptly and with particulars to be agreed.

4. Every space object shall bear marks of identification showing its origin and use call signals making it possible to identify the State under the authority of which the launching took place.

5. Every space object launched in accordance with the foregoing pro-

visions shall remain subject to the jurisdiction of the State under the authority of which it was launched.

6. The State establishing a space installation is required to ensure good order and safety at the installation. Subject to any subsequent international agreement, persons using, and occurrences at, any space installation are subject to the jurisdiction of the State having established the installation.

7. All States shall ensure that space telecommunications comply with regulations of the International Telecommunication Union.

8. States shall take appropriate measures for:

(a) mutual assistance among astronauts;

(b) mutual assistance among States on behalf of astronauts in need of assistance;

(c) prompt repatriation of astronauts after any emergency landing or rescue.

9. Appropriate measures shall be provided for by an international agreement for the return to the State under the authority of which the launching took place of space objects the launching of which has been officially notified, which bear identification marks showing their origin, and which on return to Earth have come into the possession of another State.

10. The State under the authority of which the launching of a space object takes place shall ensure that every such object is, so far as practicable, fitted with a suitable device permitting the launcher to recover it on the termination of its useful life or if recovery is not feasible as a minimum to silence radio transmission therefrom and eliminate its other effects.

11. The State under the authority of which the launching of a space object takes place shall ensure that appropriate precautions are taken against biological, radiological or chemical contamination of or from outer space or celestial bodies. International co-operation in respect of the matter should be arranged.

12. Scientific or technological experiments or tests in space which may involve a risk of modifying the natural environment of the Earth, of any of the celestial bodies or in space in a manner liable to be prejudicial to the future of scientific investigation and experiment, the well-being of human life, or the interests of another State, necessarily affect directly the interests of the whole international community.

The provisions of this resolution should be supplemented by appropriate international arrangements to forestall such risk.

13. The State under the authority of which the launching of a space object has taken place shall be liable, irrespective of fault, for any injury, including loss of life, or damage that may result. Modalities of application of this principle may be determined by special convention. Any limitation of the

417

amount of the reparation due shall be determined in the same manner.

14. In all matters not provided for in the preceding paragraphs, States are bound by general international law, including the principles of the Charter of the United Nations.

15. The principles set forth in this resolution apply to space activities undertaken by States acting individually or collectively or by international organisations.

References to States in the preceding paragraphs are to be construed as including a reference to international organisations, it being understood that the States members of an international organisation remain responsible for the space activities of the organisation.

DRAFT CODE AND RULES OF THE DAVID DAVIES MEMORIAL INSTITUTE OF INTERNATIONAL STUDIES

DRAFT CODE OF RULES ON THE EXPLORATION AND USES OF OUTER SPACE

1. In this Draft Code,
"aircraft" means any craft which depends, as means of flight upon the consumption of air, or upon aerodynamic lift, or both;
"spacecraft" means any craft, capable of orbital movement or manoeuvre in outer space and includes any craft which is being operated as a space station;
"airspace" means the volume of space between the surface of the Earth at sea level and an altitude of 80,000 metres above it;
"outer space" means space outside the airspace;
"state" includes, where appropriate, nationals of the State engaged in the exploration or use of outer space.
"international body" includes the United Nations and its specialised agencies and any other organisation or body, whether inter-governmental or non-governmental, engaged in, or having a scientific or technical interest in the exploration or use of outer space.

Comments
   (i) Like all proposed solutions of the initial problem these defini-tions use in varying combinations both physical and functional criteria, namely, the physical characteristics of airspace and outer space, and the uses to which they are, or are not, to be put. It is indeed doubtful whether any determination of boundaries in exclusively physical terms is possible.
   (ii) What seems reasonable is that any régime for outer space should cover the movement of spacecraft, orbiting the Earth, even though its perigee may be within the atmosphere of the Earth. Thus a satellite, having its perigee at an altitude where the atmosphere is dense enough to impose a "braking" effect on its flight, or a satellite designed to make a controlled return to the Earth's surface, should both while in orbit be deemed to be space craft.

At the present time the lower effective limit of perigee is in the region of the altitude of 100 miles, since below that the life of the satellite is too short to be useful, and it is possible that an altitude of about 70 miles would be the limit for effective orbiting, since below that friction would become too great. The notion of effectiveness here is to be understood in terms of the scientific uses of spacecraft.

(iii) The principle that each State has sovereignty over the airspace above its territory is now an established rule. Although the Soviet Union is not a party to the Chicago Convention, it has adopted the rule in substance in its own legislation.

Neither the Paris Convention in 1919 nor the Chicago Convention defined the altitude of the airspace, for the purpose of sovereignty, nor has it been authoratively defined elsewhere.[1]

As far as the performance of existing conventional aircraft is a guide to the definition of airspace, the ramjet which makes more efficient use of such air as is available, can "breathe" at greater heights than jet – or piston-engined – aircraft, but 25 miles is probably the outside limit of effective aerodynamic lift.

(iv) There are, however, three considerations which favour a definition of airspace yielding a more extended sovereignty than 25 miles; the fact that airspace begins to lose its character of a continuous medium only when a height of 50–55 miles is reached; the likely range of effective control of objects from the ground; and the logic of treating the frontier between airspace or outer space as being at or near orbiting altitude.

The first consideration suggests that craft may yet be designed to operate at altitudes nearer this limit than now seems possible.

The X-15 is a rocket-driven winged machine which flies as an aircraft while aerodynamic lift is available but which can be operated as if it were a spacecraft, under a different system of controls, when aerodynamic lift fails. The X-15 has already attained an altitude of 47 miles, and its descendants will certainly go higher. It is believed that such hybrid craft should be subject to the régime of that portion of space in which it is at any time operating, and that its existence does not call for any modification of the area of sovereignty.

It is now likely that control over spacecraft passing over the territory of a State, may be effectively in the hands of that

[1] See footnote 3.

State to far greater heights than was once supposed; in other words, while it was thought a few years ago that interference with, or destruction of, spacecraft from the territory over which they were passing, would at best be possible only with the greatest difficulty, diversion, destruction or even capture of spacecraft is probably now, or may soon become, quite practicable.

While 70 miles is indicated as the present limit of effective orbiting, there is a case for raising the altitude of sovereignty accordingly to perhaps 75 miles, orbiting effective for some purposes may yet be achieved at lower limits.

(v) Any particular altitude chosen as the limit of sovereignty over the airspace may appear arbitrary and be controversial, but, for the avoidance of excessive claims and by the other foregoing considerations, the relatively low altitude of about 50 miles is suggested here as the limit of sovereignty and the beginning of outer space.

(vi) "spacecraft" as defined includes missiles and passive craft.

2. 1 Outer space, and the celestial bodies therein, are recognised as being *res communis omnium*, free for exploration and use by all States in conformity with the provisions of this Draft Code, and neither outer space nor the celestial bodies in it are capable of appropriation or exclusive use by any State.

Comments

(vii) This section attempts the outline of a régime for outer space. It makes no distinction between peaceful and military purposes, beyond what is implied in the applicability of U.N. Charter provisions. It has been brought into line with General Assembly Resolutions on the uses of outer space.

(viii) The principle that outer space is *res communis* seems now to be generally accepted, though not necessarily of course in respect of outer space as defined in section 1 above; but the fact that there is as yet no international agreement as to the lower limit of outer space does not qualify the principle any more than disagreement as to the width of the territorial sea alters the status of the high seas.

(ix) It is probable that of the Earth's nearer neighbours in space only the Moon, Mars, and Venus offer chances for landing and establishing stations, though planetoids such as Eros might conceivably be converted into space stations. The proximity of the outer planets will, no doubt, be visited but their surface conditions, so far as they are known, seem to rule out the possibility of landing for a long time to come.

On September 13, 1959, the Soviet lunar probe landed on the Moon. However any consequent claim of sovereignty was repudiated by the Soviet Authorities, and Soviet writers have been inclined to favour the "common use" of celestial bodies. The General Assembly Resolution 1721–XVI unanimously adopted on December 20, 1961, is important because not only did it contain the principle that "outer space and celestial bodies are free for exploration and use by all States in conformity with international law and are not subject to national appropriation", but the United States and Soviet Union both supported it. In the absence of such an agreed principle, it would have been necessary to assert that claims to sovereignty over the celestial bodies, or portions of them, could not be recognised even as formal claims, unless they satisfied tests not less strict than those for the acquisition of territory upon the Earth.

2. 2 Subject to the provisions of this Draft Code, all States shall, for themselves and for their nationals, have equal rights in the exploration and use of outer space, including free navigation by means of spacecraft, the establishment of space stations and other like devices, astronomical and physical observations by optical radio and other methods, and the landing on and exploration and use of celestial bodies.

Comment

(xi) The principle of equal rights flows from Article 2 (1) and (2) of the UN Charter. It requires that States shall act in good faith, and with a due regard for the rights of other States, in the exploration and use of outer space and celestial bodies. In particular, mutual interference between space operations must, by due care and co-operation, be reduced to a minimum.

2. 3 In the exploration and use of outer space and celestial bodies States and international bodies (a) are bound by international law and by the provisions of the United Nations Charter and other international agreements, which may be applicable; (b) shall, to the greatest practicable extent

(1) exchange information on scientific research programmes to secure maximum economy and efficiency of operations;

(2) exchange scientific personnel for particular programmes;

(3) exchange and make freely available scientific observations, data, and conclusions from research;

(4) seek co-operation with the specialised agencies of the United Nations and other international bodies which have a scientific or technical interest in outer space;

(c) are not precluded from employing military personnel or equipment for scientific and peaceful purposes.

Comments

(xii) There is no limitation, express or implied in the UN Charter, of the applicability of Charter provisions to terrestrial activities.[2]

It may be useful to indicate briefly some of the Charter provisions which appear to be applicable to the uses of outer space:

1. General:
   Articles 1(4) and 2(1) and (2);
2. Military uses of outer space:
   Articles 2(4); 11(1) and (2) and (3); 34 and following; 39-42 and following; 51.
3. Scientific research and development in outer space:
   Articles 55(b) and 56; 59.

The position of the few non-members of the UN is that their uses of outer space, if any, would be subject to UN control under Article 2 (6) of the Charter. See also General Assembly Resolution 1721 D (preamble) -XVI.

(xiii) It is generally supposed that the Chicago Convention is confined to the operation of aircraft, defined in the Paris Convention 1919 and Chicago Convention Annexes as "any machine which can derive support in the atmosphere from reactions of the air". However, airspace is not defined and it does not follow from the definition of aircraft that airspace is to be understood as confined to that volume of space in which aircraft, so defined, can operate.[3] Thus Article 36 of the Chicago

---

[2] See for example the acceptance of this principle by the *United Nations Ad Hoc Committee on the Peaceful Uses of Outer Space:* Report (July 1959) A/4141: Part 1, para. 35: and General Assembly Resolution, A-XIV, para. 1 (a).

[3] The United States, United Kingdom and U.S.S.R. have not committed themselves to any ceiling for the airspace: see official statements by the U.S. Government and the U.K. Government cited by F. B. Schick – *Space Law and Space Politics:* 10 I.C.L.Q. (1961) 687.

Convention might be regarded as applicable to the flight "over its territory" of a machine similar to the X-15.[4] Again, if a machine of this type were to be developed, capable of being flown without a pilot, there is no reason why Article 8 of the Chicago Convention would not apply even though the flight of such machines was above the airspace.

(xiv) The ITU has already promulgated regulations governing the use of radio frequencies by spacecraft, and a conference to consider further developments is planned for 1963.[5] UNESCO has been consulted by ITU on the development of communications satellites, and is interested in the possibility of their use for educational purposes. UNESCO also intends to seek ways of improving the international network of geophysical and astronomical laboratories by exchanges of scientists and technicians and by training schemes. The use of outer space for weather forecasting and weather control also falls plainly within the ambit of the World Meteorological Organisation.[6] The World Weather Watch is designed as a co-operative global observing and prediction system based on World Centres and Regional Centres. The establishment of World Centres in Moscow and Washington has been agreed. COSPAR is already preparing a guide for World Data Centres which calls for detailed international agreements on the exchange of data and information. It is also preparing international codes for the transmission and reception of satellite data and has formulated recommendations for the rational distribution of tracking stations.

(xv) Paragraphs 2.3b and c are adapted from Articles III and 1 (2) of the Antarctica Convention 1959.

2. 4 No State or international body shall put the airspace, outer space or the celestial bodies, to uses which cause, or are likely to cause, modifications of the environment of mankind unless the prior agreement of the appropriate international body has been obtained that such modifications are acceptable.

---

[4] The X-15 is an "aircraft" within the definition cited above, though it is not at all a conventional aircraft. Cmp. also Art. 3 (b) and (c) of the Convention.
[5] See General Assembly Resolution 1721 D-XVI.
[6] See for example WMO Convention Art. 2 and General Assembly Resolution 1721 C-XVI.

Comment

(xvi) This problem is plainly urgent. The appropriate body would be one relying upon international scientific opinion and would be preferably the United Nations or an agency established by it. The standards of risk and acceptability of modifications of the environment of man would be fixed by existing rules of international law and practice and by considerations first of the protection of human, animal and plant life on the Earth, and secondly of the other uses of outer space. At the recommendation of ICSU, COSPAR has already established a consultative group, drawn from the fields of astronomy, radiation physics, atmospheric physics and chemistry, telecommunications and microbiology, to examine all experiments, carried out with spacecraft, which might have potentially harmful effects.

2. 5 No spacecraft carrying any type of warhead or otherwise designed as a weapon for use against targets on the Earth or in the airspace, shall be placed in orbit around the Earth, or celestial body, or be carried in or launched from any space station or celestial body.

Comments

(xvii) A ban upon the launching of "orbiting bombs" appears among the recent disarmament proposals put forward both by the U.S.A. and the U.S.S.R. It is possible therefore that agreement may be reached upon such a ban as part of a separate arms control agreement or of more extensive disarmament.

(xviii) The prohibition is limited to spacecraft designed as weapons whether of conventional, nuclear, chemical or bacteriological warfare.[7] It does not extend to surveillance or reconnaissance satellites, which may primarily serve military purposes, yet have the advantage that they contribute to an "open world" and so increase rather than diminish security.

2. 6 Every spacecraft shall be so designed that radio transmissions to and from it do not interfere with other telecommunications systems, and cease when its mission is completed.

3. 1 Subject to the provisions of this Draft Code, any State or international body may establish stations, manned or unmanned, upon a celestial body for its exploration or use.

3. 2 The establishment of military stations upon any celestial body and the

---

[7] See also Chicago Convention, Art. 35.

use of such stations or of a celestial body for the purposes of war is prohibited.

3. 3 The testing of any nuclear device or the disposal of radio-active waste upon any celestial body is prohibited.

Comment

(xix) Paragraphs 3. 2 and 3. 3 are adapted from Articles 1 (1) and V of the Antarctica Convention 1959. The need to dispose of radioactive waste from nuclear processes is already presenting grave problems. It is possible that, in order to avoid encumbering the Earth or celestial bodies with these dangerous substances, methods of disposal in outer space may be devised.

3. 4 In the operation and use of spacecraft, all practicable steps shall be taken (a) to prevent the contamination of any celestial body by terrestrial micro-organisms, or of the Earth by harmful micro-organisms brought back from a celestial body: and (b) not to waste or spoil mineral deposits or samples on celestial bodies.

Comment

(xx) WHO intends studying the environment conditions surrounding space travellers and the "unevaluated possibilities of the transfer of biological agents between the Earth and its extra-terrestrial environment" that are related to human biology and public health.

UNESCO already supports the work of COSPAR, the international scientific unions and other scientific bodies in planning an approach to the study of extra-terrestrial life and in examining practical implications.

3. 5 Stations on celestial bodies should as soon as practicable be placed under the supervision of the United Nations: provided that

(a) a State which establishes or permits its nationals to establish a manned station, may exercise jurisdiction over all persons in the station and in that area around it over which movement is necessary for the maintenance and use of the station;

(b) an international body which establishes such a station, may exercise a similar jurisdiction by international agreement.

Comments

(xxi) Supervision by the United Nations might be exercised initially through the Committee on the Peaceful Uses of Outer Space and later through a specially constituted international agency. It would include the right to visit and inspect the station.

(xxii) Jurisdiction is to be understood as covering the internal administration of the station and its personnel and as including a right to exclude other persons, vehicles or craft from the area, upon a reasonable belief that their entry would be injurious to the station or its use.

4. 1 No spacecraft launched from the territory of any State may at any stage of its flight enter the airspace of another State without the consent of that State: provided that

(a) such consent shall not be withheld if prior notice has been given to that State of the intended flight, and it has been shown to its satisfaction that the flight is solely for scientific and peaceful purposes and shall be so controlled as to obviate danger to aircraft;

(b) any craft capable of operating both as a spacecraft and as an aircraft shall for the purposes of its use of the airspace be deemed to be an aircraft;

(c) a manned spacecraft may enter the airspace without prior consent for the purpose of making an emergency landing, but shall be subject to the provisions of section b.

Comments

(xxiii) This paragraph establishes a controlled right of passage for spacecraft through the airspace of States, a right which in practice is likely to be exercised by spacecraft returning to the surface of the Earth in a shallow glide rather than by those taking off. It seems desirable to preserve the existing rule of air law in respect of the flight of spacecraft.

(xxiv) Prior notice under this and other paragraphs of this Draft Code might be given through an international agency, if such were established.

The notice should contain in any case a statement of the radio frequencies to be used in communication made to and from the spacecraft and a description of its means of propulsion and its orbital characteristics, including transit points.

Notice should be given not less than (14) days before the launching and could serve as the basis of the international registration of spacecraft. The UN Committee on the Peaceful Uses of Outer Space has already acquired certain regulatory functions including the registration of launchings. COSPAR has sponsored the international "spacewarn" system for the transmission of data on rocket and satellite launchings.

4. 2 Save in the case provided for in section 4. 1c, any State may divert or destroy any spacecraft which enters its airspace without the consent prescribed in section 4. 1.

Comment

(xxv) The liability of or damage to other States as a result of the diversion or destruction by State B of a spacecraft, for the launching of which State A is responsible, might be attributed either to State A alone, or to State A and B jointly. This is a matter for later agreement.

5. 1 Subject to the provisions of section 5. 2, every spacecraft shall be registered in a State, in accordance with its laws and regulations,[8] and also with the United Nations Committee on the Peaceful Uses of Outer Space.

5. 2 Every spacecraft to be launched by an international body shall be registered with the Committee on the Peaceful Uses of Outer Space, which shall issue a registration mark.

5. 3 For all purposes including that of any claim concerning the activities of a spacecraft:

(a) every spacecraft to which section 5. 1 applies shall be deemed to have the nationality of the State in which it has been registered, and whose nationality and registration mark it bears, or in the absence of such registration, of the State responsible for its launching and

(b) throughout its life shall, with its component parts, so long as they are identifiable, be deemed, in the absence of special agreement, to be the property of the State concerned under section 5. 3a or of the international body registering it, as the case may be.

Comment

(xxvi) The suggested rule as to property in spacecraft is in part to preclude any suggestion that a spacecraft, launched so as not to return to the surface of the Earth, is *res derelicta*.

5. 4 No spacecraft shall be operated by private persons or corporations save by licence granted by the State of which they are nationals. Any such licence shall include the provisions of sections 3, 6, 7 and this section as part of its terms.

---

[8] Compare Chicago Convention, Art. 19.

Comment

(xxvii) This paragraph would need considerable elaboration when private operators entered the field, but rests on the principle that the nature of space operations requires a continuing state of responsibility for them, whatever arrangements may be made between a State and private operators.

6. 1 The State or States or international body responsible for the launching of a spacecraft shall be liable for any breach of this Draft Code in which it may be involved, for any injury or loss caused by the spacecraft, or any part of it

(a) by physical impact, contamination, or otherwise, to any person or property whatsoever outside the territory of the State responsible for the flight of the spacecraft;

(b) as a result of collision or navigational interference, to any aircraft,
   1. in the airspace of another State: or
   2. of a nationality other than that of the spacecraft, without proof of negligence in the operation of the spacecraft being required.

6. 2 Liability for injury or loss under the foregoing paragraph shall not exceed in amount (fifty million U.S. dollars) or its equivalent.

Comments

(xxviii) This section does not cover injury or loss on a State's own territory, or in its airspace save in respect of foreign aircraft, and this seems proper in what is basically an international code.

(xxix) The draft also makes no provision for collision between spacecraft in outer space. Broadly it is reasonable to hold that in such a case the operating States should each bear their own loss, but in the event of an international supervisory agency being established, prior notice to it of launchings of spacecraft might be required, failure to give notice constituting fault in the case of damage to other spacecraft.

(xxx) Contamination may take broadly two forms; damage by radiation from a nuclear-powered spacecraft, and contamination of living organisms of the Earth by alien and harmful micro-organisms brought by spacecraft returning from celestial bodies.

(xxxi) The responsibility of an international body would, for the enforcement of claims, depend in part on its character and structure, and would need working out in greater detail.

7. Every State shall permit, and as far as possible assist, the recovery of a spacecraft, or any component part of it, which lands on its territory, and the return of any person travelling in it, by or to the State from which it was launched: provided that its entry into the airspace above the territory in which it lands was in conformity with section 4, and provided further that it has been registered as provided in section 5.

Comment

(xxxii) As drafted this would not exclude the recovery and return of a spacecraft which had caused damage under section 6.

8. 1 If any dispute arises between States
   (a) out of the conduct of operations in the exploration or use of outer space and the celestial bodies; or
   (b) as to the interpretation or application of this Draft Code or if any claim is made between States under this Draft Code, the States concerned shall endeavour to settle such dispute or claim amicably by consultation or other appropriate procedure.

8. 2 States undertake to accept the jurisdiction of the International Court of Justice over any dispute of claim which is covered by the preceding paragraph, and is not settled thereunder.

Comments

(xxxiii) It seems desirable to distinguish (a) and (b) so that a *casus omissus* may as far as possible be avoided.

(xxxiv) The latter part of paragraph 8. 1 is modelled on the Antarctica Convention 1959 Art. III (3).

DRAFT RULES CONCERNING CHANGES IN THE ENVIRONMENT OF THE EARTH

1. In these Draft Rules:
   "Changes in the environment of the Earth" means changes in the space around the Earth, by means of the introduction of novel elements or the disturbance of the physical equilibrium or processes which cause reactions upon, or in the vicinity of, the Earth.
   "Operations" means the use of any instrument, device or technique, on the surface of the Earth, in the airspace or in outer space.

Comment

(i) No distinction is made between the airspace and outer space, since the rules proposed are not, it seems, qualified by the fact that the airspace is subject to territorial sovereignty.

"airspace" means the volume of space between the surface of the Earth at sea level and an altitude of 80,000 metres above it;

"outer space" means space outside the airspace;

"spacecraft" means any craft, capable of orbital movement or manoeuvre in outer space and includes any craft which is being operated as a space station;

"State" includes, where appropriate, nationals of the State engaged in the exploration or use of outer space;

"international body" includes the United Nations and its specialised agencies and any other organisation or body, whether inter-governmental, or non-governmental, engaged in, or having a scientific or technical interest in the exploration or use of outer space.[1]

2.   Subject to the provisions of section 3, no State or international body shall engage in, or within the limits of its authority permit, operations which can cause changes in the environment of the Earth:

    1. if the range and scale of these changes cannot be predicted with reasonable precision; or

    2. if the changes may be reasonably expected

      (a) to have a deleterious effect upon the life, health or growth, of human beings or of animals or plants;

      (b) to modify the climate or weather of any region of the Earth: or

      (c) to prevent, or seriously hinder, scientific observation, experiment or research.

Comments

    (ii) Sub-paragraph 1 is of prime importance since it is in reckless or ill-planned operations that the greatest dangers lie.

    (iii) *Responsibility and Control.* The degree of responsibility for these changes and the measures necessary to control them must vary with the operations causing them. Among the changes must be distinguished those which are simply the cumulative result of generally permitted operations and so are the common responsibility of all the States engaged in them. Since these changes are caused by operations which are not individually forbidden, their control is a matter of public order. On the other hand the changes described may be brought about by a small number of

---

[1] These definitions are the same as those in the *Draft Code of Rules on the Exploration and Uses of Outer Space*.

space operations, or even a single operation, by a particular
State, which must alone be held responsible for them. It will
be convenient then to distinguish between issues of *public order*
and *individual State responsibility* in changes in the environment
of the Earth.

(iv) *The Public Order* of the airspace and outer space is part of
the active concern and general responsibility of the UN and
such specialised agencies as WHO, WMO, ITU, ICAO, and
UNESCO, and such bodies as COSPAR. Since the primary
task of these agencies is to promote co-operation between their
members rather than to enforce obligations, it is probable that
the changes described in section 2 would only in an indirect
way constitute breaches of the duties of membership of these
agencies. Nevertheless, in so far as they threatened to create an
international nuisance or worse, they must be controlled or
eliminated by these international bodies. Problems of public
order arise over, for example, nuclear tests in the stratosphere
and below; the increasing numbers of spacecraft and "hardware" in orbit; the progressive contamination of the upper
atmosphere by exhaust gases from spacecraft and their
"boosters"; and the exhaustion of available radio frequencies
by ground-based airborne and spaceborne users.[2]

Nuclear Tests in the Lower Atmosphere. The UN General
Assembly has often discussed this notorious problem and made
what recommendations it can. Its most recent Resolution
1762–XVII (December 1962) "viewing with the utmost appre-
hension the data contained in the report[3] of the UN Scientific

[2] For "hardware" in orbit and radio interference see paragraph 10 of the Resolution
adopted unanimously by the Institute of International Law at Brussels on September
11, 1963: "The State under the authority of which the launching of a space object
takes place shall ensure that every such object is, so far as practicable, fitted with a
suitable device permitting the launcher to recover it on termination of its useful life
or, if recovery is not feasible, as a minimum to silence radio transmission therefrom
and eliminate its other effects."

[3] See *Report of UN Scientific Committee on the Effects of Atomic Radiation* (1962) para. 48
". . . Because of the available evidence that genetic damage occurs at the lowest levels
as yet experimentally tested, it is prudent to assume that some genetic damage may
follow any dose of radiation however small." Para. 51 ". . . The exposure of mankind
to radiation from increasing numbers of artificial sources, including the world-wide
contamination of the environment with short, and long-lived, radio-nuclides from
weapons tests, calls for the closest attention, particularly as the effects of any increase in
radiation exposure may not be fully manifested for several decades in the case of
somatic diseases, and for may generations in the case of genetic damage." *Official
Records, Seventeenth Session:* 3/5216.

432

Committee on the Effects of Atomic Radiation . . . condemns all nuclear weapon tests . . . endorses the eight-nation memorandum of April 16, 1962" and calls for a settlement of differences between the three nuclear powers and a resumption of work by the eighteen-nation Committee on Disarmament. The conclusion of the Nuclear Test Ban Treaty 1963 will, it is hoped, now prevent further tests by the nuclear powers and discourage others.[4]

Objects in Orbit. With the increasing numbers of spacecraft alive or dead, and auxiliary "hardware" in orbit, there arise possibilities of mutual interference and even collision, and complication of the tasks of "tracking" instruments. Further interference with optical astronomy can be caused by their scattering of solar radiation with consequent brightening of the sky.

Exhaust Gases. The accumulation of rocket exhaust gases in the upper atmosphere, though minute in proportion to the volume of space, is significant given the very low surrounding atmospheric density, and can have physical and chemical effects which may change the behaviour of the lower atmosphere and so the weather. WMO has this problem under study.

Use of Radio Frequencies. By ITU Convention 1958, Art. 45 "Members recognise that it is desirable to limit the number of frequencies and the spectrum space used to the minimum essential to provide in satisfactory manner the necessary services". But the competition for frequencies is great and is increasing. Ground-based transmissions covering public services, commercial operations and astronomical and radio research, as well as telecommunications with aircraft and spacecraft covering control, tracking, and telemetering of information, all make demands on the radio spectrum. For example, radio astronomy has at present only one frequency band (1400–1427 mcs.) protected by ITU Regulations; again, the International Radio Regulations (May 1961) Art. 7 (1) provides that "The establishment and use of broadcasting stations (sound broadcasting and TV broadcasting stations) on board ships, aircraft or any other floating or airborne objects outside national territory is prohibited". Strictly this language does

[4] See also UN General Assembly 1884 – XVIII (October 17, 1963) against the placing of nuclear weapons or other weapons of mass destruction in outer space.

not appear to cover "pirate" space stations. The International Radio Consultative Committee has set up Study Groups, of which Study Group IV makes recommendations upon space telecommunications systems and in particular upon the allocation of radio frequencies and upon criteria for what radio "noise" and interference is permissible; for example, satellites with radio transmitters of long duration may function uncontrolled for centuries and interfere with the operations of other satellites.[5]

Weather Control. Techniques of weather control are still in an experimental stage, such as cloud-seeding, or a matter for speculation, such as extensive melting of polar ice by nuclear power, or heating of parts of the sea to induce current changes. Such operations could plainly have important consequences. It may, though it seems unlikely, be possible for a State to limit weather control effects to its own territory, and if it were so found under section 3, it would be unobjectionable.

(v) *Individual State Responsibility.* Where the changes described in section 2 can be attributed to specific operations of a particular State, the character of its responsibility will vary with the purpose of the operations involved and the gravity of their effects.

If the operations are designed, or recklessly conducted so as actually to produce changes described in section 2. 2, it is probable that an international wrong is committed. Here it is necessary to distinguish between criminal and delictual liability; see section 4 and Comment.

Secondly, the changes under any of the heads must be serious or substantial in order to engage State responsibility. Exact definition of these terms is of course impossible; but among the criteria of seriousness of changes would be their permanence, or the volume of space affected, or the intensity of their reactions upon the Earth, or the area of human, animal or plant life affected.

Examples of specific operations follow, they are obviously not exhaustive of the possibilities.

Artificial Radiation Belts. The "Starfish" bomb, with a yield of

[5] The Extraordinary Administrative Conference has been recently (October 1963) considering this particular problem.

434

1.4 megatons, was exploded by the U.S. authorities in July 1962 at a height of 250 miles above the Pacific. It was by far the largest explosion of the ten high-altitude nuclear tests which have been conducted – of these tests three have been made by the Soviet Union and seven by the U.S.A. The object of these tests is a matter of speculation, though military interest in determining how far the ionosphere or magnetic field over the territory of an enemy may be disturbed, so as to interfere with his telecommunications or satellites themselves, is apparent. In the case of the "Starfish" explosion, a significant number of the particles discharged were trapped in a thin crescent-shaped zone near the lower bundary of the inner Van Allen belt. As was not predicted, the flux here is decreasing very slowly, only by a factor of two every few months, and it will be many years before the vital question concerning the origin of the particles in the natural belt can be settled. Further, the intense artificial radiation belt, created by the explosion, caused a rapid deterioration of the solar power supplies of several satellites and is of an intensity sufficient to interfere with measurements by radio-telescope. This experiment seems then to fall under section 2. 1.

Orbiting Dipoles. The famous copper "needles", put up in the U.S. "West Ford" test belt, are designed to form part of a radio communications system in which these orbiting dipoles, about 350,000,000 in number, are used to reflect a signal, tuned to their resonant frequency, from a ground transmitter to a ground receiver. Interference with radio astronomy will be by radiation from transmitters scattered into a radio-telescope by the dipoles, and could in certain conditions be severe, though fixed world-wide allocation of frequencies to radio-telescopes would simplify the problem.[6] Interference with optical astronomy can arise through the scattering of solar radiation by the dipoles, and, since in any operational system the orbiting dipoles would be likely to be more numerous and denser than in the test belt, the interference could also be severe.[7]

[6] A. C. B. Lovell and M. Ryle – Interference to Radio Astronomy from Belts of Orbiting Dipoles (Needles); *Journal of the Royal Astronomical Society*, Vol. 3 (1962), pp. 100–108.

[7] D. E. Blackwell and R. Wilson – Interference to Optical Astronomy from Belts of Orbiting Dipoles (Needles) *Ibid.*, pp. 109–114.

3. 1 Where an operation is planned which is covered by any of the provisions of section 2 above, the responsible State authorities shall consult an international group of scientists of known competence, who shall express a reasoned opinion as to the changes in the environment of the Earth which the operation is likely to cause.

3. 2 If, in the opinion of the group, the predictable changes are confined to section 2. 2 (c), they shall recommend how the operation may be conducted so as to produce valuable scientific results without interfering with known air or space operations or known scientific researches.

Comment

(vii) This basis of consultation is that recommended in the Ratcliffe Report,[8] forming Annex II of a paper presented to Parliament by the Minister of Science in May 1963 and entitled "The Effect of High Altitude Nuclear Explosions on Scientific Experiments" (*Cmnd.* 2029).

The international group of scientists might initially be the panel already set up by COSPAR to scrutinise potentially harmful effects of the space operations. The effectiveness of such a group must depend in great part upon its being continuously informed about actual and planned operations. Its opinions should be made public.

3. 3 If, in the opinion of the group, the range or scale of changes fall under section 2. 1 or the predictable changes extend to section 2. 2 (a) or (b), the matter may be referred by any member State to the United Nations.

4. Any operation which can cause changes in the environment of the Earth, shall involve absolute liability to make good or compensate all loss or injury resulting therefrom, if it is carried out either:

(1) without resort to consultation under section 3. 1; or

(2) after the group referred to in section 3. 1 has been unable to predict the range and scale of the changes with reasonable precision; or

(3) in disregard of any recommendation of the United Nations, determining that a deleterious effect upon the life, health or growth of human beings is reasonably to be expected from such an operation.

Comments

(viii) The procedure for control suggested in Sections 3 and 4 might of course take other varied forms, but it contains two ideas

[8] This was a *Report by the Working Party on the Contamination of Space* made to the Steering Group on Space Research.

which it is believed are essential: first, such operations must be subject to international control, based upon informed scientific opinion and general human judgment; secondly, the sanction for disregard of that opinion and judgment must be as severe as it can be made.

(ix) The first principle, that such operations are of direct concern to the whole international community, is expressed in paragraph 12 of the Resolution adopted by the Institute of International Law at Brussels on September 11, 1963: "Scientific or technological experiments or tests in space which may involve a risk of modifying the natural environment of the Earth, of any of the celestial bodies[9] or of space, in a manner liable to be prejudicial to the future of scientific investigation and experiment, the well-being of human life, or the interests of another State, necessarily affect directly the interests of the whole international community. The provisions of this Resolution should be supplemented by appropriate international arrangements to forestall such risk."

(x) The principle of absolute liability for certain kinds of nuisance and for what have been aptly called "ultrahazardous" operations, is found in the legislation of so many of the industrialised countries that it can fairly be called a general principle of law which may be applied internationally in the field covered by these rules.

In the Judgment of the Tribunal in the *Trail Smelter Arbitration* (1941) 3 RIAA *at* 1965 it was said that "under the principles of international law . . . no State has the right to use or permit the use of its territory in such a manner as to cause injury by fumes in or to the territory of another or the properties or persons therein, when the case is of serious consequence and the injury is established by clear and convincing evidence", and in part rests upon the notion of abuse of rights. An analogous principle is to be found in the High Seas Convention, Article 25 (2) now in force: "All States shall co-operate with the competent international organisations in taking measures for the prevention of pollution of the seas or airspace above, resulting from any activities with radioactive materials or harmful agents", and in conventions for the prevention of oil pollution of the seas.

[9] See sec. 3.4 of the *Draft Code on the Exploration and Uses of Outer Space.*

Further, the principle of absolute liability has been adopted, with one exception, in the European Nuclear Energy Agency Convention, and in the Convention on the liability of Operators of Nuclear Ships, 1962, Art. *II, VIII*, subject to a limit of 1,500 million gold francs as the sum which the nuclear ship operator may be called on to pay in respect of any one accident.

Whether the operations, covered by section 3. 3 and 4, constitute a nuisance or, as will be considered below, a crime, they are undoubtedly "ultrahazardous" on a scale transcending any earlier industrial activity, and the rule of absolute liability for their effects seems therefore reasonable and just.

(xi) There might be operations causing changes in the environment, which involve criminal negligence since, apart from the obviously criminal operation, in which the deleterious effect is planned and intended, the effect may either be reasonably expected in which case there is a foresight and disregard of the consequences involving criminal liability, or it may be unknown or disputed in which case section 2. 1 applies and there is a reckless disregard of the consequences.

In certain cases changes in the environment might create situations covered by Article 34 of the UN Charter or even a threat to the peace under Article 39. Such cases should be dealt with by the United Nations as the Charter provides.

(xii) If a particular space operation falls under section 4, can the State responsible justify it on the grounds of self-defence? It may be observed that, in forwarding the *Report of the Working Party on the Contamination of Space*, referred to below, the U.K. Steering Group on Space Research expressed to the Minister of Science their unanimous opinion that:

"(a) serious adverse effects, both on scientific research and on other space activities (*e.g.*, communications or meteorological satellites) could result from further high-level nuclear tests above the 1 kiloton range, or from other experiments in outer space . . .

(b) the effects of such experiments may, in some circumstances, be difficult to predict . . .

(c) as far as defence considerations permit, any proposed experiments in outer space which could adversely affect scientific research should be openly discussed with the scientists whose work might be affected." (*Cmnd.* 2029 p. 3.)

The plea of "defence considerations" is broad, imprecise and given the secrecy surrounding defence measures in all countries, not subject to any objective criterion of validity. As a justification of particular operations it is at first sight not dissimilar to the claim to close areas of the high seas temporarily for nuclear tests. But such temporary closure of an area of the high seas, even if itself consistent with international law, cannot be invoked by analogy to justify a serious or substantial change in the environment of the Earth. It is difficult to see what rule of international law would prevent other States attempting, if it were technically possible, to reverse such a change. Further, if it were held to constitute an international crime, the plea of "act of State" would not apply to it.

(xiii) Two points of detail may be noticed in section 4:

(a) "any" recommendation would include General Assembly Resolution 1762–XVII: see Comment (iv), and so cover renewed nuclear tests in the lower atmosphere.

(b) while a deleterious effect upon animals or plants may not necessarily extend to human beings – the caribou of Northern Canada are known to have been seriously affected by the Strontium 90 derived from nuclear tests – section 4 would it is believed cover cases where the animals or plants affected were those upon which human beings depend for food or other purposes essential to life, and also to certain cases falling under section 2. 2 (b).

TENTATIVE PROVISIONS FOR INTERNATIONAL AGREEMENTS OF THE ASSOCIATION OF THE BAR OF THE CITY OF NEW YORK

The Association of the Bar of the City of New York had prepared in 1960 by its Committee on Aeronautics some tentative provisions for international agreements on space activities in the following terms. No decision concerning these provisions has been taken by the Association as such, but they are reproduced here in view of their intrinsic interest as tentative provisions concerning matters a number of which have not yet been regulated by international agreement.

A. Space Activities

For the purpose of this Convention the term "space activities" means all activities involving successful or attempted orbital flight about any celestial body or bodies, including the earth, or involving successful or attempted flight on a trajectory toward another celestial body than the earth, and all activities conducted on celestial bodies other than the earth. The term "space activities" does not refer to the flight of objects on a purely ballistic trajectory from one point on earth to another.

B. Freedom of Use of Space

1. The High Contracting Parties maintain their adherence to the régime of national sovereignty in air space. National sovereignty cannot be acquired in outer space.

2. (a) Subject to other provisions of this Convention, space activities may be undertaken without regard to national sovereignty in air space but may not unduly interfere with national uses of air space for security and navigation. This article shall not be taken to specify by implication the status, with respect to national sovereignty in air space, of activities not covered by the term "space activities" as used in this Convention.

   (b) States may not Exercise jurisdiction at a height of more than X miles above the surface of the earth.

C. Peaceful Use of Space

The High Contracting Parties declare their adherence to the principle that the conduct of space activities should be open and orderly. They denounce the use of space for purposes of aggression. They reserve all rights of security and self-defence conferred by or recognised under the Charter of the United Nations or otherwise under international law.

D. Prohibition of Use of Space for Mass Weapons

(a) No State shall place into orbit or station in space weapons of mass destruction.

(b) No State shall place into orbit or station in space weapons designed to inflict physical injury or damage directly or indirectly on human beings.

E. Dissemination of Space Data

In accordance with the principle of open and orderly conduct of space activities, the High Contracting Parties resolve to promote to the fullest extent the systematic and regular dissemination of information on space activities, except for information whose retention a State considers essential to national security. To this end the High Contracting Parties agree:

1. A launching State will disclose all information needed to enable others to make appropriate use of signals from space craft.
2. Data derived from space activities, including without limitation meteorological, radiological, astronomical, geodetic, geophysical, and electromagnetic data, and without regard to whether they are derived from records of signals received or from optical or other observations, will be kept accessible under reasonable conditions to any qualified researcher.
3. No steps will be taken to hinder or discourage the publication in ordinary scientific channels of the results of the analysis of data derived from space activities.
4. Upon the establishment of the World Data Center or Centers mentioned in Paragraph , a copy of all records of data derived from space activities will be deposited with the Center nearest to the place of origin of the record.
5. All High Contracting Parties will work towards the establishment of international organisations or procedures, or both, for the rapid dissemination of such information derived from space activities as may give promise of early benefit to mankind.

F. Notice of Launchings, Orbital or Flight Tracks, Re-Entries

The High Contracting Parties agree to keep the International Space Agency fully and currently informed on all objects launched or to be launched by them or under their sponsorship for the conduct of space activities, such information to include without limitation notice of the planned and actual time, place, direction, and initial velocity of launchings; planned and actual trajectory orbital elements, including significant changes as they take place and are detected; and planned and actual re-entry impact, and recovery.

G. Identification and Registration

1. The national character of launch vehicles and space craft used for space activities shall be indicated by appropriate elements of identification, including, as the case may require, visible marks, radio frequencies, and call signals, which shall be registered with the International Space Agency promptly after launching. The duty of such registration shall rest upon the State in whose territory the launching takes place or, if the launching does not take place from the territory of any State, upon the State whose nationals are in principal charge of the launching; if the launching takes place under the auspices of an international public organisation, the duty may be delegated to that organisation, with its consent, by the State which otherwise would bear it.

2. The International Space Agency shall maintain a current register of launch vehicles and spacecraft used for space activities and at appropriate intervals shall publish the information therein. Between successive editions the register may be inspected at reasonable times either on behalf of any High Contracting Party or by any other qualified researcher.

H. Repossession of Space Craft and Repatriation of Personnel

1. If the landing on the earth of any space craft or other object launched in compliance with this agreement can be controlled by the launcher, the launcher shall give advance notice if possible of any landing on the territory of a High Contracting Party other than the launching State. The re-entry into the air space, and the landing on the territory, of any State which is a High Contracting Party shall be permitted for any space craft or other object launched in compliance with this Convention. Upon any such landing, the territorial State shall upon learning of the landing notify the International Space Agency and may also notify the putative launcher. The launcher shall have the right to immediate and safe return of the space craft or other object, at the expense of the launcher.

2. Where any space craft or other object launched in compliance with this Convention is manned, the launching authority has the right of immediate and safe repatriation, at the expense of the launching authority, of all personnel landed.

I. Division of Launching Sites

A High Contracting Party engaged in launching shall set aside one or more launching sites (hereinafter called "orbital sites") for "space activities" as defined in this Convention and one or more launching sites (hereinafter called "ballistic sites") for other activities. It shall promptly notify the International Space Agency of the name and location of its launching sites, specifying which are orbital sites and which are ballistic sites.

J. Inspection at Orbital Sites

The International Space Agency may station at any orbital site qualified inspectors in reasonable numbers. Inspectors shall be afforded every necessary courtesy (including communications-facilities) and opportunity to inspect space craft, instrumentation, machinery, and installations to the extent necessary to verify compliance with this Convention and to verify the accuracy of information reported to the Agency under Paragraph . They shall report to the Agency any serious violation or discrepancy.

K. Detection at or near Ballistic Sites

The High Contracting Parties agree that upon request of the International Space Agency, they will give the Agency an opportunity to station qualified persons and appropriate equipment at locations from which launchings from ballistic sites may be observed for the purpose of verifying that "space activities" are not being conducted at those sites. The observers shall be afforded every necessary courtesy, including communications-facilities. They shall report to the Agency any serious violation.

L. International Space Agency

There shall be established an International Space Agency (hereinafter "Agency"), which shall perform the functions entrusted to it by this Agreement and other functions as agreed upon among the High Contracting Parties from time to time. Its statute shall be set out in an Annex to this Convention, which shall be an integral part thereof.

M. Co-operation with Existing Organisations

The Agency shall be empowered to co-operate with existing international organisations having to do with space activities. The High Contracting Parties agree to use their good offices to bring it about that those organisations keep the Agency fully and currently informed of the relevant parts of their work.

N. World Data Centers

The Agency may establish one or more World Data Centers to serve the

443

purposes mentioned in Paragraphs   above. The decision on the number, sites, staffing, and mode of operation of the Centers shall rest with the Agency. The Agency may conclude agreements with any State on the location and operation of a Center on its territory.

Whenever under this Convention there is a duty to notify the International Space Agency, the duty may be discharged by notice to the nearest Center maintained by the Agency.

O. Satellite Tracking Stations
If the Agency deems it necessary to build and operate on the territory of a High Contracting Party a station or stations for tracking space flights, that High Contracting Party shall make available an appropriate site or sites and facilitate the construction and operation. This shall not prevent any State desiring to do so from maintaining, or permitting any other State to maintain any other station or stations.

P. Organisation and Direction of Joint Space Programmes
If two or more High Contracting Parties undertake a joint programme of space activity, they may use the facilities of the Agency for the organisation and direction of the activity and shall in any event keep the Agency fully and currently informed of the programme.

Nothing in this Convention shall preclude any State from undertaking unilaterally any space activity not prohibited herein.

Q. Radio Spectrum Management
The High Contracting Parties agree to take all measures necessary:
(a) within the International Telecommunication Union, to assign and allocate spectrum bands so as to avert undue interference between radio transmissions to or from space and other radio transmissions;
(b) to assure, by appropriate devices for cut-off, detonation, or other means of termination, that radio transmitters in space craft will not outlive their period of useful activity;
(c) to notify the International Telecommunication Union upon the termination provided in sub-paragraph (b) above.

R. Disposal of Spent Space Craft
The Contracting Parties agree to arrange, within the limits of technical feasibility and with the aid of the Agency, for the recovery or other disposal of space craft, launch vehicles, and other earth-launched space objects when their useful life is over. The fact and details of such disposal shall be communicated to the Agency.

S. Liability for Damages

The High Contracting Parties consider that injury or damage caused by space activities should, subject to any limits to be specified in the future, be reimbursed, regardless of fault, by the State or States responsible for the space activity. They undertake to convoke a special international convention by 1968, to consider the incidence and possible limits of liability, the procedures for obtaining reimbursement, liability in case of collision, and the possible desirability of regular contributions by States or other organisations engaged in space activities to an international fund out of which such reimbursement might be claimed.

T. Contamination

The High Contracting Parties agree to take appropriate measures to minimise the adverse effects of possible biological, radiological, and chemical contamination of the earth or of other celestial objects as a consequence of space activities.

U. Territorial Claims to Celestial Bodies

Celestial bodies (other than stations, craft, vehicles, or other objects launched from the earth) shall not be subject to exclusive appropriation by any person, organisation, or State on the earth. Any exploration, occupation, development, use, and exploitation of the resources of such celestial bodies shall be conducted so as not to endanger such activities conducted by others. The High Contracting Parties agree to adopt any further decision on the subject of this paragraph that may be agreed by a two-thirds vote of the General Assembly of the United Nations.

V. Submission of Disputes

Any dispute between the High Contracting Parties as to the interpretation or application of the present Convention, not satisfactorily adjusted by diplomacy, shall be submitted to the International Court of Justice, unless the parties agree to settlement by some other pacific means.

W. Continuing Review

The Agency shall review, at least once a year, the provisions of this Convention and report the results and recommended changes, if any, to the High Contracting Parties.

PROPOSALS BY LEGAL SUB-COMMITTEE OF THE UNITED NATIONS COMMITTEE ON THE PEACEFUL USES OF OUTER SPACE, 1964

A

Proposals Relating to Assistance to and Return of Astronauts and Space Vehicles

Tentative agreement concerning the following provisions had been reached at the conclusion of the Third Session of the Sub-Committee in October 1964.

Preamble

The Contracting Parties,

Recognising that all mankind is interested in the peaceful uses of outer space,

Desiring to promote the further development of international co-operation in the exploration and use of outer space,

Recalling resolutions 1721 (XVI) of December 20, 1961, and 1884 (XVII) of October 17, 1963, adopted by the General Assembly of the United Nations,

Recognising that by resolution 1962 (XVIII) of December 13, 1963, adopted unanimously by the Members of the United Nations and entitled "Declaration of Legal Principles Governing Activities of States in the Exploration and Use of Outer Space," the General Assembly of the United Nations solemnly declared that in the exploration and use of outer space States should be guided by the principles contained in that Declaration,

Recognising that it is the duty of all States to assist astronauts and spacecraft in the event of accident, distress or emergency landing,

Prompted by sentiments of humanity and having regard for the needs of science,

Seeking to develop the international rules on assistance to, and return of, personnel of spacecraft, spacecraft and other space objects,

Agree as follows:

ARTICLE 2
Notification of accident

Each Contracting Party which receives information or discovers that the personnel of a spacecraft of another State have suffered accident or are experiencing conditions of distress or that they have made an emergency landing in territory under the jurisdiction of the Contracting Party, on the high seas, or in any other place not under the jurisdiction of any State:

(a) shall do its utmost immediately to notify the State which announced the launching, and

(b) shall immediately notify the Secretary-General of the United Nations.

ARTICLE 3
Assistance in the territory of a Contracting Party

1. If, as a result of accident, distress or emergency landing, personnel of a spacecraft are in territory under the jurisdiction of a Contracting Party, it shall immediately take all possible steps, within the limits of the means at its disposal, to rescue the personnel and to render them the necessary assistance. It shall keep the State which announced the launching, and the Secretary-General of the United Nations, informed of the steps so taken and of their result.

2. The assistance to be furnished when necessary by the Contracting Party to the personnel of a spacecraft of another State shall in no way differ from the assistance which it would furnish to its own personnel.

3. If the Contracting Party considers that the assistance of the State which announced the launching of the spacecraft concerned would contribute substantially to the effectiveness of its search and rescue operations, it shall request the State which announced the launching to co-operate with it with a view to the effective conduct of such operations, under the direction and control of that Contracting Party.

ARTICLE 6
Return of space objects

3. 1. A Contracting Party which receives information or discovers that a space object or any component part thereof has landed in territory under the jurisdiction of the Contracting Party or on the high seas or in any other place not under the jurisdiction of any State:

(a) shall do its utmost immediately to notify the State which announced the launching;

447

(b) shall immediately notify the Secretary-General of the United Nations.

(a) A Contracting Party which finds that a space object or any part thereof discovered in territory under its jurisdiction or recovered by it elsewhere is of a hazardous or deleterious nature may so notify the State which announced the launching, which shall thereupon take prompt and effective steps, under the direction and control of the Contracting Party, to recover the object or part thereof and to remove it from territory under the jurisdiction of the Contracting Party or otherwise render it harmless.

(b) If a space object or any part thereof which had landed on territory under the jurisdiction of a Contracting Party may to the knowledge of the State which announced the launching be of a hazardous or deleterious nature, the State which announced the launching shall immediately so notify the Contracting Party. If the Contracting Party so requests, the State which announced the launching shall take prompt and effective steps, under the direction and control of the Contracting Party, to recover the object or part thereof and to remove it from territory under the jurisdiction of the Contracting Party or otherwise render it harmless.

4. If in fulfilling its obligations under paragraphs   of this Article a Contracting Party considers that the assistance of the State which announced the launching of the space object concerned would contribute substantially to the effectiveness of recovery or return operations carried out by it in territory under its jurisdiction, it shall request the State which announced the launching to co-operate with it with a view to the effective conduct of such operations, under the direction and control of that Contracting Party.

5. The State which announced the launching of a space object and has requested its return shall, if requested by the Contracting Party which has discovered the object or any part thereof in territory under its jurisdiction or has recovered the object or part elsewhere, furnish identifying data to the Contracting Party.

No agreement had been reached at the conclusion of the Third Session of the Sub-Committee concerning the inclusion in the proposed agreement of certain general obligations, the return of space personnel, assistance outside the territory of a Contracting State, or certain aspects of the return of space objects. On these matters the Sub-Committee still had before it a United States proposal, an Australian-Canadian proposal, and a U.S.S.R.

proposal, with various amendments to these proposals. The proposals can be conveniently set out as follows:

General Obligations

United States Proposal

No provision.

Australian-Canadian Proposal

(Definitions Article)

(a) "Launching State" (not yet ready).

(b) "Space object" means an object or any of its component parts which a Launching State has launched or attempted to launch into outer space.

ARTICLE I

1. Each Contracting Party shall, in accordance with the provisions of the present Agreement and using every appropriate means at its disposal, assist the personnel of spacecraft in the event of accident, distress or emergency landing and (promptly and safely return them) (facilitate) (expedite) (arrange for) their earliest possible return) to the Launching State.

2. "With a view to ensuring the return to the Launching State of a space object discovered beyond the limits of the territory under the sovereignty, jurisdiction or control of that State, each Contracting Party shall, in co-operation where appropriate with other States, carry out the duties provided for in the present Agreement."

U.S.S.R. Proposal

ARTICLE I

General obligations

1. Each Contracting State shall, in accordance with the provisions of this Agreement, render all possible assistance to the crews of spaceships in the event of accident, distress or emergency landing; to this end it shall employ every means at its disposal, including electronic and optical equipment, means of communication, and rescue facilities of various kinds.

2. Each Contracting State shall foster international co-operation in the conduct of operations to find and salvage space objects launched in accordance with the Declaration of Legal Principles Governing the Activities of States in the Exploration and Use of Outer Space.

449

Appendix

Assistance Outside the Territory of a Contracting State

United States Proposal

ARTICLE 2

1. Unless otherwise requested by the State of registry or international organisation responsible for launching, each Contracting Party shall take all possible steps to assist or rescue promptly the personnel of spacecraft who are the subject of accident or experience conditions of distress or who may make emergency landings by reason of accident, distress, or mistake. Such steps shall include a joint search by those Contracting Parties which may be in a position to conduct search and rescue operations in the event personnel of a spacecraft are presumed to have made an emergency landing on the high seas or Antarctica.

2. Each Contracting Party shall permit, subject to control by its own authorities, the authorities of the State of registry or international organisation responsible for launching to provide measures of assistance as may be necessitated by the circumstances.

Australian-Canadian Proposal

ARTICLE 4

If information is received or it is discovered that personnel of a spacecraft have suffered accident, are in distress or have made an emergency landing, on the high seas or in any other place not under the sovereignty, jurisdiction or control of any State, and the Launching State is not in a position immediately to undertake effective search and rescue operations, such operations shall be conducted, in close and continuing co-operation with the Launching State, by those Contracting Parties which are in a position to do so.

U.S.S.R. Proposal

ARTICLE 4

Assistance outside the Territory of a Contracting State

If information is received or it is discovered that astronauts have alighted, owing to accident or distress, on the high seas or in any other place not under the sovereignty of any State, search and rescue operations shall be conducted by such Contracting States as are in a position to carry out these operations. These operations shall be directed by the State which officially announced its launching of the spaceship concerned or by such other State as it may request to take charge thereof.

Return of Space Personnel

United States Proposal

ARTICLE 3

1. A Contracting Party shall return the personnel of a spacecraft who have made an emergency landing by reason of accident, distress or mistake promptly and safely to the State of registry or international organisation responsible for launching.

Australian-Canadian Proposal

ARTICLE 5

A Contracting Party shall (promptly and safely return them) ((facilitate) (expedite) (arrange for) the earliest possible return) to the Launching State of the personnel of a spacecraft who as a result of accident, distress or emergency have landed in territory under the sovereignty, jurisdiction or control of that Contracting Party, or whom it has rescued elsewhere.

U.S.S.R. Proposal

ARTICLE 5

Obligation to return the crew

Each Contracting State shall do its utmost for the earliest possible return to their own country of the crew of a spaceship which was launched in accordance with the Declaration of Legal Principles Governing the Activities of States in the Exploration and Use of Outer Space and which has met with an accident, been in distress or made an emergency landing in its territory or which it has rescued elsewhere.

French Amendment to All Three Proposals

A Contracting Party shall not oppose the departure from its territory of persons on board a spacecraft which has made an emergency landing and shall do its utmost to assist them in making travel arrangements.

The present article shall not be construed as preventing juridical or administrative proceedings, or the enforcement of measures resulting from such proceedings, instituted by reason of the deeds or words of such persons after the completion of operations relating to the emergency landing.

Appendix

Return of Space Objects: Points not Dealt with in the Tentatively Agreed Text

United States Proposal

ARTICLE 3

2. Upon request by the State of registry or international organisation responsible for launching, a Contracting Party shall return to that State or international organisation an object launched into outer space or parts thereof that have returned to Earth. Such State or international organisation shall, upon request, furnish identifying data.

Australian-Canadian Proposal

ARTICLE 6

2. A Contracting Party having sovereignty, jurisdiction or control over the territory on which a space object has been discovered shall upon the request of the Launching State take all such steps as it finds practicable to recover the object.

3. A Contracting Party which has recovered a space object shall upon the request of the Launching State return the object to that State.

7. The expenses incurred by the Contracting Party in fulfilling its obligations under the present Agreement in respect of the recovery or the return of a space object shall be reimbursed by the State to which the object is returned.

U.S.S.R. Proposal

ARTICLE 6

Return of space objects

2. Each Contracting State shall, at the request of the State which officially announced the launching thereof, return to that State foreign spaceships, satellites and capsules launched in accordance with the Declaration of Legal Principles Governing the Activities of States in the Exploration and Use of Outer Space, together with the equipment they contain, or parts of any such objects, discovered in its territory or found by it elsewhere.

3. The State which officially announced its launching of the objects into outer space shall, before they are returned, furnish identifying particulars thereof at the request of the State which has discovered such objects in its territory or recovered them elsewhere.

452

Japanese Amendment to Australian-Canadian Proposal

ARTICLE 6

1. Provided that the Launching State has promptly registered the launching of a space object with the Secretary-General of the United Nations:

(b) The Contracting Party having sovereignty, jurisdiction or control over the territory on which such space object had been discovered shall upon the request of the launching State take all such steps as it finds practicable to recover the object;

(c) The Contracting Party which has recovered such space object shall upon the request of the Launching State return the object to that State.

(New Article on Reimbursement.)

The expense incurred by a Contracting Party in fulfilling its obligations under the present Agreement in respect of the recovery or the return of a space object or of the rescue or the return of the personnel of a space object shall be reimbursed by the State to which the object or the personnel is returned.

B

PROPOSALS RELATING TO LIABILITY FOR DAMAGE CAUSED BY OBJECTS LAUNCHED INTO OUTER SPACE

Three different proposals, submitted respectively by the United States, Belgium and Hungary, remained pending before the Sub-Committee at the conclusion of its Third Session in October 1964. The texts of these proposals,[1] as amended by their sponsors up to that date, were as follows:

REVISED UNITED STATES PROPOSAL FOR A CONVENTION CONCERNING LIABILITY FOR DAMAGE CAUSED BY THE LAUNCHING OF OBJECTS INTO OUTER SPACE

The Contracting Parties,

Recognising that activities in the peaceful exploration and use of outer space may on occasion result in damage,

Recalling General Assembly resolution 1962 (XVIII), entitled "Declaration of Legal Principles Governing Activities of States in the Exploration and Use of Outer Space",

---

[1] The provisions relating to the entry into force, amendment, withdrawal, registration authentic texts, etc., are omitted.

Seeking to establish a uniform rule of liability and a simple and expeditious procedure governing financial compensation for damage,

Believing that the establishment of such a procedure will contribute to the growth of friendly relations and co-operation among nations,

Agree as follows:

ARTICLE I

For the purposes of this Convention

(a) "Damage" means loss of life, personal injury, or destruction or loss of, or damage to, property.

(b) The term "launching" shall include attempted launchings.

(c) "Launching State" means a Contracting Party, or international organisation which has transmitted a notification to the Secretary-General under Article III, Paragraph 1, of this Convention, which launches or procures the launching of an object into outer space or whose territory or facility is used in such launching, or which exercises control over the orbit or trajectory of an object.

(d) "Presenting State" means a State which is a Contracting Party, or international organisation which has transmitted a notification to the Secretary-General under Article III, Paragraph 1, of this Convention, which presents a claim for compensation to a Respondent State.

(e) "Respondent State" means a launching State, or international organisation which has transmitted a notification to the Secretary-General under Article III, Paragraph 1, of this Convention, from which compensation is sought by a Presenting State.

ARTICLE II

1. The launching State shall be absolutely liable and undertakes to pay compensation to the Presenting State, in accordance with the provisions of this Convention, for damage on the earth, in air space, or in outer space, which is caused by the launching of an object into outer space, regardless of whether such damage occurs during launching, after the object has gone into orbit, or during the process of re-entry, including damage caused by apparatus or equipment used in such launching.

2. If the damage suffered results either wholly or partially from wilful or reckless act or omission on the part of the Presenting State, or natural or juridical persons it represents, the liability of the launching State to pay compensation under section 1 of this article shall, to that extent, be wholly or partially extinguished.

3. If more than one State shall be liable to pay compensation for damage in relation to any one incident under this Convention, each such State shall be liable to pay the full amount of such compensation, provided that in no event shall the aggregate of the compensation paid exceed the amount which would be payable under this Convention if only one Respondent State were liable.

4. The compensation which a State shall be liable to pay for damage under this Convention shall be determined in accordance with applicable principles or international law, justice, and equity.

Article III

1. If an international organisation which conducts space activities transmits to the Secretary-General of the United Nations a declaration that it accepts and undertakes to comply with the provisions of the present Convention, all the provisions, except Articles X, XIII, XIV and XV, shall apply to the organisation as they apply to a State which is a Contracting Party.

2. The declaration referred to in paragraph 1 of this Article shall contain a statement as to the manner in which any liability incurred by the international organisation shall be borne by constituent members once the amount of compensation has been agreed upon or established pursuant to Article VII.

3. The Contracting Parties to the present Convention undertake to use their best endeavours to ensure that any international organisation which conducts space activities and of which they are constituent members is authorised to make and will make the declaration referred to in section 1 of this Article.

4. In the event that an international organisation fails to pay within one year of the date on which compensation has been agreed upon or established pursuant to Article VII, each member of the organisation which is a Contracting Party, shall, upon the service of notice of such default by the Presenting State within three months of such default, be liable for such compensation in the manner and to the extent set forth in Article II, Paragraph 3.

Article IV

1. A Contracting Party which suffers damage as a result of the launching of an object into outer space, or whose natural or juridical persons suffer such damage, may present a claim for compensation to a Respondent State.

2. A Contracting Party may also present to a Respondent State a claim of any natural person, other than a person having the nationality of the Respon-

dent State, permanently residing in its territory. However, a claim of any individual claimant may be presented by only one Contracting Party.

3. A claim shall be presented through the diplomatic channel. A Contracting Party may request another State to present its claim and otherwise represent its interest in the event that it does not maintain diplomatic relations with the Respondent State.

4. A claim must be presented within one year of the date on which the accident occurred or, if the Presenting State could not reasonably be expected to have known of the facts giving rise to the claim, within one year of the date on which these facts became known.

ARTICLE V

A State shall not be liable under this Convention for damage suffered by its own nationals.

ARTICLE VI

1. The presentation of a claim shall not require exhaustion of any remedies in the Respondent State which might otherwise exist.

2. If, however, the Presenting State, or any natural or juridical person whom it might represent, elects to pursue a claim in the administrative agencies or courts of the Respondent State or pursue other international remedies, it shall not be entitled to pursue a claim under this Convention.

ARTICLE VII

1. If a claim is not settled within one year from the date documentation is completed, the Presenting State may request the establishment of a commission to decide the claim. In such event, the Respondent State and the Presenting State shall each promptly appoint one person to serve on the commission, and a third person, who shall act as chairman, shall be appointed by the President of the International Court of Justice. If the Respondent State fails to appoint its member within three months, the individual appointed by the President of the International Court of Justice shall constitute the sole member of the commission.

2. No increase in the membership of the commission shall take place where there is more than one Presenting State or Respondent State joined in any one proceeding before the commission. The Presenting States so joined may collectively appoint one person to serve on the commission in the same manner and subject to the same conditions as would be the case for a single Presenting State. Similarly, where two or more Respondent

States are so joined, they may collectively appoint one person to serve on the commission in the same way.

3. The commission shall determine its own procedure.

4. The commission shall conduct its business and arrive at its decision by majority vote.

5. The decision of the commission shall be rendered expeditiously and shall be binding upon the parties.

6. The expenses incurred in connexion with any proceeding before the commission shall be divided equally between the parties in the proceeding.

ARTICLE VIII

Payment of compensation shall be made in a currency convertible readily and without loss of value into the currency of or used by the Presenting State.

ARTICLE IX

The liability of the launching State shall not exceed $ with respect to each launching.

ARTICLE X

Any dispute arising from the interpretation or application of this Convention, which is not previously settled by other peaceful means of their own choice, may be referred by any Contracting Party thereto to the International Court of Justice for decision.

REVISED BELGIAN PROPOSAL FOR A CONVENTION ON THE UNIFICATION OF CERTAIN RULES GOVERNING LIABILITY FOR DAMAGE CAUSED BY SPACE DEVICES

The Contracting Parties,

Recalling the Declaration of Legal Principles Governing the Activities of States in the Exploration and Use of Outer Space adopted by the General Assembly of the United Nations on December 13, 1963, and embodied in resolution 1962 (XVIII),

Recognising that activities in the exploration and peaceful uses of outer space may from time to time result in damage,

Recognising the need to establish rules governing liability with a view to ensuring that compensation is paid for damage thus caused,

Have agreed as follows:

457

ARTICLE I

(a) The provisions of this Convention shall apply to compensation for damage caused to persons or property by a space device or space devices. They shall not apply to compensation for damage caused in the territory of the launching State or suffered by its nationals or permanent residents.

(b) The occurrence of the event causing the damage shall create a liability for compensation once proof has been given that there is a relationship of cause and effect between the damage, on the one hand, and the launching, motion or descent of all or part of the space device, on the other hand.

(c) Liability for compensation shall cease to exist in the event of wilful misconduct on the part of the applicant State.

"Wilful misconduct" shall be understood to mean any act or omission perpetrated either with intent to cause damage or rashly and in full knowledge that damage will probably result.

ARTICLE 2

"Damage" shall be understood to mean any loss for which compensation may be claimed under the law of the place where the loss is caused. Any damage suffered by a ship, aircraft or space device and by the persons and property carried therein shall be deemed to have been caused in the territory of the flag State or, in the case of a space device and the persons and property carried therein, in the territory of the launching State.

"Launching" shall be understood to mean an attempted launching or a launching operation proper, whether or not it fulfils the expectations of those responsible therefore.

"Space device" shall be understood to mean any device intended to move in space and sustained there by means other than the reaction of air, as well as the equipment used for the launching and propulsion of the device.

"Launching State" shall be understood to mean the State or States which carry out the launching of a space device or whose territory is used for such launching.

"Applicant State" shall be understood to mean the State which has been injured or whose nationals or permanent residents have been injured, and which presents a claim for compensation.

ARTICLE 3

The launching State shall be held liable for compensation for damage caused in the circumstances stated in Article 1, as defined in Article 2. If several States participate in the launching of a space device, they shall be held jointly liable.

ARTICLE 4

(a) Within two years after the occurrence of the damage, or after the identification of the State liable under Article 2, the applicant State shall present through the diplomatic channel, to the State which it holds liable, all claims for compensation concerning itself and its nationals and residents.

(b) If the applicant State or a person represented by it brings an action for compensation before the Courts or administrative organs of the State receiving the claim, it shall not at the same time present a claim for compensation for the same damage under the provisions of this Convention. The said provisions shall not be considered to require, by implication, the prior exhaustion of such remedies as may exist under the rules of ordinary law in the State receiving the claim.

(c) If the State receiving the claim has not taken, within six months after being approached, a decision considered satisfactory by the applicant State, the latter may have recourse to arbitration.

Within ninety days of the date of the request addressed to it by the applicant State, the State receiving the claim shall appoint one arbitrator, the applicant State shall appoint a second and the President of the International Court of Justice a third. If the State receiving the claim fails to appoint its arbitrator within the prescribed period, the person appointed by the President of the International Court of Justice shall be the sole arbitrator.

The Arbitration Commission shall take its decisions according to law and by majority vote. It shall make an award within six months after the date of its establishment and its decisions shall be binding.

(d) Sums due in compensation for damage shall be fixed and payable either in the currency of the applicant State or in a freely transferable currency.

(e) The periods specified in this Article shall not be subject to interruption or suspension.

(f) There shall be joinder of claims where there is more than one applicant in respect of damage due to the same event or where more than one State is liable and the damage was caused by more than one space device.

HUNGARIAN PROPOSAL FOR AN AGREEMENT CONCERNING LIABILITY FOR DAMAGE CAUSED BY THE LAUNCHING OF OBJECTS INTO OUTER SPACE

The Contracting States,

Recognising the common interest of mankind in furthering the pcefulea exploration and use of outer space,

Recalling the Declaration of Legal Principles Governing the Activities of

States in the Exploration and Use of Outer Space, adopted by the General Assembly on December 13, 1963 as resolution 1962 (XVIII).

Considering that the States and international organisations involved in the launching of objects into outer space should be internationally liable for damage caused by these objects,

Recognising the need for establishing international rules and procedures concerning such liability to ensure protection against damage caused by objects launched into outer space,

Believing that the establishment of such rules and procedures would facilitate the taking of the greatest possible precautionary measures by States and international organisations involved in the launching of objects into outer space to protect against damage inflicted by objects launched into outer space,

Have decided to conclude the present Agreement:

Article I

1. The provisions of this Agreement shall apply to compensation for loss of life, personal injury and damage to property (hereinafter called "damage"):
   (a) caused by an object launched into outer space, or
   (b) caused in outer space, in the atmosphere or on the ground by any manned or unmanned space vehicle or any object after being launched, or conveyed into outer space in any other way.

2. Liability is also incurred even if, for any reason, the space vehicle or other object has not reached outer space.

3. For the purposes of this Agreement "Space Object" means spaceships, satellites, orbital laboratories, containers and any other devices designed for movement in outer space and sustained there otherwise than by the reaction of air, as well as the means of launching of such objects.

Article II

1. Liability of the State shall not exceed . . .

2. A claim for damage may be advanced on the ground of loss of profits and moral damage whenever compensation for such damage is provided for by the law of the State liable for such damage.

Article III

Whenever damage is done to a space vehicle or object or its crew in outer space, the launching State will have no claim except in cases provided for in Articles IV and V below.

ARTICLE IV

The State shall assume full liability for damage caused directly or indirectly on the ground, in the atmosphere or in outer space, if the State is exercising an unlawful activity in outer space or the space vehicle or object has been launched for unlawful purposes.

ARTICLE V

If the damaged State produces evidence that damage has been caused in outer space because of the fault of another State, the latter shall be liable for this damage.

ARTICLE VI

If the damage has occurred on the ground or in the atmosphere, exemption from liability may be granted only in so far as the State liable produces evidence that the damage has resulted from the natural disaster or from a wilful act or from gross negligence of the State suffering the damage.

ARTICLE VII

1. Liability for damage shall rest with the State or international organisation which has launched or attempted to launch the space vehicle or object, or in the case of a common undertaking, with all the States participating in the undertaking, or with the State from whose territory or from whose facilities the launching was made, or with the State which owns or possesses the space vehicle or object causing the damage.

2. In case of joint launching or joint possession or ownership or co-operation, liability may be laid upon more than one State or international organisation; their liability towards the damaged State shall be joint.

ARTICLE VIII

If liability for damage rests with an international organisation, the financial obligations towards States suffering damage shall be met by the international organisation and by its member States.

ARTICLE IX

1. A claim for damage may be made by a State in whose territory damage has occurred or in respect of damage suffered by its citizens or legal entities whether in the territory of that State or abroad.

2. No claim shall be presented by virtue of this Agreement by any State not covered by the provisions of Paragraph 1 of this Article.

3. The provisions of this Agreement shall not apply to damage caused on the territory of the State liable or in respect of damage suffered by its citizens or legal entities whether in the territory of that State or abroad.

ARTICLE X

A claim must be presented within one year of the date of occurrence of the damage.

ARTICLE XI

The claim shall be presented through diplomatic channels. The damaged State may request a third State to represent its interests in the event it has no diplomatic relations with the State liable.

ARTICLE XII

1. In case the State liable does not satisfy the claim of the damaged State, the claim for compensation shall be presented to a committee of arbitration set up by the two States or a basis of parity. This committee will determine its own procedure.

2. Should the committee mentioned in Paragraph 1 not arrive at a decision, the States may agree upon an international arbitration procedure or any other method of settlement acceptable to both States.

SELECTED BIBLIOGRAPHY

The literature of the subject is so voluminous and is growing so rapidly that the following bibliography is necessarily highly selective; further references are given in appropriate contexts throughout the present volume.

INTRODUCTORY ACCOUNTS OF DEVELOPMENTS IN SPACE

Robert W. Buckheim and the Staff of the Rand Corporation, *Space Handbook: Astronautics and its Applications*, 1959 (still the most comprehensive general account of space technology).

Arthur C. Clarke, *The Exploration of Space*, 1960 (a new edition of a pioneer work originally published in 1951).

Andrew G. Haley, *Rocketry and Space Exploration*, 1958.

Walter Sullivan, *Assault on the Unknown: The International Geophysical Year*, 1961.

John T. Wilson, *IGY – The Year of the New Moons*, 1961.

John Glenn, Scott Carpenter, Alan Shepard, Virgil Grissom, Gordon Cooper, Donald Slayton and Walter Schirra, *Into Orbit*, 1962 (an account of Project Mercury by the United States astronauts).

Simon Ramo (editor), *Peacetime Uses of Outer Space*, 1961.

Lincoln P. Bloomfield (editor), *Outer Space: Prospects for Man and Society* (The American Assembly), 1962.

Hugh Odishaw (editor), *The Challenges of Space*, 1962 (perhaps the most valuable of recent books).

I. M. Levitt and Dondridge M. Cole, *Exploring the Secrets of Space*, 1963.

Patrick Moore, *Space in the Sixties*, 1963 (Penguin Books).

Howard J. Taubenfeld (editor), *Space and Society*, 1964.

Charles-Noël Martin, *Le Cosmos et la Vie*, (Encyclopédie Planète) 1963.

The Next Ten Years in Space, 1959–1969, United States House of Representatives, 86th Congress, 1s6 Session, Document No. 115.

The Practical Values of Space Exploration (Revised) (August 1961), Report of the Committee on Science and Astronautics, United States House of Representatives, 87th Congress, 1s6 Session, House Report No. 1276.

Selected Bibliography

OFFICIAL DOCUMENTS

United Nations

Report of the *Ad Hoc* Committee on the Peaceful Uses of Outer Space, Document A/4141 of July 14, 1959.

Report of the Committee on the Peaceful Uses of Outer Space, Document A/5181 of September 27, 1962.

Report of the Committee on the Peaceful Uses of Outer Space, Document A/5549 of November 24, 1963.

Additional Report of the Committee on the Peaceful Uses of Outer Space, Document A/5547/Add. 1 of November 27, 1963.

Report of the Committee on the Peaceful Uses of Outer Space, Document A/5785 of November 13, 1964.

Report of the Legal Sub-Committee, Document A/A.C.105/21 of October 23, 1964.)

Committee on the Peaceful Uses of Outer Space. Information Furnished in Conformity with General Assembly Resolution 1721 (B) XVI by States Launching Objects Into Orbit or Beyond. (This information is issued in a series of documents bearing the symbol A/AC.105/INF. with a final number for each document.)

Twenty-Fourth Report of the Administrative Committee on Co-ordination to the Economic and Social Council, Document E/3368 of May 10, 1960, Part V, paragraphs 18 to 21 and Annex I.

Committee on the Peaceful Uses of Outer Space, Review of the Activities and Resources of the United Nations, of its Specialised Agencies and of Other Competent International Bodies relating to the Peaceful Uses of Outer Space, Document A/A.C.105/L.12 of September 11, 1964.

International Telecommunication Union

First Report by the International Telecommunication Union on Tele-communications and the Peaceful Uses of Outer Space, Geneva, 1962.

Second Report by the International Telecommunication Union on Tele-communications and the Peaceful Uses of Outer Space, Geneva, 1963.

Final Acts of the Extraordinary Administrative Radio Conference to Allocate Frequency Bands for Space Radiocommunication Purposes, 1963.

World Meteorological Organisation

First Report on the Advancement of Atmospheric Sciences and their Application in the Light of Developments in Outer Space, 1962.

Second Report on the Advancement of Atmospheric Sciences and their Application in the Light of Developments in Outer Space, 1963.

COSPAR

Charter of COSPAR, May 1960.

COSPAR Guide to Rocket and Satellite Information Data Exchange, COSPAR Information Bulletin No. 9, July 1962.

Unified Synoptic Codes for Rapid Communication of Satellite Orbital Data, COSPAR Information Bulletin No. 9, July 1962.

COSPAR World List of Satellite Tracking Stations, COSPAR Information Bulletin No. 10, August 1962.

COSPAR Manual for the Establishment of Stations for the Reception of Real Time Telemetry Signals from Satellites, COSPAR Information Bulletin No. 15, May 1963.

LEGAL WORKS

Air Law

Lord McNair (Arnold D.), *The Law of the Air*, 1932, 2nd ed. by Kerr and McCrindle, 1953.

H. D. Hazeltine, *The Law of the Air*, 1911.

Henry G. Hotchkiss, *The Law of Aviation*, 2nd ed. 1938.

D. Goedhuis, *Handbook van het Luchtrecht*, 1943.

Alex Meyer, *Freiheit der Luft als Rechtsproblem*, 1944.

Maurice Lemoine, *Traité de droit aérien*, 1947.

J. C. Cooper, *The Right to Fly*, 1947.

Antonio Ambrosini, *Instituciones del Derecho de la Aviación*, 1949.

Alvaro Bauzá Araujo, *Principios de Derecho Aéreo*, 1955.

J. P. Honig, *The Legal Status of Aircraft*, 1956.

Min-Ming Peng, *Le Statut juridique de l'aéronef militaire*, 1957.

Julian G. Verplaetse, *International Law and Vertical Space*, 1960.

Bin Cheng, *The Law of International Air Transport*, 1962.

The leading air law journals, notably the *Journal of Air Law and Commerce* (Chicago), *Revue générale de l'Air* (Paris), *Revue française de droit aérien* (Paris), *Zeitschrift für Luftrecht* (Cologne), *Revista de Aeronáutica* (Madrid), and *Revista Latino americana de Derecho Aeronáutico* (Buenos Aires), frequently contain articles dealing with or bearing on space law.

Space Law

Philip C. Jessup and Howard J. Taubenfeld, *Controls for Outer Space and the Antarctic Analogy*, 1959.

Myres S. McDougal, Harold Laswell and Ivan A. Vlasic, *Law and Public Order in Space*, 1963.

Andrew G. Haley, *Space Law and Government*, 1963.

Legal Problems of Space Exploration – A Symposium, 1961, United States Senate, 87th Congress, 1st Session, Document No. 26.

E. A. Korovine (editor), *Kosmos i mezhdunarodnoye pravo*, 1962 (available only in Russian).

C. Wilfred Jenks, *The Common Law of Mankind*, 1958, pp. 382–407 (reproduces "International Law and Activities in Space", 1956).

—— "The International Control of Outer Space", *Eleventh International Astronautical Congress*, Stockholm, 1960, Proceedings, Vol. III, *Third Colloquium on the Law of Outer Space*, pp. 3–14.

—— "Le Droit International des Espaces Célestes", 1963, *Annuaire de l'Institut de Droit International*, Vol. 50, 128–496 and t. II, pp. 60–187.

—— *Law, Freedom and Welfare*, 1963, pp. 33–49, "The Laws of Nature and International Law".

R. Y. Jennings (Chairman) and J. E. S. Fawcett (Reporter), *Draft Code of Rules on the Exploration and Uses of Outer Space*, David Davies Memorial Institute of International Studies, 1963.

—— *Draft Rules concerning Large Scale Changes in the Environment of the Earth*, David Davies Memorial Institute of International Studies, 1964.

Charles Chaumont, *Le Droit de l'Espace*, 1960.

Eugène Pépin, *Le Droit de l'Espace*, 1962 (Institut international d'Etudes et de Recherches Diplomatiques, Paris).

Rolando Quadri, "Droit international cosmique", *Recueil des Cours de l'Academie de Droit international*, 1959.

D. Goedhuis, "Conflict of Laws and Divergencies in the Legal Régime of Air and Space Law", *Recueil des Cours de l'Academie de Droit International*, 1963.

Manfield Lachs, "Space Law", *Recueil des Cours de l'Academie de Droit International*, 1964.

Welf Heinrich, Prince von Hannover, *Luftrecht und Weltraum*, 1958.

Maxwell Cohen (editor), *Law and Politics in Space*, 1964.

Harold Valladão, *Direito Interplanetario e Direito Inter-Gentes Planetarias*, 1957.

—— *O Direito do Espaço Interplanetario*, 1959.

Aldo Armando Cocca, *Teoria del Derecho Interplanetario*, 1957.

Alvaro Bauzá Araujo, *Derecho Astronautico*, 1961.

Modesto Seara Vazquez, *Introduccion al Derecho Internacional Cosmico*, 1961.

A wide range of legal periodicals contain from time to time articles on space law. The following call for special mention:

American Journal of International Law
Proceedings of the American Society of International Law
Soviet Yearbook of International Law
International and Comparative Law Quarterly
Annuaire Français de Droit International
Recueil des Cours de l'Académie de droit international

The *Proceedings* of the Colloquia on the Law of Outer Space of the International Astronautical Federation, though uneven in quality, contain much suggestive material. The Proceedings of the First Colloquium (the Hague, 1958) and the Second Colloquium (London, 1959) are published by Springer Verlag, Vienna, those of the Third Colloquium (Stockholm, 1960) by the Organising Committee of the XIth Astronautical Congress, Stockholm, those of the Fourth Colloquium (Washington, 1961) by the University of Oklahoma Research Institute, those of the Fifth Colloquium (Varna, 1962) and of the Sixth Colloquium (Paris, 1963) by the International Institute of Space Law of the International Astronautical Federation, Washington, D.C.

There are a number of useful bibliographies of space law including the following:

Legal Problems of Space Exploration: A Symposium, 1961, United States Senate, 87th Congress, 1st Session, Document No. 26, pp. 1329–1392.

John C. Hogan, *A Guide to the Study of Space Law*, 1958.

Eugène Pépin, *Bibliographie des Travaux Publiés sur les Problèmes Juridiques de l'Espace et Questions Annexes, 1910 – 15 Septembre 1959*. (Extrait de la Revue Française de Droit Aérien, No. 4 de 1959).

SCIENTIFIC AND TECHNOLOGICAL WORKS

L. V. Berkner and Hugh Odishaw, *Science in Space*, 1961 (the most comprehensive and authoritative scientific work).

IGY Manual on Rockets and Satellites, Vol. VI of the *Annals of the International Geophysical Year*, 1958.

COSPAR Information Bulletin (issued at irregular intervals by the Committee on Space Research of the International Council of Scientific Unions).

A Review of Space Research, National Academy of Sciences (U.S.A.) 1962.

Mercury Project Summary, including Results of the Fourth Manned Orbital Flight, May 15 and 16, 1963, National Aeronautics and Space Administration, 1963.

Ari Sternfeld, *Soviet Space Science*, 1959.

Ari Sternfeld and others, *Soviet Writings on Earth Satellites and Space Travel*, 1959.

Selected Bibliography

James A. van Allen (editor), *Scientific Uses of Earth Satellites*, 2nd reviewed edition, 1958 (a second edition of the book on which the United States IGY programme was largely based).

Desmond King-Hele, *Satellites and Scientific Research*, 1960 (a good general account of the use of satellites for scientific research).

Donald P. Le Galley, *Space Science*, 1963.

Sir Bernard Lovell, *The Exploration of Space*, 1962.

Sir Harrie Massey, *Space Physics*, 1964 (particularly valuable as an account of British experiments, including satellite Ariel).

The following are studies of more specialised aspects of space science.

Sir Harrie S. W. Massey and R. L. F. Boyd, *The Upper Atmosphere*, 1958.

Harlow Shapley, *Of Stars and Men*, 1958.

Sir Harold Spencer Jones, *Life on Other Worlds*, 1940.

Daniel Q. Posin, *Life Beyond our Planet: A Scientific Look at Other Worlds in Space*, 1962.

R. A. Millikan, *Cosmic Rays*, 1939.

O. G. Sutton, *Understanding Weather*, 1960.

F. Graham Smith, *Radio Astronomy*, 1960.

R. D. Davies and H. P. Palmer, *Radio Studies of the Universe*, 1959.

J. L. Nayler, *Advances in Space Technology*, 1962.

A. L. Balakrishnan, *Space Communications*, 1963.

S. H. Reeger, *Communications Satellites: Technology, Economics and System Choices*.

Hermann Oberth, *Man into Space*, 1957.

Lt.-Col. Kenneth F. Gantz (editor), *Man in Space: Principles and Practice of Space Flight as Developed by the United States Air Force*, 1959.

James S. Hanrahan and David Bushnell, *Space Biology: The Human Factors in Space Flight*, 1960.

There are a number of technical publications issued in successive volumes at irregular intervals including:

Planetary and Space Science, Pergamon Press.

Space Science Reviews, Reidel Publishing Co., Dordrecht.

Space Research, North Holland Publishing Co., Amsterdam.

Progress in the Astronautical Sciences, North Holland Publishing Co., Amsterdam.

POLITICAL ASPECTS OF ACTIVITIES IN SPACE

Joseph M. Goldsen (editor), *International Political Implications of Activities in Outer Space*, 1959 (a leading exposition of the views of political 'realists').

F. B. Schick, *Who Rules the Skies: Some Political and Legal Problems of the Space Age*, 1961.

Leonard E. Schwarz, *International Organisations on Space Co-operation*, 1962. (a study for the World Rule of Law Center).

Joseph M. Goldsen and others, *Communication Satellites and Public Policy*, 1961.

Murray L. Schwarz and Joseph M. Goldsen, *Foreign Participation in Communications Satellite Systems: Implications of the Communications Satellite Act of 1962*, 1963.

ECONOMIC ASPECTS OF ACTIVITIES IN SPACE

Industry and Space, Report issued by Hawker-Siddely Aviation Ltd. (U.K.) and SEREB (France) in February 1961.

Eurospace, *Proposals for a European Space Programme*, 1963.

MILITARY WORKS

Henry A. Kissinger, *Nuclear Weapons and Foreign Policy*, 1957.

Lt.-Col. Kenneth F. Gantz *The United States Air Force Report on the Ballistic Missile: Its Technology, Logistics and Strategy* 1958.

Lt.-Gen. James M. Gavin *War and Peace in the Space Age* 1958.

Bernard Brodie *Strategy in the Missile Age* 1959.

Fritz Sternberg *The Military and Industrial Revolution of Our Time* 1959.

John F. Loosbrock and others *Space Weapons: A Handbook of Military Astronautics* 1959.

Herman Kahn *On Thermonuclear War*, 1960.

M. N. Golovine, *Conflict in Space: A Pattern of War in a New Dimension*, 1962.

United States Department of the Air Force, *Guided Missiles Fundamentals*, 1957.

—— *Fundamentals of Aerospace Weapons Systems*, 1961.

Raymond L. Garthoff, *Soviet Strategy in the Nuclear Age*, 1958.

General Pierre Gallois, *Stratégie de l'âge nucléaire*, 1960.

General G. I. Pokrovsky, *Science and Technology in Contemporary War*, 1959.

Marshall V. D. Sokolovsky, *Military Strategy: Soviet Doctrine and Concepts*, 1963.

Index

Aaronson, Michael, 103
Acquiescence, evidence of, 183
Adjudication in space matters, 43, 80, 107, 187, 206, 208, 260, 288, 309–312
Administrative Committee on Co-ordination, 73
Aircraft, possible interference with, 186
Airspace, passage through, 232–233
Alexander, A. F. O'D., 16
Alouette, 24
Ambrosini, Antonio, 102
American Society of International Law, 132, 137
American Telephone and Telegraph Company, 23, 75, 80
Antarctic Treaty, 106, 183, 274, 312
Appropriation of space and celestial bodies not permitted, 98–101, 200–202, 204
Arbitral Procedure, United Nations Model Rules on, 312
Ariel, 23
Armando Cocca, Aldo, 163–164
Assistance to astronauts, 246–250, 446–453
Association of the Bar of the City of New York, 131
proposals of, 440–445
Astronomical factors, 13–17
Australia–United Kingdom–European for the Development and Construction of Space Vehicle Launchers Agreement, 368–374

Babínski, Léon, 143
Bahamas Long-Range Proving Ground, 230–231
Bauzá Araujo, Alvaro, 163
Beresford, Spencer H., 103
de Bergerac, Cyrano, 10
Berkner, L. V., 12, 30, 281
Bilateral arrangements, 4–5, 82–86
intercontinental testing agreements, 85

tracking agreements, 83–85
United States–U.S.S.R. Bilateral Space Agreement, 86
United States–United Kingdom Agreement, 83
upper atmosphere research agreements, 85
Birth in space, 298
Boyd, R. L. F., 12
British South Africa Company, 201
Broadcasting, 261–263
Brüel, Erik, 157–158
Buckheim, Robert W., 21
Bulganin, Premier, 44
Bull Intercoetera, 158
Bynkershoeck, Cornelius van, 233

Capek, Karel, 313
Castrén, Erik, 157, 158
Celestial bodies,
manned stations, 273
not subject to appropriation, 98–101, 200–202, 204
CERN (European Council for Nuclear Research), 270
Chaumont, Charles, 154–155
Cheng, Bin, 103, 118
Cheprov, 133, 138, 141, 171
Cicero, 10
Cluttering of space, 218, 280–282
Cohen, Maxwell, 153
Collective security, applicability in space, 208
Columbus, Christopher, 313
Common interest of mankind in space, 192–194
Communication satellites, 198–199, 210, 255–260
Contamination of space, 113, 114, 124, 156, 186–187, 218, 280–282, 404, 410
COSPAR recommendations, 282

471